THE COMPLETE
FLASH MX
HANDBOOK

Published by Future Publishing Limited
30 Monmouth Street, Bath BA1 2BW United Kingdom
Telephone +44 (0)1225 442244
www.futurenet.co.uk
All content © 2003 Future Publishing Limited
For problems with your CD, please visit www.computerarts.co.uk/cdrom
Cover illustration by **twelve:ten** [w] www.twelveten.com

Media with passion

Welcome

We bring you a superb guide to Macromedia's award-winning multimedia development tool…

Welcome to the latest in our series of Simple Steps Guides, the Complete Flash MX Handbook. Brought to you by the team behind Computer Arts and Computer Arts Specials, it's a definitive guide to the tools, techniques and tricks that will help you make more of Flash MX.

Inside, you'll find a variety of tutorials and features. Whether you're an experienced user or a newcomer to Flash MX, you're sure to find something to help you expand your knowledge of the program. If you want to build a site entirely in Flash, for example, we show you how. Or, if you're interested in

animation, we show you how to use Flash MX to help you create 2D and 3D characters.

We also hope you'll find inspiration, which is why we've included interviews with top designers and a gallery of Flash sites designed to inspire.

On the packed CD, you'll find tutorial files as well as a trial version of Flash MX. Not only that, but we've included trial versions of other products in Macromedia's excellent MX family. Whether you're working on PC or Mac, just load the disc and away you go!

The Complete Flash MX Handbook — we had fun making it, we hope you enjoy reading it.

CHAPTER 1

Get Started with Flash MX

All the essentials you need to begin working with Flash MX. Discover what it's all about, familiarise yourself with the interface, and start building an entire Flash-based Website

CHAPTER 2

Projects

It's time to get working with examples of some real-world projects regularly tackled by designers – from creating an animated character through to building a Flash quiz...

On your CD

Essential tools and handy files

You'll find a range of essential tools on your CD. Most of the projects in this guide have graphics files you can use, plus there's a trial copy of Photoshop 6. In the unlikely event of disc problems, please visit www.computerarts.co.uk/cdrom where you'll find backup versions of our companion files. In the event of other problems, please contact our disc editor Jeremy Ford on 01225 442244 or email him at jeremy.ford@futurenet.co.uk

THE COMPLETE
FLASH MX
HANDBOOK

COMPANION DISC

CHAPTER 3

Tips

How do you speed up your work when you're using Flash MX? What are the tricks that the experts use? 101 pearls of wisdom to help you make the most of Flash MX...

CHAPTER 4

Techniques

There are means and ways of doing things. Get to grips with some key techniques for incorporating video, text effects, motion blur and a whole lot more in Flash MX

CHAPTER 5

Interview

The work of new media design agencies is increasingly a specialist field with its own jargon and heroes. Some of the world's best Flash designers demystify their work...

CHAPTER 6

Games projects

Flash games can be pretty addictive and building them is a great way to develop your knowledge and expertise of Flash MX. Our tutorials show you how

CHAPTER 7

Game techniques

Developing Flash games helps you fine-tune many techniques that you can use elsewhere — creating pre-loaders for large files or projects for Pocket PCs, for example

CHAPTER 8

Q&A

Stuck with a tricky Flash MX problem? Maybe we can help. Over these pages, our experts sort out some commonly asked Flash conundrums

CHAPTER 9

Flash Gallery

In need of some inspiration? Then browse through the following pages where we look at cutting-edge Flash work — from corporate Web pages through to experimental sites...

CHAPTER 10

Reviews

An in-depth look at some of the other programs that make up Macromedia's MX family. Plus a selection of books to improve your Web-building skills

Getting started

All the essentials you need to begin working with Flash MX. Discover what it's all about, familiarise yourself with the interface, and start building an entire Flash-based Website

Animating your site with Flash MX

What can you do to spice up your site and make your pages more animated? The answer, as we show in the following pages, is to make more of Flash MX…

Without Flash, the Web would be a far less interesting place. It enables developers to add animation, sound, interaction and general pizzazz to their pages. In a few short years, Flash has succeeded in making the Web the all singing and dancing medium it is today. What we generally refer to as Flash – the animated, interactive stuff we see on the Net – actually has a longer name. It's called Shockwave Flash, a plug-in format developed by Macromedia that was originally developed as way to play back vector animation on the Web. The development tool used to create Shockwave Flash 'movies' is now in its sixth version, and is called Flash MX. It's a mature application that's part Web-authoring tool, part drawing package and part animation program. Many others have tried to copy it. It's now common for modern drawing programs to have a Shockwave Flash export option, but none of them have the breadth of features unique to the real Flash.

Flash MX makes the most of its sophisticated features with an interface that's easy to navigate and that can be customised to your needs. The first time you start up the package you'll be

The drawing tools in Flash are comparable with dedicated vector illustration programs. It's ideal for putting static drawings on the Web too!

asked whether you wish to work like a designer or a developer. In designer mode the layout emphasises drawing and animation tools. In developer mode the bias is towards scripting and interactivity. Once you know your way around the program you can go to the Window menu and open whichever

panels you'd like to have in view, position them on screen and then save your own layout. In the centre of all these panels is the main document view where all the action takes place. This is simply called the Stage.

However you work, there are several tool panels that you'll always have

open. The Timeline appears at the top of the screen; that's where you're able to create and edit animation. The Tools panel is similar to the toolbox you'd find in many drawing packages. We'll look at each of these panels in more depth in a moment. The panel you'll visit the most is called the Property Inspector (sometimes shortened to Properties). This dynamic addition to the Flash Interface is 'context sensitive', meaning that its function changes depending on the tools or movie elements that are currently selected. If you're using the Text tool the Property Inspector panel gives you a list of styles, font choices and sizes. When the Line tool is chosen the Properties panel allows you to change the thickness and colour of the drawn line. The Property Inspector panel is also used in interactivity, allowing you to apply unique names to each element you create, which lets you refer to those objects from within scripts. Hyperlinks can also be added to buttons through the Properties panel. If you're ever stuck in Flash MX, and want to edit or otherwise transform an object – always visit Properties first.

Drawing and drawing tools

Although it's best known for its animation features, the heart of Flash MX is in its drawing tools. Flash MX is able to produce files that download fast because it relies on Vector graphics. Most of the other graphics you see on the Web are bitmaps – files that store an image pixel by pixel. In contrast, vector images are stored as a series of co-ordinates, like a join the dots picture. Far less memory space is required to store vector images, and that's one of the main reasons Shockwave Flash animations are able to download so quickly.

The Tools panel is home to the drawing tools in Flash MX. In addition to the text and line tools we've already mentioned, there are shape tools for drawing ellipses, rectangles and more complex polygons and there's a Pen tool. The pen tool is a fairly recent

New features in Flash MX

Flash MX comes with a host of special features. Here are the main highlights…

■ **MX INTERFACE** Macromedia developed a common interface for all their Web and multimedia authoring products. It made its debut in Flash MX.

■ **CONTEXT SENSITIVE PROPERTY INSPECTOR** The new 'Property Inspector' is part of the MX interface. Dreamweaver, Macromedia's HTML and Web page-building tool, inspired the idea.

■ **DIRECT VIDEO IMPORT** Reads video clips in almost any format.

■ **LAYER FOLDERS** Layers allow you to make more complex animations by stacking different elements on top of each other. The new 'Layer Folders' help you organise those layers better.

■ **SHARED LIBRARIES** Libraries are an important part of Flash. Now 'Shared Libraries' let you store the library for a movie separate from the movie file, allowing you to use the same library for multiple projects.

■ **TEMPLATES** Make your own templates or use one of the many shipped with the program.

■ **APPLICATION SERVER ACCESS** Use Cold Fusion scripting or Active Server Pages to communicate with databases from Flash movies.

■ **CUSTOMISABLE LAYOUT** Set up the Flash interface any way you like, then save that layout for your use.

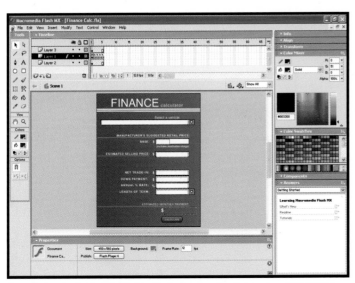

Known for its animation features, Flash is often best employed as a builder of graphic interfaces – whether they're for Web pages or multimedia applications.

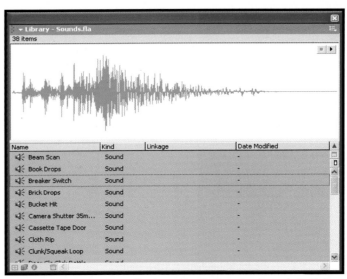

Digital music comes in many formats. If you import it into Flash you can guarantee that it will play back on 98 per cent of all computers, regardless of the platform or plug-ins.

addition to Flash, debuting in Flash 5. It enables you to make freeform curves and by inserting points onto the stage. Flash fills in the points according to properties that you specify. The program also has a unique freeform drawing tool that lets you draw directly onscreen. Your scribblings are automatically converted to vector lines, allowing you to edit them point by point.

As we'll discover, Flash can display other types of graphic and media – but vectors are the main image format used by most Flash authors. You can import bitmap graphics though if you wish. Even those can be easily converted into

Although it's best known for its animation features, the heart of Flash MX is in its drawing tools

vector format, using the Modify>Trace Bitmap option. In common with all Flash elements, these can be animated using the program's Timeline.

The Timeline is a powerful feature that lets you animate elements in Flash MX frame by frame over time. These animations can be as simple as rollover

button that change when you place the mouse cursor over it, or as complex one shape morphing or changing into another shape. The Timeline panel is further divided into layers, allowing you to stack multiple animations on top of each other, each with its own independent timeline. Although Flash

is known as a Web tool, it's possible to output Flash animation at TV broadcast resolutions – and the features available match this level of sophistication.

Flash MX allows you to create two types of animation. The first type, frame–by–frame animation is how traditional cartoons are made. You create a different image for each frame of your animation, then play them back in sequence. The second type, used more often in Flash authoring is called Tweening. This is a method that lets you define a starting frame and an end frame for an object onscreen. The frames in between are then filled

Three uses for Flash

We take a look at three of the best things you can use Flash MX for...

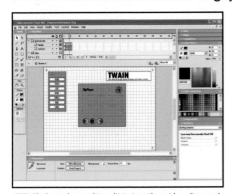

1 Flash can be used to edit to together video clips, and then put them on the Web. The Sorenson Spark import system lets you compress the size of your original clips by quite an impressive amount. Using the animation features in Flash, you can then create your own impressive transitions between clips, add titles or even scale and rotate the moving image.

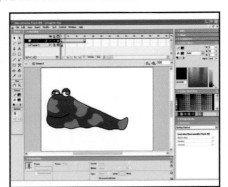

2 Ever wanted to make your own cartoons? With Flash MX you can. By using the drawing tools provided or by importing more traditionally produced pictures using a scanner, you can build animation frame by frame on a timeline. When you've created your masterpiece it can be saved for publication on the Web or, at higher resolutions, recorded on video or DVD.

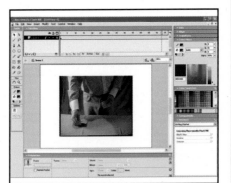

3 As broadband Internet connections catch on, the Web is becoming more animated. Flash is at the forefront of this. Forget about HTML – you can build your Web pages entirely from Flash. The program handles images, sound, video, text, hyperlinks, advanced interactivity and database connections. There's no need to mess around with multiple packages.

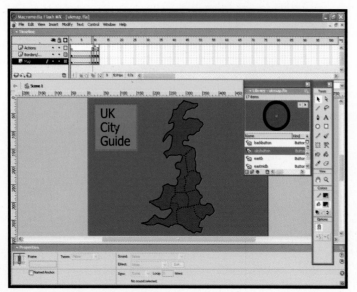

Known for its animation features, Flash is often best employed as a builder of graphic interfaces – whether they're for Web pages or multimedia applications.

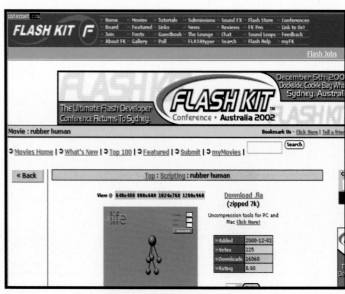

The Web is full of additional resources for Flash authors. Flashkit at www.flashkit.com provides you with free Components, fonts, example movies and more.

in by Flash MX – the term tweening is shortened from in–betweening. Flash offers a number of different ways of animating objects. You can scale them, rotate and distort them. You can move objects across the screen or change one object into another.

Multimedia, music and more

Broadband Internet connections are slowly but surely becoming the norm, and Flash MX has features that help you to put the kind of content onto you pages that users will come to expect as

Over time, Flash has developed into a full-blown, sophisticated Web development package

standard. A new Web is coming out of its cocoon, capable of supporting live video and real–time high–resolution sound. Flash can help you contribute to the creation of a multimedia Web with features supporting a variety of popular formats. Flash has been able to play

back streaming MP3 audio files since version 5, for example. The controversial sound format can compress CD quality audio 12 smaller than its original size. The program does this with very little intervention from you – you simply import the sound file

in any of the supported formats and set the MP3 export parameters when you export your finished Flash movie to the Web.

The same argument can now be put for the use of video clips in Flash. In Flash MX you're able to import video in Video for Windows, QuickTime or one of many other formats direct to the Timeline. As you import the source material into Flash MX you're able to compress it down in size significantly. Once in Flash you can treat the clip as you would any other Flash object – adding interactive elements, scripting

Buttons in Flash

Get a head start in Flash by making animated buttons for a Web site.

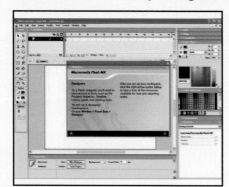

1 Start up Flash MX. If it's the first time the program has been used then you'll be prompted to choose whether you'd like to work as a designer or developer. Choose designer for now – you can always change the arrangement of the screen later if you want. Now, for the next stage, go to Window> Common Libraries.

2 Among the items listed you'll find Buttons. Selecting this launches a Library panel. Double-click on the folder labelled Ovals in this panel and select the first button in the list: Oval buttons – blue. Click and drag a copy of the button to the stage. Notice that the Property Inspector changes so that you can edit the parameters of the button.

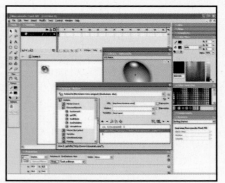

3 Right-click the button and choose Actions. In the Actions panel that appears go to Actions> Browser/Network. Double click on getURL. You type the Web address you'd like the button to take you to in the URL box. The Target box lets you specify a named frame or browser window. Go to Control> Test Movie to see how the button would work.

and even animation. It's also really easy to create playback controls using special Flash elements called smart clips that come bundled with the program. These can be accessed as a special Library – as can ready made buttons and sounds, all of which can be dragged and dropped

The use of music or video in Flash movies requires very little in the way of authoring skills. You good put music or video directly onto your Website with very little effort indeed. All that's required of you is to use the file menu in Flash MX to import the sound or video clip to your movie using the Import to Library option.

Web building

In addition to its animation and media playback abilities, Flash has always had interactive features. In earlier releases these were confined to simple Web link functions, but over time the program has evolved into a full-blown, sophisticated Web development package. At the centre of this is a kind of programming language called ActionScript. Sharing the same layout and many of the same commands as JavaScript, this language enables more advanced developers to create fully functioning applications using Flash MX. If you've played any Flash games on the Web, like those found at www.shockwave.com, you will have seen some of the things that ActionScript can do. In more recent times Flash MX has been used to develop real-time chat applications, interactive shopping systems and video conferencing tools. With special ActionScript commands that make connecting to databases easier and advanced scripting, Flash has moved on from being a simple animation tool.

The timeline is where animation happens. Here you can build multi-layered masterpieces with a little application like this example created by Alexander Olenich at www.olenich.com.

Script editing takes place using the Actions panel – and every object in a Flash movie can have scripts applied to it. The usual method employed is to attach general (or global) scripts to frames within the movie then apply specific (or local) scripts to individual objects. When pressed a button may trigger a snippet of script that moves the action in your movie to a specific frame, for example. That frame may, in turn, establish a set of variables that can be used in other parts of the script.

The scripting features may sound daunting, especially if you've little experience of programming. Don't despair if that's the case as the program comes with a Library of ready-made items called Components that make it much easier to add interactive elements to your movies. Components are special Flash elements – similar to the sound clips and button libraries we mentioned earlier. All you have to do to use them is drag and drop them to the stage, then edit their parameters using the Components Panel. Among the Components that come with Flash MX are ready-made scroll bars, form elements and advanced buttons. There are many more ready to download for free from the Macromedia Exchange that can be accessed directly through Flash.

When the building process is finished, Flash movies destined for the Web must be published to the Shockwave Flash format that can be read by the Flash Player plug-in. Using the program's Publish option you can even automatically generate a Web page complete with the code needed to embed your Flash masterpiece.

Although Flash MX is packed with features and can be used in a very advanced way, it's also easy for newcomers to get results straight out of the box. There are templates, ready-made libraries and built-in help systems make sure of that. Like all the best software, the more time you spend using it and getting to know how it works, the more you'll get out of it.

Origins of Flash

Macromedia Flash can be traced back to the early Web of the mid-nineties…

Back in the mid-nineties, FutureSplash was just a multimedia browser plug-in among many. Even though the accompanying authoring package produced vector-based animations that were smaller and faster than many of its rivals, it struggled to get the attention it deserved. Against the odds, the most popular plug-in was Shockwave for Director. We say against the odds because the earliest incarnations of Shockwave were slow and buggy, scorned by the majority of surfers. Then Macromedia did something really clever. They bought the FutureSplash and authoring tool. After the quickest of overhauls the marketing muscle of the Shockwave

name and the compact, slick animation of FutureSplash were combined. Shockwave Flash was born. The Web hasn't looked back since. Macromedia did much more than re-badge an old program though. Over the course of six different versions Macromedia Flash has gone from being a quirky vector animation package to a full-blown multimedia authoring system complete with MP3 support, a powerful scripting language and database connectivity. It still delivers files that are a fraction of the size of conventional Shockwave. All this is tied up in an easy-to-use interface that makes it great for novices and experts alike.

The Flash MX user interface

Windows are out, panels are in. This is just one of the big differences in the new Flash MX interface, but one that cuts to the core of the program…

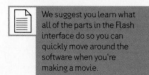

We suggest you learn what all of the parts in the Flash interface do so you can quickly move around the software when you're making a movie.

he Flash user interface has been heavily overhauled since Version 4. By far the biggest difference is that the number of panels you have to work with has been slashed down to a bare minimum.

You still have all of the old tools, but will never have to flick around multiple windows trying to track down the specific tick-box that you need, and have much greater control over exactly how everything is presented to you.

Moreover, Flash will also remember your preferred settings.

The first sign of this flexibility is a choice of three development environments – one for designers, which pushes all of the art tools to the fore, one for programmers, where the screen is organised to give you as much space for ActionScript as possible, and a general jack-of-all-trades view point. Whichever you choose, the rough design remains the same. Down the right-hand side, you have a series of

docked panels with which you can access your most important controls – such as the Components library, the colour swatch and the help system, all of which are displayed as bars that can be pulled down whenever you need the specific tool, and then ignored.

Should you need one available on a more constant basis, selecting one by the dimples enables you to drag it out onto the main screen and dock it on any side of the Flash

The interface (PC version)

Here are all of the main components of the Flash MX interface…

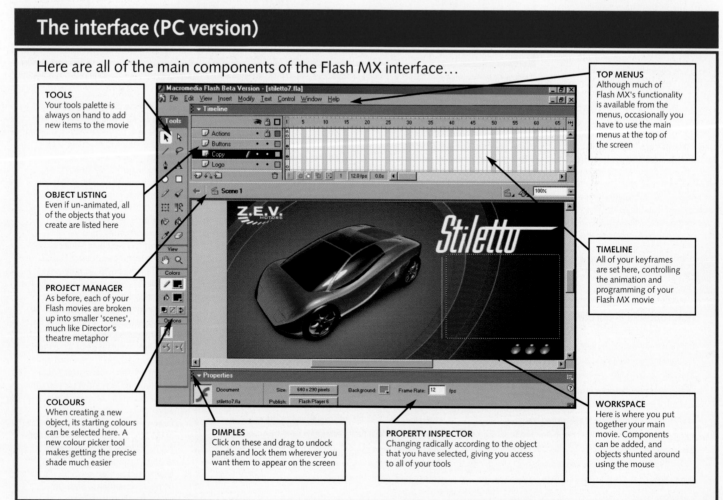

TOOLS
Your tools palette is always on hand to add new items to the movie

OBJECT LISTING
Even if un-animated, all of the objects that you create are listed here

PROJECT MANAGER
As before, each of your Flash movies are broken up into smaller 'scenes', much like Director's theatre metaphor

COLOURS
When creating a new object, its starting colours can be selected here. A new colour picker tool makes getting the precise shade much easier

DIMPLES
Click on these and drag to undock panels and lock them wherever you want them to appear on the screen

PROPERTY INSPECTOR
Changing radically according to the object that you have selected, giving you access to all of your tools

TOP MENUS
Although much of Flash MX's functionality is available from the menus, occasionally you have to use the main menus at the top of the screen

TIMELINE
All of your keyframes are set here, controlling the animation and programming of your Flash MX movie

WORKSPACE
Here is where you put together your main movie. Components can be added, and objects shunted around using the mouse

window for easy access, or simply leave it floating on the workspace.

The Property inspector

Perhaps the most important panel is the Property Inspector. This is context sensitive, only giving you relevant information on any component that you select. In the case of a shape, this could be as simple as colour, if a piece of text, the typesetting tools. While this can be moved around at will, its width means that it is best left on the bottom of the screen. Nevertheless, it combines most of the old object-related panels that Flash 5 made use of into a much more convenient package. If it doesn't contain a tool directly, it will invariably have the button that you need to bring up the necessary window.

A simple shape, for example, will offer its width, height, foreground and background colours along with the thickness of the line. A separate button, marked Custom brings up the Stroke Style window, where the Type, Thickness, Space, Jiggle, Rotate, Curve and Length settings are made available. In the case of a group, you cannot edit multiple objects simultaneously, so instead Flash MX cuts itself down to just width, height and x/y co-ordinates. The same tool when used on a Symbol or Button likewise brings up more options relating to interactivity rather than simply looks.

Video can now be imported into Flash from a variety of standard formats. The clips are compressed and distributed directly to the Timeline, so they can be controlled by ActionScript and treated exactly like any other Flash object.

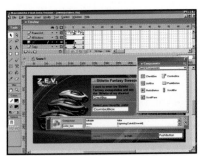

In this version, Components replace Smart Clips - they're Flash objects with editable parameters that you can drag and drop into your movies. Flash MX ships with a range of ready-to-use user interface components.

Toolbox

The toolbox is the most used part of the Flash MX interface, so it pays to know exactly what each of the tools do…

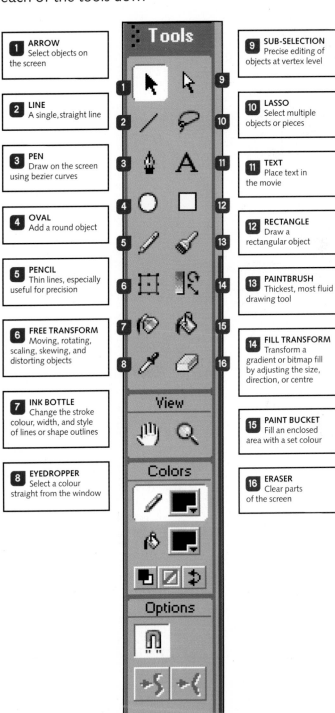

1 ARROW
Select objects on the screen

2 LINE
A single, straight line

3 PEN
Draw on the screen using bezier curves

4 OVAL
Add a round object

5 PENCIL
Thin lines, especially useful for precision

6 FREE TRANSFORM
Moving, rotating, scaling, skewing, and distorting objects

7 INK BOTTLE
Change the stroke colour, width, and style of lines or shape outlines

8 EYEDROPPER
Select a colour straight from the window

9 SUB-SELECTION
Precise editing of objects at vertex level

10 LASSO
Select multiple objects or pieces

11 TEXT
Place text in the movie

12 RECTANGLE
Draw a rectangular object

13 PAINTBRUSH
Thickest, most fluid drawing tool

14 FILL TRANSFORM
Transform a gradient or bitmap fill by adjusting the size, direction, or centre

15 PAINT BUCKET
Fill an enclosed area with a set colour

16 ERASER
Clear parts of the screen

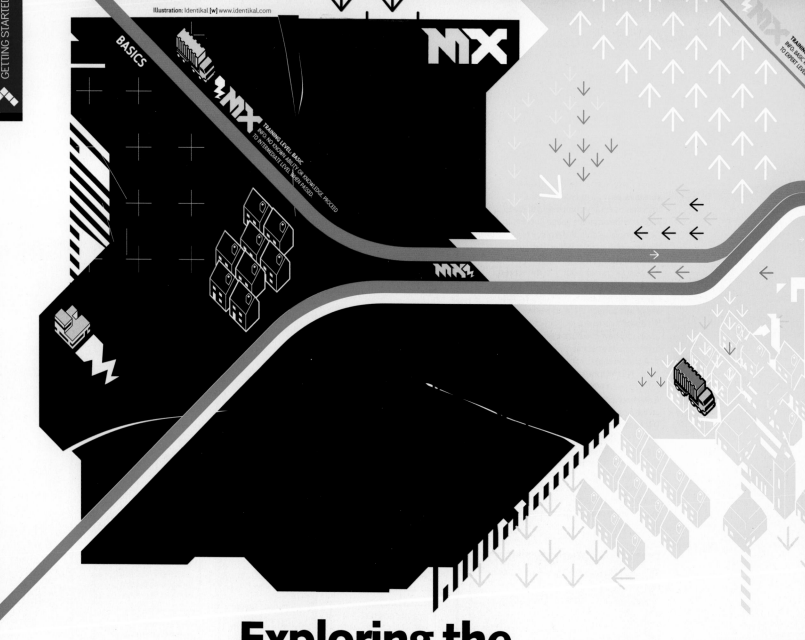

Illustration: Identikal [w] www.identikal.com

TRAINING LEVEL BASIC
INFO: NO KNOWN ABILITY OR KNOWLEDGE. PROCEED TO INTERMEDIATE LEVEL WHEN PASSED.

TRAINING LEVEL
INFO: BASIC KNOWL...
TO EXPERT LEVEL WHEN...

Exploring the fundamentals in Flash MX

Flash can be hard to learn, and even some experienced users still feel uneasy about how basic editing works. Become more comfortable with working in Flash in this tutorial for new and intermediate users…

Expertise provided by Ian Anderson of zStudio. zStudio is a new-media consulting practice that provides out-sourced Web development and training to designers and agencies. Feedback, questions or business enquiries are welcome.
[e] ian@zstudio.co.uk
[w] www.zstudio.co.uk

Flash makes Web design accessible to many designers who don't want to get involved with HTML or dealing with different browsers. It offers an excellent design environment with all the familiar tools included: rulers, guides, grid and powerful layout capabilities.

However, there are many differences between Flash and the mainstream design tools that most designers are familiar with, and these differences can result in frustration and delays. For this reason, many Flash artists shun the drawing tools in Flash and import nearly all the artwork that's more complicated than text, lines or boxes from packages such as Illustrator or Freehand.

The first part of the tutorial gets back to basics, and investigates how artwork is managed in Flash. In the second part, using the example of a simple navigation bar, you'll learn some of the design techniques. Whether you're new to Flash or have been using it for some time, this tutorial will help you to feel more confident when you're building projects.

Part 1: Creating basic artwork in Flash

First, we'll focus on how artwork is created and manipulated. If you're used to vector illustration tools such as Freehand and Illustrator, you may find some of the Flash behaviour surprising…

More about shape data

The basic artwork in Flash is called shape data, and it works like virtual modelling clay. Once you put shape data inside a container of some sort, such as a group or symbol, it becomes much more convenient to work with. The shape data is always there, though, inside the container, and you can go in and edit it at any time. Apart from imported media such as images, sounds and video, it's the shape data that will make your movie take longer to download. By storing all the shape data in symbols wherever possible, you'll keep the file size of your movie down. Shape data always sits below other objects in a given layer; to move shape data in front of text, groups or symbol instances, you either need to move it to a new layer, group it, or place it inside a symbol using Insert>Convert to Symbol.

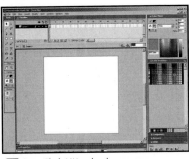

1 Open Flash MX and make sure you have a new document open. Choose View>Magnification>100%. In the Properties palette, set the stage size to W:400, H:400 and set the frame rate to 24fps. Save your document as test.fla in a location of your choice. In the Tools palette, locate the fill and stroke colour menus; set the fill to light grey and the stroke to black.

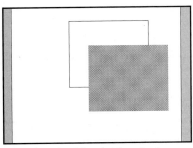

2 In the Tools palette, select the rectangle-drawing tool, then click and drag on the stage to draw a box. Try moving the box by dragging its centre; surprisingly, the outline is left behind because unlike in other drawing applications, the box is made of separate fill and stroke objects. Choose Edit>Undo. Click on each edge in turn – there are four stroke objects making the outline, and a separate fill object.

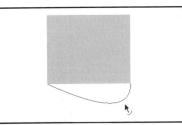

3 Double-click the edge to select all the stroke objects that are touching, and delete them with the Backspace key. Using the arrow tool, drag the edge of the unselected artwork to reshape it freely. The cursor shows a curved line when reshaping curves. You can also point to the corner of the unselected artwork to drag and reposition the connector point between two line segments. The artwork must not be selected if you want to do this; when it's selected the cursor shows a four-headed arrow that will only allow you to move the artwork.

4 Artwork in Flash can combine automatically to form new shapes. This happens when two shape elements are overlapped and deselected. To prove it, make a copy of the rectangle using Edit>Duplicate, then move the copy so that it partly overlaps the original and click away from both to deselect everything. The rectangles form a new shape. Choose Edit>Undo as often as required to separate them again.

5 Sometimes, one piece of shape artwork will punch a hole in an underlying one instead of combining with it. This happens when the fill colours are different. To show this, change the fill colour of the copy rectangle, and overlap it with the original as before. Click away to deselect, then move the copy; you'll find it has cut away an area of the underlying artwork. Do Edit>Undo until the two rectangles are whole again.

6 Objects combining or cutting like this can occasionally be useful, but more often it is an undesirable effect. To prevent it you can work in different layers or put the shape data inside group or symbol objects as we'll see in a moment. For now, choose Insert>Layer and cut and paste the copy rectangle to the new layer. You'll find it no longer joins or cuts the artwork on the first layer.

Part 2: Working with groups

Placing shape data inside group objects helps to make it easier to work with…

Tweening objects

When you're applying tweening to objects, it may not work as expected. Here are some tips:
· You can motion-tween groups, text, images, and symbol instances, but not shape artwork.
· You can shape-tween shape artwork only. Use Modify>Break Apart to render any object into its component shape data.
· Motion-tweening only works properly with one object on each keyframe.
· Tweening instructs Flash to tween the contents of two adjacent keyframes in a single layer, and is applied to the first keyframe of a pair. Make sure the contents of the two keyframes are of the same type.

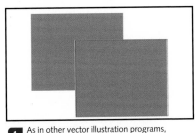

1 As in other vector illustration programs, grouping objects will help to keep them together. In Flash, grouping a single shape object with itself also prevents it from interacting with other shape artwork on the same layer. A group can be considered to be a container into which the shape data is placed. Create a copy of the rectangle you pasted to a new layer and choose Modify>Group to place it in a group object. Duplicate it, then try steps 4 and 5 again to prove that the contents of a group object are protected.

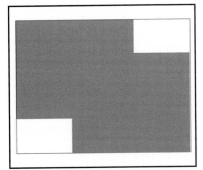

2 It is possible to create nested group objects by grouping a group object with itself or with other artwork. Select the group objects you created in the previous step and choose Modify>Group to enclose both objects in another group. The shape data is still there; it's just inside two group containers.

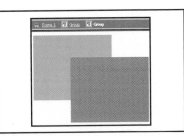

3 When shape data is placed inside a group object it can no longer be edited, although the group object itself may be scaled or transformed. To edit the contents of an object other than shape data, simply double-click it with the solid arrow tool. Double-click the outer group object, and then double-click one of the nested group objects. You can now edit the shape data, for example, to change its colour. Click Scene 1 in the breadcrumb trail under the timeline to return to the stage. >

Part 3: **Tweened animation**

Animation in Flash is easy using the motion tweening feature…

Types of artwork

There are three types of artwork that you can create in Flash itself: shapes, groups and symbols. Shape data is the actual vector artwork that you create using the drawing tools, or import from other packages. Groups are simple containers that can be used to hold shape data or other objects. Text is effectively a group object, although it has its own characteristics. Symbols are containers stored in the Library which are used for content that needs to be reused within the movie.

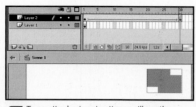

1 To practice basic animation, we'll use the group created in the previous steps. Choose Modify>Transform>Scale to make the group smaller. Position it on the left edge of the stage. We'll animate it from left to right across the stage. Click on the grey slot at frame 30 in the same layer, and choose Insert>Keyframe. A new keyframe is created containing a copy of the group. Move this copy to the right of the stage. Click on the first keyframe in the timeline and choose Motion from the Tween pop-up menu in the Properties palette.

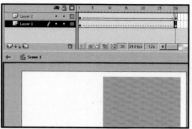

2 Press Enter on the keyboard to preview the tween in action. Now, here's a problem. Insert a keyframe at frame 30 in the first layer, and apply motion tweening to the first keyframe of that layer. When you press Enter, the timeline plays the first tween but the artwork in the first layer won't move because the keyframes contain shape data, and this can't be motion-tweened, only shape-tweened.

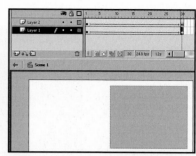

3 To fix the broken tween, select the artwork on the first keyframe and group it using Modify>Group. Do the same with the artwork on the second keyframe in this layer. Now the tweens will play in both layers, because both tweens are acting on group objects.

Part 4: **Symbols and Alpha tweens**

Groups are rarely used, because symbols offer the same benefits and have important further capabilities…

Tweening groups or text using shortcuts

If you're using the contextual menu or Insert>Create Motion Tween to apply motion-tweening and the artwork on the stage isn't a symbol instance, it's important to apply the tweening before you create the second keyframe. Both of these commands automatically convert the contents of the first keyframe to a symbol, but not the contents of any existing subsequent keyframe. This means that future edits to the symbol won't take effect in both keyframes, making it very hard to update the movie. The best option is to always convert artwork to a symbol before you use it.

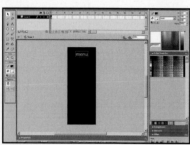

1 Create a new project using File>New. In the Properties palette, set the stage size to W:150, H:400, background colour: black. Set the framerate to 24fps. Save your document as menu.fla in a location of your choice. Set the fill colour to white and click near the top of the Stage with the text tool. Type the word menu and set the font, size and so on as you wish.

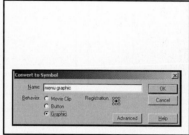

2 Switch to the arrow tool, and ensure the text is selected. Choose Insert>Convert to Symbol. Choose Behaviour: Graphic, name the new symbol and click OK. This places the text object in a new symbol object in the library, and an instance of the new symbol is placed on the stage. In the Properties palette choose Colour: Alpha, then drag the slider down to make the text transparent.

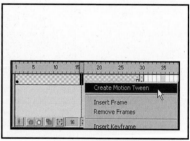

3 Click in the timeline at frame 30, and choose Insert>Keyframe. Click on the invisible symbol instance and set the Colour menu in the Properties palette to None. Right-click (Control-click on the Mac) in the timeline between the two keyframes and choose Create Motion Tween from the contextual menu. You can drag the red playback head in the timeline to see the effect of the alpha tween.

Part 5: **Sound and interactivity**

Enhance your projects using sounds and use scripting to control what happens in the movie…

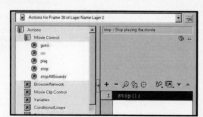

1 Preview the animation using Control>Test Movie. The movie plays back in a new window within Flash – note how the movie loops once it has reached the end. Close the Preview window to return to the movie editing window, and Right-click (Control-click on the Mac) on the keyframe at frame 30 to open the contextual menu. Choose Actions, then in the list to the left of the Actions panel choose Actions>Movie Control and double-click Stop().

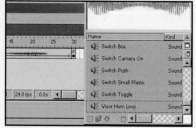

2 To apply a sound that plays automatically, click on the first keyframe of the timeline. Choose Window>Common Libraries>Sounds to open the Sounds library supplied with Flash. Locate the sound called Visor Hum Loop, and drag it onto the stage while the timeline is at frame 1. Test the movie again to see the effect of the stop action and the sound.

3 Flash can show you information about the final published movie using the Bandwidth Profiler; you can access this when you're in the Test Movie window. Choose View>Bandwidth Profiler to open the profiler. It shows a chart of the download size for each frame in the movie, and information about the movie down the left-hand side. You can use this information to help you optimise your movie so that it is as small as possible.

Part 6: User-driven interactivity

Applying actions to instances of button symbols allows the user to control their experience…

Types of symbols

A symbol can have three types of behaviour: graphic, button and movie clip. You can use the different types of symbol in different ways:

· Graphic symbols are used for individual static design elements such as text or logos.

· Button symbols can have four different states that are displayed according to mouse events. Up, over and down are the three visible states. The fourth state, hit, allows you to define a custom hit area for the button. Actions can be triggered by buttons, but are always applied to the instance of a button rather than the parent symbol.

· Movie clips are used for reusable chunks of animation and play back independently of the main timeline. Movie clips are effectively Flash movies within Flash movies, and are very powerful objects for interactivity and scripting.

1 Create a new layer using Insert>Layer. Using the text tool, type the word Macromedia onto the stage. Select it with the arrow tool, and choose Insert>Convert to Symbol. Name the new symbol Macromedia button, and choose Behaviour: Button, then click OK. Double-click the instance of the button to edit it. Click the second frame (named Over) and choose Insert>Keyframe. Change the colour of the text to a bright colour; this is how the button will appear when the mouse is over it.

2 Test the movie again using Control>Test Movie and move your mouse over the button to see it light up. You'll probably find that it's quite hard to activate the button because of the gaps in the letters.

3 To make it easier to activate, double-click the button again to enter the symbol-editing view, and add a keyframe to the fourth frame slot (named Hit). Draw a rectangle over the text to provide a solid hit area the same shape. Test the movie again to see the difference an appropriate hit state makes.

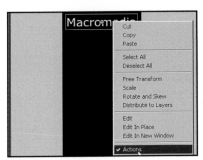

4 To define interactivity for a button, you need to apply the action to an instance of the button; you don't apply button actions in the symbol-editing view. Return to the stage. Right-click (Control-click on the Mac) on the instance of the Macromedia button on the stage and choose Actions from the contextual menu to open the Actions editor.

5 From the Actions list on the right of the Actions window, open Actions>Movie Control and double-click the On action. You can detect various mouse events, shown in the options panel; we'll accept the default, which is to detect the rollover event and execute some further action as a result. The action to be executed needs to be inserted after the first line of the On action, so that it appears within the curly braces ({}).

6 You need to ensure that the first line of the On statement is selected, and choose Actions>Browser/Network from the list and double-click the Get URL action. In the Options panel at the top of the Actions editor, type the address that the button is to link to; in this case, enter **[w]** http://www. macromedia.com and close the Actions editor. Test the movie using Control>Test Movie and try out your button if you have a live Internet connection.

Part 7: Publishing the movie

Finally, we look at how to export our work as a .SWF file and deploy it within a Website, while supporting browsers without Flash…

Using templates for compatibility

In step 3, the HTML template 'Detect for Flash 3' is chosen. As with most of the templates, this will ensure that the correct HTML is generated to play the movie in both IE and NN browsers. It also adds commands that display an alternate GIF image that is specified for export in the Formats tab for any browsers that don't support Flash or don't support JavaScript. The external links are reproduced by an image map in the HTML so that the non-Flash users and search engines can still navigate effectively.

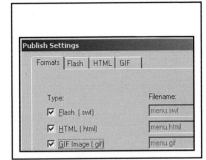

1 You need to publish your *Flash* project as a .SWF file in order to use it on the Web. This can be done at any time using Control>Test Movie or File>Export Movie, but the best way is to use Publish. Choose File>Publish Settings to open the Publish Settings dialog. This has various tabs, depending on what is selected in the first tab. Flash and HTML are selected by default.

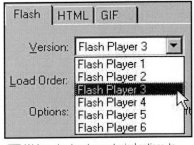

2 We're going to set some typical options. In Formats, ensure that Flash and HTML are selected, then turn on GIF as well to export the first frame of the movie as an image. In the Flash tab, choose Version: Flash Player 3. This is the most widely compatible version to export your movie in, while still allowing the essential functionality to be supported. Around 97 per cent of the Web audience can view Flash 3.0 movies, while Flash 6.0 movies have a much smaller audience share.

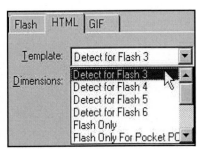

3 In HTML, choose Template: Detect for Flash 3. Click the Publish button, and Flash will output the selected formats as files in the same directory as the .FLA project file. You can then open the HTML file in your Web editing software and copy and paste the code into your final page. Make sure all the files that were exported are saved in the same folder. You can substitute the GIF file that Flash generated with another image having the same dimensions if necessary.

Illustration: Mark Thornicroft [e] mark_graphic@hotmail.com

Dynamic Websites

As we've already discovered, you can build an entire site with Flash MX. Follow this great three-part tutorial for all you need to know…

The World Wide Web is changing. Fast. With more and more people getting broadband connections, we will soon reach a point where few will be happy simply to visit text-based Websites alone.

That's not to say that we can afford to ignore usability issues or blithely assume that everyone is using state-of-the-art equipment. Nevertheless, there's a new sense of freedom in the air: maybe the Web is about to become a truly interactive, multimedia experience.

Enter Flash MX, no longer simply a tool for those from a design background,

but an invaluable, intuitive tool for anyone building a Website. Over the next 12 pages, we show you how to construct a site entirely in Flash MX.

Even if you don't choose to go down this route, but prefer to use site-building software such as Dreamweaver MX in conjunction with Flash MX, you'll still find plenty of invaluable advice that you can apply to your own projects.

Subjects covered include building a navigation system, adding content, and putting in those clever little bells and whistles that mark out the best sites, such as an MP3 player and message facilities. Enjoy…

PART ONE: NAVIGATION

Flash MX

Ready to build your Website using Flash MX? The first task is to build an effective navigation system. We show you how...

In a recent Macromedia survey, it was found that 98 per cent of Web users can play back Flash content in their browsers without having to download a plug-in. This means that Shockwave Flash is now more prevalent than Java. The only other Web-based formatting and scripting language with a similar reach is HTML. With support for more devices than ever, improved design tools and the best development features in any visual Web authoring package, Flash MX is the best tool for creating Shockwave Flash content.

Flash is well established for creating animation, site navigation and banner ads. At the higher end, you'll know that ninja coders use it to create impressive online games and experimental demos.

In this tutorial we cover the middle ground, building a Website in Flash MX from the ground up. That means building the navigation system, information architecture, content containers and layout in Flash, then deploying it across a range of platforms.

Many new features in Flash MX enable us to tackle this project in ways that weren't possible before. We'll take you through the process, step by step. In part one, we'll organise our workspace and build a navigation system for a site that has a predefined number of sections. Later on, we'll add dynamic content that can be easily updated plus enhanced interaction that HTML alone would find hard to beat. The end result will be a robust, accessible Website built entirely in Flash.

On your CD
The files to accompany this tutorial are on your coverdisc in the folder Tutorial\Webskills. Expertise supplied by Karl Hodge, [e] khodge@spodgod.com.

THE ILLUSTRATION
Artist:
Mark Thornicroft

Email:
mark_graphic@hotmail.com

Part 1: Get organised

Flash MX includes new timeline features which enable you to manage layers more easily. We put them to use alongside custom panels…

Library folders

You can add folders to the library to organise elements in your pages in the same way as you organise the timeline. Our finished layout has separate folders for background and menu elements within the movie.

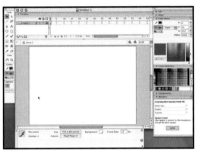

1 Flash MX launches with quite a few open panels, whether you choose Designer or Developer mode. First, get rid of those you won't need. To close a panel, grab the top-left corner, then click and drag to tear it from its dock. You can then close it as you would any window.

2 You'll need the Info, Colour Mixer, Colour Swatch and Align panels, so close the rest. Click on the 'rollup' arrows on each of the remaining panels to hide them. Click-drag on the top panel to release them all from their docking position.

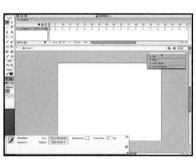

3 You may also want to float the Toolbar and Property Inspector to maximise your workspace. Tear them from their docking positions by clicking and dragging on a blank piece of the panel. Finally, maximise the document window by dragging on the bottom-right corner.

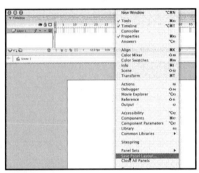

4 Go to Window>Save Panel Layout and give your layout the name Minimal Design. To use this layout in future, go to Window>Panel Sets and choose your creation from the dropdown menu.

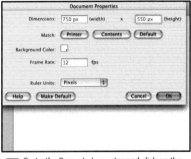

5 Go to the Property Inspector and click on the Size button. This opens the Modify Movie dialog. Set the dimensions of the movie to 750x550 and click OK. In the timeline, click on the New Folder button three times to create three folders.

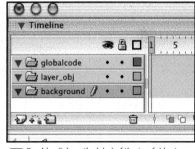

6 Double-click on the label of the top folder to edit it. Rename the folder 'globalcode'. Rename the middle folder 'layout_obj' and the bottom folder 'background'. Open the layout_obj folder and add a new layer. Rename the layer 'menu'. You're now ready to start creating the movie.

Part 2: Making a generic button

Next, we'll make a button template to smooth the process of creating multiple buttons…

Centre symbols

When creating symbols, centre them on the stage by selecting and dragging them over the crosshairs in the centre of the document window. The centre of the shape should have a registration mark that enables you to line up the middle of the object with the middle of the stage. Alternatively, select the object and use the Align panel to centre it with a couple of clicks (but be sure to toggle the Align To Stage button first).

1 Hit Ctrl+F8 in Windows or Command+F8 on the Mac to create a new symbol. In the dialog, choose Button as the Symbol type and name it 'nav_button'. You're automatically taken to Symbol Editing mode.

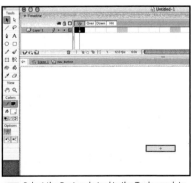

2 Select the Rectangle tool in the Tools panel. In the Property Inspector, set the Fill to white and the Stroke colour to a dark grey. Set Stroke height to 1. Draw a rectangle that's 100 pixels wide and 20 high in the centre of the stage. You can get the dimensions exact by entering them into the Info panel after drawing the shape.

3 Right-click in Windows or Ctrl-click in Mac OS in the empty Over frame. Choose Insert Keyframe from the context-sensitive menu. Select the Fill portion of the rectangle and change it to a light grey using the Fill colour selector in the Property Inspector.

Part 3: Making the menu

With the button template now completed, the next step is to assemble our navigation system…

Layer order

If elements of your menu seem to disappear when you try to align them to the menu symbol, you may have to re-arrange the order of layers within the folder. The MenuBackground layer should be at the bottom; the TempButtons Layer at the top.

Font substitute

Our original FLA used Futura as the font for text labels on buttons. If you are prompted to choose a replacement font when importing our library (or the finished example file) any sans font like Helvetica or Arial will do as a temporary replacement.

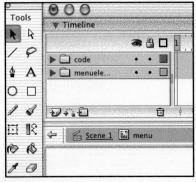

1 Hit Ctrl+F8 in Windows or Command+F8 on the Mac to create a new symbol. In the dialog choose Movie Clip as the Symbol type and name it 'menu'. Our first job is to create folders on the timeline to organise our data, just as we did in the main movie. Make two folders, naming the first 'code' and the second 'menuelements'.

2 Make a new button symbol and name it 'homebtn1'. You are automatically taken to Symbol Editing mode. Go to Window>Library to open the library. Drag and drop an instance of the button symbol nav_button to the stage. Select Tools>Text and click the cursor over the button.

3 A text box should appear. Make sure that Static Text is selected in the Property Inspector. Set the font to a sans face like Helvetica or Arial (we used Futura). Type in the label 'home'. Return to the Menu movieclip, using the Edit Symbols menu at the top-right of the stage.

4 You'll need to create additional buttons using the same technique. To save time, we've made them for you. Go to File>Open as Library and open mxtutorialbuttons.fla from the cover CD. This library contains navigation buttons and a couple of other items we'll be using to complete the menu.

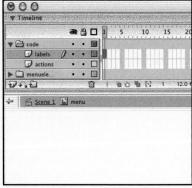

5 In the Editing window for the Menu movieclip, go to the timeline and open the menuelements folder you created earlier. Add layers named 'MenuBackground', 'TempButtons', 'Dragger' and 'Rollup'. Open the Code folder and add layers named 'Labels' and 'Actions'.

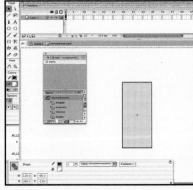

6 Create a new symbol. Select Graphic and name it 'menubackground'. Draw a rectangle that's 120 pixels wide and 260 high. Set the Fill colour to a mid-blue, with Alpha transparency at 50 per cent. Navigate back to the stage for the Menu movieclip using the Back button at the top-left of the stage.

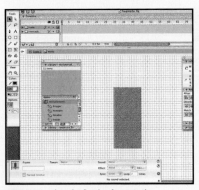

7 Next, select the first keyframe in the MenuBackground layer in the timeline. Drag an instance of the menubackground graphic symbol from the main library (not the imported library). Go to Window>Library if it isn't visible. Centre the menubackground symbol on the stage, then select the TempButtons Layer.

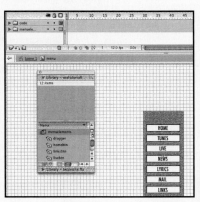

8 Go to the mxtutorialbuttons library and drag instances of homebtn, linksbtn, livebtn, newsbtn, mailbtn and tunesbtn to the stage. Arrange and space them over the menu background as illustrated, using the Align panel to centre the buttons vertically.

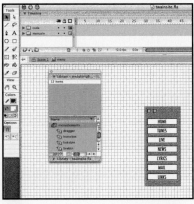

9 Finally, drag and drop an instance of the button 'dragger' from the mxtutorialbuttons library to the first keyframe of the layer labelled 'Dragger'. Similarly, drag an instance of the button rollup to the Rollup layer. Position them as illustrated.

Part 4: Animation and interaction

All those buttons have to do something. For this final step of part one, we will program a couple of them…

Snap out

To create a button that makes the menu re-appear, select the instance of dragger at frame 10, go to Modify>Transform>Flip Vertically, then edit the ActionScript attached so that it points to the frame labelled MenuOpened.

Finished symbols

In the finished example file twainsite.fla (on your CD in Tutorial\Webskills) you'll find that we've added a logo and a couple of other items to the layout. These are stored in the library as Symbols. If you wish to add these to your own movie, drag and drop them from our finished examples library.

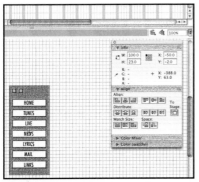

1 Continuing to work on the movieclip 'menu', click on the layer TempButtons, to select everything in the layer. Go to Modify>Distribute to Layers. Your buttons are placed on individual layers on the timeline. Delete the original TempButtons layer. Shift-click on each of the first frames in the new layers to select them all.

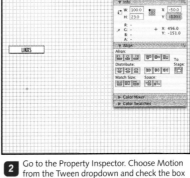

2 Go to the Property Inspector. Choose Motion from the Tween dropdown and check the box marked Sync. Click on frame 10 of the timeline and insert a Keyframe in the first individual button layer. Select the button on the layer and move it so that it's at the top and centre of the menu. Look at the position co-ordinates in the Info panel and make a note of them.

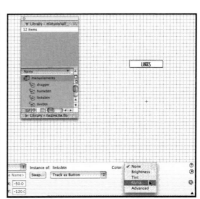

3 In the Property Inspector, choose Alpha from the Colour dropdown and set the Transparency to 0 per cent. Repeat the process for the other navigation buttons, adding a keyframe at frame 10, moving each button to the same co-ordinates as the first and setting Alpha transparency to zero per cent.

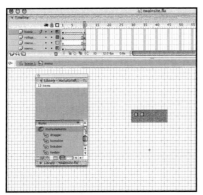

4 Now you need to select the first keyframe in the MenuBackground layer and select Motion from the Tween dropdown in the Property Inspector. Add a keyframe at frame 10. With the menubackground Symbol selected, change the dimensions of the symbol to 120x40 in the Info panel.

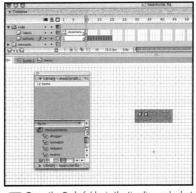

5 Open the Code folder in the timeline and select the first keyframe in the Labels layer. Type the label 'MenuOpened' into the box in the Property Inspector. Add a keyframe at frame 2 and give it the label 'CloseMenu'. Add a keyframe at frame 10 and label it 'MenuClosed'.

6 Select the first keyframe on the Actions layer and go to Window>Actions to open the Actions Editor. Insert a stop() action into the frame by selecting Actions>Movie Control>Stop. Either drag the action to the window or double-click on it to place it. Insert a stop() action at keyframe 10.

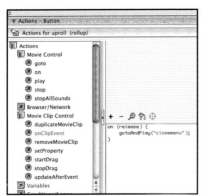

7 Select the Rollup button on stage. Add an onRelease action to the button from Actions>Movie Control>On. Below that, add a Go To action. Select Go To and Play in the editor, then choose Frame Label from the Type dropdown. In the Frame box type 'CloseMenu'.

```
on (press) {
startDrag(" ");
}
on (release) {
stopDrag();
}
```

8 Select the Dragger button on the stage. Select Expert mode in the Actions Editor by clicking on the menu arrow in the top-right corner of the panel and choosing from the menu. Type the above code directly into the editor.

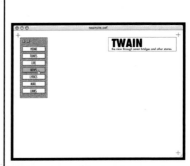

9 Finally, return to the main movie then drag and drop an instance of the completed menu to the stage. To test the menu's functions, go to Control>Test Movie. The Dragger button should enable you to pick up and drop the menu anywhere on screen, while the Rollup button closes the menu. 🔲

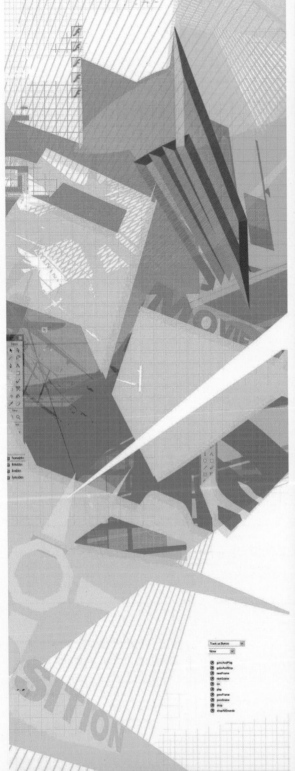

Flash MX

It's time to add some content to the Flash MX site structure we created in part one – and we're doing it dynamically…

Smart Clips were a great innovation in Flash 5. They enabled developers to create Flash elements that users could drag and drop into their pages with little mess and even less fuss. The trouble was, they were tucked away in the Window menu where no one really paid attention to them.

In Flash MX, Smart Clips have been turbo-charged and given their own panel (at a time when other elements are losing theirs). Now they're called Components, and you won't forget about them this time around.

Flash MX is bundled with a set of user interface components, and in this tutorial we'll use one of these to create an effect that we doubt

Macromedia would have anticipated when it was bundled.

And if you like free things as much as we do, you'll be happy to see that the Macromedia Exchange for Flash is being promoted far more heavily this time around. One bonus is that a second set of UI Components can be downloaded absolutely free. Just go to Help>Flash Exchange and sign up when prompted to get at the goodies.

Components aren't the only new aspect, of course. ActionScript has changed too. Savvy users will notice that the Tell Target command is nowhere to be seen in this tutorial — its use has been replaced by hierarchical dot notation. Tackle our tutorial to see what we mean…

On your CD
The required tutorial files and a completed example file can be found on the coverdisc in Tutorial\Webskills. Expertise supplied by Karl Hodge, [e] khodge@spodgod.com.

THE ILLUSTRATION

Artist	Email
Mark Thornicroft	mark_graphic@hotmail.com

Part 1: Tweaking files

Take a look at the base file to see what delights are in store…

Ready to go

This tutorial is quite complex so we've created a base file that has a lot of elements already in place. You'll have to copy the contents of the Twainsite folder directly over to your hard drive for the external elements to work properly.

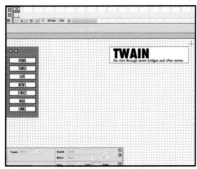

1 We've done a little tweaking to the base file since we last worked on the site. Open twainsite.fla from the Twainsite folder on your hard drive (on your CD in Tutorial\Webskills). The existing typography has been broken down into vectors. We did this by selecting the original type and hitting Ctrl+B in Windows twice (Command+B on the Mac).

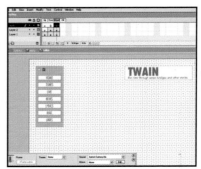

2 We've also added a sound effect to the roll-up menu window we created in the last issue. We did this by adding a sound from the Sound Library in Window>Common Libraries>Sounds direct to the Down stage of the roll-up button. It's simply a case of dragging and dropping the sound file from the Sound library to the Down frame of the button while in Symbol Editing mode.

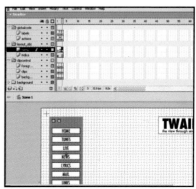

3 You may also notice that we've added some elements to the timeline. We've created a clips folder complete with new layers. Most of the things we create will be placed directly in the clipcontrol layer in the clips folder. We've also added labels and actions layers to the globalcode folder.

Part 2: Scrolling pane

The UI components that are bundled with Flash MX add a lot of extra functionality with little fuss…

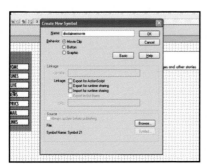

1 We're going to use the Scrolling Pane component in a way that Macromedia probably didn't intend… Start by hitting Ctrl+F8 in Windows or Command+F8 on the Mac to make a new movie clip. Name it 'disclaimermovie'.

2 Click on the Advanced button and tick the box labelled Export for ActionScript, then click OK. You should be taken to Symbol Editing mode. Go to Window>Library to open the library.

3 We've packed the library with most of the bits you'll need to complete this tutorial; all you have to do is assemble them in the right order. Drag and drop the file disclaimer.gif that's inside the library's clipelements folder to the stage.

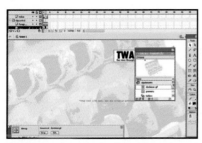

4 You now have a movie clip containing an image. Return to the main stage (clicking on the Scene 1 link in the top-left corner is a quick method) and go to the timeline. Open the folder named clips and select the second keyframe in the clipcontrol layer. Drag and drop an instance of the image disclaimer.gif (not the movie clip) to the stage.

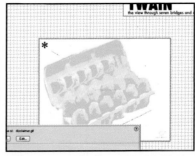

5 It's huge! You should resize it to 400x300 using the width and height boxes in the Properties panel. Next, set the X co-ordinates of the object to 165, and Y to 155. Go to Window>Components and select 'Flash UI Components'.

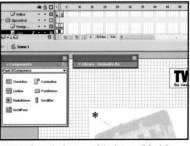

6 Right at the bottom of the list you'll find the ScrollPane Component. Drag and drop an instance to the stage. Using the Properties panel, resize the panel component to 130x180 and position it at X 585, Y 315. Give it the instance name 'scrollpane' while you're at it.

Part 2: Scrolling pane continued…

Component parts

When you add the scroll pane component to your site, you'll notice that the number of items in your library takes a significant leap. The Scrolling Pane component is a good example — adding more than 60 parts to your library. That's one of the reasons why it's important to put your library elements into separate folders.

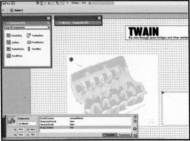

7 In the Properties panel, select the Properties tab if it's not already active. Click on the Scroll Content entry and type in 'disclaimermovie'. Set the Horizontal Scroll and Vertical Scroll entries to false. Set the Drag Content entry to true.

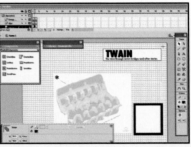

8 Click on the second keyframe within the background layer of the clips folder on the timeline. Draw a black square with the stroke set to none, and with dimensions of 150x140 position it centrally behind the ScrollPane component.

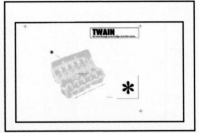

9 Hit Ctrl+Enter in Windows or Command+Enter on the Mac to test your movie. You should now have an image with a small box next to it. Click and drag within the box and you'll see that it contains a highly magnified version of the main image.

Part 3: Moving on

Those navigation buttons still need scripting – but first we have to get there…

Labels

Look in the timeline folder 'globalcode' and you'll see layers labelled 'actions' and 'labels'. We've already placed 'stop()' actions on keyframes 2 and 3 of these layers, corresponding to the disclaimer content and the main content that we create during this tutorial. These frames also have labels, 'disclaimer' and 'htcontent' that enables us to refer to them by label name in any scripts we create.

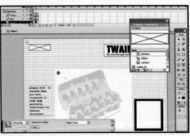

1 Return to the clips folder. Select the second keyframe in the background layer. Drag and drop an instance of the movie clip 'verifytxt' from the library to the stage. Position it left of the current content. Drag an instance of the graphic symbol 'premenu' and position that at X 30.0 Y 30.0.

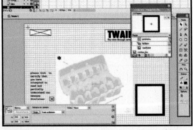

2 Click on the second keyframe in the clipcontrol layer and drag an instance of the button 'tickbox' to the stage. Position it in the bottom-right corner of the 'verifytxt' movie clip. Right-click on the button (or Ctrl-click on the Mac) to bring up the context-sensitive menu. Select 'Actions'.

3 Click on the menu dropdown icon in the top-right of the Actions Editor and choose Expert mode, then type the following code into the window:

```
on (release) {
    gotoAndPlay("htcontent");
}
```

'htcontent' is a frame label we've placed in the base file for you. Now we're going to add content to the frame that the button will take your users to.

Part 4: External content

Make a movie clip that can handle HTML formatting – and the external content that will go into it…

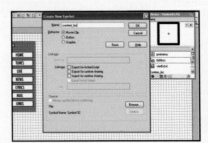

1 Still in the clips folder on the timeline, select the keyframe at frame 3 of the clipcontrol layer. One thing you'll immediately notice is that the navigation menu we made last issue is in this frame. Go to Insert>New Symbol to create a new symbol. Make it a movie clip and call it 'content_loc'.

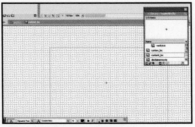

2 You're taken to Symbol Editing mode. Select the Text tool. In the Properties panel, set Dynamic Text and click 'Multiline'. Drag out a text box on the stage, approximately 560x420 pixels. When you've drawn the box, select it with the arrow cursor and use the Width and Height boxes in the Properties panel to set those dimensions exactly.

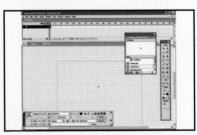

3 While you're working in the Properties panel, set the font to Courier New, size 12 and make sure the Selectable icon is toggled off. The Render Text as HTML icon right next to it should be toggled on. In the Var field, type 'dynContent'. This a variable we've already embedded in the text files we've provided.

Part 4: External content, continued...

HTML formatting

Flash has some quirks in the way it reads HTML from text files. Although it recognises and renders formatting elements like `<p>` and `<br>`, it also renders hard returns in your files as though they are new paragraphs. If you do put HTML formatting into external files for use in *Flash*, remove all the returns before you save the file.

Controlling clips

If you look at our finished file, you'll notice an extra line of ActionScript in the actions layer at the frame labelled 'htcontent':

`_root.menuclip.gotoAndPlay("menuclosed");`

This action tells the item 'menuclip' in the main movie ('_root') to go to a specific frame when executed. The frame specified is an animation that closes the menu.

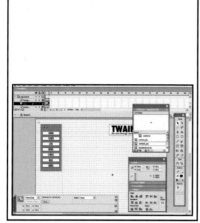

4 Before you return to the main stage, centre the text box in the document using the Align panel. On the main stage, with the third keyframe of the clipcontrol layer still selected, drag and drop an instance of the movie clip 'content_loc' to the main document. Position it at X 160 Y 100.

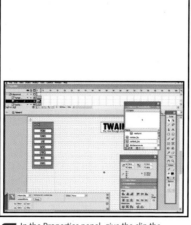

5 In the Properties panel, give the clip the instance name 'contentMovie'. This clip will be used to load HTML-formatted content from external text files. Before you can do that, you need to create the text files. Use a NotePad in Windows or use BBEdit Lite on the Mac.

6 Flash's support for HTML is pretty limited. You can create hyperlinks with the `<A>` tag, use `<BR>` and `<P>` for formatting and use `<FONT COLOR>`, `<FONT FACE>`, `<FONT SIZE>`, `<I>`, `<B>`, and `<U>` to affect the style of the rendered text.

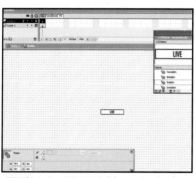

7 This isn't an HTML tutorial, so we've already created your necessary text files. All that remains is to attach the scripts that will load these files into the movie clip. The scripts will be triggered from the navigation buttons embedded in our menu. Go to the Library panel and find the first of these buttons, 'livebtn', in the MenuElements folder. Double-click on it to go to Symbol Editing mode.

8 Select the button on stage and open the Actions Editor (if it's not already open). Type the following script directly into the editor in Expert mode:

```
on (press) {
    loadVariables("content/live.txt",
"_root.contentMovie");
}
```

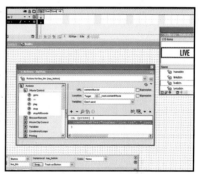

9 Let's break down what this script does: on (press) is pretty obvious, while the loadVariables command selects some content to load into a variable container. The two items that follow in parentheses are, respectively, the relative URL to the location of a text file (live.txt) and the instance name of the movie we're targeting, which is contained in the root or main movie.

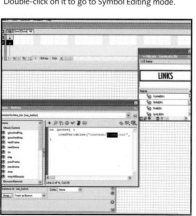

10 The buttons newsbtn, lyricsbtn and linksbtn function in the same way, so the easiest way to get them working is to paste the script from livebtn, changing the specified text file URL to news.txt, lyrics.txt or links.txt for the appropriate button.

11 Before testing whether your handiwork has been fruitful, there's one last button script to add. Select 'homebtn' and add the script:

```
on (press) {
_root.gotoAndPlay(1);
}
```

This sends the playback head of the main movie back to the start.

12 Test your movie by going to Controls>Test Movie; try hitting all the buttons to make sure you've entered the code correctly. Our finished version of the file is in the same folder as the tutorial files. Fire it up and see how they compare.

THE ILLUSTRATION

Artist   Email

Mark Thornicroft   mark_graphic@hotmail.com

PART THREE: INTERACTIVITY

Flash MX

We've built a site and added dynamic content. All we need now are interactive elements, such as an MP3 player and message facilities…

We're in the final stage of our Flash MX site project, and we're now populating the last couple of pages with interactive content. First we're going to insert an MP3 player, using external clips so that the main movie will download swiftly. Here, we take advantage of the Flash MX MP3 import capability, compressing our files before using them in the package. Use the demo of Flash MX on your CD to experiment…

Finally, we add a simple mail form to the site. Users can specify their own subject and message in the form before sending it via their own mail client. We also give you some tips on achieving a more professional result using CGI forms. See if your ISP supports CGI; chances are it already has a script you can use from your own Web space.

As you created this site you should have had a good tour of the new Flash MX interface, but we've only scratched the surface of its superpowers. Many of the new features enable a Flash 'stub' to communicate with external data and pull in resources that can easily be updated. Our site is entirely modular. Using our structure, you could overhaul the graphics and create a site all of your own, or improve on ours.

On your CD
The required files you need to complete this tutorial in the folder Tutorial\Webskills. Expertise supplied by Karl Hodge, [e] khodge@spodgod.com.

Part 1: Preparing external files

We're going to make a clip player in Flash MX that can download external files from the Net. First, we have to prepare the clips…

Playing scales

This clip player application is scalable to its function. Because the sound clips are external, you can heavily compress them for use on the Net, or go for better quality if you plan to deploy it from the desktop.

Toploader

Although Flash unloads movies automatically from the current level, explicitly adding the Unload Movie command speeds the process along.

1 The first step is to make a series of Shockwave Flash movies containing sound clips. The movies act as a wrapper for the sounds, so we can load them using ActionScript into a movie clip within our main movie later.

2 We've provided MP3 sounds on the coverdisc. You'll find them in the Resources folder within Tutorial\Webskills. Make a new document in Flash MX and go to File>Import. Browse to the first of the three sounds in the Resources folder, then choose File>Import To Library.

3 Select the first keyframe in your movie, then click on the Sound dropdown menu in the Property Inspector. Choose the sound you imported from this menu, leaving the other settings at their defaults. Go to File>Export Movie and save the file in SWF (Flash Player) format. Name the movie sound1.swf.

4 You'll notice that you can also set Sound Compression options here, but as the file is already compressed, uncheck the box labelled Override Sound Settings. Repeat the procedure with the remaining two sound clips to create Shockwave Flash files named sound2.swf and sound3.swf. Save them all in one folder.

5 In a Text Editor, type the following exactly as it appears:

infowindow1=Sound Clip 1&infowindow2=Track No. 1

Save the file as text1.txt.

6 Create similar text files for clip 2 and clip 3, naming them text2.txt and text3.txt respectively. Save them in the Content folder in the main site folder. These text files contain named field variables that we'll be setting up in the next stage.

Part 2: Loading and controlling movies

All the components for our clip player are in place. Now we apply those elements to our movie and stitch them together with ActionScript…

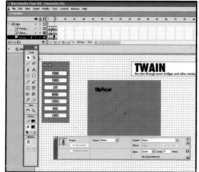

1 Open the file twainsite.fla on the CD (within Tutorial\Webskills). Select the frame 5 layer, called clipcontrol, within the timeline folder clips. In Flash, text fields enable users to input text, or they can be used to display text from an external file.

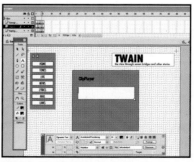

2 Select the Text tool in the toolbox, then drag and draw a text field box within in the main document. With the field still selected, go to the Property Inspector. Choose Dynamic Text from the Text Type dropdown. In the Variable box, type: infowindow1. From the Options dropdown, select Multiline and toggle the Selectable icon off.

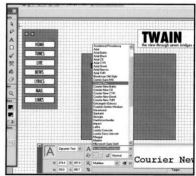

3 Draw a second text field below the first. Set the field up with the same parameters, but name it infowindow2 instead. Select the arrow cursor and then select both boxes at once (Shift-click). In the Property Inspector, set the font to Courier.

Part 2: Loading and controlling movies, continued...

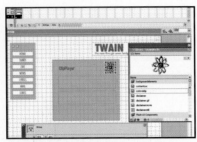

```
stop();
unloadMovieNum(1);
loadVariablesNum("content/default.
txt", 0);
```

```
stop();
unloadMovieNum(1);
loadMovieNum("sound1.swf", 1);
loadVariablesNum("content/text1.txt",
0);
```

4 Drag and drop an instance of the movie clip named controlclip from the library. In the Property Inspector, give it the instance name 'controller'. Double-click on this clip to start editing it. We've added layers labelled actions and labels to smooth things along. Double-click the keyframe in the Labels layer and give it the label 'Park'.

5 Go to the Actions layer in the clip, and select the keyframe in frame 1. Go to Window>Actions. Select Expert mode from the menu (accessed from the top-right corner of the window) and type in the code listed above.

6 Select the second keyframe in the Actions layer. Staying in Expert mode, type in the code illustrated above. Add the same code to frames 3 and 4, but change sound1.swf to sound2.swf in frame 3 and sound3.swf in frame 4. Change text1.txt to text2.txt in frame 3 and text3.txt in frame 4.

```
on (press) {
controller.nextFrame();
}
```

```
on (press) {
controller.prevFrame();
}
```

```
on (press) {
    _root.gotoAndPlay("soundPlayer");
}
```

7 Go to the library and drag and drop an instance of the button 'transport' to the stage. Position it as shown. Open the Actions window and type in the code illustrated above.

8 Drag a second instance of 'transport' from the library. With this instance selected, go to Modify>Transform>Flip Horizontal and position it next to the first. Add the script illustrated above to the new button.

9 Click on the 'Edit Symbols' on the top right of the document window, and navigate to menuelements>tunebutton. Add the code illustrated above to the button, then hit Enter to test your movie.

Part 3: Sending email

Next, we'll apply a simple method of building an interface that submits mail from your Website...

Level best

Flash movies can have many levels. In this application, our sound clips are loaded into level 1; this exists above the level of the current movie, but because the clips don't contain any graphics, this doesn't disrupt our animation. The text is loaded into variables that exist at the same level as the movie, level 0, replacing any content that's already there.

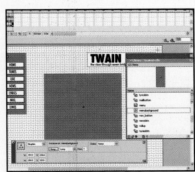

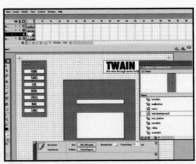

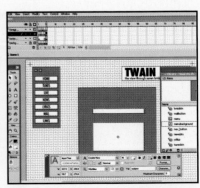

1 Continuing in the same movie, select frame 6 of the layer labelled Background within the Clips folder in the timeline. Drag an instance of the graphic symbol 'menubackground' from the library to the stage. Resize it to 340x280 pixels and position at X 230, Y 120.

2 Select frame 6 in the layer 'textbg'. Draw two white rectangles, one at 225x20 and the other at 225x125. Position them roughly as shown. Select the same frame in the clipcontrol layer. Go to frame 6 in the clipcontrol layer. Choose the Text tool and drag out two textfields corresponding to the white rectangles you created previously.

3 Shift-click to select both textfields at once and go to the Property Inspector. Set the fields to accept Input Text using the Text Type dropdown. Make the font Courier, at 16 points, in black. Select the top text field and set the Var name to 'subject'.

Part 3: Sending email, continued...

Reloader

Although our sound clips are very simple movies, the flow of our application could be optimised for use on the Web by placing an 'If frame is loaded' action in frame 1, pointing to a sound clip in frame 2. Playback of the clip could be delayed until it has fully downloaded, while a loading message displays.

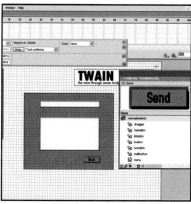

4 Select the bottom text field and set the Var. name to 'body'. Choose Multiline from the Line Type menu dropdown. Go to the library, then drag and drop and instance of the button 'Submit' to the stage, positioning it as shown.

```
stop();
recipient = "fakemail@
somefakeaddress.com";
cc = "faketoo@somefakeaddress.com";
```

5 Go to the Actions layer in the Globalcode folder in the timeline. Select frame 6 and launch the Actions window if it's not already visible. We need to set up some variables associated with the mail form. Type in the illustrated code, replacing the email addresses with your own (if you don't the code won't work).

```
on (release) {
getURL("mailto:"+recipient+"?cc="+cc+
"&subject="+subject+"&body="+body);
}
```

6 Select the Submit button you created before and type in the code illustrated above in the Actions window. Press Ctrl+Enter in Windows or Command+Enter on the Mac to test the movie. When clicked, the button should launch the user's email client with variable text already filled in.

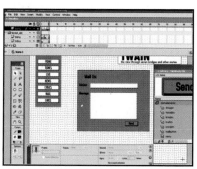

7 The same basic technique can be used to send information to a CGI mail form. You must first set up the script on a server that will enable you to execute CGI, and read the instructions to determine what field values you'll require.

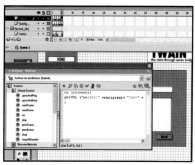

8 Some fields may be fixed values. These can be defined in the same way as we defined the fixed variable names for our simple mail form. Others, like the body of a message, may rely on user input, and these can be defined like our input form.

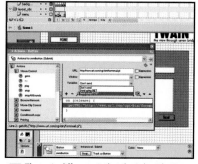

9 The main difference is that the Submit button should point to the CGI script for processing, using the getURL Actionscript command. The CGI Script processes the information from both fixed variables and those that require user input.

Part 4: Closure

Now it's just a case of tying up some loose ends – fixing, testing and clearing up...

Finished file

The file twainsitefinished.fla is on your CD. It's a complete version of this tutorial, but it will expect to find the external files sound1.swf, sound2.swf and sound3.swf, so you'll have to create these before trying it.

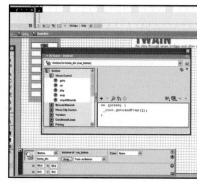

1 You may notice that the Navigation menu fails to work properly after we go to the ClipPlayer section. That's because the buttons call on a movie clip that is no longer in the current frame. Add a GoTo action to the scripts for the Live, News, Lyrics and Links buttons so that they return to frame 3, labelled 'htcontent'.

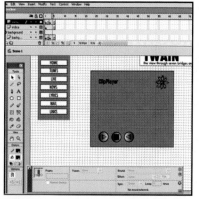

2 The design of the site is entirely modular, using clips and symbols. If you wanted to keep the same basic layout and functionality, replacing any graphics, you could do so by changing the images in the original clips.

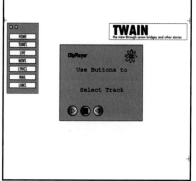

3 Finally, before committing your site to the Web, remove any unwanted symbols from the Library by choosing 'Select Unused Items' in the library menu and deleting them. Thoroughly test all links and interactive functions before publishing the finished site.

Projects

It's time to get working with examples of some real-world projects regularly tackled by designers – from creating an animated character through to building a Flash quiz…

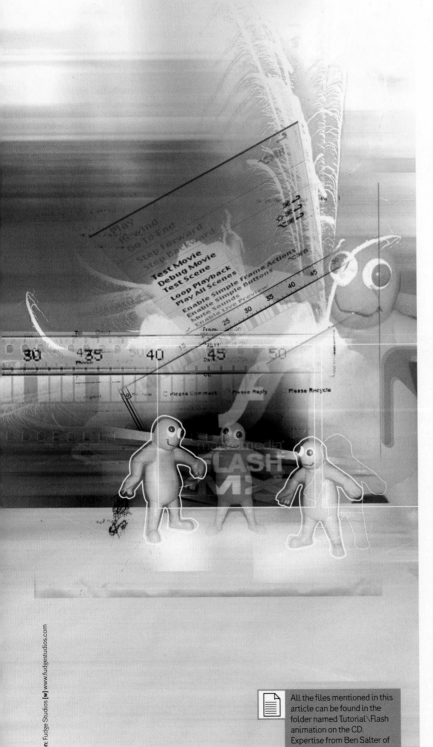

Character animation in Flash MX

Want to create your own cartoon characters?
We show you the ground rules, techniques
and tricks of professional character animation
using the ever-versatile Flash MX

Whether your subject is a cute fluffy rabbit or a giant killer robot, each one has character and needs to be carefully animated accordingly. The art of character animation takes many years to learn but now, with the advent of digital technology and thanks to wider exposure, a number of packages, Flash MX in particular, are making the art more accessible to the aspiring animator.

For this tutorial, we've ventured into the animation studios of Sprite Interactive, the company that, when you visit its Website, invites you to 'Learn to kick ass with Flash MX'. This issue and next, we'll introduce you to the main concepts behind the art of animation — which is one of the most difficult, but rewarding, art and design techniques to master — outlining the ground rules that make all the difference between a moving character and one that simply moves...

All the files mentioned in this article can be found in the folder named Tutorial\Flash animation on the CD. Expertise from Ben Salter of Sprite Interactive Ltd, www.sprite.net.

Part 1: The character

How do you bring your character to life? Expert animation tips start here

Before we begin…

Character animation is an extremely deep subject. It's a difficult but rewarding art and is worth the long hours that you'll spend planning, practising and animating. The main inspiration for an animator should lie in real life, and an animator needs more than the ability to draw – he or she should also have a keen sense of timing and movement, and have a sense of what can bring an inanimate object to life.

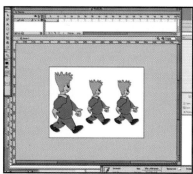

1 One of the most important considerations to make when animating a character is to develop a unique animation style. You should also consider the personality and emotional setting of your character – movements are performed differently according to emotional states.

2 It is the thought and circumstances behind an animation that makes it interesting, and one of the key things to remember is that all movements must happen for a reason.

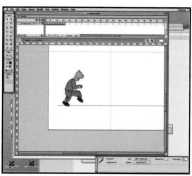

3 Exaggeration is one of the best ways to bring your character to life and is essentially a caricature of expressions and actions. It transports a character from the mechanical to the lifelike, and will, if used effectively, give your character more appeal.

Part 2: Timing

Think realistically about your character's size and weight

NTSC and PAL

PAL is the standard for television broadcasting in the UK, and NTSC in the USA and Japan. NTSC displays images at 30fps, whereas PAL runs 25fps. PAL has a better overall picture than NTSC, because of the larger number of scan lines, but the image sometimes flickers because of the slower frame rate. It's important to bear in mind the difference in frame rate when you're developing animations for television or video playback.

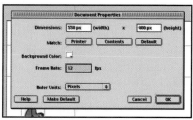

4 Proper timing and an attention to a character's size and weight are critical to conveying accurate movement during animation. As a rule, you should create everything for playback at 12fps. The action must not be so fast that the audience can't read it, but if it's too slow it will seem forced.

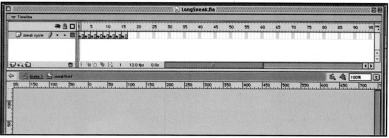

5 Traditional animation is mainly done on 'twos' (one drawing for two frames of film), or on 'ones' (one drawing for each frame of film). In the digital world, twos are used most of the time, with ones used during tracks and pans.

6 When you're deciding on the timing for an animation, you need to really think about what you're trying to convey. For example, an eye-blink can be fast to show that a character is awake, or slow to give the impression that a character is tired.

Part 3: Fluidity

Learn from your own reflection

Pixels

Computers use a square pixel format, which scales in proportion, but when taken to a TV display your images will distort, because TVs sport a different display ratio. If you scale an image on your computer to 720x480, it will look distorted on your computer, but fine on TV. You can also use third-party software to maintain scale integrity, most notably Echo Fire from Synthetic Aperture (www.synthetic-ap.com).

7 All natural movements follow an arc, or slightly circular path. To represent arcs, animations have to have fluidity, and follow smooth curved paths rather than linear ones.

8 As well as being realistic, this fluidity makes the animation flow and move from one character state to another. Each movement should be timed effectively to flow, and they should slightly overlap. Have a look at yourself in the mirror and move around – you'll see that all movements, whether arm movements, head movements or eye movements, follow an arc.

9 All actions also need to ease in or out, otherwise they'll appear mechanical. Human movement speeds up and down as it reaches beginning and end points, and Flash has the perfect tool to reproduce this: the Easing tool. We'll demonstrate how to use Easing to animate a bouncing ball, then show you how to apply squash and stretch techniques to any kind of character to bring the animation to life (you can see a finished version of this on the CD).

Part 3: Fluidity, continued...

Lip-synching

The icing on the cake for a character animator is lip-synching. Flash MX is a great tool for this, enabling you to lip-sync complicated words and sentences easily. Check out page 48 for a tutorial on lip-synching in Flash.

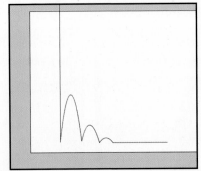

10 Open the movie football.fla from the CD. We've created a motion guide that looks like the above image. You'll see a ball that follows the motion guide and comes to a standstill to the right of the screen.

11 We've inserted keyframes at frames 6, 7, 8, 12, 13, 18 and 21 – there's a keyframe every time the ball reaches a peak or a trough in the guide.

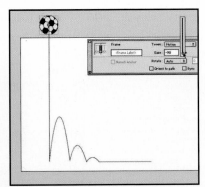

12 The animation as it stands follows the motion guide but has little life to it. Next, we'll add Easing to certain keyframes to create a gravity effect.

Volume control

One important consideration to bear in mind when you're squashing or stretching an object is that no matter how much you have to deform it, it should always appear to keep the same volume. If you don't retain an object's volume, it won't look realistic. You can see a finished version of the file you've been working on if you open footballcomplete.fla from the CD.

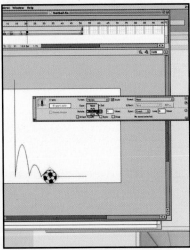

13 At frame 1, set the Easing at –90; at frame 6, set it to 0; at frame 7, to 60; at frame 8, to 0; at frame 12, leave it at 0; at frame 21, set it at 100, and then tell the ball to rotate once clockwise.

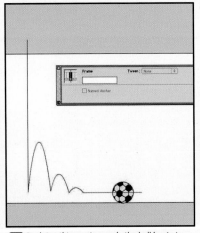

14 By doing this, you've made the ball begin to fall slowly, then speed up as it gets closer to the ground. As you've set it to Ease out on frame 7, it then bounces up; at frame 21, the Ease out effect makes the ball roll faster and then come slowly to a halt.

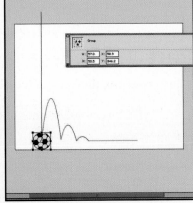

15 To squash the ball, simply use the Free Transform tool and pull the central handle down. Repeat this for all the other points where the ball hits the ground, at keyframes 13 and 18. You also need to pull the ball in the next keyframe so that it stretches in the direction it bounced in; as it bounces up, pull the top-corner handle slightly in the direction the ball is bouncing.

Part 4: Squash and stretch

Applying squash and stretch to give the illusion of weight and volume to a moving character

Video

Flash is a powerful tool for outputting content to video. It can save directly as a QuickTime video file, which is useful for when you want to feature graphic formats that are not supported by QuickTime — you can import them into Flash and then export your movie as a QuickTime file.

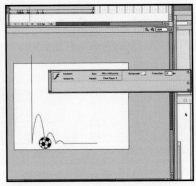

16 Now we need to add some life to the ball. Flash can do a lot of the scaling work for you, thankfully, but you still need to have a good feeling for the timing of the squash or the stretch.

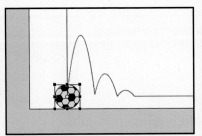

17 Stretching emphasises the speed and direction of movement, whereas squashing highlights the effect of an abrupt change of direction. The more energetic the action, the more extreme use of squash and stretch should be; more intense activities, like a bouncing ball, squash and stretch a lot before returning to their original state. It's also important to remember that an object also squashes or stretches in the direction it's travelling.

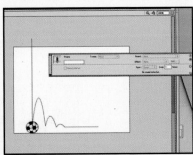

18 In this animation, we need to create the impression of the ball squashing as it hits the floor. The best way to do this is to distort the object as follows: at keyframe 7, scrunch the ball slightly so that it appears to compress as it hits the floor. You can see how much to squash it by in the screenshot above.

Part 5: **Anticipation**

How well have you grasped the laws of physics? Time for a recap…

Animals

The best way to approach the animation of four-legged animals is to tackle them as two human characters, making the back set of legs one stride out of sync from the front set; when the front right leg is forward, the back right leg is back. By experimenting with the four legs you can come up with some great walk cycles.

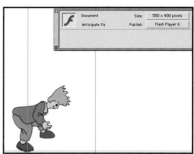

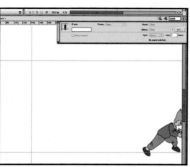

19 Newton's third law states that 'for every action, there is an equal and opposite reaction', and this is one of the most important rules to bear in mind when animating. A movement in one direction is preceded by a smaller movement in the opposite direction. Draw character animations in three stages: a static pose, an anticipatory pose in the opposite direction and then the movement.

20 Following the previous rule will bring a more natural flow to your animations. Sometimes, anticipation is needed physically. For example, before he or she throws a ball, your character must first swing his or her arm backwards. The backwards motion is the anticipation, the throw itself is the motion. When you're animating a figure who is moving a weighty object or throwing a ball, remember to use the backward motion.

21 Anticipation is a visual aid that prepares the viewer for any movement that follows. As a rule of thumb, a longer period of anticipation is needed for faster actions. However, if anticipation is correctly applied, you can make a character disappear off screen using only a few positions, and letting the audience fill in the rest.

Part 6: **Head movement**

Getting your character's eyes and mouth right is vital

Getting a head

Most people are drawn visually towards the eyes and mouth when watching animation. It's good practice, therefore, to add head and eye movement to your character. If you turn your head from side to side, you'll notice that your eyes blink as your head turns and that your pupils lead your head around in an arc movement.

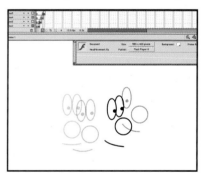

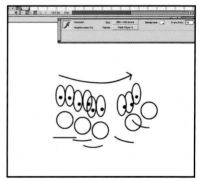

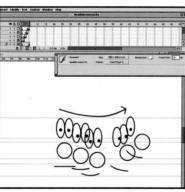

22 Open the file head.fla from the CD; this is an example of a head turning round to the side, and clearly demonstrates how the eye, nose and mouth positions change as the face turns. It also shows you that by slightly exaggerating the movement you can add a lot to the animation.

23 The animation starts with the head swinging in an arc from left to right – look at the eyes and nose line drawings in the image above, then compare how these relate to the actual facial movement and how they swing in an arc.

24 The best way to animate head and eye movements is to use guidelines to make sure the movement is even. Every facial feature should stay consistent throughout.

Part 6: **Flexibility**

An animation should flow constantly and smoothly – but how?

25 When animating a movement, parts of the body lead the animation, while others follow through. It's very important to see the body as a whole, rather than as separate, connected limbs.

26 Open the file flexibility.fla from the CD. This file contains an example of a character throwing a ball – the three stages in the file show the three main stages of the character's movements, and demonstrate how to make his limbs flexible.

27 The first stage of the animation starts with the arms, and the weight is thrown back onto the back foot. The body is poised to move forward and throw the ball; this is a good demonstration of the aforementioned 'anticipation in action'.

Part 8: Flexibility, continued...

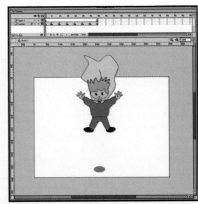

28 The second stage now sees the character transferring his weight forwards, to the front foot. Both arms are moving in a downward arc, while the one holding the ball is preparing to release it as it reaches the peak of its arc.

29 In the last stage, the character has transferred all his weight to the front foot, and both arms have completed an arc movement. The ball is now released at the peak of the arc.

30 As well as the character's limbs following through when they move, you also need to take into account what happens to objects and items associated with the body, such as clothes, hair, floppy ears or a tail. Clothing is the best example of where you'll use overlapping action – for an example, check out the file overlapping.fla from on the CD.

31 Another name for overlapping action is 'follow-through', which is a good description for it. In most cases, objects don't stop suddenly, they overshoot a little bit with inertia and then return to where they were previously.

32 In this animation, the character descends from the top of the screen wearing a cape, which billows out behind him and falls down after he's landed. You can see that in frames 1-15, the cape is fully extended behind the character as he falls.

33 As he gets nearer the ground at frame 20, the cape begins to slow, and at frame 25 when the character lands, you'll notice that the cape still hasn't settled – this finally happens a little later, at frame 30.

Illustration: Fudge Studios [w] www.fudgestudios.com

Character animation in Flash MX (continued)

What makes a successful character? We've covered the theory – now let's put that theory into practice

n the first part of this tutorial, we've explored the cornerstones of character animation, such as timing, creating natural, fluid movement and anticipation. We have also looked at the importance of your character's face, eyes, size and weight, and at using squash and stretch for speed and direction of movement. Now we conclude our guide by applying these rules and tricks, using Flash MX to animate an effective character.

So what do we mean by effective? In short, if you've ticked all the boxes we covered earlier, your character should come to life, capture the attention of your audience and appear natural.

So now we're going to show you how to make a character walk with a number of different poses, then leave the starting blocks and run free! As we established in our last tutorial, character animation is a huge subject and you can't expect to master the craft in just two tutorials, but if you apply what you learn here to your own figures, you should be able to create dynamic results that really impress.

All the files mentioned in this tutorial can be found in the folder named Tutorial\Flash animation on the CD. Expertise from Ben Salter of Sprite Interactive Ltd, **www.sprite.net**.

Part 1: The walk

To define our character's walk requires just six main phases

Toon planning

Make sure you plan your animations ahead. There's no point struggling through an animation without planning it. If you can't work out how to animate a character, stand in front of a mirror and watch yourself acting out what your character is doing — silly as it may sound (and you may look), it works.

1 The main action in any character's walk is in the legs and the lower half of the body. It's a continuous sequence which you should be able to loop into a walk cycle – more on this later.

2 Open the file walk.fla from the Tutorial\Flash animation folder on the CD, then open the library. You'll find the six main positions of the walk tucked away here, but first we need to string these single elements together to make an animation.

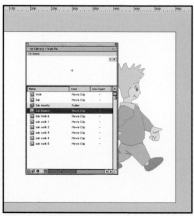

3 The animation is going to be in twos, so create a new movie clip, call it 'walk', and set up six keyframes, each two frames apart, so it matches the timeline snapshot above.

4 Now take the six walk positions and place them on their respective keyframes, using the guidelines to help you position the character. You should now have a movie clip of him walking.

5 You can see from playing the clip that all the movement comes from the character's arms and legs. As the right leg goes forward, the left arm swings backwards, and at the 'passing' position –the peak of the animation – the legs and arms are both fully extended. Then the opposite of the first position occurs, with the left leg moving forward and the right arm swinging back.

6 At the passing position, you should raise the body higher than in the other positions; this is because the leg that's below the body at the previous position pushes it up and springs the character forward. You can see an example of this in our file walkcomplete.fla in the Tutorial folder on the CD.

7 Always ensure your character's movements are balanced. When he's moving a leg or an arm, it should be counterbalanced by the opposite limb to create a natural rhythm. However, if you're looking for a funky walk style, you could swing the arms out of sequence to create some interesting results.

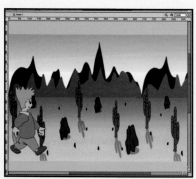

8 A walk cycle is made by looping the walk on the spot. You can then add this to a scrolling parallax background, altering its speed to create the impression of faster or slower movement. You can, of course, create your animation the other way round and tween the movie clip of the character walking across the screen, keeping the background stationary.

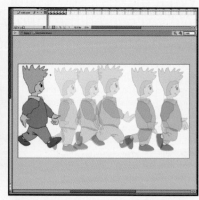

9 To create a more exaggerated effect for your walk, in the style of a character such as Mickey Mouse, you need to have two passing positions and raise the height of the character on each. This is called the 'double bounce' walk, and you can see a good example of it in doublebounce.fla on the CD.

Part 2: **Winding down**

Creating a slow, lazy walk

Centre of gravity

The best way to create the impression of a moving character is to shift its centre of gravity. If you shift it forwards slightly, it creates the impression that the figure's moving faster, as you can see from our runner animation.

10 This walk is similar to the normal walk, but tweaked to make your character look sluggish and unmotivated. Open the file slowlazy.fla and have a look at the cycle to see how it works.

11 You'll notice that the head is looking down, which takes the energy out of the character. A slow and unmotivated character should have a droopy posture, arms dangling. Again, we created this animation in twos, as you can see in the Flash file, to slow the figure's movement right down.

12 Now the tired walk, which evokes a complete lack of energy and is quite similar to our slow, lazy walk. Open the file tired.fla from the CD. For this walk to be effective, we tilted the character's torso forwards by 30 per cent – this makes the figure looks as if he's dolefully dragging his feet. In their furthest-back position, the legs nearly lock, causing the raised leg to drag its toes across the ground.

Part 3: **Sneaking about**

There are two types of sneaky walk: the short sneak and the long sneak

Appeal

Make sure your characters have something that makes them stand out from the crowd and look appealing. Avoid weak design and ensure your figures are strong and bold.

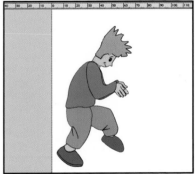

13 The short sneak is good for animating a character who creeps around another character; the long sneak, on the other hand, is a faster movement, best used when a character is trying to surreptitiously escape from danger.

14 Open the file sneak.fla from the CD – this is the short sneak. As you can see, it's a pretty simple cycle. The main movement comes from the legs, with the character creeping on his toes so he doesn't make too much noise.

15 The character's arms are raised to enhance the sneakiness, making him look almost mouse-like, and his head is lowered so he appears physically smaller – and therefore 'sneakier'.

Animation choices

There are two types of animation technique: frame-by-frame, where the animator creates an animation one frame at a time, and tweening, where he or she creates keyframes with in-between frames holding the movement. With tweening, you plan the animation; with frame-by-frame, the animation takes on a more organic feel and develops over time. Most CG animators combine the two methods.

16 We created the short sneak animation to make the sneaking action look faster and more frantic. Imagine a character sneaking about and taking small steps, travelling quite frenetically.

17 Now open the file longsneak.fla. Again, the main movement comes from the legs, but this time they extend further forwards and reach up higher. The feet aren't as pointed as before, and the character is much more flat-footed, so that he can balance as he takes the long, sneaky strides.

18 We created the long sneak in twos, which make the character's strides appear lengthy and deliberate. The long sneak transports the character along quite quickly, but because he's taking long strides, his body needs to move slowly. ❯

Part 4: Running

Time to speed things up

Sound

Using sound effectively can really bring your animation to life. Make sure the sounds you choose are realistic, though, and that they don't get in the way of the action. With Flash MX, you can create such effects quickly and easily.

19 To make your character run, take the previously defined walk cycle and exaggerate it. Open the runcycle.fla file from the Tutorial\Flash animation folder on the CD and open the library.

20 You'll see that there are five positions for the run – and now you're going to create the cycle in the same way you did the walk. First, create a new movie clip and call it 'running'.

21 This time, however, we're not going to animate in twos. Because your character is running, you want to make him look like he's moving faster, so it's best to stick to the same frame rate – and build the animation in ones. The timeline for your movie clip should look like ours above.

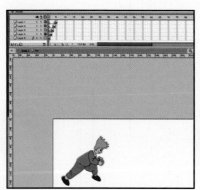

22 Place each character position 1-5 on its respective layer in the keyframe you've created and then slowly drag the playhead along the timeline. You'll now see the animation play. The first thing you'll notice is that your character's centre of gravity is much further forward, which gives the impression your figure is moving at high speed.

23 The run starts at the arms, which provides a sense of anticipation that kick-starts the run. The arms act as a lever, and the shorter you make them, the faster the character appears to go. Lean your character forward and imagine what would happen if he was to come to a sudden stop; if he'd fall over, then he's leaning far enough forwards.

24 Bear in mind that, in a run, both feet leave the ground simultaneously. In a walk, at least one foot is on the ground at the same time. Make sure you work this into your animations.

25 Also consider the environment in which your character is running. If they're running down a hill, their weight will be further backwards to keep control of the run; if they're going uphill, the weight will be further forwards to push them up the incline. Animation appears lifeless if you don't take outside elements and conditions into account.

Anticipation   Suspension   Down position

26 There are three main positions in a run: the first-contact position, where the character anticipates and prepares the audience for the run; the suspension, where the figure begins leaving the ground and both arms and legs are swinging out fully; and the down position, where the leading leg makes contact with the ground again.

Part 5: Setting off

Now we'll animate a runner leaving the starting block

Character building

When developing your characters, take advantage of Flash's library and create symbols that you can easily reuse. If you have stock character elements, this makes the animation process much smoother and easier.

27 This part of the tutorial shows you how to use anticipation to set up an effective run cycle, as well as how to recognise the difference between backward (anticipatory) action and forward action.

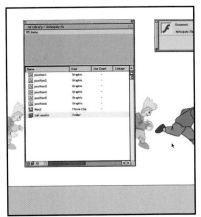

28 Open the file named runner.fla and look in the library – you'll see six positions and a movie clip called Run. This movie clip is the same as the run cycle you created earlier, and the positions 1-6 are the poses leading up to the run.

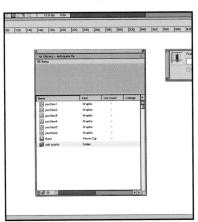

29 Create a new layer in the movie, and within this layer create six keyframes, two frames apart from each other so they look like the image above. You're setting this layer up so the anticipatory section of the animation runs in twos.

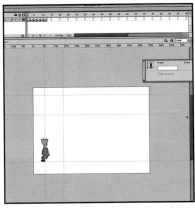

30 Put the relevant character position in each successive keyframe, ensuring each one is positioned slightly to the right of the next. When creating the anticipatory motion, you'll need to experiment with positioning to see what's effective.

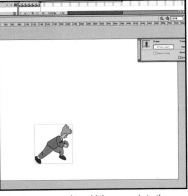

31 Now you need to add the run cycle to the animation. This has to be timed so that it starts as the last set of positions end, and can be tricky to get just right. Place it slightly to the right of the last anticipatory position and test your movie to see where the best position is.

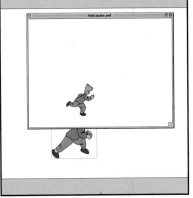

32 Now test the movie, and take a look at our finished version, runnercomplete.fla, on your CD. You'll see that the runner goes from a standing start into the anticipatory movement – and then springs forward into a run.

33 The anticipatory movement begins with the runner getting ready to spring. He crouches forward, leaning on his left knee. You can see his right leg extending backwards, then tensing up to launch his body forward – and create the anticipation.

34 Over the next two steps, the character sinks down onto his right leg and then shoots forward into the run cycle. You can clearly see the difference between the backward and forward motion. Positions 1-4 demonstrate the backward motion; the remaining positions, the forward motion.

35 You've now learnt how to use anticipation to set up a movement, and then follow through. If you apply this and the other techniques we've covered to your work, you're well on your way to creating characters that move naturally and hold your audience's attention.

Illustration: Richard May [w] www.richardmay.com

Lip-synching with Flash Amp

Blah, blah, blah. Everyone's talking about lip-synching in Flash, but it just takes so much work. Well, with Flash Amp it just got easier…

Expertise by Jerome Turner
[e] info@jerometurner.co.uk
[w] www.jerometurner.co.uk
Jerome is a freelance designer/writer and has worked on several Friends Of Ed books including Foundation iMovie 2, Foundation Dreamweaver MX and Flash MX Studio.

Files on disc
The files needed to support this tutorial can be found in the Tutorial\tech_cartoon folder on the cover CD.

Back in the day, many people treated Flash as a means of recreating traditional animation techniques such as stop-motion action. Draw a picture, draw another picture, repeat until madness sets in and someone discovers you scribbling away at a timeline as long as your arm. Things have come a long way since then. People are still creating the same kind of work but labour-saving devices such as Flash Amp combined with modern Flash MX ActionScripting can get the same job done in minutes.

If you've ever tried to animate a character's lips along an audio clip of dialogue you'll soon appreciate how useful Flash Amp can be. Typically you might spend hours listening to each frame and then making decisions on how open or closed the mouth should be for that particular drawing in the timeline. However, using Flash Amp requires only ten drawings (keeping the file size down) and it automatically works out which one should be played according to the volume of the sound at each frame. Sounds clever? It is…

Part 1: Recording dialogue

How to get the clearest conversation for use in your animations and cartoons...

Cheating
Flash Amp

If there is too much noise in your sound file, you may find supposedly 'silent' areas hissing enough to return a 1 instead of a 0 in the amplitude list. If this is the case, there are two fixes. Try to clean up the audio in your sound app so it's quieter before processing again, or simply alter a few of the values in the ActionScript arrays.

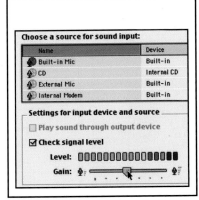

1 You'll find the voices.aiff file on the CD but feel free to record your own version. Write the script for a short conversation (four lines or less) between two people. Then make sure your audio input and recording levels are set and open your sound application.

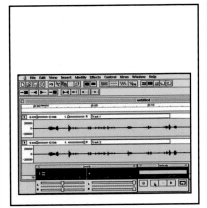

2 Record the conversation as one take with slight pauses between each new line of dialogue. Make sure the readers sound 'animated' (in other words, not monotonous) to ensure a good range of volume as this will reflect in the Flash Amp processing later on.

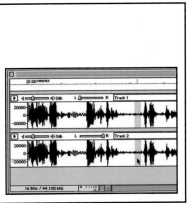

3 Trim silent areas from either end of the sound and adjust any gain or volume controls to make sure the audio is peaking around the top of the scale. If it's too high, normalise and smooth to clear up any noise. If necessary, trim out any over-long silent areas between lines.

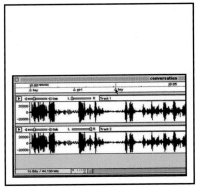

4 Insert Cue Points between 'lines' to distinguish the speaker – one before the boy starts talking, then another before the girl, back to the boy, and so on. Name them according to their characters as these will act as a switch telling ActionScript which one to animate. Save the file as an AIFF.

5 Now we'll use Flash Amp to produce a list of figures that can be used in Flash ActionScript. Open Flash Amp. Click on the question mark to select the AIFF file and hit the Continue arrow. Click it again to confirm the need for an amplitude list.

6 In step 3, tick 'cue point name list'. This will ensure the processing produces a second list of figures that run in parallel to the amplitude list, with the cue points in there indicating when the code should react. Click Continue again.

7 The 'frames per second' indicates how many volume values will be returned per second of audio, matching the fps of your Flash file. A higher number will return more values for use with a faster animation, but you must be confident that the file will cope with this speed so go for 15.

8 Step 5 sets the value scale for the readings made from your audio file. Set it to ten. This means the list will show a ten for the loudest sounds and 0 for the quietest. This also means you only need to produce 10 frames of animation from 'closed' to 'open' mouth.

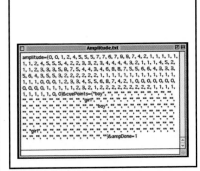

9 Finally, tick yes for 'smoothing' and in the last stage click the text file icon to process the audio. It is saved into a text file which will shortly be used in Flash MX. Feel free to open it and take a look at your conversation, now represented as an amplitude list.

Part 2: Making graphics and animation in Flash

Create your talking characters and synchronise them with your recorded speech…

Keep it clean

When you start working with background layers, characters, buttons, sounds and ActionScript, it pays to be well organised. Name your layers as you create them and place work on them accordingly. In creating and naming symbols and instances of symbols, make sure your system is clear and watch out for names like arrow, border, break and bullet which are part of the ActionScript language.

Stream sounds

Streaming sound is probably the best Sync setting for this type of work, partly because stream sound stops when the timeline stops. You could load up one long sound in chunks by periodically stopping and then restarting the timeline with user interaction, giving all the frames extra time to load up. Keep in mind that Stream sounds are 'mixed' on Exporting, so any panning across speakers will be lost.

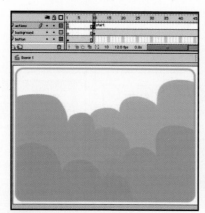

1 Open a new Flash MX file. In frame 1 of a Button layer make a button which the user must press to go to the frame "start". Then, in a Background layer, draw a simple backdrop on the "start" frame. Keep it simple so as not to detract from the main characters.

2 Create two movie clip symbols, a 'Boy' and a 'Girl'. Each one should have a face but no mouth or eyebrows. Keep in mind that simple shapes and lines (basically not too many points) will reduce the file size. Place them on the stage facing each other in a masked character layer.

3 In Boy create a movie symbol on a new layer with instance name Mouth. Inside Mouth create a graphic symbol of a fully opened mouth with the height set to 10 per cent in frame 1, 20 per cent in frame 2 and so on, up until all ten frames have been created. Also add a stop() in frame 1.

4 Add a two-frame animated symbol to Boy called Eyebrow. The Girl movie symbol should also contain an instance of Mouth – check this in flashamptut_01.fla. Then Import the conversation.aiff to the Library and drop it in a Sound layer at the 'start' frame, stretching all layers to cover the duration of the sound.

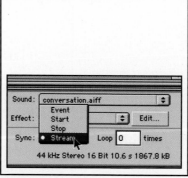

5 Select the frame containing conversation.aiff and set to Sync>Stream in the Properties panel. This means that the Timeline will always be forced into keeping up the same pace as the sound. The sound won't hang up but if Flash can't load up frames fast enough, it skips them.

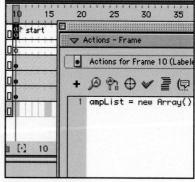

6 In the 'start' frame of the Actions layer, add the following ActionScript which starts up a new Array: ampList. This array (a list of volume values in this case) will be read in sequence as the playhead moves along the Timeline, in turn telling the Mouth clips which frame to show.

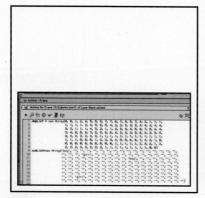

7 Now copy and paste the first list of numbers created in Amplitude.txt and place it within the array's brackets. Create another array called cueList that contains the cue point list from the same txt file, so that your ActionScript looks like this. These lists are now stored in Flash for later reference.

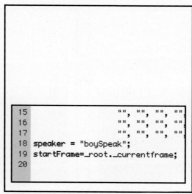

8 Under the arrays, add the following two initialising lines. As Speaker will tell the rest of the script which of the two Mouth movies to play, it needs to start on "boySpeak". The constant startFrame is set because the animated sequence of this fla actually starts on frame 10.

9 Start an onenterframe loop which starts by returning the frame number that the animation is on – gFrame. This ActionScript sits in the Actions layer from the beginning to the end of the animation, which means that the loop will also be repeated on every frame.

Bangin' choons

Now you know how *Flash Amp* works, you'll appreciate that there are a myriad of possibilities. How about a ghettoblaster in the background which pulsates along to the music it's playing? Rather than using gAmp to go to a frame, you would alter the _xscale and _yscale properties instead. Or how about a bird in the tree which sings a tune? As the volume changes, the top section of the beak _rotates.

```
1  ampList = new Array(0, 0, 0, 0, 0, 0, 0, 0, 0, 0, 0,
2                      2, 1, 0, 0, 0, 0, 0, 0, 0, 0, 0,
3                      2, 1, 0, 0, 0, 0, 0, 0, 0, 0, 0,
4                      4, 5, 5, 3, 2, 1, 3, 5, 4, 3, 2,
5                      1, 0, 0, 0, 0, 0, 0, 0, 0, 0, 0,
6                      1, 0, 0, 0, 0, 0, 0, 0, 0, 1, 0,
7                      0, 0, 0, 0, 0, 0, 0, 1, 3, 4, 5,
8                      2, 1, 0, 0, 0)
9  cueList=new Array("", "", "", "", "", "", "boy",
10                   "", "", "", "", "", "", "",
11                   "", "", "", "", "", "", "",
12                   "", "", "", "", "", "", "",
13                   "", "", "", "", "", "", "",
14                   "", "", "", "", "", "", "",
15                   "", "", "", "", "", "", "",
16                   "", "", "", "", "", "", "",
17                   "", "", "", "", "")
18 speaker = "boySpeak";
19 startFrame=_root._currentframe;
20
21 _root.onEnterFrame=function(){
22     gFrame = _root._currentframe - startFrame;
23     gAmp = ampList[gFrame];
24     gCue = cueList[gFrame];
25
```

10 The indexes (values listed) in the array are referenced with the array's name, followed by the index number required in square brackets, starting at 0. So, in adding Lines 23 and 24 to our loop, on frame 10 of the root gFrame will equal 0, so reading 0 from ampList and "boy" from cueList.

```
18 speaker = "boySpeak";
19 startFrame=_root._currentframe;
20
21 _root.onEnterFrame=function(){
22     gFrame = _root._currentframe - startFrame;
23     gAmp = ampList[gFrame];
24     gCue = cueList[gFrame];
25     if (gCue == "boy") {
26         speaker = "boySpeak";
27     } else if (gCue == "girl") {
28         speaker = "girlSpeak";
29     }
30
```

11 The following sets the variable speaker whenever gCue returns Boy or Girl to tell the ActionScript who is speaking (Lines 25-29). As Speaker was initialised as "boySpeak" it will remain so until the animation reaches a value of Girl in the cueList indexes.

```
27     } else if (gCue == "girl") {
28         speaker = "girlSpeak";
29     }
30     if (speaker == "boySpeak") {
31         boy.mouth.gotoAndStop(gAmp + 1);
32     } else if (speaker == "girlSpeak") {
33         girl.mouth.gotoAndStop(gAmp + 1);
34     }
35 }
36
```

12 Lines 30 and 31 here check Speaker to see whose mouth should be animated, and then the correct frame of either Mouth is shown. Note that a closed mouth should be shown when the ampList returns 0, but as there is no such thing as frame 0, set Mouth to go to gAmp+1.

```
30     if (speaker == "boySpeak") {
31         boy.mouth.gotoAndStop(gAmp + 1);
32         if(gAmp>=7){
33             boy.brow.gotoAndStop(2)
34         } else {
35             boy.brow.gotoAndStop(1)
36         }
37     } else if (speaker == "girlSpeak") {
38         girl.mouth.gotoAndStop(gAmp + 1);
39     }
40 }
41
```

13 Finally, lines 32-36 here show that if Boy is speaking and his voice is raised, the eyebrows follow. When the value drops below 7 again, they return to frame 1 (lowered). Now make sure all your symbol instances are correctly named, check the code against flashamptut_01.fla and test the movie.

14 As this file contains a moderately large sound file, it may be worth simulating download at different connection speeds from the Debug menu while Testing. Also tick Streaming and Bandwidth Profiler from the View menu. The movie should stream okay if the grey bars fit under the red line.

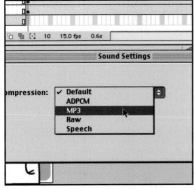

15 If the fla is too large, select the Sound file in the Library and pick Export Settings from the drop-down menu. From here, choose to compress the exporting sound as an MP3, but don't worry – you can always change this back to the original version at any time.

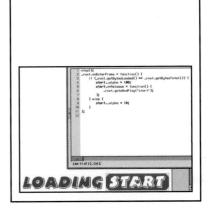

16 If size is still a problem, attach a preloader to frame 1 of the root timeline. As it currently stands, the option to press a button at the start will already stall the viewer enough to let the sound start buffering, but you can find a preloader version in flashamptut_02.fla.

17 As a finishing touch, make sure that all layers stretch right up to end of the sound file (you will see it in the Timeline) and add a stop() action on the Actions layer. You might also want to add a 'replay' button here.

18 It might seem like we've covered a lot of ground but imagine how long it would have taken to achieve the same result without *Flash Amp*! If you look at the final files you'll see how small they are, relying largely on ActionScript and being ideal for slotting into games.

Animating in Photoshop

Your images have been itching for movement, now with Photoshop and Flash, let your pictures rise from the confining page…

Breathing subtle movements into static imagery can inspire an almost hypnotic charm, as if the pictures themselves are straining to live. Macromedia Flash has extended the hand of Photoshop into a world of moving pixels, where the effects within Photoshop's interface can now be applied to the art of movement.

This tutorial is one of two parts, designed to show you how to prepare your imagery into a state of unrest. You will learn how to make your pictures vibrate and flutter. This is done by duplicating your images into a series of warped clones that will appear to animate as they fade into one another.

The first part of this tutorial will walk you through the key components of creating your animation, using the popular image–editor Photoshop. Akin to setting up carefully placed dominoes, you will create a chain of images that will fade into each other.

The specifics of having these pieces fade will be discussed in the second part of the tutorial where the entire animation will be made into a working screensaver. This is the part of the tutorial that will involve working with Flash MX.

The CD contains the workshop files needed to participate with this tutorial.

Illustration and words are provided by Vincent Marcone. You can contact Vincent at [e] vincent@mypetskeleton.com.

On the CD
The workshop files that are needed to participate in this tutorial are in the Tutorial\Animation folder on the cover CD.

Part 1: Organising image files

Keeping files clean and labelled enables the animation to move smoothly as you create your scene shots…

Folders are your friends

By organising your layers into folders, the frustration of trying to find that one lost layer among an endless line of miniature thumbnails can be avoided. Simply click on the folder icon at the bottom of the Layers palette and drag the layers you'd like to keep as a group within the new folder. To label the folder, simply double–click on the Folder layer.

1 Make sure your Photoshop files are fairly simple and well labelled. Key elements and textures should be segregated from the main backdrop. These images were created simply by taking photographs, screening a few choice textures over them, while adjusting the Hue/Saturation levels to suite the imagery.

2 Consider your plan of attack. Each illustration represents a different segment of the animation. Essentially, there are three parts to each Photoshop file: the backdrop (main image), the mid-drop (separated elements within the main image) and the foredrop (the textures screened over the back and mid-drop).

3 By grouping the layers into folders, you can see the segregated elements. In this case, the backdrop is the Statues folder, the mid-drop consists of the Hooks and Trees folders, while the foredrop maintains the textures that are screened over the other layers.

Part 2: Animating the hook within Liquify

By importing sections into the Liquify interface, you can add a random type of movement…

 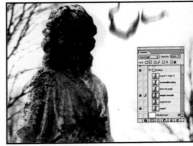 

1 To prepare the animated hook, open the file angel1.psd, and select the layer, hook1. Create a copy and label it as hook 2. Use the square Marquee tool, and select a box around the floating hook2. Make sure the Hook layer is selected within the Layers palette, and then select Liquify from the Image option on the top bar.

2 Once you're in the Liquify interface, use the Warp tool (top-left icon) to slightly push and pull different sections of the hook. Try not to move the image much more than five pixels or so. A slight displacement effects a smoother transition when the screens are eventually animated in Flash.

3 Copy the new and slightly-warped hook. Repeat the previous step three times until you have three slightly different warped versions of the same hook. You should have three hooks available to select from, each one over the top of the other.

Part 3: Blurring for motion

The Motion Blur tool works beautifully as a fade in, as well as adding mystery to the piece…

New windows

If you need to create a new window with the same dimensions, there is a simple shortcut. Make sure you have selected a visible layer, then use Command/Ctrl+A to Select all. Once you've done this, press Command/Ctrl+Shift+C simultaneously, then press Command/Ctrl+N to create a new window. Your new window will have the same attributes as the previous one. To paste a flat layer of the previous visible image from the old window, press Command/Ctrl+V.

1 Select Angel1 from the Layers palette, and copy it. Select the new copy and go to the Filters option on the top bar. Go to Blur and then highlight Motion Blur. A small interface should pop up, make sure the direction is completely vertical and disperse the pixels to about 45.

2 Label this new blurred image as Blurred Angel into the palette. Create another copy of the Blurred Angel and use the Screen option from the Layers palette. Label this as Screen Blurred Angel.

3 Go back to the Hooks folder, copy the first hook into another layer and label it Blurred Hook. Then place a small Motion Blur to it, but only disperse the pixels slightly.

Part 4: Morphing between screenshots

The fades should move into each other smoothly, so avoid abrupt changes in form and shape…

1 Only Angel Front and Angel1 should be visible within the Statues folder (all others should be turned off). Place Angel Front so that it is above Angel1, which should cause Angel1 to disappear.

2 Make a copy of Angel Front and label it Angel Morph. Once you've turned off Angel Front, go back to Angel Morph and go to the Hard Light option within the Layers palette

3 Carefully erase the inside parts of Angel Morph to reveal part of the Angel1 statue that's behind the worked layer. Don't over do it, just take enough away to display a bit of both views.

Part 5: Insert glowing eyes here

Lighting Effects can be an artist's best friend when used properly…

The Magic Eraser

This tool comes in handy when you've made a blunder that surpasses the Undo shortcut (Command/Ctrl+Z), and it's quicker than getting out your History palette. Simply hold down the Alt key (PC) or Option key (Mac) and erase over the area you wish to correct. The Magic Eraser will replace the pixels to their original state since your last save.

1 Create a duplicate layer of Angel Front within the Statue folder and label it Angel Glow. Then go to the Filters option on the top menu bar and Render, and continue to select Lens flare. When the small interface pops up, click on the 105mm prime flare at approx 30 per cent. Place the flare within the eye socket and repeat for the other eye socket.

2 Copy this layer and label it Angel Bright Glow. Then repeat the above process for each eye socket but, this time, use the 50-300mm zoom flare at approximately 45 per cent.

3 Make sure the lights within the sockets line up with each other.

Part 6: Snapshots and such…

The next steps involve using Photoshop to prepare a techno slideshow of sorts…

1 First off, open a new file that has the exact same dimensions and resolution as the working file, so that the snapshots can be copied to an outside source. Label the file Snapshots Template.

2 Go back to the original file, angel1.psd, and make the Angel1 layer visible (the only one within the Statues folder, as well as the Blurred hook from the Hooks folder. Now that you've established what the first scene will look like, select the entire image (Command/Ctrl+A).

3 Make sure you have selected one of the visible layers within the Layers palette to use the following shortcut. Press Command+Shift+C (Mac), or Control+Shift+C (PC), then go to your other PSD file, Snapshots Template, and press Command+V (Mac), Control+V (PC). This gives you a flattened snapshot from the Angel1 file. Label the layer Cell1.

Part 7: **Thinking about the elements**

It's important to have as many subtle effects going on simultaneously within each cell.
The following steps analyse all of the possibilities…

Texture changes

When considering your animation, don't concentrate on just one area of your image. Try to have a variety of things fluctuate from screenshot to screenshot. Scattering textures around from one scene to the next will provide interesting morphing effects that will be barely noticeable, and yet the effect will add to the overall ambiance.

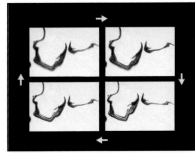

1 This is where the fun begins. You must consider all elements within the folder that have the potential to be adjusted. For example, the hook should always be changing (toggle visible layers between the four hooks within each screenshot).

2 The intensity of the textures can also affect the animation. By doubling up the Texture 2 layer, the colours will become more saturated between one fade to the next. It's all a matter of switching different visible layers for each screenshot.

3 In addition to the texture fades, the Screened Blurred Angel and Blurred Angel layers should be added. The contrast of these forms will appear as if the transformations are glowing. These screenshots will be handy in the Flash animation.

4 The morphing transition is illustrated in the above diagram. Once you've morphed from Angel1 layer to Angel Front layer, the screenshots take on a different perspective as the animations revolve around a new face.

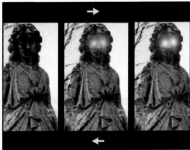

5 The layers Angel Front, Angel Glow and Angel Glow Brighter can toggle back and forth between each other when taking screenshots. It will give the appearance of a very smooth and magical glow as they fade in and out.

6 Begin taking snapshots with all of these in mind, and place them into the snapshot template PSD file as cell layers. Always have a lot going on – the more details that change within your screenshots, the more interesting it will be.

Part 8: **The angels are in your hands**

Experiment and have fun! But, keep the following guides in mind…

Burning your animation

Using the Burning tool and etching in darkness upon certain surfaces from one scene to the next, can give the illusion of fluttering shadows and the movement of light. However, make sure there isn't a drastic difference between the two scenes, less is more in this case.

1 Remember to stay consistent. Animate the hooks within each angel image as you would have within steps 1-2 in Part 2. Use the blurring effect to alter the form of the angels every once in a while. Manipulate the textures as you move from one screenshot to the next – they offer an ephemeral atmosphere within the animation.

2 The transition from one angel segment to the next is important. Once you've completed a series of screengrabs (try not to exceed over 20), take the last screenshot and import it to the next angel section. Experimenting with effects such as Colour Dodge or Hard Light (Layers option) will create a smooth transition.

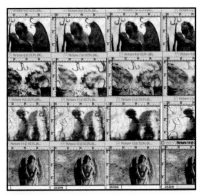

3 If you need further guidance to continue, open the file The Cells. Within this folder, you will find all of the screenshots available for viewing. Use them as a guide, but don't be afraid to let your own creative juices flow, there are several different paths that will bring life to these angels.

SOMETIMES ANGELS HAVE HOOKS IN THEIR HAIR. GOLDEN LOCKS LACED WITH POISONED METAL TIPS. TO CATCH THOSE WHO ARE NOT LOOKING. SO IF YOU EVER SEE AN ANGEL. DON'T LOOK AT THE HALO, KEEP YOUR EYES ON THE HOOKS.

BECAUSE NOT ALL ANGELS ARE FROM HEAVEN.

MYPETSKELETON.COM

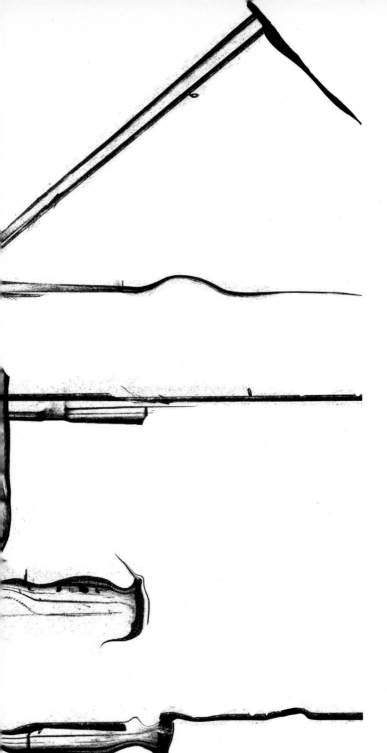

Creating a Flash screensaver

Continuing directly from the Animating in Photoshop tutorial, Flash offers you the ultimate flip book with plenty of tricks up its animated sleeve…

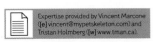

Expertise provided by Vincent Marcone ([e] vincent@mypetskeleton.com) and Tristan Holmberg ([w] www.tman.ca).

Files on CD
You can find all the files needed for this tutorial in the Tutorial\Screensaver folder on the cover CD.

The first part of this tutorial illustrated the various effects and distortions that can be used to create a series of shaped compositions. This tutorial is going to look at designing movements within controlled moments as one frame disappears and then reappears into another.

Think of the effect of a cushioned flip book that offers a smooth transition and happens to be very forgiving as one image moves to the next.

We're going to use the Photoshop images as if they were carefully placed dominoes, each piece tumbling into the next to emphasise a series of transitions.

To wrap up this animation, we'll show you how to use ScreenTime Media software to convert your animation into a screensaver for either a Mac or PC in just three easy steps. ➤

Part 1: Creating your main movie in Flash

Placing the sequenced JPEG images and animating their opacities…

Editing multiple frames

This is a great a way to manipulate many objects across many frames. By clicking the edit multiple frames icon, and dragging the frame selector within the Timeline over the desired number of frames, you can reposition, scale or apply any other transformation within the selected group.

Exporting as an AVI

If you wish to save your *Flash* animation as a different format (for example, an AVI file) it is important to understand the limitations of the program. The movie clip symbols will not be rendered in the AVI, unless you have all your tweens within the main Timeline.

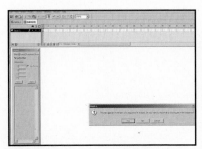

1 After saving each JPEG still for Web within Photoshop, you are ready to import them into Flash. In the file menu click Insert>New symbol (Command/Ctrl+F8). to bring up the create new symbol dialog box and select the movie symbol type. Call this movie mainmovie. Flash will then go into the Edit mode of this symbol. Go to the File menu and choose Import. Choose the first graphic of the stills that are provided on the CD (step01.jpg). Flash will prompt you to import all or only the selected graphic. Choose all.

2 We will now organise all the sequenced still images in our new movie clip. In the Timeline of mainmovie, you will notice several keyframes displayed one after another. Create a new layer in the Timeline by clicking the + icon at the bottom of the Timeline's interface. We will now place each imported still into its own layer, one at a time. After pressing the + icon you will notice a new layer with 1 empty keyframe above the original layer. Delete layer 1 by highlighting it and then clicking the trash icon. You now have one empty layer in your main movie.

3 Press Command/Ctrl+L to bring up your library that lists all the objects in your scene. Select the first imported still (step01.jpg) and drag it onto the stage. While the image is selected, use the align dialog box (Command/Ctrl+K) to position the graphic at the centre of your mainmovie clip. Make another new layer, copy the aligned graphic and paste it into this layer. With the graphic still selected on your stage, go to the File menu and click Insert>Convert to Symbol (F8) and create a graphic symbol called step01.

4 Now that we have our first still as a graphic symbol, we are going to animate its opacity. In the Timeline, click on frame 10 and go to the file menu, click Insert>Key frame (F6) to place another keyframe there. Click the first keyframe now, and go to the File menu and click Modify>Instance properties (Command/Ctrl+I) which will bring up its interface. Select opacity and drag it to 0 per cent. Go to frame 10 again and adjust its opacity to 99 per cent (this will prevent any slight movement of the graphic).

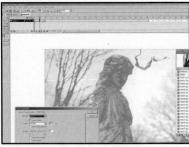

5 We are now going to animate between the still's two different opacities. Click any frame in between the two keyframes, and go to the File menu and click Modify>Frame (Command/Ctrl+F). Click the tweening tab and select motion from the combo box then press OK. You should now see a blue arrow between the two keyframes. If you drag your mouse in the Timeline over the arrow you will see the animation on the stage.

6 Now that we have our first animation, we are going to make a new layer in the Timeline, and insert a new keyframe (F6) at frame 10. Drag the next graphic (step02.jpg) from the library onto the stage filling the empty keyframe with that graphic. Be sure to align (Command/Ctrl+K) the graphic to the centre of the mainmovie. Convert the graphic into a symbol (F8) and place another keyframe at frame 20. Adjust the first keyframe to 0 per cent opacity and the last keyframe to 99 per cent opacity (see step 4). Keep placing your graphics, one after another, and be sure to position them correctly and turn them into graphic symbols so each can have their opacities fade one into another.

Part 2: Modifying frames to create the illusion of speed

Adjust the number of frames between image fades to change the speed of moments within the animation…

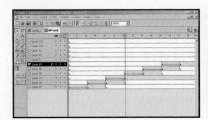

1 After you have set up all your fades (images 1-101 in the Tutorial\Screensaver folder on the cover CD) you will notice each transition takes up the same number of frames. The amount of time it takes to move from one image to another is equal. For example, you will notice that from frame 13 to 63 the ghost flies very slowly and smoothly off the screen. To create a sense of speed, you must eliminate intermediate frames.

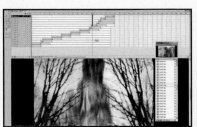

2 To manipulate this time frame, select a frame between the two animated keyframes (the frames marked by the blue arrow) and move the scroll bar of the Timeline up to the top. Hold the Shift key and click the top frame such that the entire column of layers is affected. Now press Shift+F5 to delete 1 frame from all those selected layers. Keep pressing Shift+F5 to quicken the selected animation.

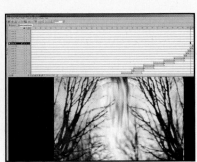

3 If you run the movie you will find that the ghost now whips off the screen in this section of the movie. You can also add keyframes to the animations by pressing just F5 instead of Shift+F5 while a column is selected in your Timeline.

Part 3: **Around and around we go**

How to make your movie clip loop seamlessly…

Opacity tweening

When dealing with graphic bitmap symbols for a smooth transition (without any possible unwarrented movement) do not use a value of 100 per cent when fading in, rather use 99 per cent. This will ensure a proper fade.

1 Highlight the first layer and copy the first key frame in your "mainmovie" clip. Make a new layer at the top of the stack and place an empty key frame in the very last frame of that layer.

2 Highlight and copy the first frame of the bottom layer (in the file menu click Edit>Copy frames). Paste it into the recently created empty key frame at the top of the stack (in the file menu click Edit>Paste frames).

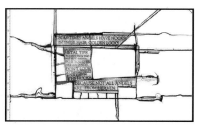

3 Skip 10 frames ahead and place a new key frame (F6) there and adjust the first key frame opacity to 0 per cent and the last to 99 per cent (Command/Ctrl+I). Add a new frame (F5) to the layer below the very last key frame. If you run the movie you should see the end of the movie fade into the opening image at frame 1.

Part 4: **Preparing backdrop and masks**

Planning the position of your masks on the backdrop in Photoshop…

Align Tool

In Flash press Command/Ctrl+K to bring up the align object box. Using this feature you can quickly orient your objects within the scene or space objects evenly apart. Make sure you have the Match page size checkbox checked. This is a useful tool to evenly separate objects from one another.

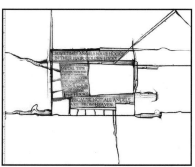

1 The first thing you need to do is decide what dimensions your screen saver is going to be. Generally a canvas size of 1024x768 will produce consistent results among a variety of resolutions. Open the prepared backdrop.jpg in Photoshop.

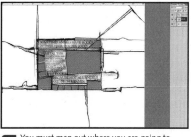

2 You must map out where you are going to want your animations on the backdrop graphic. Make a new layer and mark out the areas with the Lasso tool. Once you are confident with their placements, fill the selection with red. This will be your designated mask. For your convenience, there is a mask layer available in the Photoshop file (theangelscreensaver.psd).

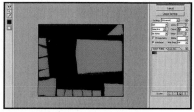

3 Highlight the mask layer and press Command/Ctrl+C which will create the appropriate selection. Now make a new document by pressing Command/Ctrl+N, which will keep the dimensions consistent for your mask. Paste the layer into this new document Command/Ctrl+V. Make a new layer underneath the current one and fill it with black. Save this file as mask.gif with two colours only (use Export to Web option and select GIF with two colours in the options box); red and black.

Part 5: **Invite the moving imagery into your design**

Set up your dimensions and import your objects into the Flash movie…

The Inspector

Press Alt+Ctrl+I or Option+Command+I to bring up the Inspector. This interface is great for quickly gathering information about specific objects in your scene. As you highlight various elements within your composition the Inspector will relay every detail about them.

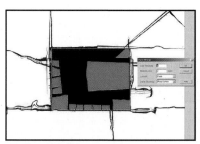

1 Go to the File menu and choose Import. In the dialog box, pick the location of the images you saved earlier and select the backdrop image (backdrop.jpg). This will automatically place the graphic into your scene. Press Ctrl+Alt+I (PC) or Option+Command+I (Mac) to open the Inspector dialog box, and under its position values, enter 0 for both the x and y textfields.

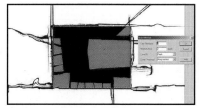

2 Make a new layer and import mask.gif into it. Press Command/Ctrl+K to align the mask.gif directly on top of the backdrop.jpg. In the File menu, click Modify>Trace bitmap and use these settings: colour threshold=4, minimum area=2, curve fit=pixels, corner threshold=many corners and press OK. The mask.gif is now a vector image, you can select the black and press backspace to delete it. Select one of the masks and press Command/Ctrl+X to cut it from the scene. Make a new layer and paste in place (Command/Ctrl+Shift+V).

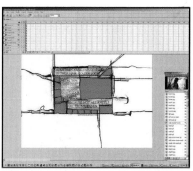

3 Make a new layer for each mask, cutting and pasting each one in place on their respective layer and name them accordingly. You are now ready to place your mainmovie clip into the scene under the main mask. ➤

Part 6: Prepare to give life to your scene

Placing your movie within the backdrop…

Naming layers

It's a good idea to name your layers in Flash. Make it a habit to name each object as you create them. This makes navigating much easier as your scenes can get very complicated. Naming a layer in relation to its position on the stage is a great example of helping you identify and orient your scene's objects.

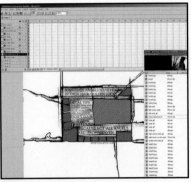

1 Make a new layer under the mask that will reveal the mainmovie clip. Drag from the library your symbol called mainmovie and place it onto the stage. (When placing objects onto the scene, be sure you have the correct layer selected!).

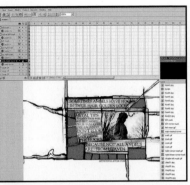

2 Position the mainmovie clip under the mask. Right-click (PC) or hold-click (Mac) the mask layer and select mask. You will now see that the masked mainmovie has integrated with your backdrop.

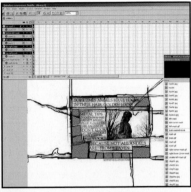

3 Go to the + icon and make a new layer under each mask. This will prepare you for the various movie clips that will be placed within the backdrop.

Part 7: A collage of movement

Be resourceful by duplicating your animation into a series of miniature movies within the design…

Using the Library

Try to avoid editing your symbols on the stage. Instead, always keep your library open. Press Command/Ctrl+L and edit the symbols from within this interface. This will prevent you from unintentionally moving a symbol within the stage.

Locking layers

Keep your layers locked at all times. This will prevent you from editing the wrong object. Edit only the layer you are working on, and once finished, lock it again. You can lock all layers simultaneously by clicking the lock icon located at the top left of the Timeline.

1 In the library, right-click (PC) or Option-click (Mac) on the mainmovie clip and choose duplicate movie clip. Give it an appropriate name, that will reflect its location within the design (for instance, top right mask). Now right-click (PC) or Option-click (Mac) on the mainmovie clip in the library and choose edit.

2 Once you have identified a favourable segment within the mainmovie clip, extract it by highlighting a block of frames by clicking the first keyframe. Hold the Shift key and click the last keyframe. This will create a block selection around that period in the Timeline. In this case, the ghost animation was been extracted. Now press Alt+Ctrl+C (PC) or Option+Command+C (Mac) to copy those frames. Note: do not select more than 50 frames per mini clip.

3 In the library go to the new movie clip you created, right-click (PC) or Option-click (Mac) on it, and choose edit. Select the empty keyframe in the clip and press Alt+Ctrl+V (PC) or Option+Command+V (Mac) to paste the frames of animation you just copied. Make sure that you loop the animation as previously described earlier in the tutorial.

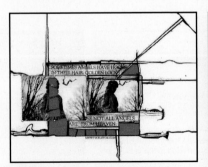

4 Drag that clip onto the stage beneath the appropriate mask and right-click (PC) or hold-click (Mac) on the mask layer and choose the Mask option. You may want to scale the duplicated clip so that it fits the mask's composition. To scale the clip, right-click/Option-click the clip on the stage and choose Scale. You can also flip the image in any direction using the Scale tool.

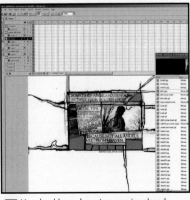

5 You should now have two movies placed within your backdrop.jpg. Repeat this process until each mask is occupied by a different segment of the mainmovie clip.

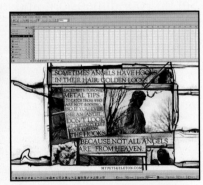

6 Be careful when putting your mini clips into the scene. If your screensaver contains too many animations that are too large it will be too CPU-intensive for most machines. The end result: the movie will lose its smooth flowing quality and appear to chug from image to image.

Part 8: Adding the final touches

The hooks shall now make their appearance…

Hiding layers

Use the Transparency option (the eyeball icon) in the Timeline for positioning layers. This comes in very handy when overlaying movie clips on bitmap backgrounds to align them correctly. Repeatedly toggle a layer's visibility to ensure correct placement, and zoom in.

Matting the screensaver

If you designed your screensaver to be locked at 1024x768, then there will be matting for monitors displaying at a higher resolution. To set the matting colour, simply click Modify>Movie and select a colour from the colour box located at the bottom right of the dialog box.

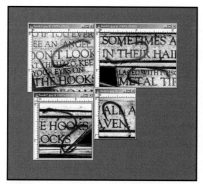

1 The final steps involve incorporating the design and the animations by adding movement to the interface. A series of hooks will be placed to relate to the typography and the animations as they randomly appear and disappear. Import the hooks from the Hooks folder within the CD and place it on its own layer in Flash.

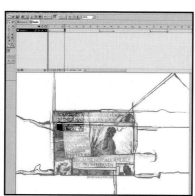

2 Make sure that the layer is matched up with the type and make each hook image a movie clip symbol (see Creating your main movie in Flash for reference). Edit each movie clip symbol and make a graphic symbol of the hook so that you can fade them in and out.

3 Create a unique Timeline (for example, make each hook movie a different length) so that during the animation's playback, the hooks will appear and disappear randomly over time. Try not to animate all the hooks at the same time, because it's CPU-intensive and will reduce the overall performance of the animation.

Converting the Flash movie into a screensaver using Screentime

Screentime is a quick and efficient way to convert your Flash animations into a screensaver format for both Mac and PC...

For PC

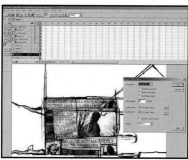

1 Go to the File menu and click File>Export movie. Choose SWF as the format and 50 per cent JPG quality to conserve on filesize. Pick a name and location for the SWF.

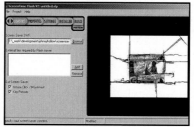

2 Load the *ScreenTime* application. You'll find a demo at [w] www.screentime.com. You will see five tabs: content, properties, settings, installer and build. In the content tab, select the location of the SWF. In properties, name your movie and either use the SWF as a thumb or make your own to be displayed during the screensaver installation.

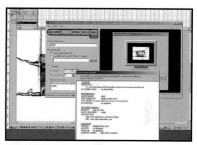

3 Adjust your settings to your liking in the settings and installers tab, and finally click Build to make the screensaver. You will be prompted to save your Screentime settings, then click continue. You will now have an executable ready to be installed on any PC system!

For Mac

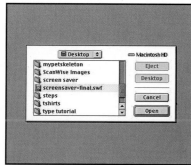

1 Open the SWF file in the the Flash player and save it as a Projector file. After this has been completed, close the Flash player. A diamond-shaped icon should appear on your desktop.

2 Open the application ScreenTime (you'll find a demo at [w] www.screentime.com) and under the File menu, select Convert Projector. Browse for the file that you have created and open it, give it a name, and convert the file.

3 Once the file has been converted, a new icon (a movie reel) will appear on the desktop. Simply drag the icon into your Control Panels. You can set the idle time of your screen saver by double-clicking the file.

Illustration: Bryn Owens [w] www.bluntdog.co.uk

A Flash quiz game

With the release of Flash MX, we show you how to build a quiz game that takes advantage of the new features…

Back in the early days of Flash, the application was used to create specific site elements — especially animations and intro splashes. Having developed into Flash MX, it can now be used to create all sorts of interactive experiences. One area where you can apply MX straight away is in the creation of quiz games.

We've teamed up with Sprite Interactive to bring you this tutorial, in which you'll use ActionScript and some Flash design skills to structure a quiz. The questions in the quiz itself are all Flash-related, so you may even have fun taking trying it out before you work on the tutorial.

Here, you'll learn how to use all the new Flash user interface components, such as radio buttons, drop-down menus and push buttons. We'll also show you some of the new ActionScript functions, most notably the new dynamic loading of sound into the movie.

Flash MX Quiz was created by Sprite Interactive at [w] www.sprite.net

Files on disc
In the Tutorial\Quiz folder on the cover CD you will find the quiz.fla file containing all the assets you will need to complete the tutorial, as well as a free demo of Flash MX in order for you to build your game.

Part 1: Creating your Flash MX quiz game

Follow this tutorial and use the files in the Tutorial\Quiz folder on the CD to build your game...

XML

XML (eXtensible Markup Language) is a great way to interchange structured data in Internet applications. We have used XML in this quiz to format the questions so they can be read by *Flash* in a standard format. In XML, as with HTML, you can use tags to mark up or specify a body of text. In XML, you define tags that identify a piece of data, which enables the same XML document to be used and reused in different environments.

1 First of all, prepare your movie. Create six layers and name them – from top to bottom – Question Display, UI Components, ActionScript, labels, and background, then import the background graphic onto the background layer: background.swf from the folder on the CD.

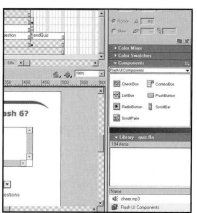

2 We need to put our user interface components on the stage. Select the UI Components layer, open the Components panel and drag a new ComboBox component onto the stage. This will be used to select the number of questions to answer.

3 Select the new ComboBox and open the properties panel. Here, enter two values in the Labels field and corresponding values in the Data field. Give the ComboBox the instance name numQuestions.

4 Next, drag a new CheckBox component onto the stage and label it, Give me the hard questions. When this is selected by the player an alternative set of questions will be used. Give the CheckBox the instance name hardQuestions.

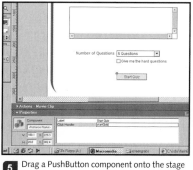

5 Drag a PushButton component onto the stage and give it the label Start Quiz. Since you want the button to actually perform a function, you need to add a Click Handler – this is an ActionScript function that is called when the push button is clicked. To assign a handler set the Click Handler field to startQuiz.

6 Now add the script from code1.txt in the Tutorial\Quiz folder on the CD to the first frame action of the Actions layer. This code defines the startQuiz function that is used to load the questions for the quiz and start the game.

Part 2: Adding the questions

The next step is to add the questions to your quiz game...

1 The function uses the getValue() function to get the number of questions selected from the ComboBox. It loads the appropriate set of questions by calling the getValue() method on the CheckBox, it will return true if checked.

2 The questions are loaded from an XML file. The file contains a number of elements. Each element defines a question, its possible options and its answer. Refer to the comments in code1.txt for more details on the XML functions that are used for the quiz, and refer to question_easy.xml for an example of the XML format.

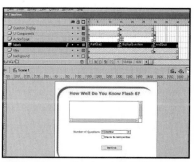

3 Once the questions have been loaded, you need to start the quiz. On the Labels layer create keyframes on frames 1, 15 and 30. Give the first frame the label startQuiz, frame 15 displayQuestion and frame 30 endQuiz. These will be used to control the quiz. ➤

Part 2: Adding the questions continued…

The new Flash MX environment

Flash MX boasts a whole new environment that, although monitor-intensive, offers a lot more flexibility to the Flash developer. Gone are the dockable panels that were the bane of so many Flash developers' lives. These have now been replaced with a context-sensitive properties panel, to bring Flash MX in line with Macromedia's other products, such as Dreamweaver. Flash now also has a new Answers window close-to-hand, which gives you quick access to support material and ActionScript reference. A great new feature in the Timeline is the ability to organise your layers into folders, and the colour mixer panel has had a new overhaul to make it easier to use.

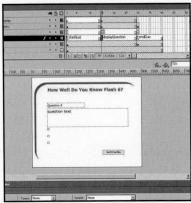

4 The displayQuestion frame is used to display the current question, the text for a question, its possible answers and a button to move onto the next question.

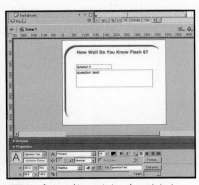

5 You first need to create two dynamic text fields: one to display the question number, and another to display the question. Create these on the Question Display layer and give them the variable names questionIndicator and questionText. Make the questionText field multi-line so that it displays the questions correctly.

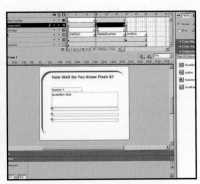

6 Drag three RadioButton components onto the UI Components layer underneath the questionText field. Select the first RadioButton and set its Data field to 1, set the second one to 2 and the third to 3. The Data field is the value returned for the selected radio button when the getValue() function is called on the radio button group.

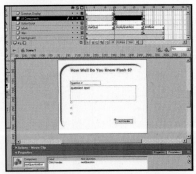

7 Name the RadioButtons option1, option2 and option3. Drag a new PushButton onto the stage and give it the label Next Question, and the instance name nextQuestionPattern. With the RadioButtons and PushButton in place, the layout for the question display is complete.

8 Add the code from code2.txt on the cover CD to the frame action on frame 15 of the Actions layer. This disables the next question button by calling the setEnabled() function of the PushButton component. It then updates the questionIndicator display with the current question number.

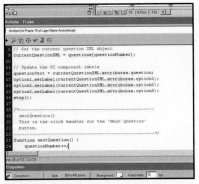

9 To display the question, the code retrieves the current question from the array of XML question objects that you loaded at the start of the quiz. The values for a question can then be retrieved by accessing the attributes object of the question.

Part 3: Adding the answers

Now that all the questions are in place, we need some answers…

Flash Components

Flash MX lets you quickly develop advanced user interfaces by using a number of preset components. These reusable objects are movie clips that have associated parameters, and behave a lot like their counterparts in Dreamweaver. Flash MX includes all of the most commonly-used operating system interface elements, such as radio buttons, drop-down menus and push buttons, and they can be integrated into your movies in a simple drag-and-drop fashion.

1 Using this method, the question text is displayed in the question text field and the radio button labels are updated to display the question's possible answers (the values of .attributes.option1 etc.). To set a RadioButton label, the setLabel() function is used on each of the three radio buttons.

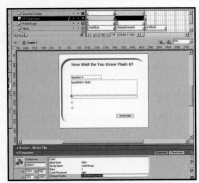

2 To re-enable the button once they've selected an answer you need to add a Change Handler to each radio button. In the Change Handler field of each radio button add the value enableNextQuestion, this will be the name of the function to call when they select an answer.

3 Add the code from code3.txt to the frame action on frame 15. This code defines the enableNextQuestion() function which uses the setEnabled() function to re-enable the Next Question button.

Part 3: Adding the answers continued...

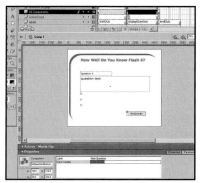

4 You need to add a Click Handler to the Next Question push button. To do this change the value for the Click Handler field of the button to nextQuestion. Add the code from code4.txt on the cover CD to the frame action on frame 15. This code defines the nextQuestion() function.

5 This function first increments the current question number. It then checks if the answer selected is correct by comparing the values of getValue() result from the radio button group with the defined correct answer for the question. If identical then the player score is increased.

6 The function then checks if the player has answered all their questions, if they have it jumps to endQuiz. If not, the radio buttons are all deselected and the displayQuestion frame is repeated to display the next question.

Part 4: Adding the sound files

All that now remains is to let the players know how well they've done...

Sprite Interactive

Sprite is the developer of this Flash MX quiz game. Based in Fetcham, Surrey, Sprite Interactive Ltd is a new media company specialising in Web-based solutions. Sprite builds cutting-edge solutions for a wide range of high-profile clients, including TONI&GUY, TIGI, Philips, Schnieder Electric, Pirelli, ESPN and Disney Interactive, for whom it has developed a number of Web-based games and applications. Sprite is publishing a book on *Flash* animation techniques through Focal Press this Easter. For more information on Sprite, and to play the games it has developed, visit **[w]** www.sprite.net or email **[e]** info@sprite.net.

1 This is done on the endQuiz frame. On this frame create a multi-line text field with the variable name welldone – this will display the end of quiz message. Next, drag a push button from the components panel onto the stage and give it the label Play Again and the Click Handler restartQuiz.

2 Paste the code from code5.txt into the frame action of frame 30. This generates a message depending on the player's score and displays it in the welldone text field. It also defines the restartQuiz() function used to restart the quiz.

3 If the player gets a good score a sound clip will be played. To import the sound select File> Import and select cheer.mp3. Next, open the library and select the Linkage option for the imported sound effect. Check Export for ActionScript and give it the identifier cheer.

4 To play the sound a new sound object is created and the cheer sound is attached using the attachSound function. The sound is played using the start() function, and the new onSoundComplete handler is used to automatically restart the quiz when the sound clip finishes.

5 To attach the onSoundComplete handler the code defines the function stopCheer() and uses the line cheer.onSoundComplete = stopCheer to attach the function. The stopCheer() function performs the same function as restartQuiz.

6 Now drag a ScrollPane component onto the stage. Next, open the library and create a new movie clip called Instructions to hold the contents of the scroll pane. Write the instructions into this movie using the Text tool and, using the Linkage option, check Export for ActionScript and give it the identifier Instructions. To attach the Instructions movie clip to the scroll pane, select the ScrollPane component you created and open the properties panel and enter the value Instructions for the Scroll Data field.

soundclip·org

SC

artists   forums   contact   links

Illustration: Bryn Owens [w] www.bluntdog.co.uk

Build a virtual radio

Time to put your skills to the test, by using Flash, Fireworks and Dreamweaver to build a Website…

Over the next ten pages, we combine Flash with other members of Macromedia's software family, Fireworks and Dreamweaver, to create a Website that is also a virtual radio.

We've used Fireworks to plan the layout of the site, using its prototyping features to get a design that we were happy with before we started to bring it across to Dreamweaver and Flash.

Next we used Flash to create the 'radio' bit of the site. In this part of the tutorial we show you how to pull in MP3s to a SWF shell and use a bit of ActionScript to create some playback controls so that your visitors can be in charge of the streaming sound.

The last leg of the tutorial enables you to create a bulletin board where your visitors can chat and exchange views on the clips they've just heard. This section takes Dreamweaver UltraDev (now part of Dreamweaver MX) and shows you how to build a bulletin board that uses .asp (Active Server Pages) technology.

First up, let's look at Fireworks' layout capabilities and take you step by step through the process of exporting Dreamweaver Libraries from Fireworks.

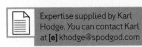

Expertise supplied by Karl Hodge. You can contact Karl at [e] khodge@spodgod.com

Files on disc
The files that accompany this tutorial can be found in the Tutorial\FW layout folder on the cover CD.

Part 1: Assembling the page

Use Fireworks' drawing tools and layout capabilities to put a page interface together…

Adding edge

You'll notice in your finished version of the layout that the navigation bar has diagonally sliced ends. These are shapes we cut off using the knife tool and duplicated from the end of the diagonally cornered rectangles in our layout.

Importing fonts

If you get a message asking whether you wish to replace the fonts used when you import any of the PNG files mentioned in this tutorial, choose Maintain Appearance. This recreates the paths of the original font used, and is fine for export.

1 Starting with a paper-based design, we created logo elements and a colour scheme for our page layout in Fireworks. You join the process just as we're getting ready to create the layout. Make a new document in Fireworks MX at 800x600 pixels. Go to View>Grid>Edit Grid and set the grid to 10x10 pixels, ensuring that snapping is on.

2 Open the file logostrap.png from the cover CD. Switch back to your new window and go to Modify>Canvas>Canvas Colour. Choose Custom and use the eyedropper tool to sample the background of logostrap.png. Switch to logostrap.png and click and hold the main image. It's a graphic symbol, so you can drag and drop a copy to the main window.

3 Position the logo symbol at X:20, Y:10. Open the file smalllogo.png from the cover CD and drag a copy of the main symbol over in a similar way. Position that at X:730, Y:20. At the co-ordinates X:20, Y:130, draw a rectangle that's 760 pixels wide and 30 pixels high. Go to the Properties panel with the new rectangle selected and sample the yellow colour from the logo as its fill. Set Stroke to transparent.

4 At co-ordinates X:20, Y:160, draw a second rectangle that's 290 pixels wide and 20 high. Select the Subselection tool (the white arrow) in the toolbar and click on the top-right corner of the new rectangle. You'll be prompted to turn the shape to vector paths. Click OK. Move the top-right corner point 20 pixels to the right to form a diagonal corner.

5 With the newly transformed rectangle still selected, go to Edit>Duplicate. Select the duplicate and go to Modify>Transform. Choose Flip Vertical then Flip Horizontal, then position the rectangular shape at X:470, Y:110.

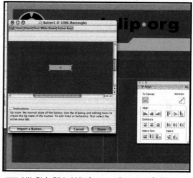

6 Hit Ctrl+F8 in Windows or Command+F8 on the Mac to create a new symbol. In the dialog that appears give the symbol the name Button1 and select Button as the symbol type. When you click OK you're taken to symbol editing mode. Draw a rectangle 90 pixels wide by 20 high. Go to Window>Align and use the panel to centre the button on the canvas.

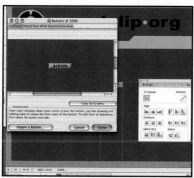

7 Add the text 'artists' to the button using Arial Black (or Arial set to Bold with the horizontal scale set to 120%), the font size at 14. Centre it in the button with the Align panel. Click on the Over tab and select Copy Up Graphic. Add an Inner Bevel effect to the button at this stage, using the effects menu in the Properties panel.

8 Add a Down state for the button in the same way, then close the symbol editing window. Position the button at X:360, Y:170. Drag three more instances of the button from the library to the stage and arrange them in a horizontal line. Select the first new instance and go to the Properties panel. In the Text box change 'artists' to 'forums'.

9 Change the text labels on the remaining buttons to 'contact' and 'links' in the same way. Add a simple footer to the layout by drawing a black rectangle at the bottom, 760x20 pixels, with a yellow rectangle above it at 760x10 pixels. Duplicate a copy of the rectangle with the diagonal corner and position it as shown. ❯

Part 2: Export for authoring

Tidy up loose ends and export page elements for direct use in Dreamweaver...

Relative root

Fireworks isn't smart enough to alter relative URLs when saving Dreamweaver Libraries, so you have to add the relative path yourself. Putting ../ at the beginning of the path points to the folder above the Library folder.

Naming slices

You don't have to name each slice or alter the export settings in the way we did – but the technique we used here generates images that have meaningful names you can easily find and edit in the future, rather than images with names like slice_r2_c4.gif...

1 By now you should have a near-complete layout. You can continue with the file you've been working on or switch to our version: sounclippartial.png. Select the logostrap symbol and go to Edit>Insert>Slice. When the slice is in position, hover the cursor over the right edge and stretch the slice out to 700 pixels wide.

2 Next, select the slice tool in the toolbar and draw a slice around the small logo. Use the guides to position the slice exactly next to the first. It should be 60 pixels wide, 99 pixels high and positioned at X:720 Y:10. The slice after that should cover the top of the divider, be 720 pixels wide, 61 high and positioned at X:20 Y:209.

3 In the 'row' below that, our buttons have already been sliced by Fireworks. You need to create three more slices: one of 300x20 pixels at X:20, Y:170, the second of 40x20 pixels at X:320, Y:170 and a final slice of 60x20 at X:720, Y:20.

4 The final slice to be made is over the bottom divider. Marquee around the objects that form the bottom divider to select them all, then go to Edit>Insert>Slice to create a slice around it. The next thing you need to do is name the slices and add URLs where necessary.

5 Select the first slice and go to the Properties panel. In the left corner there's a text box with the label Slice above it. Type in the name logostrap. Select the slice around the small logo and name that one 'smalllogo'. In the Link box for that slice type in ../index.htm. Continue to give the remaining slices individual, meaningful names.

6 Add URLs to the buttons in the same way you added a link to the small logo slice. Add the link ../artists.htm to the artists button, ../forums.asp to the forums buttons, ../contact.htm to the contact button and ../links.htm to the links button.

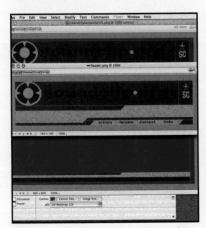

7 Save the file you have been working on, then marquee around the header elements – those in the top half – to select them. Go to Edit>Copy then File>New to create a new document. Paste the copied elements into the new document. Save the document as header.png – then go to File>Export.

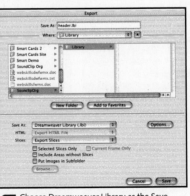

8 Choose Dreamweaver Library as the Save As type, then navigate to the folder you want to develop your site in. Create a new folder called Library and choose that as the save directory. Click the Options button when you return to the original dialog, then click on the Document Specific tab. You'll see a series of drop-down menus that govern how the exported slices from your layout are named.

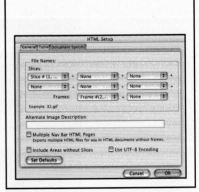

9 To make things as simple as possible, begin by setting them all to None. Then set the top left drop-down to Slice # and the bottom left (in the Frames row) to read Frame #. In the Save As text box, name the file header.lbi and click Save. Repeat stages 7 to 9 to convert the footer into a Dreamweaver Library.

Tune in to Flash radio

As part of our site, we create a pseudo Flash radio using the Sound object to pull MP3 files into a SWF shell…

Although there are methods of creating actual streaming MP3 radio stations using software such as ShoutCast, these are costly affairs in terms of development, hosting and management. Establishing both the server and client elements takes valuable programming time, but you need to ensure you have the right amount of bandwidth available for such a feature as visitors may stay permanently 'tuned in'. Add to that the time and dedication needed to create constantly new broadcast material and you'll start to realise the amount of work that's involved.

What we're creating over the next few pages is a budget alternative based around a larger and more flexible model being developed by track5 that plays back a sequence of MP3 files. We only have enough room to show you the basics involved in pulling MP3 files from outside of the controlling SWF with some elementary playback controls,

although the principle can be easily modified so that not only the sound files are being referenced but also any supported content.

To minimise repetitive stages, we have only two tracks playing on our playlist, but you'll easily see how this can be expanded to include as many tracks as you find necessary.

By using standardised filenames for the sound, copy and imagery, it's possible to develop the principle here to allow the average client to have full control over the track listing and playback order without having the slightest understanding of either HTML or Flash.

As with all streaming formats, the user will benefit from more stable playback through a broadband connection. However, by using the Sound object model, we can easily read the sound properties so that tracks will play all the way through before moving onto the consecutive MP3 file regardless of the width of their pipe.

Expertise provided by Chris Schmidt at track5.
[e] chris@track5.co.uk
[w] www.track5.co.uk

Files on disc
The PNG and MP3 files used in this tutorial can be found in the Tutorial\Flash radio folder on the cover CD.

Part 1: Importing Fireworks

With a design already produced in Fireworks, you need to import the elements and keep their identities…

Credits

The MP3 files used in this tutorial, which can be found on the cover disc, have been kindly provided with permission by track5 clients Joanna MacGregor and The Brodsky Quartet. Please respect their copyright and only use the clips as part of this tutorial. The clips used are taken from Joanna MacGregor's SoundCircus release 'Neural Circuits' (SC008) and from the Brodsky Quartet's CD of Britten and Tchaikovsky String Quartets (CC72106). The former can be bought from [w] www.soundcircus.com and the latter from [w] www.brodskyquartet.com.

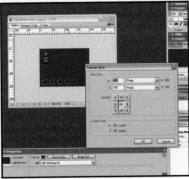

1 We've been given the Fireworks interface.png file from the site designer to use the basic layout and buttons for our radio. Open the file to discover the file dimensions of 200x150 pixels. Then create a new file in Flash matching these dimensions and matching the background colour.

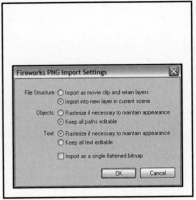

2 Import the interface.png file into Flash via File>Import and choose the options as above to retain the existing symbol status and keep paths editable. Click OK to continue.

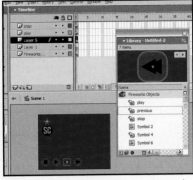

3 Notice how each element has been imported as its own symbol in Flash's Library. Go through each item and rename it to something a little more descriptive than the default filenames. Then create similarly named layers for each symbol to isolate each object.

Part 2: Loading and detecting external sounds

Create the SWF shell that references external MP3 files and recognises when they've finished playback…

The Sound object

The Sound object is a Flash-defined class whose methods control the playback behaviour and whose properties help control its timing. You need to create the Sound object by using a constructor function to provide its identity. When the Sound object is named, it is then possible to use it to play and modify sound files that you associate with it.

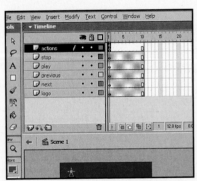

1 Add frames to these layers extending the timeline to frame 10. Create a new layer, call this Actions and drag this to the top of the layers order. Select the first frame of this layer, open the Actions panel and include a Stop action.

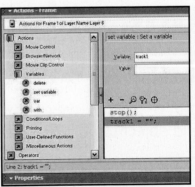

2 With frame 1 of this layer selected you need to create a global sound object by choosing Actions>Variables >Set Variable. In the Variable field enter the name track1 and click the value field.

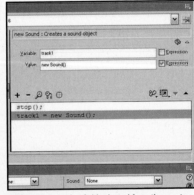

3 With the Value field selected from the previous step, choose the Objects>Movie>Sound>new Sound option and check the Value expression box.

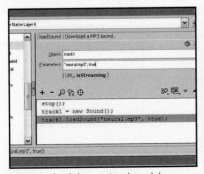

4 To load and play an external sound choose Objects>Movie>Sound>Methods>loadSound and enter the name of your sound object: track1. In the parameters field enter the path to the neural.mp3 file as neural.mp3. The true attribute specifies streaming properties.

5 Test your movie and you should hear the track playing back. As soon as your movie begins, it creates a Sound object, then loads the MP3 file into it and plays.

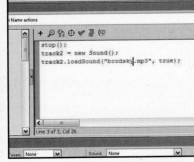

6 Create a keyframe in the Actions layer at frame 10 and copy the script settings you've just completed. You can manually edit these through in the Actions' panel Expert Mode setting so that all track1 entries become track2. Revise the MP3 filename to brodsky.mp3 as above.

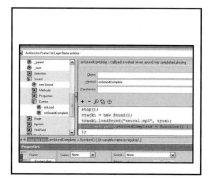

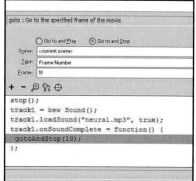

7 With two individual keyframes calling back the external MP3 files, you need to create an event that detects the end of playback and sends the timeline to the next clip. Select the first frame and choose Objects>Movie>Sound>Events> onSoundComplete.

8 In the Object field, enter the name of your Sound object, track1, to associate the clip with the command. Then add a Go To and Stop command pointing to frame 10 in the current scene.

9 Repeat this step for the equivalent keyframe at frame 10 changing the Sound object info to track2 and the Go To and Stop command pointing back to frame1. Test your movie and the clips should then play back-to-back on completion.

Part 3: **Controlling playback**

Add standard playback controls for stop and play, and allow the user to move forwards and backwards between tracks…

Play it again Sam

After you stop a loaded sound, there are two methods of making it play again, depending on whether the sound file has been synchronised to an event or streamed. Streaming sounds must be reloaded with the loadSound () method. Event sounds, however, must use the start () method.

Going round in circles

If a sound is looping, the onSoundComplete event is triggered when all the loops have finished.

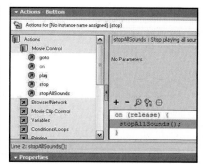

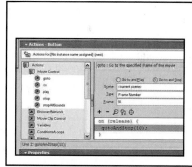

1 Back in the Actions layer at frame 1 place an instance of Actions>Movie Control> stopAllSounds after the initial Stop value and before the script loading the sound file. Repeat as step 7 above. This ensures tracks don't play over each other if the user skips tracks with the controls we are about to add.

2 Next select the Stop button and assign an onRelease event handler embedding the same stopAllSounds command as we added in the previous step. There is no need to add further keyframes to the Stop layer as the same command is relevant at all stages of the movie.

3 Adding commands to the Next and Previous buttons in the Controls layer is a simple case of specifiying Go To and Stop frames for the relevant tracks. Add a keyframe at frame 10 to provide buttons back to the first or any subsequent tracks.

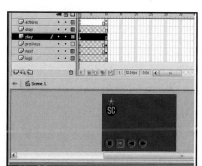

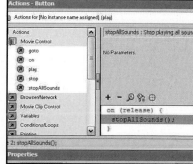

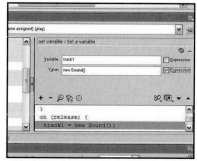

4 Assigning values to the Play button is a little more complex as you need to ensure you don't activate a duplicate sound clip. As the Play button will be used after playback has been stopped – and the Stop button has cancelled the loaded sound – it must be configured to load the sound again.

5 With the Play button selected at frame 1, create a standard onRelease action followed by an Actions>Movie Control>stopAllSounds action to cancel any playback that may be currently streaming and avoid a duplicate.

6 Next you need to create a global sound object within the play button by choosing Actions>Variable>Set Variable and entering track1 as the variable and Objects>Movie>Sound>new Sound as the value, remembering to check the Value expression box. ➤

Controlling playback continued...

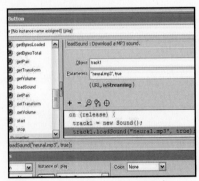

7 To associate the external sound choose Objects>Movie>Sound>Methods>loadSound and enter the name of your sound object, track1, in the object field. The parameters field requires the path to the neural.mp3 file using the neural.mp3, true command.

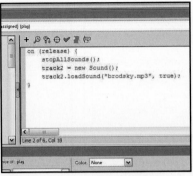

8 Duplicate the Play button by adding a keyframe at frame 10. Then, either run through the previous two steps or manually edit the script from frame 1 through the Actions panel Expert Mode to reflect the correct track, file and frame references.

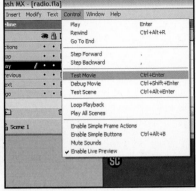

9 Test the movie again making sure all the buttons function as expected, no duplicate sound clips are played and the tracks move onto each other consecutively.

Part 4: **Getting interactive**

Provide basic listings on currently playing music and offer links to more information...

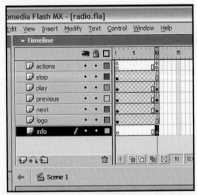

1 So far you have the functionality and playback controls in place. You now need to add information displayed with each track offering basic details on the current track playing. Create a new layer called 'info' adding keyframes to frame 1 and frame 10.

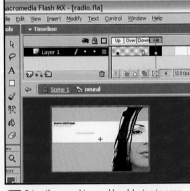

2 Bring the neural.jpg and brodsky.jpg images into your movie from the CD via the File>Import option and add these to the library as button objects. For each button leave the Over and Down states clear creating keyframes in only the Up and Hit states.

3 Add the button containing the neural.jpg image into the first frame aligning the image button with the top and centred within the movie. Replace this with the Brodsky image button at frame 10.

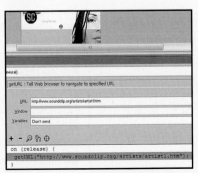

4 By adding a simple GetURL action to the image button we're effectively making the artwork into one big button that can prompt a regular HTML page. This provides more detailed information about the track or CD than is possible through the minimal radio interface.

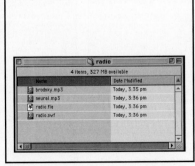

5 To integrate the radio into the main site, you need to copy the SWF and MP3 files into the same directory because this is how the relative locations of these independent files are specified from the shell Flash radio.

6 You can then prompt the radio to be displayed in a pop-up window matching the dimensions of the SWF file. This allows the radio to be left playing in the background without being too visually intrusive.

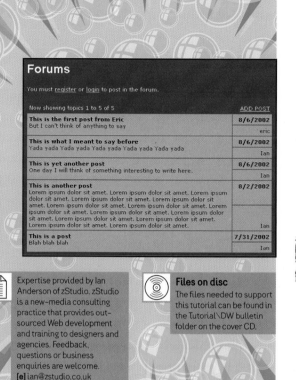

Forums

You must register or login to post in the forum.

Now showing topics 1 to 5 of 5   ADD POST

This is the first post from Eric But I can't think of anything to say	8/6/2002 eric
This is what I meant to say before Yada yada Yada yada Yada yada Yada yada Yada yada	8/6/2002 Ian
This is yet another post One day I will think of something interesting to write here.	8/6/2002 Ian
This is another post Lorem ipsum dolor sit amet. Lorem ipsum dolor sit amet. Lorem ipsum dolor sit amet. Lorem ipsum dolor sit amet. Lorem ipsum dolor sit amet. Lorem ipsum dolor sit amet. Lorem ipsum dolor sit amet. Lorem ipsum dolor sit amet. Lorem ipsum dolor sit amet. Lorem ipsum dolor sit amet.	8/2/2002 Ian
This is a post Blah blah blah	7/31/2002 Ian

Expertise provided by Ian Anderson of zStudio. zStudio is a new-media consulting practice that provides out-sourced Web development and training to designers and agencies. Feedback, questions or business enquiries are welcome.
[e] ian@zstudio.co.uk
[w] www.zstudio.co.uk

Files on disc
The files needed to support this tutorial can be found in the Tutorial\DW bulletin folder on the cover CD.

Building the bulletin board

In order to make the site more interactive, we build a simple bulletin board where visitors can leave messages for other people to read…

There are many good pre-built solutions available for adding your own discussion groups, forums or bulletin boards, most of which are shareware and will cost just a few dollars to license once you've evaluated them. However, one of the problems is that they can be too comprehensive for what you need.

Dreamweaver MX incorporates the dynamic data publishing features of Dreamweaver UltraDev. Using these, we create a simple bulletin board that offers all the functionality needed while avoiding unnecessary complexity.

Here we use Microsoft Active Server Pages as the dynamic page technology and Microsoft Access as the database, simply because these are the easiest to host and the most widely available options. If you're using different technologies, you should still be able to follow most of these steps. The tutorial assumes you're using a Windows PC with Personal Web Server or IIS enabled. If you're on another platform, you'll need to set up your application server according to the instructions provided by Macromedia or your software vendor.

Part 1: Setting up the system to work with dynamic data

Copy the site folder to the computer, publish it and set up a data source…

1 Copy the folder called soundclips_start from the CD to your computer. This folder contains copies of all the files created in the previous tutorials. If you wish, you can replace these with your own versions. This folder contains the site we'll be working with.

2 First, you need to publish the folder with Personal Web Server or IIS. This can be installed from your Windows CD. Choose Advanced, then set up a virtual directory called soundclips, pointing at your copy of the soundclips_start folder. This makes the folder available by pointing your browser at [w] http://localhost/soundclips

3 Create an ODBC data source name (DSN) pointing at the Access database in the site folder. Open the ODBC control panel, choose System DSN, Add, then choose Microsoft Access Driver (*.mdb) and click Finish. Select the forum.mdb data file in the soundclips_start folder, and name the DSN 'forumDSN'.

Part 2: Setting up Dreamweaver MX

The first thing to do when starting any project in Dreamweaver is to set up a site…

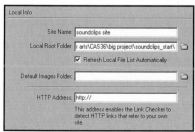  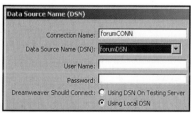

1 Launch Dreamweaver, and choose Site>New Site. In the Site Definition dialog, click the Advanced tab. In the Local Info category, enter the name soundclips site, and browse to your copy of the soundclips_site folder for local root folder.

2 Choose the category Testing Server on the left, and then choose ASP VBScript as the Server Model. From the Access list menu, choose Local/Network. In the URL Prefix field, amend it so that it reads http://localhost/soundclips. Click OK.

3 In the Application panel group, bring the Databases tab to the front. If necessary, create a new untitled document to make the options active. Check the first three steps have ticks beside them, then choose Data Source Name (DSN) from the plus menu, name it forumCONN, and choose forumDSN from the list of DSNs on the system. Click OK. >

Part 3: Creating the forum page

The forum page will be a simple results list, created using a Recordset to query the database and a Repeat Region server behaviour to repeat the latest entries in a list down the page…

Keep your files together

Remember to always keep your files for a Web project in one folder, and set this up as a site within Dreamweaver. Doing this helps Dreamweaver to manage the site, and prevents annoying warning messages.

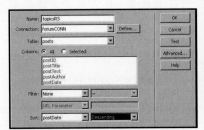

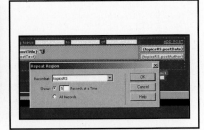

1 Open forums.asp. In the Application panel group, switch to the Bindings tab. From the plus menu, choose Recordset. Enter the name topicsRS. From the Connection menu, choose forumCONN. Check the Table menu is set to posts, and that Columns: All is selected. From the Sort menu, choose postDate and Descending. Click OK.

2 Open the new Recordset by clicking on the small plus sign beside its name, and click in the left hand orange cell on the page. Click on postTitle in the Bindings palette and click Insert at the foot of the palette. Click after the title and press Shift-Return to enter a line break. Insert a placeholder for postText under the title, then add one for postDate to the top right orange cell and one for postAuthor to the lower right orange cell. Make the title and date bold.

3 Highlight all the orange cells by carefully dragging through them with the mouse, then switch to the Server Behaviours panel. From the plus menu, choose Repeat Region. Ensure that topicsRS is selected and set Show to 5 Records at a Time. Preview the page in a browser using F12.

Part 4: Creating a page for users to post messages

This page inserts a new record into the Posts table, which adds a new entry to the bulletin board…

Microsoft Access 2000 database

The database for this project was created in Microsoft Access 2000, but has a very simple structure. You should be able to create it in another RDBMS if you need to. The data structure consists of two tables; here are the field names and Access data types: PostspostID – primary key, autonumber, postTitle – Text field, postText – Memo field, postAuthor – Text field, postdate – Date/Time field with auto-insertion of current date Users: userID – primary key, autonumber, username – text field, password – text field, email – text field

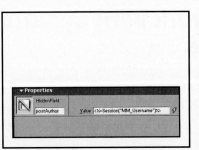

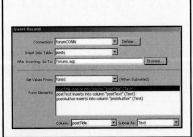

1 Open post.asp. Inspect the form; there are two text fields, one named postTitle and one named postText. Click beside the button at the bottom of the form and choose Insert Objects>Hidden Field. In the Properties, name it postAuthor and for Value enter the following code: <%=Session("MM_Username")%>. This will label all messages with the author's login name.

2 In the Server Behaviours palette, choose Insert Record from the plus menu. From the Connection menu, choose forumCONN, and select 'posts' for Insert Into Table. Enter forums.asp in After Inserting, Go To. Check that postTitle, postText, and postAuthor are all inserting into columns of the same name, and click OK.

3 Preview the page in a browser by pressing F12. You can't try inserting information though, until you have constructed a login page and logged into the site. This is because the page is trying to write the login name into the database but, as you haven't yet logged in, the field is empty. Sending the form results in an error message at the moment.

Part 5: Creating a subscription page

The subscription page allows a new user to register to post messages on the site. Add a new user to the Users table in the database, and check to make sure that their chosen username is unique…

Form validation

In a production site, it would be essential to apply Dreamweaver's form validation to the insert forms to ensure that the required fields are completed correctly. Dreamweaver can check that fields have been completed, and that email addresses are in a valid format.

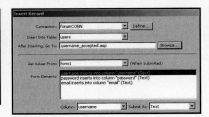

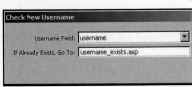

1 Open register.asp. Inspect the form, and you'll see three text fields named username, password and email address. In a real site, you would ask the user to enter their password twice (and you'd write JavaScript code to check that the two entries matched) but we'll omit this step to keep the example simple.

2 In the Server Behaviours palette, choose Insert Record from the plus menu. From the Connection menu, choose forumCONN, and select 'users' for Insert into Table. For After Inserting, Go To, enter username_accepted.asp. Check that username, password, and email are all inserting into columns of the same name, and click OK.

3 In order to ensure that users have unique login names, get Dreamweaver to check for duplicates. From the Server Behaviours palette plus menu, choose User Authentication>Check New Username. Check that username is selected for Username Field, and enter username_exists.asp for If Already Exists, Go To. Click OK, and try out the form using F12. If you enter the same username on two separate attempts, it will reject the second instance.

Part 6: Protecting the post page and allowing users to log in

We have decided that users should sign in before posting, which offers a limited measure of accountability. Create a login page, then protect the post.asp page from being viewed unless the user is logged in…

Nuisance post

Requiring the users to register before posting cuts down on the level of nuisance posts that could be experienced, but it doesn't really provide proper accountability. In production sites, we often implement systems where the password is automatically generated and emailed to the recipient. This at least gives the site administrator one valid email address for the poster, and is useful for marketing purposes. It still doesn't prevent malicious posting, since anyone can sign up for free Web-based email, but it increases the hassle factor that discourages casual mischief on bulletin boards.

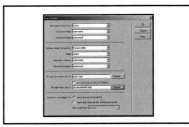

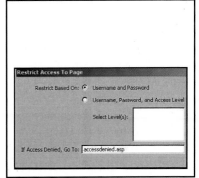

1 Open forums_login.asp. From the Server Behaviours palette plus menu, choose User Authentication>Log In User. Check that 'username' and 'password' are selected for Username Field and Password Field. Choose forumCONN for Validate Using Connection; choose 'users' for Table; set 'username' for Username Column and 'password' for Password Column. For If Login Succeeds, enter post.asp. For If Login Fails, enter accessdenied.asp. Click OK when you're done.

2 Open post.asp. From the Server Behaviours palette plus menu, choose User Authentication> Restrict Access To Page. For If Access Denied, Go To, enter accessdenied.asp. Click OK.

3 That's it – view the site in your browser by going to http://localhost/soundclips. You should be able to try out the radio, navigate the site, register for the forum and post messages. You can also view the finished site at [w] www.soundclip.org.

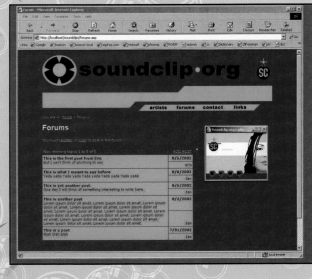

How the project was brought together

To produce the site, we used Dreamweaver MX, which offers superb integration options with both Flash MX and Fireworks MX…

Once the design had been finalised in Fireworks, the next step was to optimise and export it. In this case, we chose to export from Fireworks as Dreamweaver library items, one for the header and one for the footer. Doing this offered a great way of easily keeping the artwork up to date.

Within Dreamweaver, we used the Library items as part of the construction of a template, and used the template as the basis of the pages within the site. Templates allow the entire layout to be controlled, rather than just the individual parts of the page that can be controlled using Library items. Using both together in this way offers incredible design control with very little work. We also used Cascading Style Sheets, so that the appearance of the type can be controlled centrally, independently of the templates.

The Flash movie was imported into a new HTML document that had the same background colour as the rest of the site, and the page margins set to zero to prevent the unattractive page border showing up. We then used Dreamweaver's Open Browser Window behaviour to launch the HTML page in a new window. The point of doing this is to be able to control the width and height of the new window precisely.

When using the Open Browser Window behaviour, we had to apply it to a link in the page that would act as a trigger, but we didn't want the main window to do anything when the link was clicked. One way to prevent this is to create a link that consists of a hash (#), but this means that non-JavaScript browsers can't access the content. Instead, we chose to link to the Flash page, but to disable the link using JavaScript. This means that everyone can access the content; JavaScript users get the new browser window, while non-JavaScript visitors will receive the content in the main window.

And that's pretty much that for our virtual radio project — happy developing!

Tips

How do you speed up your work when you're using Flash MX? What are the tricks that the experts use? Here are 101 pearls of wisdom to help you make the most of Flash MX…

TIPS

101 Flash Tips

That's right – 101 hand-picked tips that'll get Flash working for you faster, and more efficiently…

Flash MX is a complex program that combines authoring, Web development, animation and a drawing package. It's easy to become an expert in a narrow area while paying scant attention to other parts of the program. So, we've put together these tips — 101 of them guaranteed to take you into every nook and cranny of Flash MX.

Our watchword has been workflow; these pearls of Flash wisdom are designed to get you working faster and more efficiently with the package. Your movies should benefit too, as they'll now be more compact and run better than they did before. In our section about including other media in your masterpieces, you'll get tips on using sound in ways you wish you'd thought of eons ago. Plus, our Timeline workout will have you working in a more organised and effective manner as soon as you fire up Flash. Photocopy them and tape them up next to your monitor — these are the Flash commandments... ➤

TIMELINE

1 Naming Layers
As you build up your Flash movie, make a habit of naming each new Layer you create, making sure that the name is both descriptive and concise. Properly naming Layers will cut down on the time you spend looking for specific objects or snippets of script.

2 Label liberty
Use a Label layer to add labels to key events in movie clips and in the main Timeline — even if you don't need to refer to them in ActionScript. It helps to keep track of what's happening where, especially when you have to juggle several clips in a single movie.

3 Action Layer
Putting your Timeline ActionScripts on a separate layer labelled Actions is a good idea.

4 Layer folders
Layer folders in Flash MX let you organise material into categories. Create a folder to put non-visible items like Labels and Actions to keep them separate. You may want to differentiate static stage objects from animated elements.

5 Movie Modification
Quickly access the full properties dialog for the current movie by double-clicking on the frame rate on the Timeline.

LIBRARIES

6 Common libraries
Go to Window>Common Libraries and you'll find a range of ready-made objects, graphic symbols and sounds ready to drag and drop into your own Movies.

7 Open as Library
Add custom Libraries to the Common Libraries menu. Create a new Flash file and add any symbols or items you wish. When you're done, save the file to the Libraries folder inside the Flash program folder. You can continue adding to the Library by reopening the original file in Flash.

8 Multiple libraries
You can open multiple libraries in Flash MX and easily keep track of them. They automatically dock in the main Library panel and can be retracted or expanded as you wish by clicking on the arrow next to the Library label.

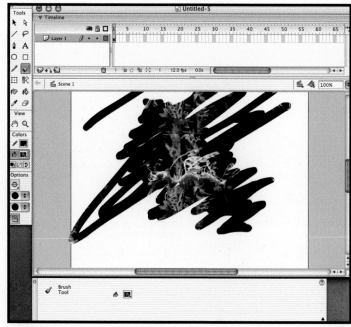

Paint with bitmaps may produce interesting effects but remember that you'll increase the size of your published file.

9 Shared Libraries
Shared Libraries are item collections that are stored in an external Flash movie. You can update items across a range of movies using a Shared Library by making any necessary changes to the library file then clicking Update.

10 Selective memory
In Flash MX, if you add a Library item from another movie's Library, Flash remembers where that item came from. If you later update the original movie, the changes can be applied to any other movie where the items are used.

11 Quick symbol
In Flash MX you're able to convert any object into a symbol by selecting it and dragging it directly to the library. A dialog enables you to select what type of symbol you wish to transform the item into.

12 Higher resolution
When importing media into the Library, make it as hi-res as you can. You can then compress items individually in the Library or set global compression options when you publish. In either case, this enables you to publish multiple versions of your files, targeting users with different bandwidth requirements if necessary. Compression is often accumulative — this will help you retain as much quality as possible in media files and bitmaps.

DRAWING

13 Bitmap Fills
You can use a bitmap as a Fill, and paint with it just as you can paint with a gradient or solid colour. Import a bitmap into the current scene and select it. Go to Modify> Break Apart, then choose the Eyedropper tool and click on the bitmap. The current fill is changed to the selected bitmap.

14 Combining shapes
Shapes placed overlapping each other in the same layer, which are of the same colour, are joined together automatically. An overlapping shape of a different colour can be used to cut a piece away from another shape. Both these techniques can be used to create complex images using simple elements.

15 Group hug
If you don't intend to edit an image any further, or you want to preserve it exactly as it is while you work on something else, use the arrow to marquee select the object and then go to Modify>Group to group it. This will prevent you from accidentally selecting either the stroke or the fill of the object while you work on other parts of your project.

16 Gradient editing
Gradients can be moved within an object using the Transform Fill tool in the toolbox. This

Putting your Timeline ActionScripts on a separate layer labelled Actions is a good idea

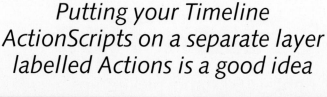

Applying the Modify>Break Apart command to text splits it into characters on the first application, then transforms those into vector shapes on the second.

17 STAR TIP

Drop shadow

Create a drop shadow under an object by creating a duplicate (Command/Ctrl+D). While the duplicate is selected, choose a dark grey fill colour from the Toolbar. With the object still selected, group it by going to Modify>Group and in the Colour Mixer panel, and set the alpha transparency of the group to 70 per cent. Place the duplicate on a layer below the original and position it so it's offset by between 4 and 8 pixels. Go to Modify>Shape>Soften Fill Edges and accept the default settings in the dialog. Don't try this on objects that are too complex as softened edges are made up of duplicated, progressively lighter vector objects and can add a lot to the eventual size of your published file.

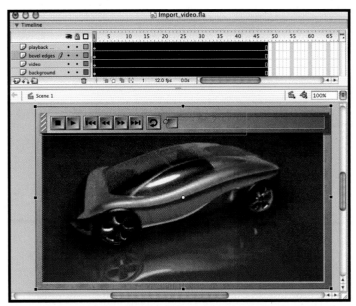

One of the most impressive additions to Flash MX is the ability to import video clips directly onto the Flash Timeline. Treat converted video as you would any other Flash object.

enables you to resize, rotate or change the centre of the gradient applied to an object on the stage.

Flash in Fireworks

The vastly improved support for the Fireworks PNG format in Flash MX means that it's possible to take advantage of the drawing tools to create Flash designs. Stick with vector-based designs, then import into Flash using whichever settings yield the best results.

What a smoothie

You can reduce the complexity of an object or group by going to Modify>Curves> Optimise. Smooth out the object, reducing the number of micro-curves. In most cases you won't see much difference, but you will optimise the movie for export — resulting in a smaller file size.

Straighten up

Select an object and click the Straighten icon on the toolbar to iron out any curves. The effect is accumulative so you can continue pressing the button until the effect you want has been achieved. The same is true of the smooth button.

Rounded corners

You can set how round the corners of a rectangle are using the Round Rectangle Radius option button in the toolbar when the Rectangle tool is selected. If you prefer to set the corner radius visually, draw your rectangle and — without releasing the mouse button — press the up and down cursor arrows on your keyboard to alter the roundness of the corners.

Pixel precision 1

To place an object with pixel precision, select it then enter exact X and Y co-ordinates in the Property Inspector.

Pixel precision 2

Flash MX introduces Pixel-Level Snapping. If you zoom into a movie sufficiently, a 1x1 pixel grid automatically appears, enabling you to manually move objects into place with pixel perfect accuracy.

Lines to Fills

While lines and bézier curves are easy to adjust and edit, fills can have gradients, textures or bitmap tiles applied to them. Just select the line you want to convert and go to Modify>Shape> Convert Lines to Fills.

Bitmap editing

If you select a bitmap image in the Library, you can launch Fireworks to edit the image and have it automatically updated in Flash. If Fireworks is not available on your system you're able to specify an alternate image-editing package.

WORKFLOW

You need hands

If, while drawing, if you find that you're running out of

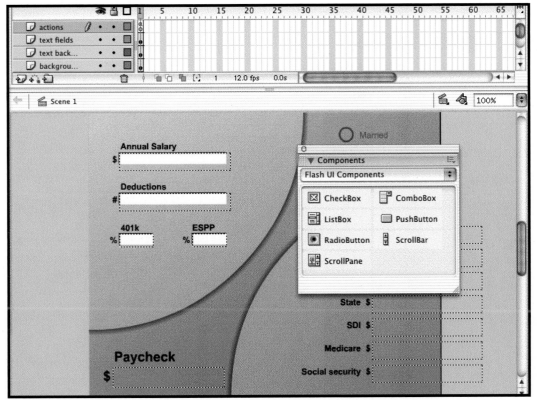

Having a set of interface components ready to drag and drop into your movies is just the ticket when you're pressed for time. All the graphics in component parts are editable.

27 STAR TIP

Common shortcuts

Make using *Flash* easier with these commonly required shortcuts:

V = Arrow/Cursor

R = Rectangle

O = Oval

M = Magnifier

F5 = Add Frame to Timeline

F6 = Add Keyframe

F8 = Convert to Symbol

Ctrl-click + drag = duplicates current object

SHIFT click with Eyedropper = selects current colour for both fill and stroke

Command/Ctrl+1 = Reset view to 100 per cent

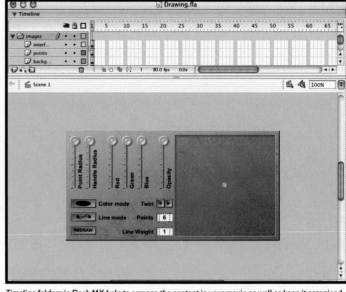

Timeline folders in Flash MX help to arrange the content in your movie as well as keep it organised.

canvas or the object you're working on disappears off the edge of the visible work area, you can temporarily switch to the Hand tool by pressing and holding down the spacebar. The Hand tool enables you to pick up and move the work area around the screen much more quickly than scrolling.

 Visual Layers
When working with multiple Layers, you may sometimes need to isolate elements as you work on them. There are different ways to do this depending on the type of object you're editing and the number of layers

in the movie. The quickest way to isolate a single layer is to click on the Show/Hide All Layers symbol in the Timeline, then make the layer you want to work on visible.

 Symbolic focus
If you want to work on a Library object, double-click on it and you'll be taken to Symbol Editing mode, with the rest of the movie greyed out.

 Edit in Symbol Mode
To isolate the symbol in its own editor, right-click in Windows or CTRL-click on the Mac to

Creating separate layouts for drawing, animation, design and so on will speed things along

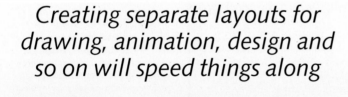

The ability to show and hide layers in the Timeline lets you cut out the clutter while you work.

bring up the context-sensitive menu. Choose Edit.

 Outlines only
Another way to visually isolate individual elements is to turn on Outline Mode. Go to View>Outlines. Everything on stage is rendered as outlines only, with colour coding that you can edit by going to Modify>Layer. Individual Layers can be set to Outline view from the Outline column in the Timeline.

 Movie Explorer
In Flash MX, another way to navigate through movies is to make use of the Movie Explorer. For the best results, go to Window>Movie Explorer and make sure Show Frames and Layers is switched on — this lets you choose which specific frame and layer you want to work on without having to scroll through the Timeline.

 Back and forth
When you go to Symbol Editing mode or switch to another scene, Flash MX displays a link back through the preceding screens at the top left of the document window, enabling you to quickly return to the main screen.

 Float the toolbar
By default, the toolbar in Flash is docked in the Windows version of Flash. You can float the toolbar by clicking then dragging on an empty area. This detaches it from its docked position, giving you a larger work area.

 Detach all panels
All the panels in the Windows version of Flash MX can be detached in a similar way, including the Property Inspector and the Timeline. Use this feature to set up the screen the way you like it, then go to Window>Save Panel Layout. On the Mac, all the panels are already floating, except the Timeline window which is docked with the stage.

 Bespoke layouts
Use the Save Panel Layout feature to set up panel layouts for different tasks. Flash is a complex application, and creating separate layouts for drawing, animation, scripting, design and so on will speed things along nicely.

 Keyboard shortcuts
Use the Edit>Keyboard feature to create key combinations that enable you to quickly switch between the custom panel layouts that you've created. You'll find it under Flash>Keyboard Shortcuts on the Mac.

 Banish panels
When all the panels in your layout are floating, you can quickly banish them by hitting the TAB key. To bring them back, press it a second time.

 Panel parameters
To save time while entering a lot of parameters in a single panel, you can use the TAB key to confirm the entry that you've typed

in, as well as automatically move to and select the next parameter that is to be entered.

 Leave space
When creating a new movie, always leave the first few frames empty. This will enable you to put in content like a simple loading clip or splash screen later on — but won't affect the flow of the movie if you decide against it.

 Edit multiple frames
Next to the Onion Skin icons on the Timeline is a little noticed icon that enables you to edit multiple frames at once. You should select this if you need to reposition either an instance of an object or across an entire series of frames simultaneously.

TEXT

 Device fonts
Flash includes three default font types that search for common font types on a user's system. These are _sans (Arial, Helvetica, Verdana etc), _serif (Times, Garamond) and _typewriter (Courier). Choose the font type from the font drop-down as

normal — there's no need to specifically select a Device Font option in MX.

 Font embedding
Not all fonts can be embedded in your Flash files when publishing, and when viewed on another system the font may be replaced by an alternative that may change the look of your movie. You can determine whether this might be a problem by going to View>Antialias Text — if the font still looks jagged the outline can't be exported.

 Break apart
One way to make sure that your type comes out the way you intend is to convert text to vector shapes before saving by selecting the text and choosing Modify>Break Apart twice.

 HTML Format
Flash MX supports HTML 1.0 formatting options in documents, even within editable text. Use the same common sense approach to font definitions as you do with HTML pages and you won't go too far wrong.

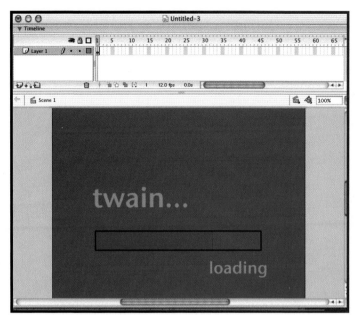

A loading screen doesn't have to be fancy - as long as your user knows that the file is on its way and you give them something pretty to look at in the meantime.

layers by selecting the text object and choosing Modify Break Apart. When applied to text this function divides the object into separate letters rather than shapes in Flash MX. With the characters still selected, choose Distribute to Layers.

Each character can then be separately animated.

ACTIONS

 All inclusive
Long ActionScripts can be stored as external text files with an .as extension. To use them in a movie, you'll need to place an 'include' in the file that points to the file. This enables you to reuse complex routines in movies, or build up a library of common scripts.

 Functions
The ECMA syntax from Flash 5 has been expanded in MX so you can now predefine functions in ActionScript. Use the function command (find it under Actions>User–Defined Functions in the Actions Editor) to create a new function from a series of commands. Use call function to use the function later.

 Calling all
As well as calling named functions, you can also call the script content of a specific keyframe in Flash MX — this enables you to store reusable ActionScripts in sections of your movie and call on them when required.

 Stage manager
Flash MX enables you to directly control the size of the current movie with the stage.height and stage.width commands.

 Fast animation
Quickly place individual characters on different

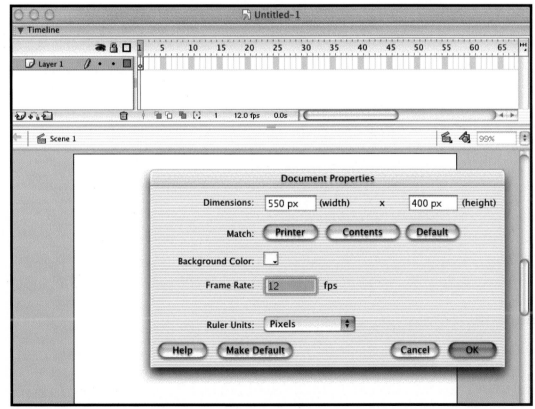

In Flash MX you can make changes to the properties of the current movie in either the Property Inspector or the traditional Modify Movie dialog.

51 STAR TIP

Hotspots

Flash doesn't have a hotspot function, but you can mimic one by using a transparent button symbol. Turn off line drawing by selecting the line drop-down in the Colour Mixer and clicking on the No Colour icon. Draw a shape around the area that you want to make hot; it's best to use the Pen tool to do this so that you can get an exact match to the area. When you've drawn the area, go to Insert>Convert to Symbol and choose Button as the symbol type in the dialog that appears. Double-click on the shape to go into Symbol Editing mode and set the Alpha transparency of the button to 0 per cent in the Colour Mixer. Hotspots are ideal for complex image areas and bitmaps.

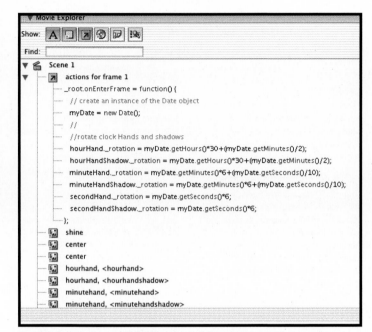

The Movie Explorer gives you a hierarchical view of all the elements present in your movie.

Nice device

The Capabilities object, found in Objects>Core> Movie enables you to interrogate the browser your movie is downloading to. The range of properties available include screen DPI, resolution, colours, audio support and so on. Use this to serve different versions of your movie to different devices, or adjust the properties (scaling, audio support) of your movie directly.

Automatic drawing

The new set of drawing functions in Flash MX enables advanced coders to create vector graphics using ActionScript. Animations that mimic real-world physics, or draw objects in response to user interaction, benefit as you no longer have to predefine objects or animations on the stage.

Hints

To get hints on using a specific ActionScript command within Flash, place the command in your script then hover your cursor over it to see a pop-up with information about its usage.

MOVIE CLIPS and SYMBOLS

Movie clip clutter

Simple animation can be embedded in a clip and frozen using the Stop command. Embed the clip in a movie and use the main Timeline to trigger the animation. This leads to less clutter in your movies.

Load Movie

The Load Movie command doesn't just work for Movies, it can be called within Movie Clips too. You can use this knowledge to replace Movie Clips on the stage dynamically by loading in a new SWF format clip from an external source in response to user actions or events in the Timeline.

Clip hierarchy

Flash movies can have many levels and the same is true of Movie Clips. If you choose the default 'Level 0' to load the new clip into, it'll replace the current content of that clip. Selecting Levels 1 or above will leave the content of the clip in place and simply superimpose the new clip over the top.

Speed things along

Although Flash unloads movies automatically from the targeted level, explicitly adding the Unload Movie command speeds the process along. You can also use the command to clear levels below or above where you place new content.

Surplus symbols

At the end of a big animation project you may find yourself with several extra symbols

Why embed the whole font when you only need half of it? In Flash MX you'll have to click on the Character button to enter the dialog that enables you to edit how fonts are embedded.

60 STAR TIP

Bitmap to Vector

Convert simple bitmap images to vectors using Flash's Trace Bitmap function. Select the bitmap you want to convert, then go to Modify>Trace Bitmap. Adjust the settings according to the result you want: the less complex the final vector conversion, the smaller the resulting file size will be. Curve Fit decides how smoothly the outlines of the shape will be preserved, while Corner Threshold does the same for sharp edges. The Colour Threshold slider in the Trace Bitmap dialog sets the level that Flash will use to generate colour areas. Setting the Colour Threshold to 10 will mean that Flash will treat two pixels with colours that have a RGB colour variance of 10 as though they were the same. You can enter a value between 1 and 500 — the higher the value, the smaller the file size.

that aren't actually used in the movie. You can get rid of them by going to the menu in the Library panel and choosing Select Unused Items

Use Folders

Create folders to store common symbols together to make them easy to track in complex movies. You may want to create separate folders for text, bitmaps, buttons and so on, or it may be more valuable for you to place all the parts that went into the creation of a specific clip in one folder.

Stop

Remember that movie clips loop by default. That means that you'll need to put a Stop action in both the first and last frames unless you want them to loop forever in your movie...

Full paths

When publishing movies that include external content, alter URLs so that they contain the full path to clips and other external items to increase reliability.

Symbolic gesture

Create generic symbols that can be reused. A blank rollover button can be given a new text label when an instance is dragged to the screen from the Library, and an instance of direction arrows

Transform all your graphics into symbols and name them to keep track of them

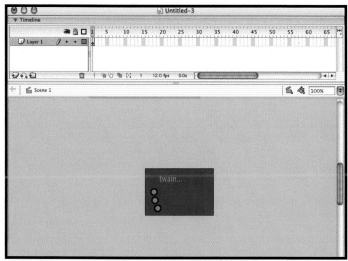

When your movie is composed of vector shapes you can save valuable bandwidth by creating it on a small stage in flash and scaling it up in your browser.

can be rotated on stage to create a new button.

Graphic symbol

Transform all your graphics into symbols and name them. This makes it much easier to keep track of them in the Library and Movie Explorer. They can also be more easily isolated for editing as symbols.

Quick components

The UI Components in Flash MX are smarter than you might think. To create a scrolling text field, for example, draw a text box on the stage, change it to Dynamic Text or Input Text, then drag and drop an instance of the ScrollBar component to the stage. Align the top-left edge of the ScrollBar with your text field and the component will snap against it, resizing to the dimensions of the text field.

Long division

If your movie is composed of a series of interactive pages that each contain their own unique set of scripts, think about breaking them down into separate movies. Use the loadMovie ActionScript command to load each segment as required (in response to user input). This will make your movie load much faster and conserve processor power.

Bookmarks

As well as placing labels in movies and movie clips, you can now put bookmarks in Flash MX authored movies. These let your users click on the back and forward buttons of their browser to revisit sections of your movie.

CLICHÉS

Text Zoom

Avoid Zooming Text. Flash enables you to zoom in and out of scenes at any level of magnification — that's the power of vectors. The first time someone realised that you could do that with text it looked pretty good. The wow factor wears off pretty quickly though.

Spotlight

Forget spotlight effects. Flash enables you to create a layer mask so that you can show one small part of an image at one time. Lots of designers have used this to create spotlight effects where a search beam highlights bits of the image. Now that

you can control masks using ActionScript, you should expect more.

Gradient spheres

The gradient sphere is the classic computer art cliché, but it's a simple 3D effect.

Looping animation

Just like animated GIFs before them, some people use Flash to create short animation sequences that loop forever and ever and ever... try not to be one of them. After a while it can begin to get on your nerves.

The pointless splash screen

For all the wonderful things that Shockwave Flash can do and has been used for, it's still popular for creating intro screens to Websites. If your splash screen downloads quickly and adds to the experience of using the site, then great. More often than not they're just there for the sake of it.

STREAMLINING MOVIES

Two stage launch

Keep the initial file size super small. You can use a stub movie to load in background graphics quickly which then calls a second external movie if you have a lot of bitmap graphics, scripting or a sound track to load.

Get out clause

Make sure that your intro or splash screens have a button that appears, as the rest of the file downloads so that users can skip past any non-essential sections.

Loading screens

Simple loading screen solutions include a looping animation or small bit of text telling the user the size of the file with a estimated download time.

Individual compression

Flash enables you to set general compression options for sound and bitmaps on export. You can tweak the individual settings for bitmap and sound objects within Flash by selecting the object in question in the Library, then choosing Properties from the Options menu in the panel.

Smaller with symbols

Try bringing down movie file sizes by constructing

animations using generic shapes that you've converted to graphic symbols. Draw simple shapes like circles and generic triangles and choose Insert>Convert to Symbol to place them in the Library. Build up components in a scene using them.

Scale up
Save file space by creating your movie at a smaller size than you intend it to be displayed in the users browser. When you embed the file into a Web page, set the dimensions larger than the original stage. You can create a movie at 150x100 then scale up to 600x400 in the Web page. This works best when your movie is composed entirely of vector objects.

Own devices
Using Flash device fonts keeps down the eventual size of the published file by taking the font information direct from the user's machine.

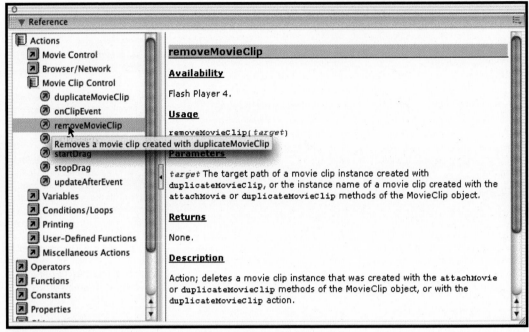

Flash MX now has a full ActionScript reference panel built in. Go to Window>Reference to launch it.

Partial embedding
In the Property Inspector while text is selected, you can choose to only embed those parts of the font that are going to be used in your movie by selecting Character and typing the letters you'll need into the dialog.

Reduced fonts
The more fonts that you use in a movie, the more that will need to be embedded and the larger the resulting file size will be. Try using one main font for content

Short snippets of looped sounds reduce file sizes and improve performance

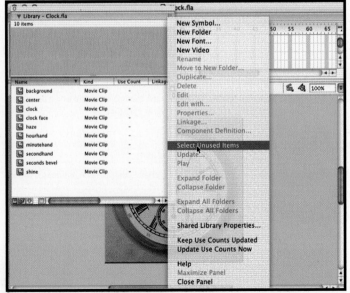

It's easy to miss – the Select Unused Items option can be found in the menu of the Library panel.

and breaking down headers and logos into vector shapes.

ANIMATION

Shape Hints
Use Shape Hints when tweening from a simple shape to a more complex one, like a letter. To use them, select the first keyframe in a shape-tweened animation sequence, then go to Modify>Transform>Add Shape Hint. Move the Shape Hint to the point you want to mark. Go to the last keyframe and add a corresponding hint. Continue alternating between the first and the last frames as you add further hints.

Logical placing
Shape Hints work best if you place them in the same logical order in both frames. That means making sure that the sequence of numbered hints is the same at both ends of the transition. Failing to do so can generate some odd effects.

Named tweens
Turn shapes or groups into movie clips before you animate them with tweening. Flash does it automatically for you, but the naming system it uses (tween1, tween2 etc) can soon clutter up your library with symbols that it's difficult to keep track of.

Ghost objects
If you use Tweening to fade out an object with Alpha transparency, the object's final state may still be faintly visible on screen on some systems. Place a frame with the object removed in the Timeline after the fade to get rid of ghosts.

Balance the load
The more separate items you have animating on screen at any one time, the more load you'll put on your user's computer. Try to plan ahead and stagger the triggering of clips in your movie. Minimise the number of distinct items that are animating simultaneously.

Break it down
Long animation sequences can be managed more easily if your break your movie down into separate scenes. There's a tendency to overlook this capability, but Flash makes it easy to communicate data between scenes, so there's no reason not to use it. Storyboard your animation and create a new scene whenever there's a natural break in the action or a new background.

MEDIA

Streaming sound
Flash movies can play back at different speeds over different systems, making it difficult to synchronise soundtracks. To deal

with this, adjust the properties of your sound and set the Sync option to Stream. If the animation slows down, Flash will drop frames to stay in sync with the audio.

 Dynamic media
Both MP3 and JPEG files can now be in placed Flash MX movies as external media which are called during runtime. Use this feature to keep initial files sizes to a minimum or create movies with updateable elements.

 Loop the loop
Short snippets of looped sounds reduce file sizes and improve performance in comparison with long clips. You can download free, ready looped sounds from Flash resource sites like [w] www.flashkit.com.

 Video
Video imported using the new Sorenson compression option in Flash MX can be easily manipulated using the same tools as any other object. This means you can distort it, resize, scale or skew video, applying those effects to the entire sequence simultaneously.

 Sound and vision
Try not to trigger a large sound file at the same time as important animation events. Sounds take a moment to initialise — and could delay the playback of the movie while you're waiting.

PUBLISHING

 Modify movie
You can now modify your basic movie settings without going to the Modify menu. Just click away from any objects and the Property Inspector lets you change the background colour, dimensions, frame rate and publication settings for the movie.

 Browser resize
Flash movies are vector-based and therefore scaleable by nature. If you link directly to a Shockwave Flash file, it will automatically resize to the dimensions of the user's browser. Alternatively, you can go to Publish Settings and set the movie dimensions to a percentage of the browser window in the HTML file your movie is embedded within.

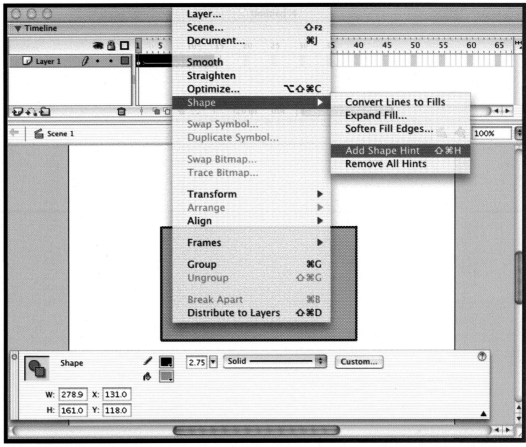
Use Shape Hints to guide complex tweened animations but be careful or you could end up with more of a mess than you started with.

 Bitmap integrity
Prevent bitmaps embedded in resizable movies from distorting by ensuring that they are given absolute dimensions rather than percentage-based attributes in Flash. For best results, ensure that images are placed within your Flash movie at their original dimensions.

 Retro save
You can use the enhanced development capabilities of Flash MX and still export to Flash 5 format to ensure that your movies play on as many platforms as possible. Some features may not be supported.

 Consistent playback
Flash movies may play back at different speeds on different systems. If it's important that you get consistent playback speeds, try placing a short, looping sound file in your main movie. Set the sync option to stream and make it loop for the length of time you want your movie to last. This hack takes advantage of Flash's sound streaming features that will drop frames if necessary to synchronise the movie to a sound file.

 Comprehensive reports
In Flash MX, it is now possible to generate a comprehensive report detailing the impact that various objects in your movie have on the size and performance of the finished. To do this, you should check the box labelled Generate Size Report in the Flash Publish Settings dialog.

 Development features
If you haven't used many of the new development features of Flash MX in creating your movie, you should consider publishing your file in Flash 5 format. As more users install the new Flash Player, this tip will become less relevant. But, for now it is worth considering that the majority of your users will probably still be using Flash Player 5.

101 STAR TIP

Sound pieces
A long soundtrack can add a lot to the bandwidth overhead for your movie. If you really want music playing in the background, try to break it down into its component parts. Most tunes are made up of repeated phrases. In a sound editor try to break your soundtrack into an intro, verse riff, chorus riff and fill sections. You can then trigger and loop these sections in Flash to recreate your soundtrack without having to load a huge file. Make sure that all your pieces are of a uniform length so that you can mix and match between them.

A similar approach is to use the channels in Flash MX to loop separate instrument tracks. Create one loop with a bass part, one with a drum section, and others with differing melody lines. As long as they're all in the same key and the same length, you should be able to loop them, overlaying sections to create new tunes.

Techniques

There are means and ways of doing things. Get to grips with some key techniques for incorporating video, text effects, motion blur and a whole lot more in Flash MX

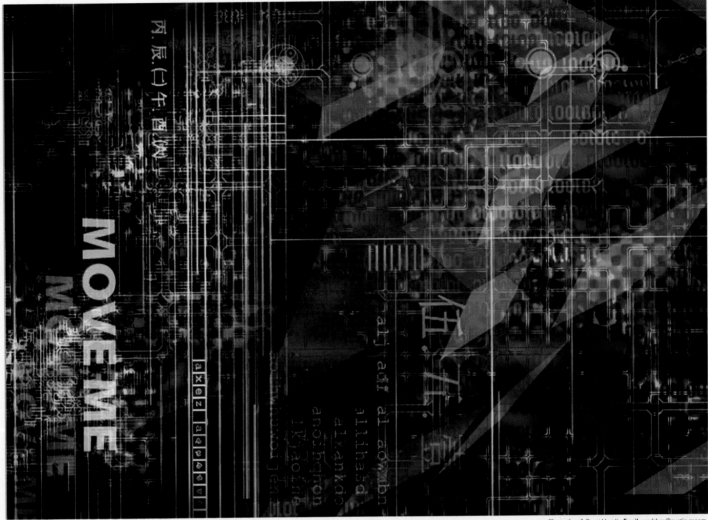

Illustration: J. Scott Hamlin **Email:** rendrboy@austin.rr.com

Funky text

Funk up your interface's buttons with some rollover and rollout animations, which we'll create in Flash MX…

Scripting with ActionScript often gets the lion's share of attention these days. And with improvements to ActionScript, the Actions editor and the Debugging panel in Flash MX, that's not likely to change. While most of the new power features are in the Actions and Debugging panels, there are a few things for designers to cheer about in MX.

In this tutorial we'll utilise the new Distribute to Layer feature along with Flash MX's new improved UI to create some funky rollover and rollout animations for buttons on an interface. You can create any number of effects with Distribute to Layers, but we're going to look at the possibilities and share a few tricks along the way.

Most of the new features for designers are really just designed to minimise the tedium inherent in designing with Flash. But the new Distribute to Layers feature is one definitely worth shouting about, as it takes an ungrouped object and distributes the pieces to layers.

This feature is useful for animated text effects. For example, if you break apart some text, each individual letter remains editable. So, you can break apart text, distribute each letter to a separate layer in one easy step, and then apply animations to the layers. So, keep reading and get funky.

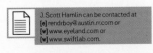
J. Scott Hamlin can be contacted at
[e] rendrboy@austin.rr.com or
[w] www.eyeland.com or
[w] www.swiftlab.com.

Files on CD
The ecorp2.fla file needed for this tutorial is on the cover CD in the Tutorial\Funky text folder.

Part 1: Flash MX's Distribute to Layers feature

Leveraging the new Distribute To Layers feature to create animated text effects on individual letters...

ecorp2 interface from Flash Web Foundry

The ecorp2 interface comes from Eyeland Studio's Flash Web Foundry CD. Flash Web Foundry is a collection of over 100 interfaces, and more than 100 animations and much more for Flash. It can be found at **[w]** www.eyeland.com/fwf.php.

Layer folders

Now you can make the Timeline as manageable as the Library. Flash MX enables you to put layers in folders much like the folders in the library. You can even nest folders within folders. You can also lock and hide folders — saving you the trouble of locking or hiding individual layers one at a time.

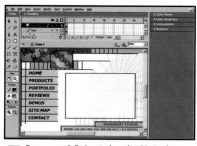

1 Open ecorp2.fla located on the CD (in the Tutorial\Funky text folder) in Flash MX. Save the file to your directory with the name ecorp2_mod.fla. Scroll down the layers until you locate the Text layer on the Timeline. Select the Text Layer and click on the Insert Layer button to add a layer above the Text layer. Rename the new layer Text MCs (for Text Movie Clips). Select the Text layer again and press Command/Ctrl+C to copy. Now select the Text MCs layer and then press Command/Ctrl+Shift+V to paste in place.

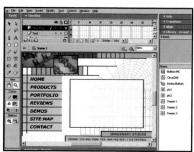

2 Press Command/Ctrl+T, Command/Ctrl+K, Command/Ctrl+L, and Command/Ctrl+I to open the Transform, Align, Library and Info panels respectively. Put these four panels in the right panel bar in Flash MX. Remove all of the other panels such as the Color Swatches and Components panels from the panel bar on the right. Open the Library panel on the bottom so that you can see more of it when you expand it out. Expand out the Transform, Align, and Library panels.

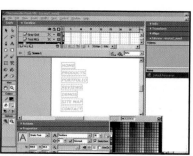

3 Click on the folder icon in the Library panel to create a new folder. Name it Default Resources. Drag all of the movie clips, graphics, and bitmap resources into the Default Resources folder. Hold down the Option/Alt key and click on the dot underneath the eyeball icon in the Timeline next to the Text layer to make the other layers invisible. Open the Properties panel (below the stage), select all the text elements on the text layer and change them to light grey colour (Hex value #CCCCCC).

4 Option/Alt-click on the dot underneath the eyeball icon in the Timeline next to the Text MCs layer to make all of the other layers invisible. Select the HOME text. Press F8 to open the Convert to Symbol dialog. Enter Home Main MC for the Name, set the Behaviour to Movie Clip, leave Registration at the centre, and click on the OK button. With the Home Main MC movie clip selected on the stage, press Command/Ctrl+E to edit the movie clip. Zoom in on the text.

5 Select the Home text. Press Command/Ctrl+B to Break apart, and then press Command/Ctrl+Shift+D to Distribute to Layers. Change the name of Layer 1 to Actions. Select the letter H on the H layer. Press F8 to open the Convert to Symbol dialog. Enter Home MC H for the Name, set the Behaviour to Movie Clip, leave Registration at the centre, and click on the OK button. Turn the O, M, and E into movie clips naming them Home MC O, Home MC M, and Home MC E respectively.

6 Click on the folder icon in the Library panel to create a new folder. Name it Home Text. Drag the Home Main MC movie clip into the Home Text folder. Click on the folder icon in the Library panel to create a new folder. Name it Home Letters. Drag the folder into the Home Text folder. Drag the Home MC H, Home MC O, Home MC M, and Home MC E movie clips into the Home Letters folder.

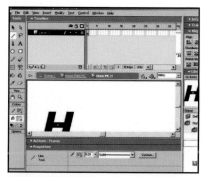

7 Select the Home MC H movie clip and press Command/Ctrl+E to edit it. Select the H text and press Command/Ctrl+B to break apart. Select View>Magnification>800 per cent. Adjust the stage so that the H is over to the left leaving some white space to the right of the letter H. Press N to select the Line tool. Open the Properties panel and change the Stroke Height to .25. Change the colour to red.

8 Hold down the Command/Ctrl key and draw a straight horizontal line that is about twice as wide as the letter H. Draw the line a little bit above and the right of the letter H. Press the V key to select the Arrow tool and select the line. Press Command/Ctrl+D five times to duplicate the line five times. Drag the fifth duplicate down below the letter H. Select all of the lines. Open the Align panel. Align the lines to the left edge (far left button under Align in the Align panel) and distribute them to the horizontal centre (second button to the left under Distribute in the Align panel).

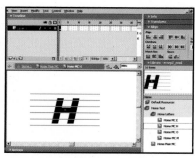

9 Press Command/Ctrl+G to group the lines. Press F8 to open the Convert to Symbol dialog. Enter Lines for the Name, set the Behaviour to Movie Clip, leave Registration at the centre, and click on the OK button. Press the To Stage button in the Align panel and then centre the Lines movie clips vertically and horizontally. Press Command/Ctrl+B to break apart. Select any portion of the letter H and you will see that we have sliced the shape up with the lines. ➤

Part 2: Creating a funky Shape Tween effect

Creating nested Shape Tween animations for each of the letters and then adding tween effects to the results…

Shape Tween variations

You can get some interesting variations with Shape Tweens by experimenting between the Distributive or Angular Blend options. You can also play with the Ease option to change the pace of the effect. Negative values ease the tween in and positive values ease the tween out. Easing in means you will see more of the effect towards the end of the tween, and easing out means you will see more of the effect towards the beginning of the effect.

Toggle on and off Panels

You can easily expand and close a panel with its shortcut key. For instance, pressing Command/Ctrl+T repeatedly will act as a toggle to expand and close the Transform menu when it's nested anywhere on the Macromedia Flash interface. When a panel is not nested, the shortcut key will do three-step toggle: open, expand, and close.

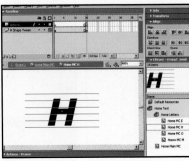

1 Rename Layer 1 H Shape Tween. Click on the Insert Layer button to add a new layer and rename the new layer Actions. Select frame 15 on both the H Shape Tween layer and the Actions layer. Press F6 to add a keyframe to both layers on frame 15. Select frame 15 on the Actions layer. Open the Actions panel. Open Actions>Movie Control. Double-click on stop to add a stop action **stop();** to the keyframe. Minimise the Actions panel.

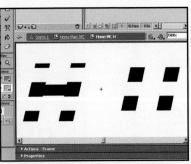

4 Minimise the Properties panel. Select frame 1 on the H Shape Tween layer. Select All and press Command/Ctrl+B. Select the Arrow tool. Select all of the red lines and delete them. The red lines will also be broken apart wherever they overlap or touch the H shape. You will have to select all of the line pieces to delete them as well. Some portions of the red lines might be as small as a dot, so double-check that you have selected them all.

7 Click on the OK button in the Preferences dialog. Click on frame 5 on the H layer and press F6. Click on frame 5 and select the Home MC H movie clip. Expand the Transform panel and enter 180 degrees in the Rotation field. Expand the Properties panel and change Colour to Alpha. Set the Alpha to 0 per cent. Now click on any frame between frame 5 and 15 on the H layer. Set the Tween field to Motion in the Properties panel. Leave all of the Tween options at the defaults. Select frame 1 on the H layer and delete the Home MC H movie clip.

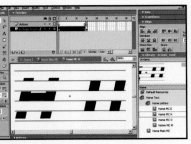

2 Select Frame 1 on the H Shape Tween layer. Select View>Magnification>800 per cent. Press M or Z to select the Zoom tool. Click on the Enlarge option and click once in the centre of the H to zoom in closer. Press V to select the Arrow tool. Hold down the Shift key and select the pieces of the H between the top two lines, the two middle lines and the bottom two lines. Hold down the Shift key and nudge the pieces to the left 20 times. Now Shift-select the remaining pieces, hold down the Shift key, and nudge them to the right 20 times.

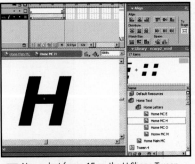

5 Now select frame 15 on the H Shape Tween layer. Select and delete all of the red lines. Once again, be sure to delete all of the pieces of the red line. You can check to see if there are any remaining lines by scrubbing between frames 1 and 15. If you see any red lines in the Shape Tween you know there are still some red lines on frame 1 or frame 15. When you are done there should only be black shapes morphing from one side to the other.

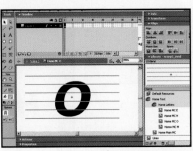

8 Repeat from Part 1, step 7 through to Part 2, step 7 on the Home MC O, Home MC M, and Home MC E movie clips. However, instead of drawing new lines as described in Part 1 steps 8 and 9, drag and drop the Lines movie clip onto the stage and centre it over the letter shapes. For instance, edit the Home MC O movie clip, break apart the letter O, drag and drop the Lines movie clip onto the stage, centre it, and break it apart over the letter O shape. Otherwise apply the same Shaped Tween with the same settings to each letter movie clip.

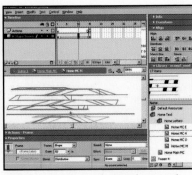

3 Click on any frame in between frame 1 and frame 15 on the H Shape Tween layer. Open the Properties panel and change the Tween option to Shape. Change the Ease field to –50. Later we will apply a alpha transparency fade to this movie clip so we're delaying the Shape Tween a little so that we can see more of the effect when the movie clip is visible. Leave the Blend mode on Distributive.

6 Return to the Home Main MC movie clip. Add 30 frames to each of the layers. Press Command/Ctrl+U to open the Preferences dialog box. Deselect or turn off the Span Based Selection Option. The Span Based Selection option makes it very difficult for us to select specific frames within a span. Clicking on frame 5 on the H layer, for instance, would select the entire span on the H layer rather than just frame 5. Turning off the Span Based Selection makes it much easier for us to add keyframes to layers.

9 In the Home Main MC movie clip, offset the tweens for each letter by 5 frames. For instance, start the tween for the Home MC O movie clip on the O layer on frame 10 and end it on frame 20. Start the tween for the Home MC M movie clip on the M layer on frame 15 and end it on frame 25. Start the tween for the Home MC M movie clip on the M layer on frame 20 and end it on frame 20. Be sure to delete the movie clips from the first frame of each layer.

Part 3: **Rollover and rollout animation effects**

Create a rollover and rollout animation using invisible buttons that
control the text movie clips…

Exploiting an anomaly or bug in Flash

When you use the Reverse Frames option in Flash MX, tweens tend to get broken. Flash gives you an indication that there's something wrong on the last frame of the reversed Tween. There is a small warning sign in the Properties panel telling you that the tween won't occur because of ungrouped symbols (even though the symbols are still grouped). However, this results in a pleasing effect. Rather than getting the same effect in reverse with a RollOut event, we get a different effect. So we get a richer variety of effects with no extra effort.

1 Select the Actions layer and click on the Insert Layer button. Rename the new layer Labels. Click on frame 1 of the Labels layer. Open the Properties palette and set the Label to Rollover. Add 35 more frames to all of the layers. Select frame 35 on the Labels layer. Press F6 to add a keyframe. Set the label on frame 35 to Rollout.

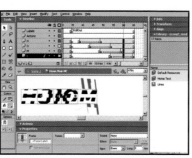

2 Select the Arrow tool and drag over frames 1 through 30 on the H, O, M, and E layers. Press Command+Option+C (Mac), Ctrl+Alt+C (PC) to copy the frames. Now select frames 35 on the H, O, M, and E layers. Press Command+Option+V (Mac), Ctrl+Alt+V (PC) to paste frames. Flash MX will add unnecessary frames on the H, O, M, and E layers from frame 65 to frame 94. Select these and press Shift+F5 to Remove Frames. Select frame 60 on the H, O, M, and E layers and press F5 to add a frame.

3 Select the Arrow tool and drag over frames 35 through 65 on the H, O, M, and E layers. Select Modify>Frames>Reverse. Now add keyframes to the Actions layer on frames 30 and 65. Add Stop actions to frame 1, 30, and 65 on the Actions layer. Now we have an animation for Rollover and Rollout. Unfortunately, we're not finished. If Reverse Frames worked properly we would have the same stair-stepped pattern for the tweens between frames 35 and 65 as those between frames 1 and 30 (only reversed). So, we have a little more work to do to make it right.

4 Add a keyframe to frame 40 of the M layer, frame 45 of the O layer and frame 50 of the H layer. Select frames 35 through 40 on them layer. Right-click (PC) or Option-click (Mac) on the frames and select Clear Keyframe. Repeat this operation for frames 35 through 45 on the O layer and frames 35 through 50 for the H layer. The stop action on frame 1 prevents the viewer from seeing anything. We need to add event controls to an invisible button so that people will be able to see the animations when they rollover or roll off the button.

5 Return to the main scene. All of the layers, except the Text MC's layer, should be invisible. There should be a white dot above the Products text. This is the movie clip that we have been working on. Flash represents any movie clip that has no graphics in its first frame as a white dot. Click on the white dot with the Arrow key and open the Properties panel. Change the instance name to home.

6 Now Option/Alt-click on the dot below the Eyeball icon next to the Buttons layer (third layer below the Text MCs layer). This layer contains a series of light blue rectangles. These are all invisible buttons. The light blue rectangle is how Flash represents a button with no artwork in the Up State. The light blue shape is a representation of what is in the Hit State. The light blue boxes for the buttons will not be visible when you play the movie. Select the top button.

7 Open or expand the Actions panel. Notice that there are already on (RollOver) and on (RollOut) event handles assigned to the button. Click inside the Actions palette and press Command/Ctrl+Shift+E to change to Expert Mode. Place the cursor at the end of the **_root.one.gotoAndPlay("OUT");** line of code, press enter and then add **_root.home.gotoAndPlay(2);** to the on (RollOver) code. Next place the cursor at the end of the **_root.one.gotoAndPlay ("IN");** line of code and **_root.home.gotoAndPlay ("RollOut");** to the on (RollOver) code.

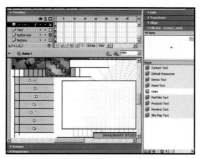

8 Minimise the Actions panel and press Command/Ctrl+Enter to test the movie. Rollover the Home button and observe the results. Rollover and roll off the Home button to observe the Text animations. Notice that the animations do not act the same when you rollover as they do when you roll off. See the margin note for more info on this. Close the test movie window. Perform the same basic procedure on the text for each of the other buttons.

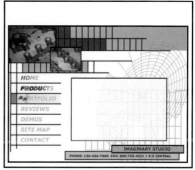

9 To save time, copy and paste frames between movie clips that contain the same letter. For example, Portfolio has the letter o in it three times. You can copy and paste the Products MC O to the Portfolio MC O movie clip. The new Distribute to Layers feature opens the doors to many more text animation effects. Experiment and have fun. If you're not having fun, you're not doing it right.

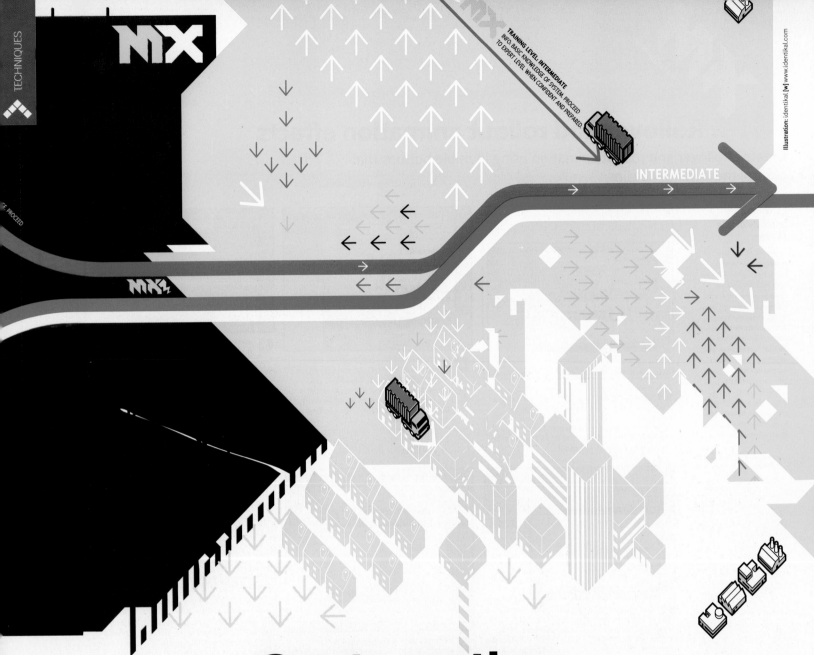

Illustration: identikal [w] www.identikal.com

INTERMEDIATE

TRAINING LEVEL INTERMEDIATE
INFO: BASIC KNOWLEDGE OF SYSTEM. PROCEED
TO EXPERT LEVEL WHEN CONFIDENT AND PREPARED

Create motion blur in Flash

There is more to motion than framerate, as our tutorial will demonstrate…

Expertise is provided by Jason Krogh, who is the lead developer at zinc Roe design. You can contact Jason at
[e] jkrogh@zincroe.com
[w] www.zincroe.com

Files on disc
The files needed to support this tutorial can be found in the Tutorial\Motion blur folder on the cover CD.

Once you have mastered the process of creating simple motion tweens, there are a few good tricks that can help you create professional-looking motion. One very simple animation technique is the use of motion blurs. Fast moving objects appear to be blurred because of our persistence of vision. This effect is captured when shooting live-action using film but it has to be simulated when creating animation.

We are limited in what we can do with motion blurs because they require the use of bitmap images, and Flash is a vector-based format. Each bitmap we use adds to the overall file size. However, it's impressive what we can accomplish with just the use of one or two bitmap images.

We are going to modify an existing animation to use the blur motion effect. We will take artwork from Flash, into Photoshop for processing, and then back into Flash. At the same time we will introduce a couple of other simple techniques to create professional-looking motion within Flash.

Part 1: Blurring foreground elements

Making good animation better with blur effects, easing and follow-through…

Motion tween

The original animation is created with simple motion tweens. Flash has the ability automatically to position an object at various points as it moves from one position to another on the screen. The tween can also create a smooth transition in transformations applied to the artwork such as scaling, rotation or transparency.

1 Open the motionBlur.fla file provided on the cover CD. Examine the timeline and then select Test Movie from the Control menu to watch the original animation.

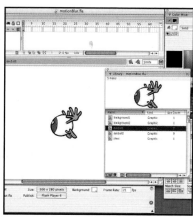

2 Open the library by selecting Library from the Window menu. Double-click on the eyeball1 symbol to edit it.

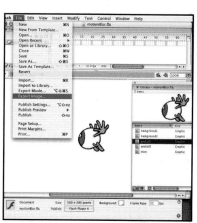

3 First you need to create a bitmap file of your artwork. To do this, select Export Image from the File menu.

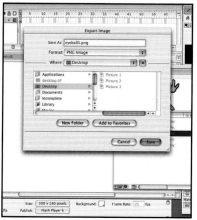

4 In the Export Image window enter the file named eyeball1.png and choose the PNG format. This is a great file format for working with bitmaps within Flash because it is lossless and supports transparency.

5 In the Export PNG window select Minimum Image Area, 24 bit with alpha channel, and None for Filter. Select the Smooth checkbox and leave the others unselected.

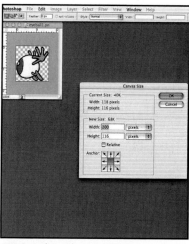

6 Open the newly created PNG file in Photoshop. Select Canvas Size from the Image menu. Set the width to 200 pixels and click OK.

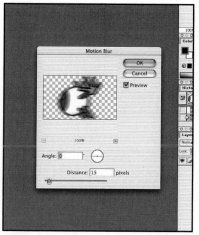

7 Select Motion Blur from the Filter menu. Enter 0 for the angle and 15 for distance.

8 To create a new PNG file select Save for Web from the File menu. Under Settings select PNG and transparency. Save the file as eyeball1_blur.png.

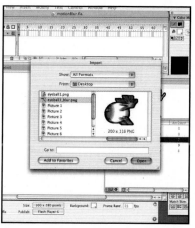

9 Move back to the motionBlur.fla file and select Import from the File menu. Select the eyeball1_blur.png file. ➤

Blurring foreground elements continued...

Swap button

The Swap button provides a handy way to switch to a new symbol while retaining the instance's position and any transformations that have been applied.

Easing in and out

In real life, motion is based on acceleration (the gas pedal) and deceleration (the brakes). By default, Flash creates tweens which reflect a perfectly even speed. In Flash, the term Ease In means to start slowly and speed up. Ease Out means to start quickly and slow down. Note that, strictly speaking, the terms are used differently in traditional animation.

Anticipation and follow-through

When animators studied the way people move they noticed that most movements are preceded by a slight motion in the opposite direction. This effect is commonly exaggerated in animation and is called anticipation. A similar effect is used when motions come to a sudden halt. The moving object is carried a little too far and then snaps back to a final resting position.

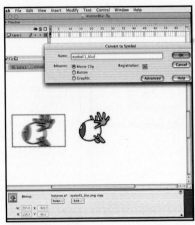

10 Select the newly imported image and then select Convert to Symbol from the Insert menu. Enter eyeball1_blur and select Movie Clip in the Convert to Symbol window. Now delete the newly create symbol instance on the stage.

11 Move up to the main timeline by clicking on Scene 1 just below the timeline. Move to frame 13, where the first tween begins. Select the symbol instance on the stage, press the Swap button in the Property Inspector and select the eyeball1_blur symbol.

12 Move to the next keyframes in this layer and use the same step to swap each of the instances. Do this for the keyframes on frames 23, 32, 40, 46 and 52.

13 Repeat steps 2-11 for the eyeball2 symbol – export a PNG file and open this in Photoshop. Use an angle of 15 when using the motion blur filter. Import this PNG back into Flash and create a symbol containing the blurred bitmap. Then swap the symbol instances found on frames 62, 71, 113, and 120.

14 You have now added the motion blur effect to both animation sequences. Use Test Movie under the Control menu to see the results.

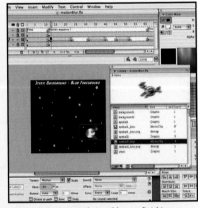

15 Now we are ready to add some finishing touches. Select the keyframe on frame 13. In the Property Inspector enter an easing value of -50. This will make the object accelerate as it moves. Add the same easing value of -50 to frames 62 and 113.

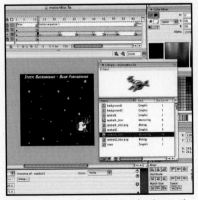

16 Move back to frame 12, select the object in the eyeball layer and nudge it to the right 10 pixels (Shift+right arrow). Now the object takes a step back as it takes off. This effect is called anticipation.

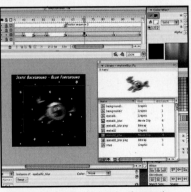

17 Move to frame 71, select the object in the eyeball layer and nudge it up 10 pixels and to the right 20 pixels. This creates a follow-through effect. Now move to frame 113 and move the object down 10 pixels and to the left 20 pixels.

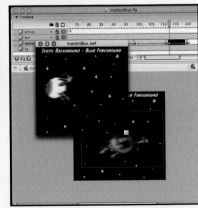

18 Finally, test your movie. You can continue to adjust the speed, pacing and easing until you are happy with the results.

Part 2: Creating a continuous scrolling background

Charge things up with a blurred background that just keeps going…

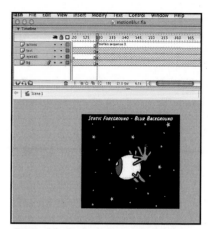

1 Scroll the timeline to the area labelled motion sequence 3 (frame 130). We are going to use another approach to create the illusion of motion – a continuous scrolling background.

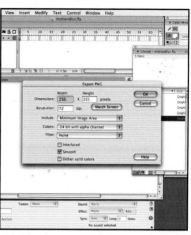

2 Select the stars movieclip in your library and use Export Image to create a PNG file of the stars called stars.png.

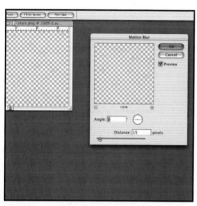

3 Open this PNG file in Photoshop, select Canvas Size under Image and set the width to 300 pixels. Now apply a motion blur using 0 for the angle and 15 for the distance. Use Save for Web to save the blurred image as a bitmap called stars_blur.png.

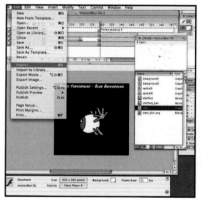

4 Move back to the motionBlur.fla file and go to the main timeline on frame 130. Select and delete the stars on the stage. Then import the newly created stars_blur.png file.

5 Select the newly imported bitmap and use Convert to Symbol under the Insert menu. Give the new movieclip the name starfield.

6 Double-click on the starfield symbol in the library to navigate inside the symbol. Now select the bitmap image and select Duplicate under the Edit menu. Move this new copy to the left so that its right edge touches the left edge of the original bitmap. Align the two bitmaps vertically.

7 Move back to the main timeline by clicking scene1. Select the starfield on the stage and use Convert to Symbol under the Insert menu. Name this new Movie Clip symbol starfield_pan and click OK.

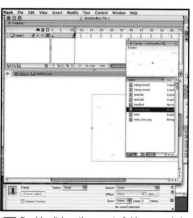

8 Double-click on the new starfield_pan symbol in the library. Once inside, select frame 8 in Layer 1 of the timeline and then select KeyFrame under the Insert menu. Select the starfield in frame 8, open the Info window (Command+I or Ctrl+I) and enter an X value of -30.

9 Select the first keyframe in the timeline and set the Tween to Motion in the Property Inspector. Now use Test Movie to see the finished results.

Illustration: Magictorch [w] www.magictorch.com

Video in Flash MX

Flash MX enters a whole new arena with support for embedded video…

 With the introduction of Flash MX comes the ability to embed video clips directly within your Flash projects. Macromedia worked with Sorenson to develop a new codec called Spark, which is designed specifically for Flash. The Flash MX authoring tool includes the Spark video encoder and the decoder is built into the Flash Player.

Developers using Flash 5 who needed video content had few choices. One option was to create movie clips containing a series of bitmap images. Anyone who has used this approach will instantly appreciate the power of the new video features with Flash MX. The new video playback is smooth, the quality is good and the file sizes are amazing.

The great news is that once embedded within a movie clip you can manipulate the video like you would any other Flash asset. So, you can move, mask, and control the playback of the video using ActionScript. This opens up a whole range opportunities for Flash developers to incorporate video into less traditional interfaces.

We're going to start by importing video clips in Flash MX. We will then move on to using ActionScript to build a playback controller that will enable the user to start, stop and advance through the video clip. The final stop will be looking at masking to create a video kaleidoscope. ➤

 Expertise provided by Jason Krogh, a *Flash*-based developer and trainer. You can contact Jason at [e] krogh@zincroe.com.

 Files on disc
The code needed for this tutorial is on the cover CD in the Tutorial\Video folder.

Part 1: Importing Video

Delivering video online is like coaxing an overweight elephant through a kitchen pipe…

Codecs: temporal and spatial compression

A codec is an algorithm used to compress and decompress video. Cinepak and Sorenson Video are examples of popular codecs. Two techniques are used to compress the video. Spatial compression works much like JPEG compression to create a small description of an image. Temporal compression uses the similarity across frames to squeeze file sizes down even smaller. The Sorenson Spark codec used in Flash MX employs both approaches.

Video keyframes

A keyframe in video compression is not the same as keyframes in the Flash Timeline. Interframe compression takes advantage of the fact that a set of video frames are often very similar, or that the active part of the frame may be restricted to a small area of the screen. When Flash compresses the video it starts with a complete description of the very first frame. Subsequent frames are then described in terms of their differences from this frame. The process of looking at all the proceeding frames in order to render a frame can be very taxing on your computer. So, periodically, the encoder will store a single complete frame called a keyframe.

1 You can, of course, use your own movie clip. The one we're using, snowboard.mov, has been reduced in size to 320x240 and the frame rate cut to 12.5 frames per second. But even still it is nearly 16MB – far too large for delivery online.

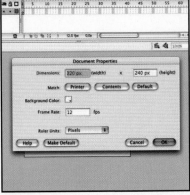

2 We are going to prepare a simple Flash movie containing a single compressed video clip. Create a new Flash file then click the stage size button in the Property Inspector and change the dimensions to 320 wide and 240 high.

3 Select Import from the File menu. If you have QuickTime 4 installed, Flash will enable you to import video in a MOV, AVI and MPEG formats. Select your movie file and click OK.

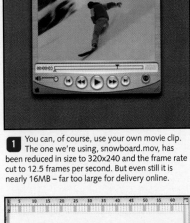

4 When importing QuickTime files Flash will check to see if you want to embed the video into your project or link a Flash file to a QuickTime file as a new track. Select the embed option.

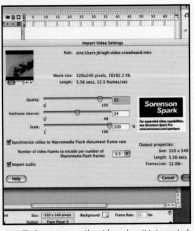

5 Flash compresses the video when it is imported and not when the SWF file is generated. The first setting you will come across is the quality slider. Set the quality to 85. Values below 75 normally result in poor visual quality.

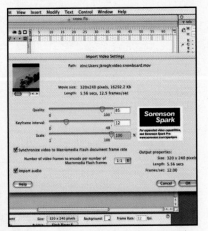

6 Enter a value of 12 for the Keyframe Interval and 100 per cent for the scale. The Keyframe interval marks how frequently a complete frame is stored. A lower value for the interval creates larger files but also enables faster seeking during playback.

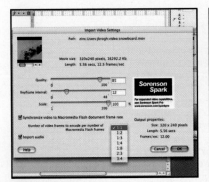

7 Set the frame ratio to 1:1. This will compress the video with a frame rate of 12fps whereas a setting of 1:2 would use a frame rate of 6fps. For online delivery there is rarely a need to use a rate higher than 12fps.

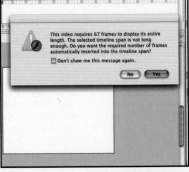

8 Imported video is automatically added as a library symbol much like bitmaps and audio clips. Flash MX will also place a copy on the active layer and display an option to add frames to make space for the video.

9 Position the newly imported video to align with the stage area. You will notice that there is no audio playback of video assets from within the authoring environment. Use the Test Movie option under the Control menu to see (and hear) the compressed video.

10 Select the video asset in the Library panel and use the drop-down menu to open its properties. You can use this Property window to reimport the video if you make changes to the video or want to use different compression settings.

11 Another option in the Properties window enables you to export video symbols to FLV files. These compressed video files can be imported directly into other Flash projects.

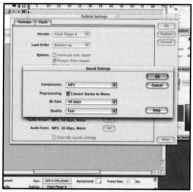

12 Now that we are done let's publish the finished SWF. Pay special attention to the audio quality settings. The audio track from imported video is compressed according to the publish settings for the audio stream.

Part 2: Video Playback Controller

A little ActionScript can go a long way in creating a sophisticated video controller interface. All code required is in the Tutorial\Video folder on the CD…

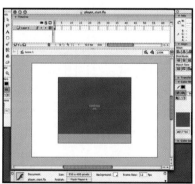

1 Open the player_start.fla document from the CD. This file contains all the interface elements and the basic structure of our video player.

2 Double-click on the player movie clip to edit it. You will see that the first frame is displayed while the video is loading and the second is used once the load is complete.

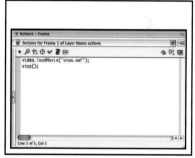

3 Select the first keyframe in the Actions layer and open the Actions window. Add the code above, which is in the Tutorial\Video folder on the CD. The first line initiates the load of the swf file already created. The next line stops playback.

4 Add the rest of the code here (also on the CD). This code calculates the percentage of the video file that has been downloaded. When the entire file is loaded it advances the movie clip to the next frame.

5 Now advance to the second frame. Notice the appearance of the three playback control buttons as well as the volume slider. Select the stop button and add the code seen here.

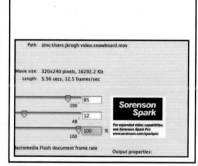

6 Select the play button and add the code:
```
on(press) {
  video.play();
}
```

Part 2: Video Playback Controller continued...

Go lossless

Every time the footage is copied, digitised or recompressed you can expect to see a drop in quality. Just as with JPEGs each time you recompress the video new artifacts are introduced. When you need to store digital video at maximum quality use QuickTime Pro's animation codec. This is only practical for shorter clips because of high file sizes, but it will store the video with a lossless compression scheme.

Progressive download

In most cases it is safe to let the user start viewing the video before the entire clip has been downloaded. As with other Flash content the video is streamed into the player. In this case we are preloading the entire clip because the user can scrub the video to any point in the video right away.

7 Select the reset button and add the code:
```
on(press) {
    video.gotoAndStop(1);
}
```

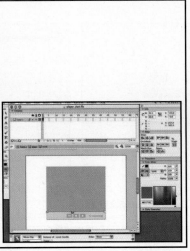

8 The horizontal line and diamond shaped button are the scrub controller. This lets users advance to any point in the video. Double-click the scrub movie clip and select the marker movie clip.

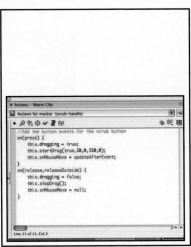

9 Open the Actions editor and add the code displayed above (also on CD). The startDrag action enables the user to slide the marker and also sets up a mouseMove event to force a screen update as the marker is being moved.

10 Now add the rest of the code for the marker. When the user releases the mouse button we stop the drag and remove the mouseMove event. Note that Flash MX enables you to use both button and clip events on movie clip instances.

11 Navigate back up to the player movie clip and select the second keyframe in the Actions layer. Add the line of code displayed here. This will stop the video playback when it is initially loaded.

12 Now add the remainder of the code displayed here. This code is used to keep the scrub marker and the video in sync. If the marker is being moved by the user then we queue the video according to its position. Otherwise we reposition the marker according to the position of the video.

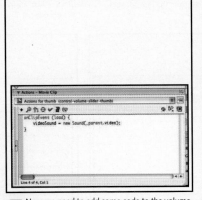

13 Now we need to add some code to the volume slider. Double-click on the volume-slider movie clip and select the volume-thumb movie clip. Add the code in the Actions editor. This establishes a sound object associated with the video clip.

14 Now add the rest of the code for the volume-thumb movie clip. Most of this is similar to the code used for the Scrub Marker. Note the setVolume action used to change the sound level after the user has moved the thumb marker.

15 Now that all the coding is complete, we can try the Test Movie option under the Control menu. If you run into a problem compare your work with the player.fla file in the finished folder.

Part 3: Video kaleidoscope

You don't need to be a programmer to have some fun with video in Flash. You can apply masks, tweens and colour transforms just as you would for other artwork…

Spark Pro

If you're using a lot of video in Flash you may want to check out Spark Pro – a video encoder which offers improved compression options. You can find Spark Pro at [w] www.sorenson.com/sparkpro.

1 We are going to use the same snowboard footage again for this project. Create a new document and import your movie file using the Import to Library option under the File menu.

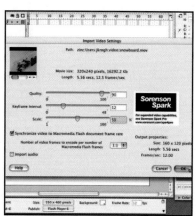

2 In the video import window set the quality to 100, the keyframe interval to 12 and the size to 50 per cent. We won't need the sound so deselect the import audio option.

3 Open the Library window and create a new movie clip symbol named wedge. Drag an instance of the video clip into the new movie clip. You will be prompted to add more frames for the video. Click OK to add the frames.

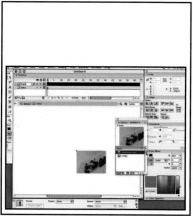

4 Add a new layer in the Timeline using the insert layer button. Name the bottom layer video and the upper layer mask.

5 Double-click on the Layer icon to open the Layer Properties window. Set the top layer to mask and the bottom layer to masked.

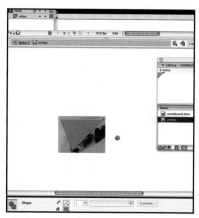

6 Draw a triangular wedge shape on the mask layer. The sides of the wedge should be at a 45 degree angle. Adjust the mask and video so the wedge's tip lines up with the crosshairs on the stage.

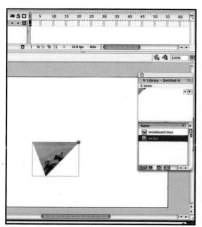

7 Navigate up to the main Timeline and drag an instance of the wedge movie clip onto the centre of the stage.

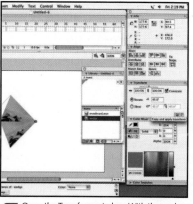

8 Open the Transform window. With the wedge selected enter 45 degrees in the rotate field and press the Copy and Apply button. Press this several more times until you have eight instances arranged around the centre.

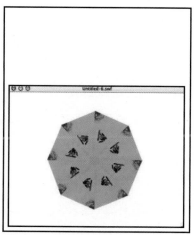

9 Now use the Test Movie option under the Control menu to view the result.

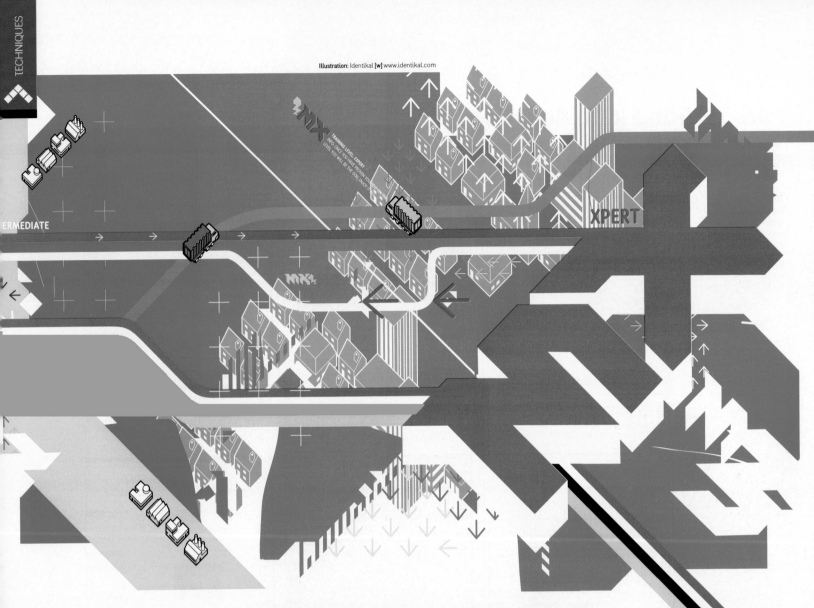

Illustration: Identikal [w] www.identikal.com

Using sound to control moves in Flash

Flash MX's microphone tools open up a new world of interactivity. Forget the mouse and keyboard. Now you can play with a shout...

Expertise provided by Patrick Gardner and Perfect Fools, [e] info@perfectfools.com [w] www.perfectfools.com

Files on disc
In the Tutorial\Flashmic folder on the cover CD you'll find the freeware typeface Pixel for both PC and Mac. Install this font and open cb_start.fla to begin. Also on the CD are ActionScript files you'll need during the tutorial.

 f you have a bent for testing new types of interactivity and stretching the edges of the Internet envelope, you'll love Flash MX's deliciously innovative microphone tools (for more information on Flash Communication Server MX, see page 240).

In this tutorial, Stockholm's Perfect Fools shows how it used the new features to craft a simple platform game with a twist. In CrashBaby you help your 'baby' navigate a bizarre hallway obstacle course by, well, doing a little whoopin' and hollerin'.

The tutorial details how to build the game from the ground up in classic Pong style. You'll learn how to make a fully functional platform game engine in Flash, as well as how to access MX's microphone features to add a new level of interactivity to your repertoire.

You should have at least basic proficiency with Flash MX. Before starting, install the freeware typeface Pixel included on the cover CD.

Part 1: Structuring the movie

A few quick steps get your game off to a good start…

All-in-one clip

Perfect Fools structures its Flash movies with everything in one master movieclip at frame 1 on the main timeline. Why? Because of Flash's infamous 'Failed to save' bug. Occasionally when working intensively with a .fla, a request to save is met with the cheeky response: "Failed to save document." With everything in one clip it's easy to copy over to a new file.

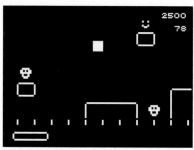

1 Throughout this tutorial we refer to files found in the Tutorial\Flashmic folder on the cover CD. A copy of the finished game, complete with lots of helpful ActionScript comments, is included on the CD in the Tutorial\Flashmic folder (filename cb_final.fla). When you've finished, your game should look like the above image.

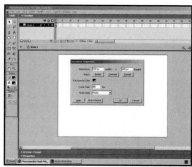

2 Begin by opening cb_start.fla from the cover CD. This file contains most of the graphics you'll need to build your game. Under Modify>Document, set Background Colour to black and Frame Rate to 40 frames per second.

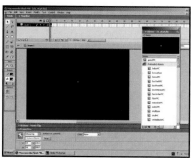

3 Create a new symbol with Insert>New Symbol. Name the symbol gameMC and choose Movie Clip Behaviour. Return to the Scene 1 timeline, open the Library, and drag gameMC into frame 1. Using the Properties Inspector, set gameMC's position to X:275, Y:200.

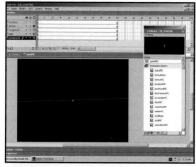

4 Double-click on gameMC to edit it in place (a small circle will indicate the movieclip's position in the middle of the stage). Once inside add 49 blank frames and four new layers. Rename the layers, from top to bottom: functions, actions, foreground, baby, background.

5 Add keyframes to your layers as follows: functions and actions layers, frames 10, 20, 30 and 40; foreground, 20, 30 and 40; baby, 30 and 40; background, 40. On the functions layer you need to label your five keyframes in order from left to right: setup, gameStart, gamePlay, gameOver, and clearing.

6 Now it's time to add some ActionScript. Select frame 1 of the functions layer, open the Actions panel, and paste in the script found in the file 6a.txt in the Tutorial\Flashmic folder on the cover CD. On the actions layer add the script from 6b.txt to frame 20, and 6c.txt to frame 30.

Part 2: Building the platform game

With the background player you can create hallway segments, which are pulled randomly during the game.

Mike issues?

While Flash's microphone functions are groundbreaking, they may have one or two quirks. When the movieclip containing the microphone stream leaves the timeline, objects from the previous keyframe sometimes (mysteriously) appear in the new keyframe. That's the purpose of gameMC frame 40: to 'clear' the screen before restarting the game. Another issue is when you change Record Volume in the microphone settings panel, the new level seems to last only temporarily.

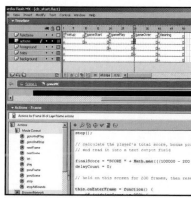

1 Your game's structure is now largely complete. Frame 1 initialises variables and contains game functions. 10 is where the movie holds while waiting for new games to start. 20 manages play, while 30 handles the game ending (see the margin note 'Mike issues?' to learn what frame 40 is for).

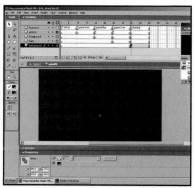

2 Next we need to construct the movieclip that animates the randomly changing background through which our baby moves. At background layer frame 40, draw a black rectangle with no outline. Set the rectangle's size and position using the Properties Inspector: W:550.0, H:400.0, X:-275.0, Y:-200.0. Copy the rectangle.

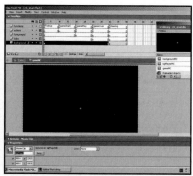

3 Paste the rectangle into frame 1. Choose Insert>Convert to Symbol. Name the symbol backgroundMC, Behaviour Movie Clip. Position backgroundMC at X:-275, Y:-200. Select backgroundMC and Insert>Convert to Symbol once again. Name the new symbol bgPlayerMC. In the Properties Inspector, give it the instance name bgPlayer. ▶

Part 2: Building the platform game continued...

Platform engine

CrashBaby's platform engine is simple but flexible. Customise your own graphics to create an entirely different look. Add a layer to backgroundMC and place more advanced obstacle graphics over the existing barebones surfaces. The game shown here was built with the same engine.

No microphone?

If you've got a pair of headphones, you can plug them into your mic adaptor and use them as a simple sound input.

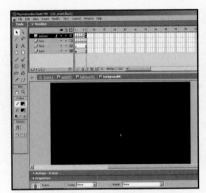

4 Double-click on bgPlayerMC to edit it in place. Repeat with backgroundMC. Insert five frames and three layers. Name the layers, from top to bottom: actions, fore, floor, and back. On both the actions and fore layers, add keyframes to frames 2-6. Frames 5 and 6 should be named startScreen and endScreen respectively.

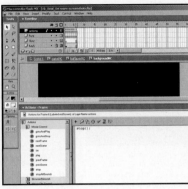

5 backgroundMC contains the game's various screens. startScreen and endScreen are for game start and ending. Frames 1-4 hold play segments, pulled randomly during the game. Go to actions layer frame 1, open the Actions panel, and type the action stop();. Copy this action to each of the other five frames.

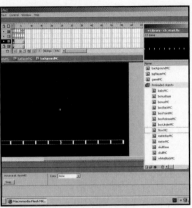

6 Now let's give our baby a floor to crawl on. First, since we'll be doing lots of work above it, lock the layer named back. Open the Library and drag floorMC onto frame 1 of the floor layer. Set floorMC's position to X:-250, Y:120.

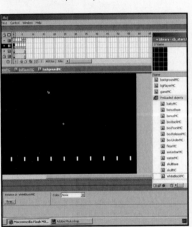

7 Next we want to add the surfaces over/around which the baby manoeuvres. Most of these are already in the library, but to show how these were made we'll create one from scratch now. Begin by dragging whiteBlockMC from the library to frame 1 of the layer fore.

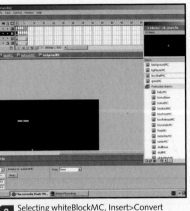

8 Selecting whiteBlockMC, Insert>Convert to Symbol. Name the symbol boxShelfMC. Double-click on boxShelfMC. Select whiteBlockMC and open the Actions panel. Paste in the ActionScript from file 14.txt. This controls how the surface interacts with the baby. Return to backgroundMC's timeline. Resize boxShelfMC to 45 pixels wide by 5 high.

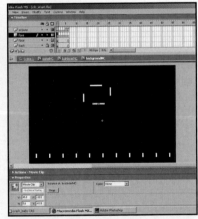

9 Along with a top (boxShelfMC) your obstacles need a front, back and – if they're not sitting on the floor – bottom. Drag boxFrontMC and boxBackMC onto the fore layer and size them to 5 pixels wide by 30 high. Add boxUnderMC, resized to 45 pixels wide by 5 high.

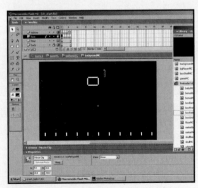

10 Arrange the four surfaces as a box, with corners almost touching. Position this group anywhere above the floor. Finally, add to the fore layer the object that tells your baby when to 'fall' off the obstacle. Position boxReleaseMC 30 pixels to the right of, and 35 pixels above, boxBackMC.

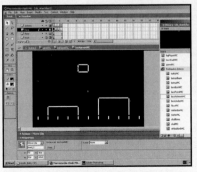

11 Copy this group and paste it as many times as you like throughout frames 1-4. Resize the surfaces to create a variety of obstacle environments (see cb_final.fla for examples). When you're done, give all of the surfaces unique instance names: front1_2 (for example, frame 1 instance 2), shelf3_2, under2_2, back4_3, etc.

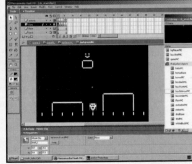

12 Now that your obstacle course is ready, let's add some bonuses and nasties. Drag bonusMC and skullMC onto the fore layer. As with the surfaces, you can copy these as many times as you like throughout frames 1-4. Just remember to give each instance a unique name: bonus4_3, skull2_1, etc.

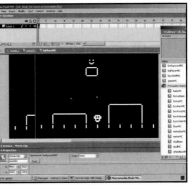

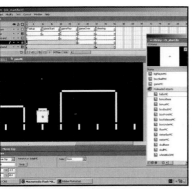

13 Go to frame 6 (endScreen), fore layer. Create a text field with: Text type Static Text, Font Pixel, Font Size 40, colour white, style Bold, alignment Centre. Write GAME OVER into this field. Copy the field. On the copy, reset type to Dynamic Text and link to the variable _parent._parent.finalScore.

14 You can always add more game segments by inserting more frames to backgroundMC. Just be sure that startScreen and endScreen stay at the end. Now return to the bgPlayerMC timeline. Select backgroundMC and give it the instance name backGr2. Copy and paste this movie clip.

15 Position the new copy at X:-825, Y:-200. Give the copy an instance name of backGr1. Exit to the gameMC timeline. To complete the game elements drag babyMC from the library to frame 1 of the layer baby. Position babyMC at X:-12.5, Y:85.0 and give it the instance name baby.

Part 3: Adding microphone interactivity

With Flash MX, adding audio interactivity to your productions is as easy as typing Microphone.get()…

Player Settings Window

Whenever you use Flash MX's new features to access local resources like the microphone, a dialog called the Player Settings Window pops up to ask the user for authorisation. This dialog is a movieclip that's built into the player, and as far as we've been able to tell there's no way to disable it. To access resource settings while the movie is playing, right-click and choose Settings....

Perfect Fools

This tutorial was developed by Perfect Fools, the interactive production company based in Stockholm, Sweden. From an island stronghold in the heart of Stockholm harbour, it continues to hatch its megalomaniacal plot to conquer the world, one brand at a time. Visit Perfect Fools at [w] www.perfectfools.com.

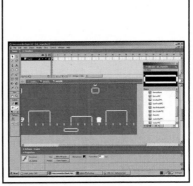

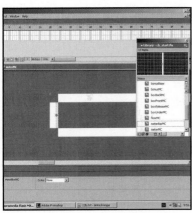

1 Enable the game elements with ActionScript. Go to frame 1, functions layer, open the Actions panel, and copy the contents of file 22a.txt from the CD into the gap following the variable list. Jump to frame 20, actions layer, and add the script from 22b.txt to the space after this.onEnterFrame = function() {.

2 And now the fun part: connecting the microphone input to the game. First, we need a meter to display the microphone's activity level. From the Library, drag meterMC to the lower-left corner of the stage at frame 1, foreground layer. Double-click on it to edit it in place.

3 To ready meterMC for use as a readout, insert one layer and name it meterBar. Drag meterBarMC from the Library onto this layer. Position meterBarMC at X:4, Y:5, and give it an instance name of meterBar. Exit to the gameMC timeline, select meterMC, and set its instance name to meter.

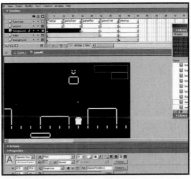

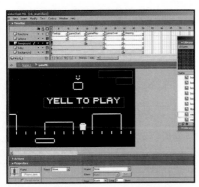

4 Time for the bits of ActionScript that exploit Flash MX's microphone object. Open the Actions panel, select actions layer frame 10, and paste in the contents of file 25a.txt from the Tutorial\Flashmic folder on the CD. Go to actions layer frame 20 and, in the gap after this.onEnterFrame = function() {, paste the script from 25b.txt.

5 Finally, place two text fields on frame 1 of the foreground layer. In the Properties Inspector choose: Text type Dynamic Text, Font Pixel, Font Size 20 points, colour white, style Bold, alignment Right, Selectable off. Link the fields to variables bonusPts and elapsedTotalSecs respectively.

6 Copy the fields together with meterMC and paste them in place on frame 20. Back at frame 1 create another text field. Set Text type to Static Text, Font to Pixel, Font Size to 40 points, style to Bold, and alignment to Centre. Type YELL TO PLAY into the field.

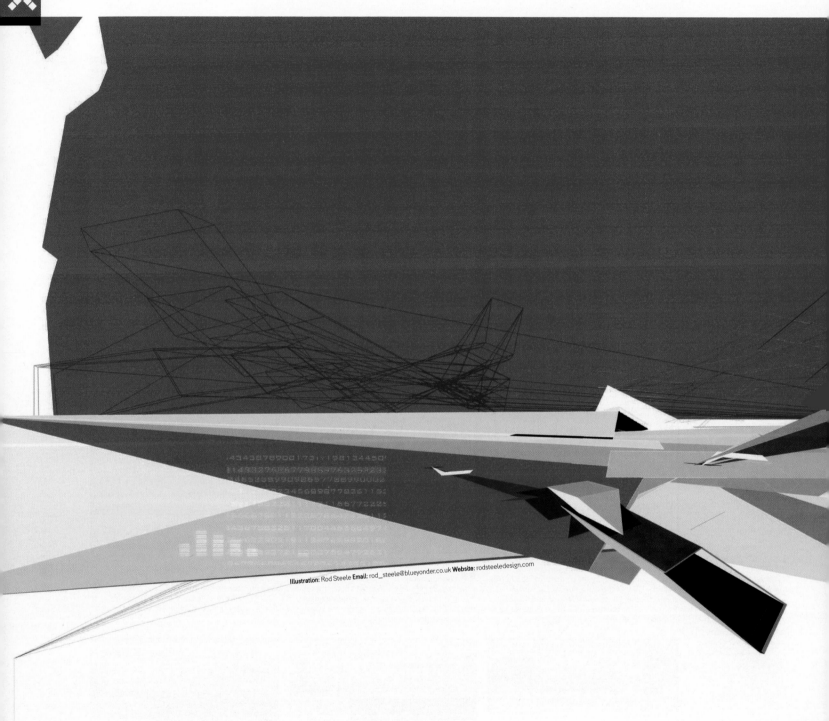

Illustration: Rod Steele **Email:** rod_steele@blueyonder.co.uk **Website:** rodsteeledesign.com

XML in Flash MX

You say tomato, I say <entity name="tomato"/>.
Power up your static Flash MX with a little XML
spice in this real-world tutorial…

et's face it. Dynamically updating sites are what clients want — and they want them cheap. With Flash MX, you can deliver them, and include all the usual design flare expected of a Flash-based product.

We've teamed up with the fledgling second generation new media agency Webziggy to bring you this tutorial which demonstrates how to set up a site in Flash MX using a Web server that delivers database content as XML. It's a technical job, to be sure, but puts a lot more power at your fingertips. Using similar techniques, you'll be able to deliver Flash sites to clients that enable the clients themselves to update the actual site content.

The tutorial is based on Webziggy's

site for A–Bomb, which is at [w] www.a-bomb.co.uk. Webziggy has kindly set up a dummy XML news feed that you'll be able to use within your ActionScript. They'll show you how to access that within the Flash MX interface and put some finishing touches to the Flash movie and tell you about publishing your movie and the security implications surrounding that.

There is also a small supporting site for this tutorial, which you will need to visit to set up your dummy XML news feed. You can access it at [w] http:// share.webziggy.net/. The site will be kept up to date as feedback comes in from readers about the tutorial. So, let's get started. It's quite straightforward. ➤

Files on disc
Supporting files for this tutorial can be found in the Tutorial\XMLFlashMX folder.

Expertise provided by Alan Ogilvie, Technical Director of Webziggy. You can contact him on [e] alan@webziggy.net or visit [w] www.webziggy.net

Part 1: Setting up your XML news feed

Get all of your data to be used on your site ready, so it can be pulled into and manipulated within Flash MX…

Which browser?

It's best to use Netscape 6.2, or another standards compliant browser when viewing XML on the Web. However, you'll find IE 5 or greater is okay. Don't worry if you can't see anything in step 5, *Flash MX* will still be able to retrieve the XML. The supporting Website should work okay on Netscape 6.2, Netscape 4.7x, and IE 4+ on PC and Mac — but this hasn't been tested to breaking point.

Propeller-heads unite!

Providing the News Feed like this enables you to successfully complete the Flash movie without server knowledge. However, if you go to the supporting Website, [w] http://share.webziggy.net/, you will find a Propeller–heads section. It explains how you can set up a local copy of the Database and XML feeds using Microsoft IIS 5, Microsoft Access, and spot of Active Server Pages in JavaScript.

What is XML?

It's a way of sharing data, a way of marking data up. If you like, XML is to data what HTML is to text. Where HTML marks up text and a browser reads and understands it to present the text visually, XML marks–up data which a client (browser) understands and can use – it enables you to delineate fields in a database rather like in a database. XML is much more than this, but it gives you an understanding for the tutorial. to read more info about XML head to the Propeller–heads section of [w] http://share.webziggy.net/.

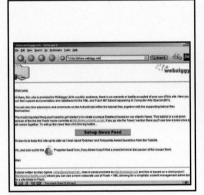

1 Visit **[w]** http://share.webziggy.net/ and read the first page, finally clicking through to the News Feed set up page (**[w]** http://share.webziggy.net/generate_newsfeed.asp). Since our Flash movie will be pulling XML data from this site, we will need to set up a unique ID, and subsequent screens will help you do this.

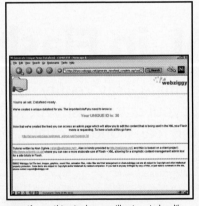

4 If everything is okay, you'll get a window like the one above telling you that everything is set. The important thing is that you make a note of the unique ID the site has generated for you. In the example here, it's 30.

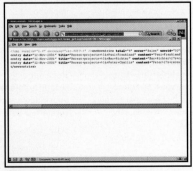

7 Use your browser to go to **[w]** http://share.webziggy.net/news_get.asp?userid=XX. You should put your user ID where we have XX in the URL. For example, it should be something similar to **[w]** http://share.webziggy.net/news_get.asp?userid=30 – the feed we just set up.

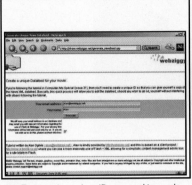

2 To generate a unique ID, you need to supply an email address and a name. Please note that we need a unique email address, so if we set up a news feed using **[e]** bob@somewhere.com then you will be unable to set up another feed using that email address. In the screenshot we have supplied **[e]** alan@webziggy.net. We next hit the button marked Generate.

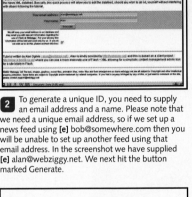

5 Further down this Web page you'll see a link to your own unique admin page. This page is essentially what A-Bomb sees when it wishes to edit its News section.

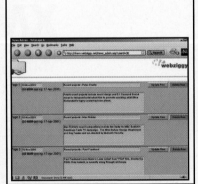

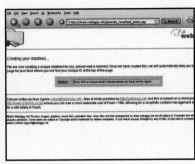

3 Depending on the speed of your Internet connection, you may see another page at this point. This page, called Creating your datafeed, is where we have to set up the datafeed. Check the Status field, which is on an orange background. The server will update this field with important information about what it's doing. If this phrase appears on your screen "Error: Not a unique email address please go back and try again", then hit the back button on your browser and enter a different email address.

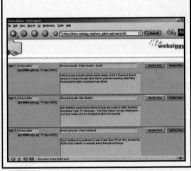

6 Try editing one of these news articles. Pick a row and make some editorial changes. Hit the green button on the right to submit your changes. We've made a change to the title of the first news article, try putting your name in there, this will appear in your Flash movie. Further down you can add a new article.

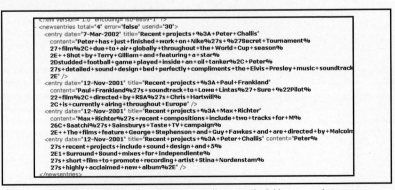

8 Have a look through the XML above. Here you see what was in the fields on your admin page represented in XML. Note that each article has been extracted into <entry> nodes with attributes for date, title and content. XML is similar to HTML, except it is far more powerful. The content for each article has been URLEncoded so that it doesn't prove a problem within the XML. There are other ways to do this, but this is the easiest.

Part 2: Flash, ActionScript and XML

Use the supporting files on the cover CD in the Tutorial\XMLFlashMX folder when working along with this tutorial…

Need files?

We would recommend creating a new folder on your desktop, and copying all the files from Tutorial\XML on the cover CD into there. The important file you are looking for to start this section is skeleton.fla.

Notice anything different?

If you've been used to the Flash 5 interface, you know how frustrating it can be when you are trying to use design tools and ActionScript at the same time. The Actions panel or the Output panel clutters your display — you just couldn't get a clear view without pulling panels around all the time. Thankfully, Flash MX has had a rethink. The screenshots show our set up of panels of which Macromedia conveniently provides some default layouts for panels which are split between Designer and Developer. Here, we've chosen Developer [1024x768] Panel Set from the Window menu. Flash MX deals with the old clutter by making these panels dockable into/onto the sides of the main window. They even have nifty minimisation buttons like WindowShade.

The debugger gets a facelift

One of the biggest issues we had with Flash 5 was the debugger, and in Flash MX it's good to see it's had a bit of an overhaul. You can interactively set Breakpoints, which you can also do through the Actions panel. Although we haven't used Remote Debugging extensively with Flash MX we're hoping that with the Debugger improvements the link for Remote Debugging will be better.

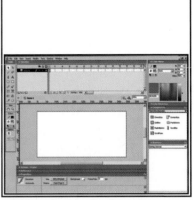

1 Open the tutorial file skeleton.fla from the cover CD in Flash MX. Take a good look around the new Flash MX interface and bring up the Actions, Reference and Properties panels from the Window menu. (See the Notice anything different? margin note).

2 On the first frame in the Timeline, on the actions layer, you'll see the ActionScript associated with this frame in the Actions panel. You should read the comments made at the top of the ActionScript, and bring up the Reference panel.

3 The first thing to do is to look for the Properties section and – with your unique ID in hand – amend the ActionScript: **var userid = 30;** so that it equals your unique ID (we have highlighted this above). Just beneath you will note the property newsfeedURL which has the URL of the News Feed on the server and where our XML request and response will be passed to.

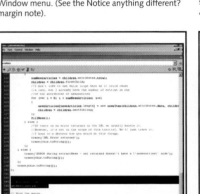

4 The flow of control within this may not be familiar to you. First, it relies on Events; when used to load data, the XML object fires an Event that essentially tells another function to execute. In the screenshot we have highlighted the line: **getNews(userid);** to kick start our XML request.

5 Now find the function getNews() and you will see that it creates a new XML object (xmlquery) and puts your unique user ID (userid) in there. The real meat in the getNews() function is the line: **xmlquery.sendAndLoad(newsFeedURL, xmlresponse).** This line sends out a request to our server and gives it your unique ID.

6 Then on the line: **xmlresponse.onLoad = extractNews;** we see our Event Handler which *Flash* will execute when the sendAndLoad has completed and returned data into our xmlresponse object. And that's really as complicated as it gets.

7 Once our XML has been returned back into our Flash movie, we can then manipulate it. This is what happens when our Event Handler executes. We call the function extractNews() which then goes through the returned XML and generates some friendly ActionScript Arrays and Objects for us. We have highlighted this function in the screenshot. There is an Array called newsArticles which will now be available to us.

8 At this point, you might like to test your movie in the debugger, by going to Debug Movie. For Flash 5 users, you'll notice that the debugger has had a significant upgrade. When we start the debugger, it immediately pauses the movie. However, we just want our movie to run so that you can look at the Variables defined in _level0. So, click the Green Arrow to get the debugger going again and wait.

9 If all is well, you'll see some XML in the Output window. You should click on the _level0 movie in the Debugger window, and then pick the Variables tab and have a look at the contents of the newsArticles Array. The movie has requested the XML and has traced this into the Output window, and then using our Event Handler, extractNews(), we have transformed this into a simple ActionScript array called newsArticles. ➤

Part 3: Enough code? Let's look at design

Now that all the coding is complete, we can take a look at the overall appearance of the site…

The design

A–Bomb has a very clean brand, with a white background and sparse colour use. The red that we used was #CA2819 and the green was #4C541B in case you want to copy the colour scheme.

Better breadcrumbs

With all these nested symbols running riot in Flash, you'd think there would be a better way to navigate? Flash MX to the rescue. Gone are the bad visual feedback animations of Flash 5 when you edited a symbol directly nested in another – now you get a nice zoom feeling which helps you subconsciously know where you are. Also there is a new movie navigation system, just beneath the Timeline is a Breadcrumb navigation to help you when editing symbols. This is an improvement over **Flash 5** which had something similar above the Timeline on the PC version, but we never found it worked all that well.

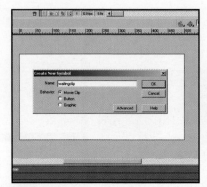

1 Dock your Actions panel and we'll start putting some text fields, movies and buttons into our movie. First, we'll need something that will announce to our users that we are waiting on the content coming from the server (the XML Feed). Insert a New Symbol, make it a Movie. Name the symbol waitingclip.

2 On the symbol add a text box with Please Wait... We are retrieving the latest news in Arial 12 pts. The screenshot above gives an example of how to lay it out.

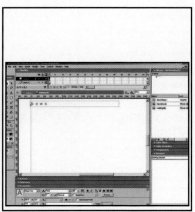

3 Insert another New Symbol, make it a movie also. Call the symbol newsmovie. You'll need to make 4 text fields. The first is just a heading, News, so Arial 12 pts again.

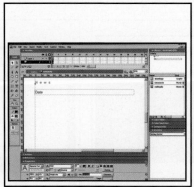

4 Below that make another Arial 12pts field, this time make it a piece of Dynamic Text by using the Properties panel. On the Properties panel for this text field, link this Dynamic Text to the variable named newsdate. This field will hold our Date for each item of news.

5 Now create another text field, same text size just below that, this time it should be Dynamic Text and its variable should be newstitle. This field will hold our Title for each item of news.

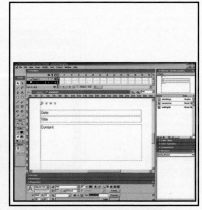

6 Beneath that, create a bigger multi-line Dynamic Text field, and link it to the variable newscontent. This field will hold our Content for each item of news.

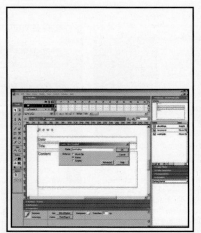

7 Insert another New Symbol, this time make it a button. Call it next button.

8 You can see that we made a fairly simple button to go with our client's clean looking brand. It's just the word Next in Arial 14pts and then a greater than sign.

9 Using the Library, edit the newsmovie that you created. Drop the next button onto the page somewhere on the bottom of the screen, just beneath the Content box is a good place to put it as we have done in the above example.

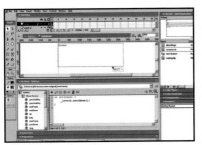

10 To tie our next button to our ActionScript you should open your Actions panel for the next button instance and give it the following ActionScript. We use the Expert mode editing, which you can find in the Options drop-down on the Actions panel at the top-right hand corner of the screen:

```
on (release) {
    _level0.nextNews();
};
```

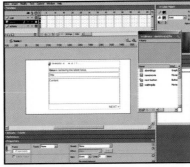

11 Edit the root scene, add three layers. Using the library of Symbols you have just made, drag and drop the newsmovie onto a frame on an empty layer, in the Properties panel give the movie an Instance name of newsmovie. Drag and drop waiting clip in a similar fashion, giving it an Instance name of waitingmessage.

12 If you look in the Library you should see a graphic called abomblogo, this is A-Bomb's Logo and can be placed on another layer and scaled. For those used to Flash 5, use the Free Transform tool in MX. Place it on the left-hand side.

Part 4: Testing, publishing and security

Now that your site is all in place, all that needs to be done is check to make sure that it works properly…

Sandbox

Security is important within Flash, and you should be aware that there is an important constraint on movies that use XML on other domains. If you Test this movie in the Standalone Flash 6 Player you will have no problem. If you publish the movie to HTML and then view it locally using a browser over the filesystem, you will have no problem. However, if you put the HTML and your SWF file onto a Web server... then it will not work. This is called Same-Domain security which says that you cannot access data from another domain (i.e. a different server) when Flash Player is embedded within an HTML page on a Web server. This security SandBox stops people pilfering data from sites. There is a common workaround for this at [w] http://share.webziggy.net/.

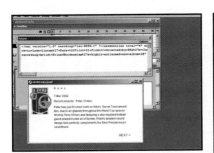

1 Now you are ready to test your creation. Assuming that you have followed our naming techniques outlined in Flash, it should work when you Test Movie from the Control menu. You should initially get the message, Please wait text while the movie retrieves the XML News Feed. You need to be connected to the Internet for this to work.

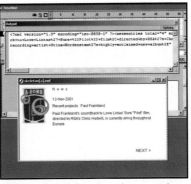

2 Once the first piece of news has appeared, click the Next button to cycle through all your data from your News Feed.

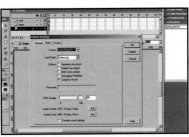

3 You may want to publish this movie, but you should read the comments about Sandbox opposite. However, if you set your publish settings to export for Flash Player 6 and Compress Movie (another godsend that we've all been eagerly waiting for), and then hit Publish you can then load the resulting HTML into a browser with Flash Player 6 installed.

4 Here's what it should look like. Don't forget to try changing the data on the server using the content admin tool described in Part 1. But watch out for your Browser Cache as both Netscape and IE will cache the XML, so you'll need to clear your cache if you change the data on the server.

5 If you're a bit uninspired and you need some help, you should take a look at another site the has been built using extensive XML transactions with more on their way. Go to [w] www.joshandpecs.com/journal.asp and click on the filofax after it detects Flash.

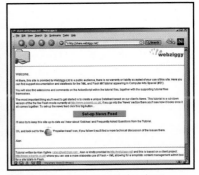

6 More information about Flash and XML interactivity is available from the Webziggy Website at [w] http://share.webziggy.net// where there are also links to other sources.

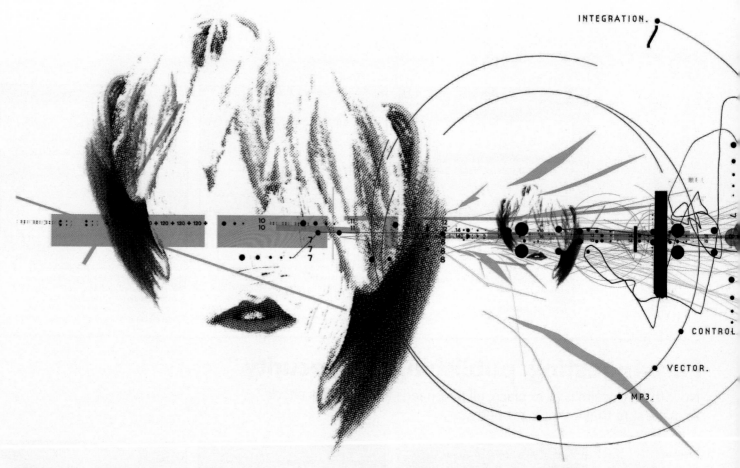

INTEGRATION.

CONTROL

VECTOR.

MP3.

The new powers of ActionScript

Scripting has evolved in the new version of Flash. Find out just how much has changed with this analysis of the new scripting features and take your first steps into Flash MX scripting…

Flash MX is promoted by Macromedia as being more than just a new version of Flash; it's claimed to be the first step in a new way of developing rich applications for the Web and other interactive platforms. Only time will tell exactly how justified this claim is. It's clear that Flash is only the first of the Macromedia product family to receive the MX treatment.

It's hard to assess how significant some of the changes to Flash MX are because they relate to server products that haven't been released yet. The vision emerging, though, is one of a powerful integrated platform consisting of both server and client applications that will enable the rapid development of rich applications, including real-time messaging and the ability to stream a variety of content through a Flash MX front end.

Flash MX will also make life easier for users by helping developers to create accessible, consistent, high-performing interfaces. Most of the power to achieve this lies in functionality that is accessed through ActionScript.

Raising the bar

One of the consequences of the changes to ActionScript in Flash MX is that it is now a little less obvious how to do simple things, especially if you are just beginning to get to grips with applying Actions in Flash. The Actions menu is now formally arranged, with everything in its correct location. In Flash 5, the Actions menu was similarly strictly organised, but it also offered a Basic Actions menu that contained the most commonly used commands.

The Basic Actions menu may have been a mishmash of commands from all over the place, but it was a useful subset for beginners to focus on. That menu has gone, and some beginners may well be put off by the formal language and complexity of the restructured Actions menu. The important commands for beginners (such as goto, getURL, stop and play) are easy enough to find provided the user opens the Actions category in the menu pane. In the pane are sensible titles like Movie control, Browser/Network, and Movie Clip Control which group together related commands.

The interactive features of Flash have been greatly enhanced in the new release, but not in the completely earth-shattering way that one might expect from the description of Macromedia's aims for the new product.

And that's a good thing. For anyone who invested time and effort in learning Flash 5 ActionScript, that investment has been protected in Flash MX. Much of ActionScript remains unchanged in this release, and the many improvements to the language are essentially incremental in nature. Nothing should break when you bring Flash 5 scripts into Flash MX.

Aside from the new features, Macromedia claims that the speed of ActionScript has been greatly improved in certain key areas, such as string, XML and array handling.

See the boxout on page 90 for more highlights of the changes to scripting in Flash MX.

Changes to the ActionScript Editor

The Actions editor still has the Normal and Expert modes that were introduced in Flash 5. In Normal mode, Actions have to be inserted from the list or

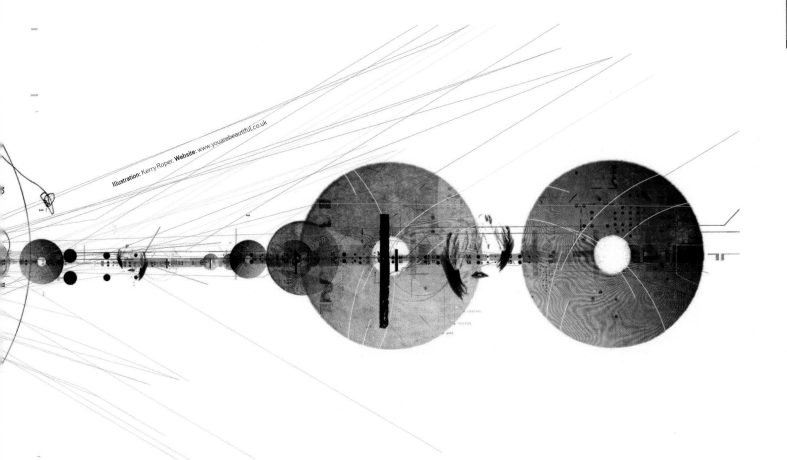

Illustration: Kerry Roper. **Website:** www.youarebeautiful.co.uk

menu, and customised using the Options panel, which has been moved to the top of the Actions palette. Working in Normal mode is slow and prone to errors when constructing complex commands such as If...Else statements. In Expert mode, you can type freely into the Editor window in addition to choosing from the menu options. But, until now, there's been no interface in Expert mode to help you write the commands.

The new pop-up, Code Hints, offers the perfect compromise, enabling you to work in Expert mode but offering valuable help with syntax and options. If Flash recognises the command you're typing, a pop-up code hint window appears (after a user-definable delay) to remind you of the required syntax or choose from a list of modifying attributes.

As well as a range of buttons for common tasks like find and replace, the editor window now offers a script navigation menu, which lists all the locations where scripts are likely to be defined in the movie. This means you don't have to spend so long hunting for elements in the movie to check or change their actions. You can also pin the current script in place, so that you can select other items on the stage without losing sight of the script you're editing at that moment.

The addition of line numbering in the Editor is welcome in Flash MX, as is the customisable syntax colouring and the customisable auto-formatting for code layout. Small details, such as the editor automatically indenting nested lines of code and moving closing curly braces ("}") back to the left margin, make coding in the new version a real pleasure compared to Flash 5.

Anatomy of the Actions palette

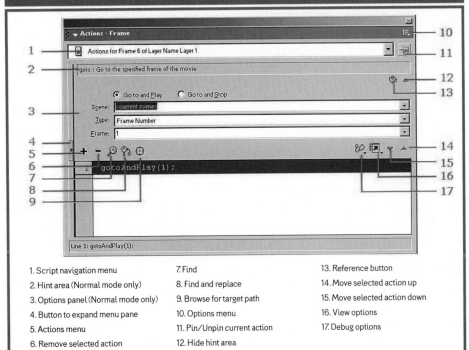

1. Script navigation menu
2. Hint area (Normal mode only)
3. Options panel (Normal mode only)
4. Button to expand menu pane
5. Actions menu
6. Remove selected action
7. Find
8. Find and replace
9. Browse for target path
10. Options menu
11. Pin/Unpin current action
12. Hide hint area
13. Reference button
14. Move selected action up
15. Move selected action down
16. View options
17. Debug options

Helpfully, the Editor now remembers whether it is in Normal or Expert mode, instead of remembering the last mode it was set to for individual objects.

The Actions menu, accessed through the left pane or the plus menu, has been revised substantially in this release. It's now much more hierarchical, and methods, properties and events are listed under separate menus for each object. The Basic Actions menu is gone, and the commands it contained have been redistributed into the hierarchy. Some, like the venerable Tell Target, have been relegated to the new Deprecated menu.

Reference panel

When the code hints aren't enough to help you use a command, or when you are exploring the commands in the hierarchical menu pane, you can use the new reference panel to obtain a detailed description of the command and its usage.

The Reference panel contains the same information as the ActionScript reference in the manual and online help, but it's integrated into the Flash environment so that information on any command is presented with the press of a button. Because you're not juggling an open browser window as well as the Flash interface, it's easier to make convenient use of the information.

You can summon the relevant information for any command in ActionScript by clicking anywhere in the

name of the command and clicking the Reference button in the Editor toolbar. You can also highlight an option in the menu pane in the Actions palette and obtain reference information about it without having to use it in the editor.

The online help has not been made obsolete by the Reference panel. The information in the Reference panel essentially contains general information about the command, whereas the ActionScript Dictionary in the online help gives more detailed information.

Components

Flash MX introduces a revamped version of the Smart Clips from Flash 5. Called Components, these are scriptable interface elements that you can add quickly to your project to create common widgets like scrollbars, radio buttons, select menus, and so on.

A basic selection is supplied with the product, and an enhanced set is available for download from the Macromedia site.

Components are designed to be reused without much coding, and can speed up interface work in Flash. They can be customised with user-definable skins so that they can be easily integrated into the visual style of your project.

Each type of component has a substantial set of methods that can be used to control component

elements via scripting. The components have a standard API (Application Programming Interface), which enables developers to access and control properties such as whether an individual element is enabled, its size, the registration of new skin elements and so on. For most uses, you don't need to add additional code. Components self-configuring as far as possible, so you'll only need to use the commands in the API when you want to move beyond the basics.

Data integration

Macromedia has put a lot of thought into the integration of Flash with data-driven applications, and there are several new ActionScript features that empower this sort of development. However, some of these features are designed to integrate with a new series of server products that aren't yet available. Flash MX offers data integration in the following ways:
• Loading information into variables or sending data through HTTP request/response (same as in Flash 5)
• Loading information into variables or sending data through a direct connection with the server, either using XML through a socket connection or the new LoadVars data API
• Loading information from or storing data in local data structures, using the new SharedObjects feature (similar to browser cookies).

Named anchors

One of the biggest drawbacks with Flash Websites arises from the way the browser treats a Flash movie as a single element within a Web page. This means that although the movie may contain many pages of information, the user's navigation through that content is not part of the browser history. Clicking either Back or Refresh in the browser will lose the user's place in the movie: firstly, the browser will load the page before the one containing the Flash movie; and secondly, the browser will reload the page. In either case, this resets the movie to its beginning and impairs the user experience when navigating Flash content. It's been impossible to give someone a URL to take them directly to a particular piece of content in the movie — until Flash MX, that is.

In Flash MX, you can set a frame label to be a named anchor. When the user clicks a button to take them to that destination in the movie, the browser is actually given a new URL to load which consists of the page name followed by a hash (#) and the name of the frame label. It's formed exactly like an HTML page anchor. The Flash 6 Player takes that information from the browser and uses it to display the correct information within the Flash movie.

The effect of this is to restore the functionality of the back and forward buttons in the browser even when navigating within a single Flash movie, provided that named anchor frame labels are used as destinations for all internal navigation. This also enables the bookmarking of Flash content, and the ability to send someone a more accurate URL to take them to a certain part of the movie. To make using this feature easier, Flash can automatically give the first frame of each scene a named anchor frame label.

To make this feature work when the page is published, you need to publish the movie in an HTML page exported using the appropriate template (Flash with Named Anchor) in the HTML Publish Settings. This simply has the effect of listing all the named

The changes to ActionScript in Flash MX serve to consolidate the excellent scripting features of the previous version

New ActionScript highlights

Editor

Revised interface, line numbering, customisable syntax colouring, auto-formatting of code layout with customisable settings, object selector menu, ability to 'pin' scripts in view so that they remain visible when editing other objects.

Components

Reusable, scriptable, prebuilt interface components such as scroll bars, menus, and radio buttons are now supplied, with more being available for download.

Named anchors

Frames in the Timeline can now be labelled with named anchors enabling the use of the browser Back button, making Flash movies more accessible to screen reader software.

Drawing API

New drawing methods enable the creation of artwork at run-time via scripting.

System capabilities

System features such as screen resolution can be detected at runtime, and changes made to layout or functionality accordingly.

Reference panel

Complete language reference now available within the Flash environment, with links to the code editor so that you can look up features of a command as you use it.

Data integration

New server API and event model will allow real-time display of data through the Flash front end. Flash now has the ability to store data on the client machine for use on other occasions using SharedObjects.

Dynamic content

Dynamically download and play JPEG images and MP3 sounds at run-time without embedding them into Flash first.

Event and object model

Create new listeners for mouse, data and keyboard events. Textfields and buttons are now scriptable objects, with their own new properties and methods available for use.

Using the drawing API and dynamic content features

```
createEmptyMovieClip("logo",1)
with (logo) {
  beginFill((0x333366,60);
  moveTo(0,300)
  curveTo(200,500,400,100)
  curveTo(175,450,0,300)
}
```

1 We'll start by creating a new empty movie clip. In Flash MX, we don't need to use an existing clip as a container; we can create one completely from scratch. In the beginFill method, the second parameter is the alpha transparency of the fill. The drawing methods operate when the movie is played. The drawing commands operate in a similar way to PostScript, effectively moving an invisible pen around the drawing space.

```
createEmptyMovieClip("sandy",1)
sandy.createEmptyMovieClip("image",1)
loadMovie("sandy.jpg",_root.sandy.image)
```

2 Using the Load movie command, we can import a JPEG image in the same way as SWF files. In this example, we use the createEmptyMovieClip action to create an image clip inside a container movie clip. We then replace the image clip using the loadMovie command and a target path.

```
createEmptyMovieClip("logo",2)
with (logo) {
  beginFill((0x333366,60);
  moveTo(0,300)
  curveTo(200,500,400,100)
  curveTo(175,450,0,300)
}
createEmptyMovieClip("sandy",1)
sandy.createEmptyMovieClip("image",1)
loadMovie("sandy.jpg",_root.sandy.image)
```

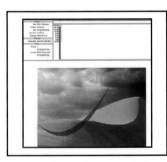

3 By combining the previous two examples, we can create a whole layout completely through scripting.

```
createEmptyMovieClip("logo",2)
with (logo) {
  beginFill((0x333366,60);
  moveTo(0,300)
  curveTo(200,500,400,100)
  curveTo(175,450,0,300)
}
createEmptyMovieClip("sandy",1)
sandy.createEmptyMovieClip("image",1)
loadMovie("sandy.jpg",_root.sandy.image)
sandy.setMask(logo)
```

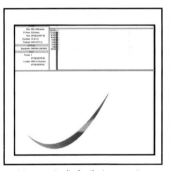

4 Finally, we call the setMask method of the container movie clip for the image, using the logo clip as a mask. This is why we used two nested clips for the dynamic image; once the imported image has replaced the image clip, it no longer has the properties and methods of a normal movie clip, and the setMask method is not available for the image clip.

anchors from the Flash movie as empty anchor links in the HTML, which is required for the browser to pass the anchor information correctly to the player.

Dynamic content

One of the biggest benefits of Flash for Web design is the way that once a movie has loaded, navigation within the movie is instantaneous. However, if the movie contains a great many images or sounds, downloading all the data in the movie can make the initial loading process take too long.

There is a particular problem if different visitors to the site are going to use different bits of the content; this means that any one visitor is going to have to download much more content than they will actually need. Until now, the solution has been to structure the movie as separate SWF files and use Load Movie actions to link it all together, which brings its own problems of download delays and editing complexity.

In Flash MX, you can use the new dynamic content features to script the movie so that JPEG images and MP3 sounds are downloaded separately from the SWF file; they still play back as part of the Flash movie. This means that the project can be created as a single movie without the download penalty that used to be associated with this option, and you can use variable data to reference the images or sound files as external content. This result is that both the images or sound data and the information about the references and file names can be loaded dynamically at run-time.

To dynamically display an image, use the loadMovie command, referencing a JPEG image instead of a SWF file. To dynamically load a sound, define a sound object as usual in the script, then use the loadSound method of the sound object to reference the external MP3 file.

Drawing API and graphical scripting

The graphical abilities of Flash have been extended in unexpected directions in Flash MX. Chief among the new features here is the introduction of a drawing API, which includes methods for drawing straight lines, curves, strokes and fills via scripting. For developers familiar with how PostScript operates, the new drawing methods will be second nature.

Macromedia has also introduced scriptable masks, which means that using scripted behaviours, designers can create dynamic masking effects that selectively hide or reveal artwork. See the sidebar for an example of these new features in action.

Event and object model

Flash MX boasts a revised event model, together with new Listener objects that detect the mouse, keyboard and data events in a more predictable, consistent and intuitive way. Listeners can be defined for movie clips, buttons and other objects — each class has its own listeners that capture specific events related to the object in question. Listeners don't have to be defined in the objects to which they relate, you can create listeners anywhere, such as in the main Timeline.

Text fields are now instances of a TextField object class, which has an interface enabling properties like size, text formatting, colour, border, tabbing and so on to be controlled by scripting. There is also a TextFormat object that offers control of text appearance.

One implication of this change is that dynamic and input text fields now have instance names as well as being bound to specific variables. This is much clearer to work with than the previous situation; for example, we can now set the scroll property of the text using the name of the text field rather than that of the text variable inside it. However, for backward compatibility, setting the scroll property still works if you set scrolling using the variable name.

Buttons are now scriptable objects in their own right, and have their own properties and methods as well as event handlers.

Movie clips now understand mouse events directly, which greatly simplifies the structure of interface objects that used to require buttons nested inside movie clips in order to provide mouse event detection. Movie clips with mouse event handlers applied to them are now known as button movie clips.

Even the movie properties are scriptable using the new Stage object. This offers properties such as stage alignment, width and height, and the scale mode for scripting, as well as a new onResize event which fires when the onscreen size of the movie changes.

The only apparent lack in the new object model in Flash MX is the absence of properties and methods for controlling embedded video. The new Video object only contains one method, clear(), which removes a movie with a given instance name from the stage, but only if it isn't playing. If the movie is playing, the effect of the clear() method is simply to skip a frame.

The intention appears to be that video objects should be embedded into movie clip timelines, which means that you can use normal timeline controls such as stop, goto and play to control the movie clip and thereby the embedded video.

System capabilities

Where device-specific information is required about the environment within which the Flash movie is running, there's a new system capabilities object which enables the detection of characteristics like screen width and height, the colour depth, and other factors such as the availability of sound and video support.

This information can be used to customise the movie, or to control whether certain assets are going to be displayed or not. This is going to be of increasing importance, as we see Web and Flash content being deployed for a greater range of devices, such as the new Pogo PDA, PlayStation 2, PalmOS, Windows CE, and so on. Using a simple Flash movie, we can detect the capabilities of the device and decide what to deliver to it without necessarily creating several independent versions of the content.

Conclusion

Overall, the changes to ActionScript in Flash MX serve to consolidate the excellent scripting features of the previous version. By exposing more of the object model to scripting, through the new drawing API and graphics features and with the revised event model, Macromedia has set the stage for a new generation of cutting-edge design. Over to the Flash community to take the new features and run with them...

 Expertise provided by Ian Anderson. Ian is available for hire as a freelance developer and trainer, and welcomes feedback or questions. [e] ian@zstudio.co.uk [w] www.zstudio.co.uk.

New ActionScript commands

Flash MX has many new ActionScript commands. For information on any item, locate it in the Reference panel menu pane using the alphabetical Index list. Or, look in the Flash MX online help in the ActionScript Dictionary...

#initclip	system.capabilities.hasVideoEncoder	movieClip.onDragOver	textField.getNewTextFormat()	textField.onSetFocus
#endinitclip	system.capabilities.pixelAspectRatio	movieClip.onEnterFrame	textField.getTextFormat()	new TextFormat()
setInterval	system.capabilities.screenColor	movieClip.onKeyDown	textField.removeListener()	textFormat.getTextExtent()
clearInterval	system.capabilities.screenDPI	movieClip.onKeyUp	textField.removeTextField()	textFormat.align
==	system.capabilities.screenResolutionX	movieClip.onKillFocus	textField.replaceSel()	textFormat.blockIndent
!=	system.capabilities.screenResolutionY	movieClip.onLoad	textField.setNewTextFormat()	textFormat.bold
switch	key.addListener()	movieClip.onMouseDown	textField.setTextFormat()	textFormat.bullet
default	key.removeListener()	movieClip.onMouseMove	textField.autoSize	textFormat.color
case	key.onKeyDown()	movieClip.onMouseUp	textField.background	textFormat.font
call function	key.onKeyUp()	movieClip.onPress	textField.backgroundColor	textFormat.indent
method	mouse.addListener()	movieClip.onRelease	textField.border	textFormat.italic
_focusrect	mouse.removeListener()	movieClip.onReleaseOutside	textField.borderColor	textFormat.leading
arguments.caller	mouse.onMouseDown()	movieClip.onRollOut	textField.bottomScroll	textFormat.leftMargin
arguments.length	mouse.onMouseMove()	movieClip.onRollOver	textField.embedFonts	textFormat.rightMargin
Array.sortOn()	mouse.onMouseUp()	movieClip.onSetFocus	textField.hscroll	textFormat.size
Function.apply()	movieClip.createEmptyMovieClip()	movieClip.onUnLoad	textField.html	textFormat.tabStops
Function.call()	movieClip.createTextField()	selection.addListener()	textField.htmlText	textFormat.target
Function.prototype	movieClip.getBytesLoaded()	selection.removeListener()	textField.length	textFormat.underline
super	movieClip.getDepth()	selection.onSetFocus	textField.maxChars	textFormat.url
accessibility.isActive()	movieClip.setMask()	sharedObject.getLocal()	textField.maxhscroll	video.clear()
button.getDepth()	movieClip.beginFill()	sound.getBytesLoaded()	textField.maxscroll	new LoadVars()
button.tabEnabled	movieClip.beginGradientFill()	sound.getBytesTotal()	textField.multiline	loadVars.getBytesLoaded()
button.tabIndex	movieClip.clear()	sound.loadSound()	textField.password	loadVars.getBytesTotal()
button.trackAsMenu	movieClip.curveTo()	sound.duration	textField.restrict	loadVars.load()
button.useHandCursor	movieClip.endFill()	sound.position	textField.scroll	loadVars.send()
button.onDragOut	movieClip.lineStyle()	sound.onLoad	textField.selectable	loadVars.sendAndLoad()
button.onDragOver	movieClip.lineTo()	sound.onSoundComplete	textField.tabEnabled	loadVars.toString()
button.onKillFocus	movieClip.moveTo()	stage.addListener()	textField.tabIndex	loadVars.contentType
button.onPress	movieClip.enabled	stage.removeListener()	textField.text	loadVars.loaded
button.onRelease	movieClip.focusEnabled	stage.align	textField.textColor	loadVars.onLoad
button.onReleaseOutside	movieClip.hitArea	stage.height	textField.textHeight	XML.getBytesLoaded
button.onRollOut	movieClip.tabChildren	stage.scaleMode	textField.textWidth	XML.getBytesTotal
button.onRollOver	movieClip.tabEnabled	stage.showMenu	textField.type	XML.contentType
button.onSetFocus	movieClip.tabIndex	stage.width	textField.variable	customActions.get
system.capabilities.hasAccessibility	movieClip.trackAsMenu	stage.onResize	textField.wordWrap	customActions.install
system.capabilities.hasAudio	movieClip.useHandCursor	textField.addListener()	textField.onChanged	customActions.list
system.capabilities.hasAudioEncoder	movieClip.onData	textField.getDepth()	textField.onKillFocus	customActions.uninstall
system.capabilities.hasMP3	movieClip.onDragOut	textField.getFontList()	textField.onScroller	

Interview

The work of new media design agencies is increasingly a specialist field with its own jargon and heroes. Some of the world's best Flash designers demystify their work…

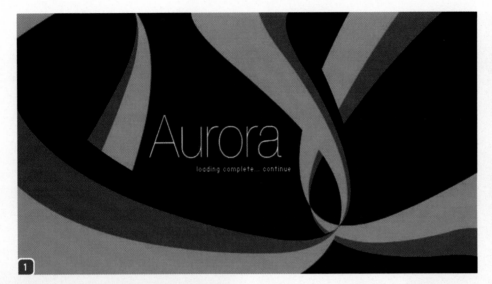

Pixelfury

"It's probably the best Flash upgrade I've seen…"
Pete Barr-Watson discusses the development of
MX-based content…

It seems incredible that a company formed in January 2002 should so quickly have built a client list including Channel 4, Microsoft and EMI, but pixelfury was no ordinary start-up. With Flash guru Pete Barr-Watson as its founder, the company boasted well-established links with the Web design community, as well as unbeatable Web and multimedia skills.

Pete came to prominence as a founder director of Kerb, working with the company from its humble beginnings in a squat in 1996, through to its expansion to a 22-strong corporate outfit.

"The company had become more commercial and market-driven, which suits it really well, but it wasn't challenging for me personally any more," he says.

Surprisingly, Pete has no formal art training. After a variety of dead-end jobs he was made redundant in 1995: "At the time, the Internet was this strange thing that got mentioned on the news," he remembers "I got a 9600 baud modem, an Internet account, got hold of Photoshop 2.5 and Hotdog and started designing Websites. Initially, it was for my own amusement, then I started doing some for local companies.

"I strongly believe that screen design is a discipline in itself," he continues. "I don't know if I had settled into print whether I'd have been as successful. For that I do think you need more formal training."

Having followed the progress of Flash since its launch, Pete began working with version 4 of the software. He is now a prominent member of the Flash community, has graced several advisory and design panels, and contributed a chapter to the hugely influential New Masters Of Flash publication.

Despite his pedigree, Pete found the first couple of weeks of pixelfury's life something of a worry: "We did loads of PR and meetings, but nothing seemed to come of it. But then, literally in our third week, we got work doing a microsite for Channel 4, and then the contract for a major job for EMI to produce one of the flagship Flash MX sites for this country.

"MX is probably the best Flash upgrade I've seen," he adds. "With the improved workflow it's taken a massive leap. We now even create most of our illustrations directly in Flash."

Another key project for the studio was a Flash-based music video. For the record label the benefits are obvious, with far lower production costs than that of a 3D-rendered CG music promo.

"Flash lends itself to motion graphics. Take that and add the ability to export to broadcast standard and it opens up a whole new marketplace. But it's not as easy as it sounds. Talking to people in the Flash community, we realised it was something they'd been trying to do for ages. The problem is that when you try to export any animation embedded in a movie clip it won't play properly. We've developed a way around that, so you can create a video for the Web, and then easily drop it out at high quality."

With several other projects currently under way, Pete is always looking for new challenges "The next step is to take the focus of our services away from the Web," he says, "and move it further into mobile devices and interactive TV."

 You can contact pixelfury via email at [e] info@pixelfury.com, or you can view some of its work at [w] www.pixelfury.com.

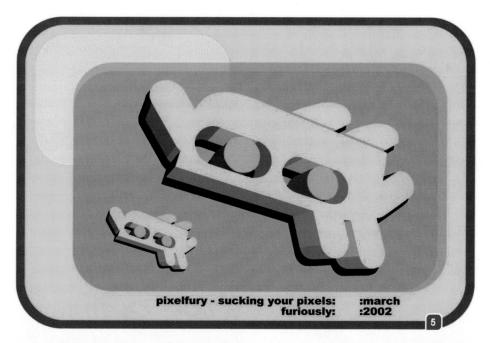

pixelfury - sucking your pixels: :march
furiously: :2002

5

newyorkx3:sanfranciscо:cannesx3:linzx3:amsterdam:chamonix:toronto:::12months

6

welcome to
SNOWDAY
the best snow game
for girls only...

play
instructions
high scores

7

8

1 The swirling technique of this different-looking preloader is reminiscent of gymnasts' ribbons. Again, departing from the normal way of doing things in Flash.

2 "Most purists hate using bitmap images when building Flash applications. But for a subject such as Aurora, who has such amazing publicity material, it's a no-brainer. So, rather than fight it, we embraced it and in the process came up with some pretty cool visual effects. This screen demonstrates a focus shifting effect. When the mouse moves over one of the three group members, the focus highlights them."

3 This was a site for EMI Music for the group Aurora, viewable at [w] www.aurora.mu. The site was built entirely in Flash MX and has two versions available: one for Flash 5 users, the other taking advantage of the extra features of MX. "It's a very visually-led site, with lots of graphical effects that you don't normally see in a Flash application," says Pete. "The photos and audio are pulled in when the user views the site so that the audiovisual content is always up to date, without any special server technology."

4 Pixelfury's dedication to support the Flash community is reflected in this area of its Website. The company wanted to create something with a similar feel to Dreamless.org when it shut down last summer. "We created this section of our site where some of the industry's top creatives can mix it up and chat away from the public boards. It sounds elitist, but it isn't. Well, maybe a little bit."

5 After one of his team turned up for work wearing a T-shirt from a rival company, Pete decided to design a pixelfury alternative. "This is from the 'sucking' variety T-shirt, with the main graphic on the front, a pixelfury label at the bottom corner, text and graphics on the sleeve, and the same on the back. We may even sell them on the site."

6 This is one of the images that appeared in the redesign of pixelfury's own Website. "The integration of vector graphics and photo imagery is something that fascinates me, so we're looking into this as much as possible for the redesign. Everyone who has seen this image assumes that the picture was taken in Japan, but it's actually New York. I find it interesting that you can influence people's perception with a few well placed graphics."

7 pixelfury's Flash-based Snowday game was developed for a clothing brand. "Teenage girls are a tough audience to engage with online games. But we've come up with something a bit different."

8 One of pixelfury's Flash game projects. It's an idea that the company has been thinking about for a long time. It started off as a gameplay experiment and has expanded. It's Flash 4-compatible and iTV ready, and utilises scripting almost entirely for the gameplay.

Atticmedia

From an attic flat living room to spacious offices in Islington, Atticmedia has come a long way. Its secret? "Mixing technology and interaction in a completely new way…" says CEO Mark Weber…

When Atticmedia opened for business in the lounge of Mark Weber's attic flat some six years ago, Baddiel and Skinner were singing about three lions on a shirt and the Conservatives were still in power. Since then, the change from Tory sleaze to Labour spin may have been barely perceptible, but fortunes at said digital media company have definitely changed for the better.

Its philosophy of offering technology-led design proves popular with clients like the BBC, Channel 4, PriceWaterhouseCoopers, Dazed & Confused, Viacom and Ribena, to name a few. Founder Mark Weber believes that Flash is one piece of the jigsaw the company couldn't live without (along with Director and Shockwave). The team regularly produce games, Websites, animations, promotions and educational content in its bid to make the world more interactive.

Mark thinks his team has an edge because his staff all have practical experience. He says: "We started as an enthusiastic bunch of programmers and designers; we're self-funded and have grown through new clients and projects." It's 40-odd staff now reside in Islington. Says Mark: "We've always specialised in combining technology with design — knowing about the technology, but at the same time making things look as good as possible. Combining Shockwave and Flash with server side technologies is important to us."

The f-word

Ah yes, Flash. Atticmedia is enthusiastic in its use of Macromedia's flagship, even though it thinks that there's still plenty of room for improvement. Mark continues: "Director is still my favourite software for the sheer versatility of Lingo — but once Lingo is in Flash, then it will win…" And there are many recent projects that have been given the company's Flash/Shockwave treatment, not least the Tracy Beaker site for the BBC and the Soundplan project.

Mark says: "The Tracy Beaker site for Children's BBC is aimed at 6–11 year olds, and is an enormous Website of over 80 Flash-based activities." The team's brief was to make the site educational, but in a fun way that would draw kids in. "It was a great challenge: kids play games, see animations and then write stories. Tracy Beaker is a site that's all about content — it's fun, entertaining and lively."

Another ongoing Flash project is Soundplan, a game that Atticmedia has produced to promote business entrepreneurship in the UK. "The game is a virtual reality world where you play the role of the band manager," enthuses Mark. "But even though the game is virtual, the bands are real." Does this mean he's about to spawn a few more Nikki Chapmans and Simon Cowells? Not quite. "We're auditioning for bands to join us, and we'll be selecting ten bands to be

featured in the first game – all of them unsigned – and they'll be promoted by the game."

Such a not-for-profit funded game — aimed at promoting grass roots music talent and teaching kids about the music industry — is as far removed from Pop Idol as you could get, and Mark is excited at being involved. He sees it as a step in the right direction for both the company and the Internet, where content is king and it's entertainment for a mass audience. "It's been a lot of work, but it's the future," he adds.

Other work the company has done is varied. Try a virtual reality simulation training programme for PriceWaterhouseCoopers, the build of the Flash/Flash Generator engine for the Dazed& Confused Website, a Ribena desktop character, interactive kiosks for Trouble TV, as well as numerous online games for companies such as Lost for Channel 4, to accompany the TV series of the same name.

Game on

Gaming is a major part of what Atticmedia does, both for educational and entertainment purposes. And creating games has been enhanced by the company's favourite part of Flash — the scripting. "With Flash 5 and the JavaScript type code, Flash can make high level games now," state Atticmedia's

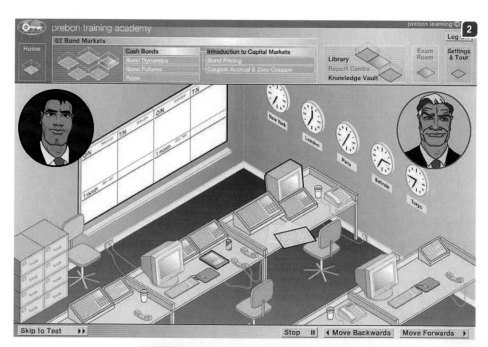

1 Still in development, Soundplan is a virtual band management game where you manage a real band within a virtual world. The whole team are excited by the commission, which aims to promote grass roots music, uses real bands and gives kids an insight into the industry. The project utilises Flash, ASP and SQL Server.

2 An online training tool for a firm of trainee financial brokers, this project was two years in development and took a lot of work – it provides 60 hours of training in all. The team used Director, Flash, HTML, JavaScript, PHP and XML to put it together, and Mark says the finished piece went way beyond the client's expectations.

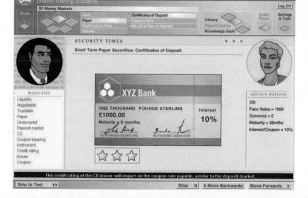

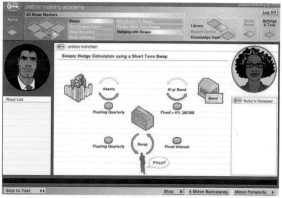

3 "A fun engaging promotional for Jimmy Neutron and Dairylea Lunchables," is how Mark describes this piece of work that takes in the likes of Shockwave, Flash, HTML, JavaScript, ASP and SQL Server. The project had a large team and a tight three month schedule.

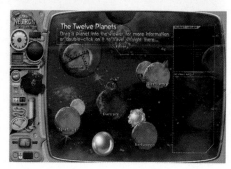

4 Another Flash project, JuiceUp sponsors an online TV station, and this is the Website of the kids running the TV station. They want your help to contribute material to be featured on JuiceUp TV. "It's lasted about ten months and still has a loyal audience," says Mark. "But with hindsight, we'd like to have done more with the characters."

5 A promotional microsite for Cheestrings, this also tied into the Nickelodeon site. Atticmedia employed the powers of Flash, HTML and JavaScript in the month-long project, and also composed the music, which Mark says was a lot of fun.

6 For this project, the team was asked to produce two RAF games – each took two months to complete. The games, Search and Rescue and T.A.L.O. (Tactical Air Land Operation) were produced using Shockwave with 3D effects with Flash, HTML and JavaScript. "It was very easy to get carried away in the whole virtual reality of these games," laughs Mark.

7 The Website for the BBC's Tracy Beaker took the team six months to complete and included more than 80 adventures, each containing an animation, game and story writing activity. The site, produced to entertain and educate, was developed using Perl (server side), Flash, HTML and JavaScript.

8 This promotional game for Wall's Fruit 5s on Nickelodeon is a Flash-fuelled feast that clocked-up hundreds of thousands of visitors in just a couple of months.

You can contact Atticmedia at [w] www.atticmedia.com, [t] 020 7490 8789 or email [e] mark@atticmedia.com The Tracy Beaker site is at [w] www.bbc.co.uk/cbbc/tracybeaker, and Soundpland is at [w] www.soundplan.co.uk.

There are some files to accompany the walkthrough for this profile in the Tutorial\Atticmedia folder on the cover CD.

Flash designers and programmers. "We can build an entire game without even touching the work area." Games are usually Flash content in a Shockwave shell. Atticmedia sorts the ideas, concept, design, coding and hosting, and its games often get a few hundred thousand users.

To create its smorgasbord of work, the team employs a whole bunch of software and technologies. ASP/SQL server 7 and other server side technologies – Flash Generator and UltraDev for a start, along with HTML, JavaScript, Dreamweaver, Director, Flash, Photoshop and Illustrator.

And it says there are pluses and minuses to all software. One key thing that the whole company would like to see solved in future versions of Flash is the debugger.

"It's poor and difficult to use, to say the least," says Mark. "If you've got serious arrays it can even freeze or crash you out. Plus, it refreshes on each frame, meaning you can't get to the bottom to view values. It's a major headache."

Mark also states that Flash doesn't work well with Illustrator, but the team uses Fireworks or Photoshop for compression, and they're happy using Soundforge. "Cooledit is very helpful as well". The company also favours Macs over PCs, and – like vodka and red bull – the other must-have item to go with your Mac is Photoshop. "I don't remember who said it, but the sentence 'Photoshop is the best game for the Mac' had something right!" he laughs. As for Flash into the future — well, Atticmedia hasn't used Flash for iDTV or PDAs yet, but Mark reckons that time will come within the next year.

"These are exciting times in the industry, and we're only just beginning," he concludes. "We want to work with anyone who will buy into an interactive vision, and as a company we'd like to have some influence over how the Internet develops."

Flash tips

Take it from the experts — here are Atticmedia's top Flash hints...

1. Get the illustrators to export to Flash. Even opening up Illustrator takes ages.

2. Use shared libraries — it's a major memory saver.

3. Keep a folder of any code you've done and name the files clearly so you can find code to be reused again.

4. Save every major change as a new file – space is cheap, and Flash files are small – so that mistakes can be easily rectified. We can often have more than 150 versions of a game by the time it's finished.

5. Buy some decent JavaScript books. They'll stick to just the code better than the Flash books out there, which try to cover everything.

6. Get a printer. Sometimes you need to print out code to look at it properly, and get a pencil to go with it. Go and sit somewhere away from the computer.

7. A good night's rest makes a major Flash problem so much easier. A problem that's confused you at the end of the day can often be solved with in a few minutes with a fresh head. With coding, breaks are essential.

8. Check code constantly.

9. Start off small and break down a problem. There are a lot of different ways to get to the final work, but it's best to start with paper and a plan. Build one bit of programming at a time, check it, then add to the whole.

10. Get some memory. Flash testing is a nightmare if you don't have a decent amount of memory.

Prototyping a MovieClip

What

With OOP (Object Orientated Programming), an object is basically just a collection of attached methods (which are functions that are assigned to your object) and properties (values).

Why

When creating objects, ActionScript keeps their individual components separate. So an object functions independently of others, meaning increased speed of execution (fps). For example, a function becomes part of an object and is called using "this", instead of lots of calls to one function.

How

When an object is constructed it inherits its properties from its class constructor, and this is done with the prototype property. It is possible to override where an object looks for its prototype. The __proto__ points to an object's prototype that it wants to use.

Conclusion

We now have a self-contained object (or number of objects) that have inherited and can use these new methods, as if they were normal MovieClip methods, like _droptarget(), play(), gotoAndPlay() etc.

By using prototyping you can redefine built-in Macromedia MovieClip object's methods, for example, giving all MovieClip objects _x more functionality or built-in intelligence.

1. In the example here, the man object is first placed on the stage, and given an instance name of man.

2. We then create Man Class, this is just an empty constructor.
```
Manclass = function(){
}
```
We then assign Manclass' prototype to that of MovieClips, therefore getting all its functionality (for example, Flash's MovieClips methods are made available to Manclass). This is done by:
```
Manclass.prototype.__proto__ =
MovieClip.prototype
```
The man's prototype is then set to that of Manclass (which is itself set to MovieClips). This means the man object has MovieClip methods available to it.
```
_root.man.__proto__ =
Manclass.prototype
```

3. We can now set the methods for Manclass.
```
Manclass.prototype.canMove =
function(xDir, yDir){
// Code that checks to see if can move.
}
Manclass.prototype.move = function(){
// Code that moves object.
}
```
These can therefore be called directly by the man object like this:
```
this.canMove(xValue, yValue)
this.move()
```
– where "this" refers to the man object.

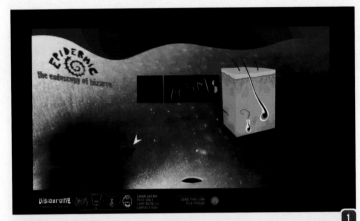

Oeil pour Oeil

"Today, it's time to get serious." These French Flash masters are looking forward to a revived and animated industry…

mbitious and brash, this agency is out to be seen by as many people as possible. "We specifically work in content dedicated to large audiences," says Laurent Tricart, Design and Communication Manager. With a name that translates as an eye for an eye, Oeil Pour Oeil has completed a growing number of entertainment-based projects for leading companies including Virgin, Sony and Honda, as well as organisations including the French Ministry for Youth and Sports — large audiences assured.

The company was established in November 1996 by a team of four designers. These days, Oeil Pour Oeil consists of 60 people working in three areas: Web and new media, games for PC and console, and online communities. Oeil Pour Oeil Productions concentrates on the Web content, particularly Flash animation and interactivity.

Content created by the company includes snowboarding demos, music-oriented Websites and a long-running adult series called *Visiodrome*, which attracts 20,000 visitors a month. "We'd describe our work as brilliant, fun, trashy and off the planet," says Laurent. He admits that the team's inspiration comes from the past and present — American comics, Japanese animation, psychedelia, rock-'n'-roll, electronic music and hip-hop. "We're the digest of all these influences. A mix between underground culture from the 70s and 80s and a creativity that is possible in today's media."

Much of the company's work, from Web to television, is created in Flash. Laurent explains its progression towards the software. "We discovered Flash in 1998 while creating a Spanish site, and we were immediately impressed. Before that we worked mainly in Director." Four years ago, Oeil Pour Oeil was one of the first agencies to be producing such content. "Flash was a revolution — our own site was an event in France and, today, it is still a reference for many Web designers. A Website we made for comedian Alain Souchon, was one of the first Flash sites to capture a large audience in France and we're proud of it."

An exciting and recent opportunity for the company's Flash designers is the production of a number of series for television broadcast. Loana et ses Amis is one of the first animated series to be shown on television. The 32 one-minute episodes each took three days to produce. "With the TV standard, you work differently — more complex animations, more elaborate, longer frames and slower lip sync." But despite the difficulties, it was a positive experience. "Flash gives you more freedom when working for TV. You can take the entire package to its limits before converting the files to QuickTime, then Betacam."

Oeil Pour Oeil shares a regional affiliation with some of the leading new media agencies in France.

1 Visiodrome is an ongoing interactive comic project that Oeil Pour Oeil has invested much time and effort into designing. The brash characters and colours demonstrate excellent manipulation of Flash.

2 Designed for television, L'Epine de Succession was also created in Flash, marking a great opportunity for Flash designers to expand their audience.

3 The team also developed a Website for NAUSICAA, an organisation in aid of sea-life conservation. The site, which can be found at [w] www.nausicaa.fr, features innovative navigation and imagery.

4 Oeil Pour Oeil has animated a number of cartoons for television using Flash rather than high-end broadcast software. Featured here are scenes from Le Secret Minceur (The Secret of Slimming) and Murder et Scoty, both series have aired on French TV.

5 When French songstress Françoise Hardy needed a site to reflect her changing career since the 60s, Oeil Pour Oeil came up with an elegant and attractive site with great audio at [w] www.francoise-hardy.com.

In the North Eastern region surrounding Lille, reside TEAMcHmAn ([w] www.teamchman.com), NOCOPY ([w] www.nocopy.com), T.O.K.T.O. ([w] www.tokto.com) and AnalogiKS-IndianS.com ([w] www.analogiks-indians.com), each carving its own particular niche in the Flash, gaming and interactive media industry. Despite the potential overlap, they all know each other well and often participate in joint projects. "We have worked together in different Webjams such as WebDaysigner and Vector Lounge and we go to shows as a group," says Laurent. "It's a community — with friends, lovers and all. Nevertheless, we are still competitors and try to keep loyal."

And it's all set to get even better. Laurent alludes to a Flash and Shockwave 3D convergence in the near future which, from his perspective, makes the future look distintcly bright. "We're collaborating with companies who want to launch big and serious projects," he says. "There was an hysterical period within the industry that was closely followed by a downfall. Today it's time to get serious."

You can take a look at Oeil Pour Oeil's online portfolio at [w] www.oeilpouroeil.fr. View some of its design collaborations at [w] www.vectorlounge.com and [w] www.tokto.com/webdaysigner

Grey Digital

You won't be able to stop playing G-MAX Skateboarding – the game that's won two Flash Film Festival awards and has achieved cult status on the Web. "The key thing is it has to be addictive," says its creators…

1 G-MAX has an intro that captivates and prepares the audience for the task ahead – just what every game should have,

2 Remaining faithful to real-life skateboarding, the team at Grey Digital built Flips, Methods, Christs and other popular tricks into G-MAX.

For those of us a little less 'extreme', who prefer to spend time surfing the Web rather than the streets, G-MAX Skateboarding brings all the excitement of Ollies, Nollies, Roastbeefs and Madonnas, without the grazed knees and frequent hospitalisation.

A simple yet completely addictive game from Swedish design company Grey Digital, G-MAX Skateboarding was brought to the attention of many when it won in two categories at the Flash Film Festival held in New York in August 2002. Winning Best Game (an honour previously bestowed on Electrotank's awesome Mini-Golf) and possibly even more importantly, the People's Choice Award, the game has become a cult phenomenon on the Web, visitors constantly juggling for a better position on the high score table. The premise of the game is simple — score as many points as you can by performing all manner of halfpipe tricks using the Z, X, and Cursor keys. Playing this game, as with the best games in any medium, really is a mixture of enjoyment and sheer frustration.

The company behind G-MAX Skateboarding is Grey Digital, a design firm with a client list that includes the likes of Nokia, Procter & Gamble and Electrolux. One of the men behind G-MAX itself is Jesper Wahlström, Art Director at GD. We asked him how the idea for G-MAX was conceived.

"It started as an experiment, like most of our creative ideas do. We wanted to do something for ourselves to promote the fact that we are a serious competitor in the market for online game development. G-Max is a non-violent sport game for all ages and we just wanted to make a game that was easy to understand and really fun to play."

In development for around three months, Grey Digital started experimenting with different styles of graphics and animation. Jesper explains that even though the skater is only 35 pixels in height, a lot of effort was put into the animation, making sure movieclip transitions were as smooth as possible.

The game enables you to change the skating environment and even the type and design of skateboard. Considering the board is no more than a few pixels in size, this really shows Grey's attention to detail and the user experience. The in-game graphics are original and stylish, fusing illustrative elements with 3D-like effects. Jesper explains: "Like most of my graphic ideas, I start out with pen and paper; just some raw sketches of the framework and key elements of characters and functionality. Then I transfer all my sketches to Illustrator to make all the vector art and the basic elements to work on within Flash. The last adjustments and effects I then add on directly in Flash, together with the animations."

For all of the 3D animation in G-MAX, Grey used Electric Rain's Swift 3D, with basic 3D animation being created in the app before being touched-up in Flash MX. ActionScripting on the project was completed by Grey Digital's Einar Nilsson.

Worth the work

G-MAX Skateboarding certainly found a huge audience on the Web — after nearly six months online over two million people had played it. And the secret of success for Flash-based games? "The key thing is it has to be addictive," says Jesper, "you must get the feeling of just wanting to play the game one more time. The game engine has to be smart, lightweight and

optimised to make your graphics come alive with the right dynamics and physical motion."

Jesper's inspiration and influences include all kinds of media — TV commercials, movie intros, retro games and new console titles. He tells us that he tries to keep his eyes open to new technical progress and ways in which Grey can improve its graphics. Jesper also gives credit to Nordic colleagues, Titoonik, who he says are "true masters of animations and Web-based character designs for the Web". Jesper's ideas for new Web-based Flash games seem to focus almost completely on the user's experience. The reason behind this approach is clear. "I look back and see what caught my attention in the 80s," he says. "When we didn't have the mega graphic cards and 21-inch screens, we played our games on a Commodore 64 with a small TV as a monitor, but we could stay for hours and play the same game over and over again."

Starting out as an art teacher and freelance illustrator, Jesper became involved in Web design when a company emailed him a proposal for working with something called the Internet. This triggered Jesper's love for interactive design.

"I started out with Flash and by the end of 97 I was creating small animations and Web effects" he says. "I'm basically a graphic artist and I had been stuck in Photoshop for all my creative Web work. Then Flash came along and for the first time a non-technically minded person such as I could combine art with interactivity and functionality on the Web."

Jesper and Grey Digital are currently laying down the plans for G-MAX II which, Jesper tells us, will be more complex and will feature a lot more gameplay, as well as a new high score application. Expect to see it hitting the Web sometime this year.

Contact Grey Digital on [t] +45 (0) 8 458 0901. You can email Jesper at [e] jesper.wahlstrom@grey.se. Alternatively, check out [w] www.greydigital.se and [w] www.gmaxskateboarding.com.

What makes a game playable?

It's all very well creating excellent in-game artwork. Likewise, you can have an entire ActionScript dictionary built into your brain, but these combined do not equal a great Flash game. Like any game on any console, Flash games for the Web must be playable, because if they're not, and they're not addictive, visitors won't return. G-MAX Skateboarding has everything a Flash game needs — great graphics, playability and that 'want another go' feel to it. We asked Jesper exactly what he thinks makes an online game playable.

"I believe in instant action. You can't let the player go through all kinds of intros and game descriptions in the beginning and believe he or she has still got their focus on the game when it really starts. On the Internet with online games you don't have more than a few seconds to get the attention you want."

He continues: "You have to convince the player from the beginning that the game is easy and fun but at the same time a challenge. You have to practise to master it and become a top ten player. The game must give you a competitive feeling and make you want to climb the high score list."

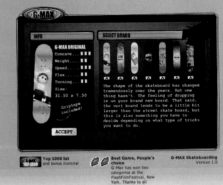

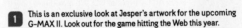

 This is an exclusive look at Jesper's artwork for the upcoming G-MAX II. Look out for the game hitting the Web this year.

 The ability to choose one of seven skateboards is a great example of the amount of detail that Grey Digital put into G-MAX.

 A Christmas greeting from Grey Digital — a G-MAX spin-off enabling you to guide a snowboarder down a treacherous slope.

 Three different halfpipes are on offer at the G-MAX skatepark, all with different characteristics.

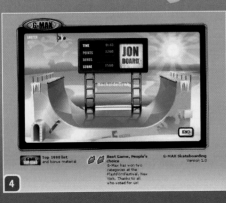

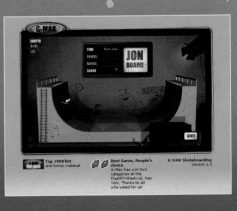

Kerb

"Many 8-bit games can be recreated in Flash, with better graphics and sound," says Kerb's Jim McNiven. We ask him how to make Flash games and why his Website became one…

Founded in 1996, Brighton-based Kerb is well known within the world of new media design. High-profile clients such as BT, Disney and the BBC have been won over by the company's innovative and creative stance. While initially concentrating on illustration and animation, Kerb has now ventured into television, music videos and Flash games.

Perhaps logically then, the latest incarnation of Kerb's Website is a Flash game. As Creative Director, Jim McNiven, explains: "We had a nightmare thinking of how to present the services we offer. It was hard to generate a theme to casually explain that we create Websites, games, viral campaigns, music videos and our own television series."

Website exploration

With a team keen on gaming, they decided to create an imaginary version of the Kerb offices and let users explore via an 'old skool' platform game. Coding groundwork had been done while creating the Travel Sick game for Bravo, so most additional work involved integrating a database for regular news releases, to keep the site fresh.

Responses to the Kerb site have been positive and some clients had to be dissuaded from wanting something identical themselves. "Unsurprisingly, feedback from designers has been mixed," says Jim. "Some appreciate the extravagance, style and tight coding but others bitched about it being complicated and too time-consuming to navigate, claiming it would scare potential clients."

As Jim says, the latter point is moot — Kerb targets Web-savvy markets rather than SMEs (Small-to-Medium Enterprises) wanting 'generic' Website design. "To that end, representing our work via a game was probably a no-brainer."

The site contains many quirky features, including a Blade Runner-inspired top floor, and clients being tortured on the ground floor, according to Jim, "as visual representation of the pain they go through with us."

Long-time gamers will also detect a hint of nostalgia within. "The game is retro, based on a C64 game I used to love called Pyjamarama," explains Jim. Despite being an ex-member of C64 and Amiga demo crews, Kerb's use of such game ideas is not down to rose-tinted spectacles. "Many 8-bit games had great gameplay," says Jim. "And they can mostly be recreated in Flash, with better graphics and sound."

Jim reckons Flash is an excellent environment for developing games, setting a level playing field that mirrors the competitive environment of days passed. "It's versatile and cross-platform," says Jim. "Everyone has to push it as far as possible until a new version appears. We're constantly discovering amazing new stuff by people like Titoonic and wondering how things were achieved."

1 The ground floor of the first level of Panik In Chocoland. In this arcade-style platform game, you have to collect bombs to progress through each level.

2 Another image from Panik In Chocoland, which shows the top of the first level. Here, you can see the escape door that appears once you've collected all the bombs, and the head of the almighty Bob Dobbs.

3 Travel Sick is a platform adventure game consisting of three levels of increasing difficulty. In level one you can give this watermelon-obsessive the object of his desire and swipe his pliers when he's getting 'stuck in'.

4 Travel Sick's gameplay relies on a mix of lateral thinking, problem solving and quick reactions to negotiate the terrain. In this image we see Loaded magazine and TV's very own Grub Smith mere seconds away from meeting an icy death.

5 This is the second level of Travel Sick. The mission is to give the cat a Viking funeral. Depicted is the 'victim', but first you have to work out how to poison it.

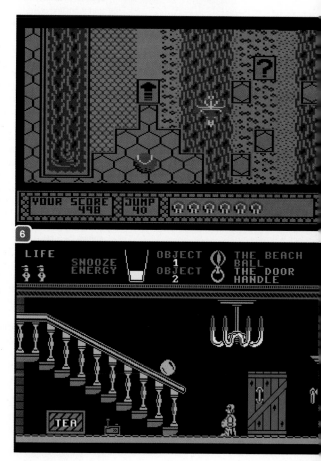

So what makes a great Flash game? "It shouldn't need instructions and must have a perfectly weighted learning curve," claims Jim. "A sense of humour is helpful, and while you might get frustrated with your ability, that shouldn't be the case with the game itself. Truly great games always give you that 'one more go' feeling. That's why I love Nintendo. Its designers know how to grab you and turn up the heat to keep you hooked but not so much that you switch off." But he admits that creating online games is rather different to authoring for consoles or PCs: "Budgets for Flash games are often non-existent. Therefore expectations are lower, although we hope people playing our games get good value with regards to investing their time."

Programming tips

As for making the games themselves, programming comes first. This means programmers can work with dummy graphics until satisfied with frameworks. Meanwhile, illustrators design in-game graphics in Flash itself, which gives them clean lines and reduces file sizes. Finished graphics are then integrated, programming polished, and, finally, sound and high-score tables added.

Common problems include game speed and parallax scrolling. "Flash is fairly processor intensive and too much on-screen action causes things to lag," says Jim. He advises keeping moving objects to a minimum and using flip-screen scrolling. To speed up parallax scrolling, Jim recommends breaking apart objects on each layer: "Instead of scrolling multiple objects, Flash only has to deal with one per layer." Further tips include loading levels in the background while players are exploring, and extra content only when specifically requested. "Also nip over to [w] www.flashkit.com if you're a beginner, and study the tutorials," says Jim. "I won't pretend to know much about ActionScript but from what I can gather, it's useful to have good resource books and a really big book on applied physics!"

Making games can be fun and it can also be profitable. "We mostly create promotional content for brands," explains Jim. "Although we've also built games in-house, which were licensed to content sites for a fixed 'rental' fee."

Undoubtedly, a budget pays dividends with the games themselves. "Bravo's decent budget for Travel Sick is a case in point," says Jim. Kerb was able to make something that looked stunning, and was extensively play-tested. Many Flash games suffer from a lack of play-testing — this keeps budget lows but makes it harder for companies to create playable games.

Regardless, Kerb continues to develop Flash games. "I can't say much about our next project, as it's all 'hush hush'," says Jim. "But I can reveal it's a healthy mix of Flash, database stuff and community gaming. Our most recent Flash game was for BT Broadband, which involves the BT pigs flying through a pipe (Internet connection), collecting files and being slowed down if they don't get Broadband." Now that's entertainment.

You can see Kerb's games at [w] www.panikgames.com, [w] www.bravo.co.uk/travelsick, and [w] www.kerb.co.uk. And you can contact them at [e] info@kerb.co.uk, [t] 0870 013 0040 and [f] 01273 682 637.

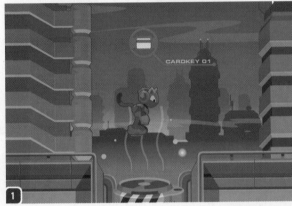

1 The top floor of the Kerb Website. Hovering on the updraft enables you to grab a key-card, which can be used to unlock a door later on in the site. The game/site was programmed in Flash and arrays were used to define each room and floor.

2 While the Kerb site is chock-full of useful information, all easily updateable via a back-end CMS, there's also plenty of nonsense, such as this locked room. It harbours a disk that contains screen savers; however, the disk must be inserted into a terminal elsewhere in order to access them.

3 Insert a battery into the shrink-ray device and you'll shrink to be able to enter the mouse hole. Inside, you can view the psycho vegetables from Kerb's television show, *Hellz Kitchen*.

4 *Panik In Pogoworld* is a tile-based game. It includes a level editor, so that the owner can design and add their own levels – multi-dimensional arrays were loaded into Flash from a text file.

5 This game is based on the 3D animated Robbie Williams video from a while back. You control Robbie and go shagging around three different levels of scenery, each with parallax scrolling. The icy third level was made particularly tricky.

Kerb's flashiest moments

Jim McNiven tells us more about the best of Kerb's Flash games…

Based on classic 8-bit platform game Pyjamarama, Travel Sick succeeds thanks to slick graphics and the game's 'feel'. After concepts and puzzles had been worked out for each level, graphics and code were created within Flash.

Panik In Chocoland also thrives on a mix of playability and polished graphics. "Dave was messing around with the physics for ages and pretty much built the game in his free time," comments Jim. "Then Dantoo came up with a sketch of a boy in a rabbit costume that Dan redrew and animated in a cleaner style. Zeb finished it off by adding some backgrounds." Apparently, when displayed within a cabinet for Melia in February, people were genuinely surprised it was done in Flash.

Another 'Panik' game is the third on Jim's list, namely Panik In Pogoworld. Inspired by the unique Commodore 64 platform game Bounder, Jim cites its main quality as being really addictive. "It's also our first Flash game creation with a level editor, so the game goes on infinitely," says Jim. Sensibly, a password system was introduced for higher levels, so you don't have to return to the start each time you play.

Finally, while Kerb's Website isn't strictly a game, it has a large following nonetheless. "We got huge traffic from Spanish gaming sites, resulting in numerous emails from easily-pleased Spanish gamers," comments Jim. He continues: "We hope it showcases nice graphics and tight coding, combined with database skills and a sense of humour."

Unsurprisingly, the site, created between paying projects, rapidly spiralled out of control. "It almost killed Sermad, who did the bulk of the coding," says Jim. "Every time he had it nailed, someone would think up more features!"

As for why it was created, Jim states: "We were trying to create a visual representation of what we do."

Titoonic

Titoonic knows a thing or two about how to develop Flash games. It's not all about technology, though. "Keep attention to detail and to expression," says Creative Director Peter Holm…

Copenhagen's Titoonic is one of the best-known games developers in the interactive design industries. Back in 1989 it was a mere freelance operation, formed by Tomas Landgreen, but in August 2000, Titoonic's current incarnation came about in partnership with Peter Holm. Then in autumn 2001, Henrik Mou, the company's current MD joined, and not long after it became a private limited company.

Titoonic's senior management comes from a post-production background, creating 3D material for broadcast and feature films. But this is a long, pernickety way to spend one's waking hours according to the company's Creative Director Peter Holm.

"At some point we lost interest in doing all this hi-res 3D with a lot of textures and mind boggling lights and all this," he explains. "We'd had enough of this long process. We wanted to get into the animation quicker and we could do that by creating stuff for the Web."

Capturing the imagination

Although the company has developed PC games using technology like C++ and Visual Basic, it is the company's cartoon-style Flash games that have captured the imaginations of its domestic and international clients. The list includes Lego, window maker Velux, telecoms company Telia, ISP Chello and confectioner Ferrero. The company employs around 17 people, all of whom have their specialities, although many work across disciplines like design, animation and programming. When projects are underway, they're all divided into teams to make it easier to share information. "We also try to emphasise the importance of asking for help or advice," Holm adds. "We aim at grabbing all the opportunities we get to teach each other and share our knowledge."

There are a few good reasons for Titoonic's extensive use of Flash for games development, as opposed to more complex technologies like Shockwave. First, Flash has a huge installed user base and second, it enables a great deal of creative freedom within a small file. Finally, scripting makes it possible to add complex functions. On the other hand, while Shockwave games are more full-featured and include such aspects as 3D interaction, they have a much narrower installed user base. Furthermore, the plug-in is more difficult for many users to get to grips with. "Lately we've had big clients explicitly stating that they did not want Shockwave games for these reasons," Holm adds.

Titoonic's creatives find inspiration in a number of sources. Much of it develops from technical experiments. This, for example, is how one of the company's mainstays, its Snowboard game, came about. According to Peter Holm, the company was experimenting with ways to create fake 3D. It was highly successful and Titoonic has now sold around

25 customised versions to various companies. While the snowboard game was developed primarily in 3dsmax and output to Flash using Swift 3D or Vecta 3D ("I can't remember which one," Holm apologises), old-school techniques are all important at Titoonic.

"Inspiration comes from a lot of very different places," Peter Holm explains. "Sometimes it comes from a dirty pencil-sketch on a napkin that no one was supposed to see but sees anyway. Other times we sit down and think hard for 45 minutes and nothing happens — but the funny thing is, the day after, those who attended the fruitless thinking session will be bursting with ideas."

Tools of the trade

Titoonic's equipment is equally split between digital and analogue. There are lots of PCs: 800MHz PIIIs and 2.4GHz P4s running Windows 2000 and Windows XP, most of which are equipped with GeForce3 graphics cards. There's also Flash 5, Flash MX, Photoshop, 3dsmax, Swift 3D, Dreamweaver and Ultradev. Music and sound effects either originate from "a cheap microphone and a cardboard tube" or are specially commissioned from Hans Landgreen at BabyCuts ([w] www.babycuts.dk) or Jeppe Juul at Cooloop ([w] www.cooloop.com).

"Other than that, the list of important hardware is: paper, pencil, ball pen, digital camera, Wacom tablets, a good bicycle and a nice bed," Holm says, smiling.

Gear is one thing but at Titoonic it's the art of animation, rather than an emphasis on technology, that is most prized.

"I think the trade secret on our part is to keep attention to detail and to expression," says Holm. "Keep an animator's approach. Of course you should

Crumb Crumbsworld

Brad

1 Peter Holm is especially pleased with the animation-like programming of the Spider game. In it, you take on the character of the eponymous arachnid and your survival depends on the number of bugs you eat. It was one of those Titoonic projects that started out as a technology experiment but evolved into a highly playable game.

2 One of the more well-known versions of the Snowboard game is Titoonic's Powerade game for Coca Cola, found on the Get Up, Stay Up microsite. It's very easy to spot the similarities between the original game and its custom made, client-led variation.

3 Crumbs World is a Titoonic in-house project with its own Website. The company has a view to develop the idea for children's television. In short, it's the story of Brad the pumpkin farmer, his dog, Biskit, and an alien called Crumb, all searching for Crumb's long-lost brother on an Earth-like planet. It was sketched by hand and scanned into Flash.

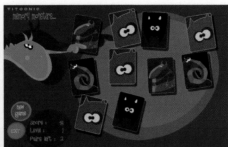

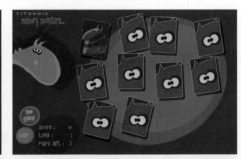

4 Another of Peter Holm's favourites is the Memory game. It's a simple game of pairs, but the illustration and unique interactivity add an extra dimension. As Holm explains, "Basically, it illustrates that we try to do simple, enjoyable games, but add more life to them."

5 Titoonic developed a system for moving a Flash-based character around in a 2D/3D space. It dubbed its system the "Isotoonic engine" and it's been used for a number of projects, including one for the Danish National Museum. It's not a multi-player game, but its database integration enables children to interact with virtual objects based on physical materials.

DIN EGEN UDSTILLING

DIN EGEN UDSTILLING

The key is co-operation

Titoonic's clients also include other agencies. The company worked with Framfab on a microsite for Coca Cola…

Titoonic's Powerade game typifies the company's work in many ways. It was part of a campaign designed by Framfab for Coca Cola called Get Up, Stay Up. The site of the same name is designed to promote Coca Cola's energy drink Powerade, and part of its requirement was a game in Flash. That's where Titoonic came in.

Framfab was pretty specific about what it needed. The basic Snowboard game needed to be modified to include sports like kite surfing, rollerblading and mountain biking. Much like the original snowboarding game, their central character was built in 3dsmax and rendered into Flash. All animation was done in 3dsmax as well: "Just with good old manual keyframing, not using Character Studio or anything like that," Holm says.

The backgrounds were sketched by hand and then imported into Flash, with the outlines traced with red or green bright hairlines. "Sometimes some of our people prefer to use Illustrator for this process, but most of the time we do it directly in Flash," Holm recalls. It's a fun and simple idea with plenty of longevity.

worry that the code works properly, but it's important for us that our programmers have a certain insight in how animation works, and what will make animation work. For instance, take the Spider game. The spider moves in an 'alive' way, but it's programmed, not animated. That sort of illustrates the idea."

The future holds even more games, using more than Flash. Titoonic is finalising its Java game engine, for instance, and the company hopes to get into console and Game Boy Advance content. While that sounds daunting, when Peter Holm sums it up, it sounds less like work and more like a joyful walk in the park. "More games, more animation, more stories, more trouble, more fun," he says. Amen.

You can see Titoonic's games at [w] www.titoonic.dk, www.getupstayup.com, www.crumbsworld.com. [t] 00 45 35 35 93 30.

COMPUTER arts special
COMPLETE PROJECT

STEP-BY-STEP PROJECT

BRAND iDENTITY

Everything you need to create stationery, advertising and logos for your company

HOW TO...
- Design the perfect logo
- Produce stunning business cards
- Create great print and banner ads

TUTORIAL FILES AND SOFTWARE ON THE DISC

ON SALE **3 APRIL**

Flammable Jam

When Spank The Monkey was first launched on the Web it was downloaded more than 700,000 times in one weekend. "Think about it – that's ridiculous," Flam Jam's Hoss Gifford demonstrates the power of Flash…

 f Flash could save the universe, you'd find Hoss Gifford and his Flammable Jam team involved somehow — probably applying the finishing touches to some super-hero code. For the past few years, this Glasgow-based new media outfit has been pushing the envelope and cutting many an edge, turning Flash into a powerful branding and marketing force for a powerhouse of clients including The Edinburgh Film Festival, the BBC, Toyota, and Scottish Widows.

It's a full-on, big name list, but Hoss isn't one to shove it in your face. "We aren't impressed by big names," he moots, "it's the person that commissions us and the briefs they write that we are really interested in." But Flam Jam is lucky enough to have only worked with big brand names.

The five founding members came from one of Scotland's top new media firms where they were used to working with international clients on high-profile jobs. When they left to form Flam Jam to focus on funky Flash stuff, a lot of their clients moved with them.

Client base

But being born with a good client base hasn't made Flam Jam unappreciative. "We get really good briefs from insightful clients that give us scope to push the technology, and each other, really hard. Having such good clients that really believe in what we are doing makes Flam Jam a great place to work," says Hoss.

Hoss is happy that his clients share Flam Jam's belief that Flash is the best tool to achieve their goals. Mind you, Flam Jam has the experience to prove it. The company's talented individuals have done the full multimedia dance, creating viral campaigns, Websites, CD-ROMs, and Web games. They're even dipping their toes into interactive TV and wireless applications, albeit in an R&D capacity. "Basically [we do] any digital, screen-based medium that we can get our hands on that allows us to build our clients' brands online," says Hoss.

But that almost makes Flam Jam sound like a hum-drum company. Flam Jam is different. It has personality. In addition to a sticky name, the company possesses a quirky sense of fun, mixed with a canny sense of what works and what can work for its client. A quick glance through its project titles is enough to raise a chuckle. There's Trash Hotel — the tossing-tellies-out-the-window game and Beermat — a flicking beer mats game. Perhaps the company's masterpiece is a peeing-in-the-urinal game for S1 Play ([w] www.s1play.com/takeaim) although Hoss is rather partial to Spank the Monkey, a game that he created for VectorLounge — [w] www.vectorlounge.com.

"Spank The Monkey was launched on a Thursday evening at Flash Forward in Amsterdam, and the following weekend it was downloaded more than 700,000 times. Think about it — that's ridiculous," he says with just a smidgen of pride sneaking through his modest exterior.

Flam Jam's work isn't just funny or superficially slick. "The unique quality of a Flammable Jam project,

1 The best games can come from simple concepts – flicking beer mats, for example. And then you build it in Flash.

2 Even selling toilet seats online can benefit from the interactive nature of Flash

3 Flam Jam created a Flash microsite for the Channel 4 TV show The Priory. "They wanted something that was easy to maintain and was more on brand for The Priory," reflects Hoss.

4 "Rock, scissor, stone is the most stupid game that ever existed," opines Hoss. "We were doing some really in-depth games for BBC Choice and decided to do something incredibly simple. This is simple but hugely addictive. Try it."

more often than not, is based on the concept," explains Hoss, losing some of his bashfulness. "We like to pervert the traditional viewpoint on things, drop the standard marketing bollocks, and honestly reflect the way things are."

It all helps Flam Jam's reputation as the "mad bastards from Glasgow," as Hoss laughingly puts it. It's a reputation clients seem to love. "But the big thing is that clients feel comfortable putting their brands in our hands. They can see we've done work for Toyota, for example, and they know their brand is in safe hands."

Fluent in Flash

The company's competence using Flash has helped accentuate this reassuring environment. The technology plays a major role in almost everything Flam Jam does. They've been using the program since version 3 and there's little they don't know about it.

"With Flash 5, we got to that really comfortable position of being able to do most stuff without thinking too hard about how we were going to do it," reflects Hoss. "The good thing about this is you can concentrate on what you want to do to achieve your clients' objectives, rather than getting caught up with what you are capable of doing. When you aren't fluent with a technology, it is all too easy to get excited about the technology itself rather than what it can do. Once you get your shit down pat, it is much easier to focus."

When he isn't knee-deep in code, Hoss is either talking about Flash at industry conferences, writing books about Flash, or crafting technical reviews of He was an official tester of Flash MX for Macromedia. According to this grand master of Flash, version MX rocks. "It's lush," he enthuses. "It fixes all the things that pissed us off about Flash 5, and gives us the vast majority of our wish list for new features. We've been using it for a few months now, and there is no going back."

"A lot of work has gone into subtle things that dramatically improve efficiency of workflow — especially on larger projects," he continues. "The other big thing is the ability for us to truly abstract our code engines from the graphics and animations. It's a code-head's dream. It also helps us stay profitable as a company, because building projects in this way makes code highly reusable."

Flam Jam is currently making the most of MX's advantages, creating a number of Flash Websites. So how about the future? "Our balls may be big, but they aren't made of crystal," jokes Hoss "The one thing we've learned is anything can happen, and although you can try and steer in a general direction, you've got to take new opportunities as they appear and go for a wander now and then." Just so long as Flash is there for company.

You can contact Flammable Jam by phone [t] 0141 204 5269, email [e] turnmeon@flamjam.com, or by visiting its Website at [w] www.flamjam.com, which features a comprehensive client list and links to all the company's work.

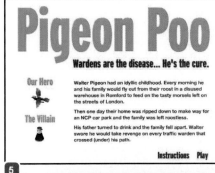

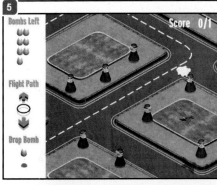

Watering hole

Flammable Jammer Hoss takes you through the making of the game's soundtrack...

The soundtrack is an important aspect of animation or games. The urinal game for S1 Play had to sound like you were relieving yourself into an aluminium urinal. The realistic sound effects were created with ActionScript.

"I started off by recording the sound of water being poured from a bottle into my kitchen sink," explains Hoss. "I recorded three samples from when the water was being poured onto the left, middle, and right of the sink.

The Flash movie attaches three samples to three sound objects: pish_left, pish_mid and pish_right. A function continually checks the x position of the mouse and adjusts the volume of each sound object accordingly. "When the player aims all the way to the left, the pish_left object is played at 100 per cent volume, and the other two at 0 per cent. As the aim moves to right, the volume of pish_left decreases and the volume of pish_mid increases."

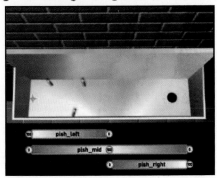

"The code means that wherever the aim is in the urinal, the volumes of all three samples always adds up to 100 per cent, giving the effect of a truly 3D sound. Isn't technology wonderful?"

5 This is a game for anyone who hates traffic wardens. Be a pigeon and see how many you can poo on. The sound effects in this are hilarious. "Sound is so integral to the stuff we do. We put a lot of work into it," says Hoss. Flam Jam tend to use Sonic Foundry's ACID and SoundForge to create their own sounds and make use of free sound samples found online.

6 "We did this when we were experimenting with putting video into Flash," explains Hoss. "It's actually a series of bitmaps in Flash made to look like video. Now, using MX, we'd actually use video, the file size would be smaller and the video would be smoother. Using video in Flash MX is a doddle."

7 "This is a really good concept," says Hoss "It's about somebody on a swing that falls off. The idea came when we were being photographed for an article appearing in The Scotsman. We went down a swing park and played on the swings. We were swinging really high and I got scared. I think I've lost the lack of fear you have when you're young."

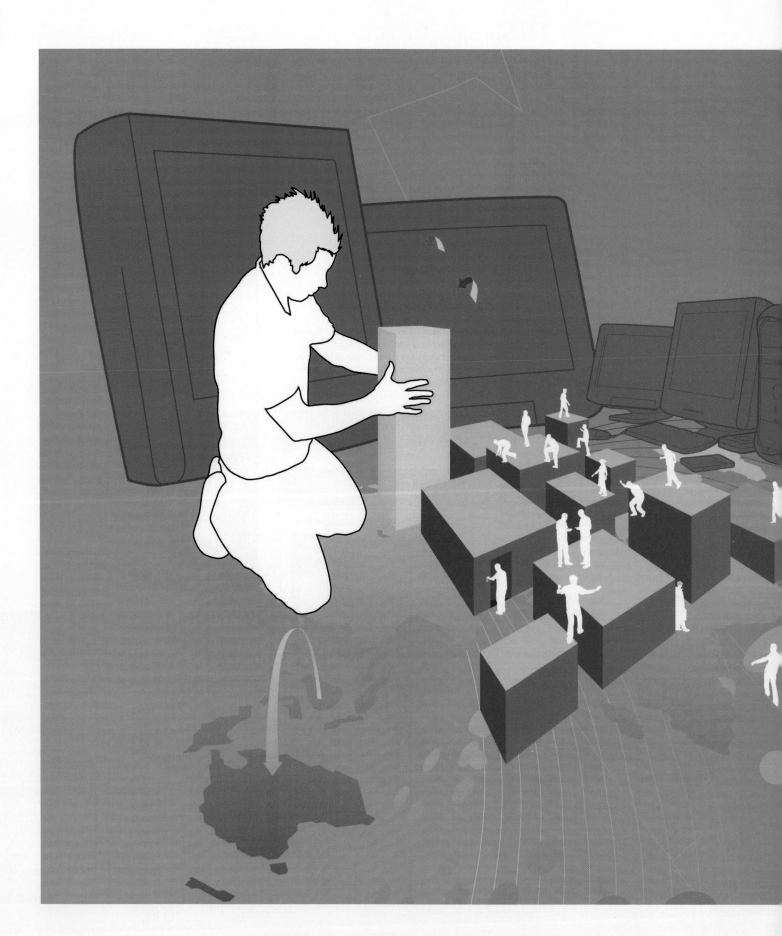

Games projects

Flash games can be pretty addictive and building them is a great way to develop your knowledge and expertise of Flash MX. Our tutorials show you how

Ten blinding Flash games

With Flash now a standard for online entertainment there are more games created with it than ever before. But what makes a great online game? Is it originality, gameplay or a combination of all these factors and more? We take a look at ten top games…

As Macromedia continues to develop Flash into an ever-more powerful rich media tool, there are greater opportunities for creating better and more diverse games. So what marks a game out to be great?

"First of all, it should load fairly fast," says Ferry Halim, creator of online games company Orisinal. "There are lots of people who are still on a 56k modem." Halim goes on to explain that the best games are simple, easy to learn, yet hard to master. Most important is the gameplay itself, and those games that have the ability to change dynamically as the player progresses are clear winners.

Glen Collins, Managing Director of Digital Outlook believes that a game has to be addictive. "There is always the opportunity to add in a multi-user aspect, which is hugely compelling," he explains.

The multi-user idea crops up repeatedly, with many gamers saying that this is the next stage of the Flash game, especially since Macromedia's release of the Flash MX Communication Server.

"Multi-player for me is what makes a game that I will keep and play for a long time — you just can't beat human interaction," says Jamie Madden, Creative Director of Australian developer BatteryHead. However, Madden says it'll be interesting to see how many people learn to harness the server since many Flash developers are designers, not coders.

Another key winning point is the subject of the game. Parodies of current affairs or those based on hot topics of the day make for very good viral games that spread across the Web like wildfire. Intelligent user interfaces are another plus. "Before releasing a game, you should let users test it and listen to their feedback," says Jobe Makar, Director of Electrotank. He also highlights the fact that the

most popular games are often the best looking: "Graphics definitely make the first impression. Gorgeous graphics can help you get a lot of first-time players," he says, adding that the best games are also the ones with non-offensive sound effects and music, with the option to turn these off.

As well as the brainstorming sessions common to most online projects, developers often get their ideas from tried and tested games on other platforms.

"Most of our games have some sort of elements to them that have already been proven in some form or other," says Rene Boutin of Spore Productions, although he adds, "We stay away from what has obviously been done to death." Some developers steer clear of older gaming ideas altogether, though.

"There must be an original idea to build a real Flash game, not just creating on top of an old concept," says Nicolai Chauvet, Artistic Director of Studiotanuki. However, clients often want variations of games they've seen, and as budgets for Flash games are usually tiny, this is normally what they get.

Most designers also agree that it's hard to come up with purely original ideas. "In reality there are only a limited number of game types to work with, be it platform, maze, shooter and so on," says John Lyons, Interactive Director at Egovision. "What makes a game stand out is the twist that you put on it, the plot, characters and set."

Contacts

StudioTanaki www.studiotanuki.com
Spore Productions
www.sporeproductions.com
Wheel www.thewheelgroup.com
Kerb www.kerb.co.uk
Electrotank www.electrotank.com
Orisinal www.ferryhalim.com/orisinal
Hyperlaunch www.hyperlaunch.com
Digital Outlook www.digital-outlook.com
Edition Interactive
www.editioninteractive.co.uk
Egovision www.egovision.com
BatteryHead www.batteryhead.com

 Expertise provided by Michael Burns. You can contact Michael at [e] burns@dircon.co.uk

Bubble Bees

Company: **Orisinal**
Website: **www.orisinal.com/games/bubble.htm**
Designer: **Ferry Halim**
Development time: **Two weeks**

Bubble Bees is a popular Flash game in which players try to put flying bees into bubbles. The more bees you get, the better your score. There's also a time limit to the game.

"I was experimenting with the drag-and-drop feature in Flash when I got this idea for a game," explains designer Ferry Halim. "At first it was just a bubble-making game, but then I added the bees to make it more fun. I always try to make something different and new — it's not easy, but luckily, so far I've managed to produce some quite 'different' games."

Halim doesn't have specific stats for each game, but says that the Orisinal Website has around one million unique visitors each month.

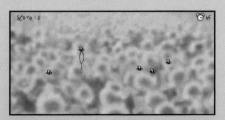
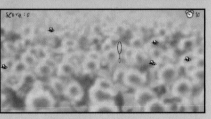

What makes this a great online game?
"It has a different concept. It's fun. And it's the most popular game on Orisinal." **Ferry Halim**

Barstar

Company: **Egovision**
Website: **http://polstarvodka.com/games/barstar**
Designer: **John Lyons (Art Director) and Anna Hague (Lead Illustrator)**
Development time: **Four months**

In this game you are a barman and the onus is on you to make a roaring success of a night out, keeping the punters, the owners and your own libido happy. The only way to do this is to make sure the punters get their favourite tipples without too much waiting.

"The game was for a luxury vodka brand with an established sexy image off-line," says John Lyons, Interactive Director at Egovision. "We devised the concept of a bar simulation game with a sexy twist, making the player rely upon a keen knowledge of cocktails and flirting to achieve a high score."

After concept and styling, the game engine was built to cross-reference internal databases of cocktails and a number of ingredients. The

character AI and dialogue were then developed, and it was decided that the game would also form the basis of an enhanced data music CD with a Flash front-end, brand new cocktail recipes and a number of exclusive funky bar tracks.

What makes this a great online game?
"It was innovative and had a lot of depth. The cocktail list had over 100 entries, many of which were devised specifically for the game, and the visual style took the product into a new direction." **John Lyons**

Stuntman Stunts

Company: **Hyperlaunch New Media**
Website: **www.hyperlaunch.com/stuntman/**
Designer: **James Humphrey (Creative Director) and Mark Birch (Production Director)**
Development time: **Four weeks**

Hyperlaunch New Media created a teaser game for the PlayStation 2 title Stuntman, featuring four different stunts designed to give the player an online feel for what the actual PS2 game is all about. The stunts are easy to get the hang of, but very hard to master.

"Ideally we look for elements of the title that we think would make a great game," says Marketing Director Don Jenkins. "A number of ideas are generated and storyboarded for the client. When an idea is agreed, assets are made and animation added. This asset is then handed over to technical in order to integrate the game into a site, link it to a high score table and add 'mail-a-mate' functions to it."

The game has been a great success. After the launch of Stunuman Stunts on 4 September, 2002 an average of 8,500 visitors a week clicked through to the game.

What makes this a great online game?
"The stunts are great fun and I think they really do give a great taster of the concept of an original PS2 title." **Don Jenkins**

Pinpin

Company: **Studiotanuki**
Website: **www.studiotanuki.com/pinpin/**
Designer: **Meko**
Development time: **Two months**

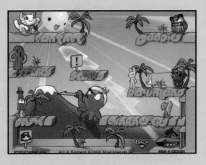

In Pinpin, you play a crazy rabbit who adds a rather personal brand of humour to a platform game. Users have to jump across stages, driving the rabbit around monsters using only the keyboard direction arrows. The Manga cartoon style is of very high quality, as is the amount of control the player has over the character of the flatulent rabbit.

"We wanted to create a lot of animations and possibility of moves for our character, so we built a script that allows animation for each instance," says Nicolai Chauvet, Artistic Director and Game Designer. "All our animations are made up entirely of Flash interpolations." This approach has been very successful and this wacky, high-quality game received over one and half million hits in two months, with 200,000 pages served.

What makes this a great online game?
"Pinpin's responses, once the user understands how to command them." **Nicolai Chauvet**

Chariot Race

Company: **Edition Interactive**
Website: **www.channel4.com/history/microsites/H/history/rome/index1.html**
Designer: **Nick Kuh**
Development time: **Four weeks**

Chariot Race is a 3D action game designed to boost traffic to Channel 4's History site. The player clicks around a 3D Roman Circus and moves into Play mode by zooming down into a packed arena. They start the game with 100 per cent energy, which is reduced each time they collide with debris or competitors, while points are gained for each avoided obstacle. The space bar activates the whip and players get bonus points if they whip their competitors as they overtake them. Edition's Nick Kuh designed the 3D interface and created the 'zooming' effect in Swift 3D, then exported it as an swf file to be brought into Flash.

"3D graphics tend to weigh down swf files so I had to make some sacrifices in export quality to keep the overall file size below 500KB," says Kuh. "The main challenge I met when programming was the collision detection script as this needs to activate only at the moment when the chariot racer appears to be passing the obstacles."

What makes this a great online game?
"The key to the popularity of this game is that it's fast paced and very difficult to achieve a good score. It is also a php/mySQL database-driven game with a high-score board." **Nick Kuh** >

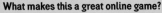

Eelextrix

Company: **Wheel**
Website: **www.hulahoops.com/eelextrix**
Designer: **Catherine Gray**
Development time: **Three weeks**

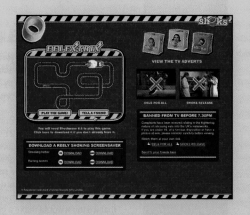

Based on the classic Scalextrix car-racing product, Wheel has developed an eel racing game for a Hula Hoops Shoks campaign. Players construct their own track from water pipes and race against an evil eel. A vicious plumber tries to make life even more complicated for the intrepid eel racers.

"We were briefed to develop online concepts that worked with the launch of Hula Hoops Shoks," says Chris Clarke, Creative Director at Wheel. "The advertising featured electric eels being released into the water system. We started thinking about eels struggling to escape from water pipes and came up with the idea of making the eels race each other. Classic compulsive games in the Tetris mould work well for older target audiences," Clarke continues. "For younger groups, an irreverent and slightly surreal design style is key."

What makes this a great online game?
"You can build your own track and race a friend. Also, there are lots of creative details that give the game a strong narrative flavour." **Chris Clarke**

Panik

Company: **Kerb**
Website: **www.panikgames.com**
Designers: **Dave, Dan, Zeb and Dantoo at Kerb**
Development time: **One month**

This Bombjack-style game presents the player with three or four screens on each level where they have to collect all the bombs within a set time limit. Later levels have air ducts which need to be jumped on in order to access higher areas.

Panik's was conceived as part of a portfolio of games created in-house to license to third parties. After creating Panik the Rabbit's move controls, the team added the platforms, then the background and foreground graphics to the game. "We then fixed the baddies, then the bombs," says Jim McNiven, CEO of Kerb. "It was important to make sure that once the bombs were collected they didn't reappear when Panik went back to that screen."

More tricky obstacles like the moving platforms and the conveyer belt with a saw blade were included as each new level was built. "With the bulk of the gameplay complete, we inserted the sound effects, sorted out the intro screen, preload and instructions at the start and a Game Over sequence at the end," says McNiven.

What makes this a great online game?
"We had it running on a PC in an arcade cabinet on our stand in Cannes (Milia) this year and people were playing it constantly. When people are on the stand asking you if it would be possible to create something similar for Websites, you get the feeling that it looks the part." **Jim McNiven**

Fruit Smash

Company: **Electrotank**
Website: **www.electrotank.com**
Designer: **Robert Firebaugh (Creative Director)**
Development time: **Four weeks**

Fruit Smash is a grid-based fruit-matching puzzle game with a new and fun twist. Occasionally, instead of a new fruit, a different kind of icon will appear — a bomb, fire, geyser, ice, bug or mallet — representing one of six types of supermoves. A supermove icon acts like a wild card, so it can match with any two identical fruit.

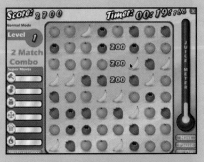

"This game started with an experimental engine that handled everything but the supermoves," says Jobe Makar, Director of Electrotank. "We talked about the different directions that we could go with this game engine and decided to bring it to a higher level by adding in the idea of supermoves. When we settled on this idea we documented the entire game and then started to build it to completion." Development wasn't without problems though. Makar adds, "As with all games, along the way we decided on a few changes because of technical problems and playability problems."

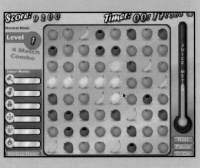

What makes this a great online game?
"The addictive nature of searching more matches and applying supermoves. Supermoves are really what makes this game fun and unique." **Jobe Makar**

Spore Cubes

Company: **Spore Productions**
Website: **www.lilgames.com/cubes. shtml**
Designer: **Rene Boutin**
Development time: **Two weeks**

"A client wanted a couple of games where they could 'reveal' photographs gradually," says Rene Boutin of Spore Productions, explaining the origins of Spore Cubes. "They initially asked for a Breakout/Arkanoid-type clone, but that's an action game and is over-done." Boutin convinced the client to go with his new concept and it turned into a major hit.

"By now, the concept is easily recognisable as the 'click groups of same-coloured blocks to destroy them'," Boutin says. "The end-goal is to clear the entire screen of blocks." Boutin's inspiration was a shareware game which followed a similar concept. "I felt it was the type of game that could be simplified and would translate perfectly to an online format for the general mass market."

The game remains the most popular at Boutin's game site, LilGames.com. "Stats I've gathered show that a majority of the players are female and there is also an unexpected high number of seniors who love it," he reveals.

What makes this a great online game?

"Spore Cubes can be considered a veritable Flash game classic now. It was released in the summer of 1999 and shortly thereafter I started seeing clones of the concept appearing. Today, there doesn't seem to be a Web game developer or game site without some sort of variation of the concept. I humbly think the balance and simplicity of Spore Cubes *keeps it as one of the more addictive of its genre."*
Rene Boutin

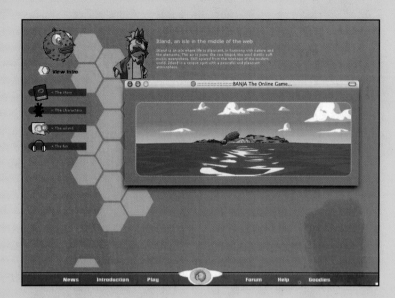

Banja

Company: **TeamChman**
Website: **www.banja.com**
Designer: **Seb Kochman, Stephan Logier, Tony Derbome, Gauthier Malou and several others**
Development time: **Two years of initial production, then updated constantly since 1998**

Banja is the first community adventure game in 3D Flash, evolving in real time and exclusively on the Web. The goal is to explore ItLand as you attempt to help Banja keep the magical island pure and vibrant, discovering new games, places, music and surprises with every episode. Chat rooms and other integrated community tools, as well as arcade games and a media server, all add to the user's gaming experience.

Damien Giard of chmAN, Banja's developer, says the team are all hardcore gamers from the Web design world who spent extensive amounts of time on LAN games, picking up tips on what was effective in a game, and what to leave out. In the creation of this graphics intensive world, special attention has been given to making the results as fluid for the player as for the viewer, who can watch the game as if it were an actual cartoon. Banja also integrates 3D-specific technologies, using 3DS Max and Flash to ensure that there's a perfect render with both 3D depth and vector smoothness.

As for success, there are more than 200,000 registered players on the French servers, more than 150,000 on the Spanish/Latin-American servers and already more than 30,000 on the recently launched German servers.

What makes this a great online game?

"Banja is unique! There is nothing comparable on the Web or in any video game. From the adventure games, you collect objects, solve enigmas and discover new scenes with an emphasis on graphics and scenario. From the RPG games, it has dialogue and interaction with the characters, as well as a system of knowledge points. Mini game modules are also integrated in the story, with running, fishing, climbing, logging, motor biking, kiting and even a cooking game! The good spirit of Banja *is also very important: positive and peaceful. Unlike most online games, the aim is not to conquer a territory or to exterminate the enemy, but to discover all the secrets of this mysterious isle, as well as living in a community, learning to control energy and preserving the environment."* **Damien Giard**

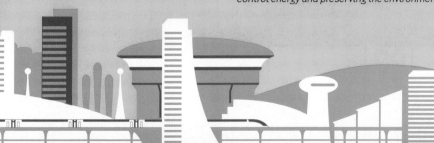

●GAME STATUS

●LEVEL

●CLEARED LINES

●SCORE

●HIGHSCORE

●NEXT

Build a Tetris-style Flash game using ActionScript

In this tutorial we show you how the object-oriented features of ActionScript can be used to create a versatile and modular game…

This might be the first time you have come across an object-oriented approach to ActionScript, so you need to understand the underlying concepts before you begin writing code. You need to understand what an object is, what a class is, how objects and classes are related and how they communicate by using messages. This approach is the same for all object-oriented languages and scripts.

What Is an object?

If you look around you now you'll see many examples of real-world objects, such as your dog, your computer, your phone or your book. These physical objects have two characteristics: they all have properties (variables) and behaviour (functions). For example, cats have different properties (name, colour, hunger) and behaviour (purring, meowing and licking).

In Spriteris we have a game board. This is the area on which the pieces are stored and which dictates the position and rotation of the active falling piece. The board has properties (rows, columns, pieces, lines cleared, level) and behaviour (move piece, rotate piece, shift piece, check board, create new piece and so on).

Software objects are modelled after real-world objects. A software object

---

This article and tutorial has been provided by Sprite, who are working on exciting projects in mobile marketing, VR and on the Web. For more info, [e] alex@sprite.net [w] www.sprite.net.

Files on disc
All the files for the tutorial can be found on the CD. The Flash file is called spriteris.fla, and the code for the tutorial can be found in tutorials/gm_tetris

---

PAUSE ROTATE RIGHT LEFT FASTER START

▲SPACE　▲ARROW UP　▲ARROW RIGHT　▲ARROW LEFT　▲ARROW DOWN　▲RETURN

●CONTROLS (PLEASE USE YOUR KEYBOARD)

▲108 ▲253 ◆047 ◆098 ▲182 ▲205
●STATISTICS

maintains its state in one or more properties (variables). A software object applies its behaviour as functions. The board object has an active piece, which is an instance of a piece object. The active piece is moved down the board until it lands on the bottom or another piece and then another piece is chosen randomly and created in order to start the process again.

In object-oriented programming, you might want to represent real-world cats as software objects in an animation program. You can also use software objects to model abstract concepts. For example, an event is a common object used in ActionScript to represent the action of a user pressing a mouse button or a key on the keyboard.

Everything that the software object knows (properties) and can do (behaviour) is expressed by the variables and the methods within that object. A software object that modelled your car would have variables that indicated the car's current state: its speed is 10mph, its engine speed is 2000rpm, and its current gear is fifth. These variables are formally known as instance variables because they contain the state for a particular car object, and in object-oriented terminology, a particular object is called an instance.

In addition to its variables, the software car would also have different methods to make it start, go forward, reverse, steer and brake. These methods are known as instance methods because they inspect or change the state of a particular car instance.

What is a class?

In the real world you often have many objects of the same kind. For example, your piece is just one of many pieces in the game. Using object-oriented terminology, we say that your piece object is an instance of the class of objects known as pieces. Pieces have properties (rotation, colour, structure) and behaviour (rotate, width, height, getData) in common. Each piece's properties are independent of and can be different from that of other pieces.

When building pieces, the programmer takes advantage of the fact that pieces share characteristics, building all the pieces from the same scheme. It wouldn't be very efficient to produce a new scheme for every individual piece created.

In object-oriented software, it's also possible to have many objects of the same kind that share characteristics. Like the 'piece' creator, you can take advantage of the fact that objects of the same kind are similar and you can create a scheme for those objects. A software scheme or blueprint for objects is called a class.

What is inheritance?

Generally speaking, objects are defined in terms of classes. You know a lot about an object by knowing its class. Even if you don't know what a Rover Mini is, if I told you it was a car, you would know that it had four wheels, two doors and a steering wheel. Object-oriented systems take this a step further and allow classes to be defined in terms of other classes. For example, BMW, Ford Escort and SAAB are all kinds of cars. In object-oriented terminology, BMW, Ford Escort and SAAB are all subclasses of the car class. Similarly, the car class is the superclass of BMW, Ford Escort and SAAB.

As you follow through the Spriteris game, we take you through a step-by-step introduction to designing and implementing a game using Object-Oriented ActionScript. If you're feeling adventurous you could even extend the game with your own pieces or create a multi-player version!

The same process of development also applies for Java development. The above illustration features Sprite's Tamogotchi pets running on mobile phones.

By developing in an object oriented environment it is very easy to develop for deployment on a number of different platforms.

The same methods used for developing content for a desktop PC can be applied to the Pocket PC, bearing in mind size and playback restrictions.

Part 1: The game basics

The first step is to create the building blocks of the game…

The history of Tetris

The game *Tetris* was first developed in Moscow in 1985. Later that year its creator, Alexey Pazhitnov, converted it for the IBM PC, and the game still remains a firm favourite among gamers worldwide. The arcade version of *Tetris*, released in 1987 through *Tetris*'s main developing and distributing company, Spectrum Holobyte, enjoyed extreme popularity and *Tetris* was included with all Nintendo Game Boy systems when the handheld was launched.

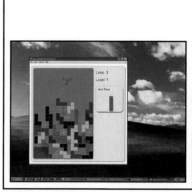

1 This tutorial will show you how to build a flexible Tetris-style arcade game using object-oriented ActionScript. Start by opening spriteris_empty.fla. This is an empty movie with the required library items.

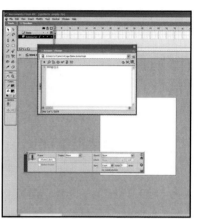

2 Create two layers named Game and ActionScript. On the ActionScript layer create a keyframe containing a single stop() action. The game will be stored in a separate movie clip.

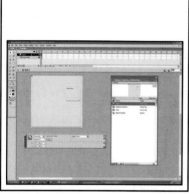

3 The next step is to create a movie clip to hold the game. By creating your game in a separate movie it's easy to add it to other Flash documents and scale to fit other movie sizes. Give the new movie the instance name 'gameboard'.

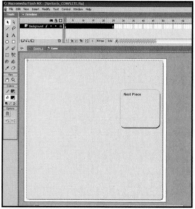

4 Open the gameboard movie and create a new layer named Background. Copy the movie clip 'Background' from the library onto the stage. This will be the static background for the game.

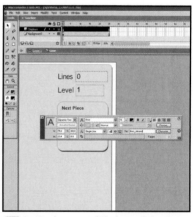

5 Create a layer named Displays and place two dynamic text fields on it, next to the Lines and Levels labels on the background. These will be used to display the status of the game.

6 Give the Lines text field the 'Var' value 'lines_cleared' and the Level text field the value 'levels_cleared'. These variables will be used to update the text fields.

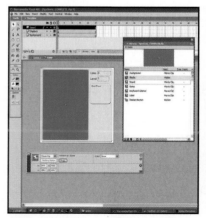

7 Create a new layer named Board and then place the Board movie clip from the library onto the first frame. This will be the background for the game board.

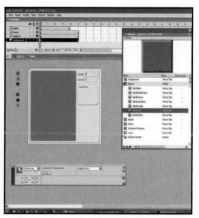

8 The pieces used in the game are built up from a number of simple blocks that are duplicated by ActionScript to display each piece. The building blocks are located in the Blocks folder in the Library.

9 Create a new layer named Blocks and place an instance of each block from the library off to the left of the stage. Give each block the instance names block0, block1, block2… up to block6.

Part 2: Creating the game pieces

Next we take the plunge into ActionScript objects and create the Piece class…

1 On the Blocks layer, create an instance of the 'Keyboard Listener' movie clip from the library. Later in the tutorial this movie clip will be used to detect keyboard events and perform game actions.

2 The whole game is based on object-oriented ActionScript, with ActionScript objects used to represent different elements of the game. The elements of this game are based on the Piece, Board and Game classes.

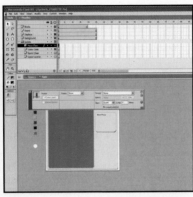

3 To help organise the code you should create four layers: Piece Class, Game Class, Board Class and Game Control. The first three layers will contain ActionScript used to define each object class while the game control layer is used to control the flow of the game.

4 A class is defined by creating a function with the same name as the class and placing variables and functions associated with that class within the function. For example: function MyClass() { … }. To create a new object of the class you would use the 'new' keyword; for example: myObject = new MyClass();

5 Within the class, variables can be defined by using the 'this' keyword; for example: this.type = 0;. Functions can also be defined within classes; for example: this.calculate = new function(x, y) { … } This function could then be called from the new object; for example: myObject.calculate(1,2).

6 The first class to create is the Piece Class. A Piece object will be created for each different type of piece used in the game. In this case there are seven. Create a keyframe on frame 1 of the Piece Class layer and add the code from Code1.txt to the ActionScript window.

7 A Piece object contains the data for each rotation of that piece. The setPiece() function is used to set the piece structure for each rotation, the structure being specified using a two-dimensional array, similar to an image of the piece.

8 Create a keyframe on frame 1 of the Game Control layer and add the code from Code2.txt. This code is used to create each different piece used in the game and place them in an array. Refer to the comments in the Piece Class code for more details on the setPiece() function.

9 The Piece Class also offers functions to rotate the piece, get the array structure for the current rotation and retrieve other information about the piece, such as width, height and type.

Part 3: Creating the game board

Now we'll look at creating the Board Class to hold the game board…

Naming conventions

It's a good idea to learn the object-oriented programming naming conventions. A class always starts with a capital letter. When naming a function or a variable you need to start the name with a lower case letter, then if it is two words make sure the second word begins with an upper case letter. For example, movePiece(). You also need to give your variables meaningful names so that someone editing your code can come to grips with it easily.

1 Now you have the game pieces, you need a board to place them on. For this, the Board Class is used. A Board object will manage the game board, control the active piece and check for complete lines and collisions. Create a keyframe on frame 1 of the Game Class layer and add the code from Code3.txt to the ActionScript window.

2 The Board class contains many functions that will be covered in this tutorial. When creating a new board, the number of rows and columns must be specified, along with the name of the block movie clip used to display the pieces, and the width of the block. The board creates an array to hold the status of the game board.

3 The reset() function of the board clears all the data from the board. The setOffset(x,y) function is used to align the display of the board from the top left corner of the main movie. On the first frame action of the Game Control layer, add the code from Code4.txt.

4 This code creates a new board of 24x16 blocks, assigns it to duplicate the "block#" MovieClips, resets it and sets the offset to display it at. This will form the basis of your game.

5 Finally add the code from Code5.txt to frame 1 on the Game Control layer. This will pick the first piece to display. The first frame of this layer is used to initialise the game, while the second frame performs the main game processes of moving the active piece, updating the board and creating new game pieces.

6 The Board object has an active piece, which is the piece being controlled by the player. To set a new active piece, the setActivePiece(newpiece) function is used to set it to the one specified. To check if an active piece already exists on the board, the activePieceExists() function is used.

7 Create a new keyframe on frame 2 of the Game Control layer and add the code from Code6.txt to the ActionScript window. This code checks whether an active piece exists on the board, and if so, whether it can be moved down.

8 The board.moveActivePiece() function is responsible for moving the active piece down the board. It first checks for collisions with existing blocks before updating the display. If a collision occurs, the active piece is registered on the board and then deleted so another one can be created.

9 The Board class contains a two-dimensional array to represent the game board, where each element of the array corresponds to a block on the board. The registerActivePiece() function is responsible for registering the active piece in the array when the piece has landed. After it has been registered, the active piece is deleted using the deleteActivePiece() function.

Part 3: Creating the game board, continued

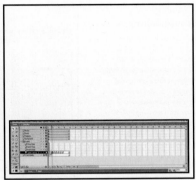

10 If a new active piece is needed, the board.setActivePiece() function is called with the next piece to create. After it's created, another piece is randomly chosen to be the next piece.

11 At the end of the moveActivePiece() function, the checkBoard() function is called. This function is used to remove any filled rows from the board array and to update the game board on screen. Every time a row is cleared, the linesCleared variable of the board object is incremented. Each time five lines are cleared the levelsCleared variable is incremented.

12 The levelsCleared variable is used to control the speed of the game, so the higher the level the faster the pieces fall. Create keyframes at frames 4, 6, 8, 10, 12 and 14 on the Game Control layer.

Part 4: Adding game and user controls

Adding keyboard control for the user and making the game more challenging…

Using layers

When building a movie of this complexity, you'll find it easier if you create each ActionScript class on its own layer. This helps to break up the structure of your movie, meaning you won't have to scroll through hundreds of lines of code to find the class you want. Flash MX's new function that allows you to organise your layers into folders also proves useful, keeping your movie as uncluttered as possible.

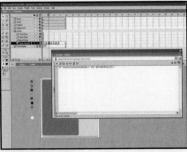

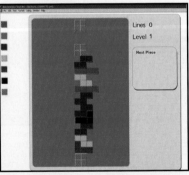

1 Open Code7.txt and follow the comments in the code to paste it into the appropriate frames on the Flash file. Each keyframe checks if the levelsCleared variable of the board object is above a certain level. If so, it'll immediately repeat frame 2 to drop the active piece down one step. The higher the level, the sooner it repeats.

2 By testing the movie at this point you'll see that the pieces fall into a column on the board. The next step is to add some control for the player. The active piece will be controlled by the keyboard using the cursor keys.

3 Select the Keyboard Listener movie clip on the Blocks layer. Open the Object Actions and paste into it the contents of Code8.txt. The code uses an onClipEvent(keyDown) { … } block to detect when a key is pressed, and Key.isDown() checks to find out what key was pressed.

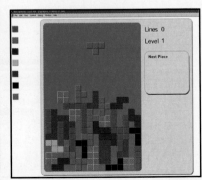

4 When the left or right cursor key is pressed, the function board.shiftActivePiece(dir) is called. This function moves the active piece on the board in the direction specified, either -1 for left or 1 for right. Pressing the up cursor key calls the board.rotateActivePiece() function. This function rotates the active piece to its next position and updates the display.

5 The down cursor key is used to drop the active piece until it lands. It does this by repeating the board.moveActivePiece() function until it returns to 0, meaning that it has landed. When it has landed, the game is restarted at frame 2 to generate the next active piece.

6 By testing the game at this point you'll see that it's getting more playable. The next step is to provide a display of the next piece and update the display of the number of lines and levels cleared. A Game object is used for this.

Part 5: Finishing touches

Adding the essential features to create the complete game…

Commenting

Make sure you comment all your ActionScript so other members of your team can understand your movie. You need to use '//' tags or '/* ...*/' blocks to comment your code. Don't forget that the Commenting tool is a great way to store code that you want to use in your movie but don't want turned on at the time you write it.

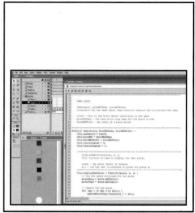

1 Create a keyframe on frame 1 of the Game Class layer and paste the code from Code9.txt into the ActionScript window.

2 The Game Class provides two functions. The first is displayNextPiece(piece,x,y) and this is used to update the display of the next piece. It accepts three arguments: the first is the Piece object to display, and x, y are the top left co-ordinates to display the piece at.

3 The second function, updateStats(), updates the Lines and Levels text fields to display the status of the game. To create a new Game object, add the code from Code10.txt to the end of the ActionScript on frame 1 of the Game Control layer.

4 The Game Class functions need to be called on the second frame, whenever a new piece is created. Replace the code on frame 2 of the Game Control layer with the code in Code11.txt.

5 All that now remains is to control when the player runs out of board and it's Game Over. Create a new layer named Frame Labels, create a keyframe on frames 1 and 20 and give them the frame labels 'start' and 'gameover' respectively.

6 On frame 20 of the Game Control layer, add the code from Code12.txt. This code stops the game and displays the Game Over message. It does this by attaching a movie clip from the library with the linkage name gameover_panel. The message is then positioned over the board.

7 The message is attached dynamically to make it appear on top of the existing blocks on screen, since all graphics on the timeline will appear beneath duplicated movie clips.

8 Create a new layer named Game Over and a keyframe on frame 20. On this keyframe, place an instance of the New Game button from the library and then add the ActionScript from Code13.txt to it.

9 Now simply compile and play the game! Open spriteris.fla to see a complete version.

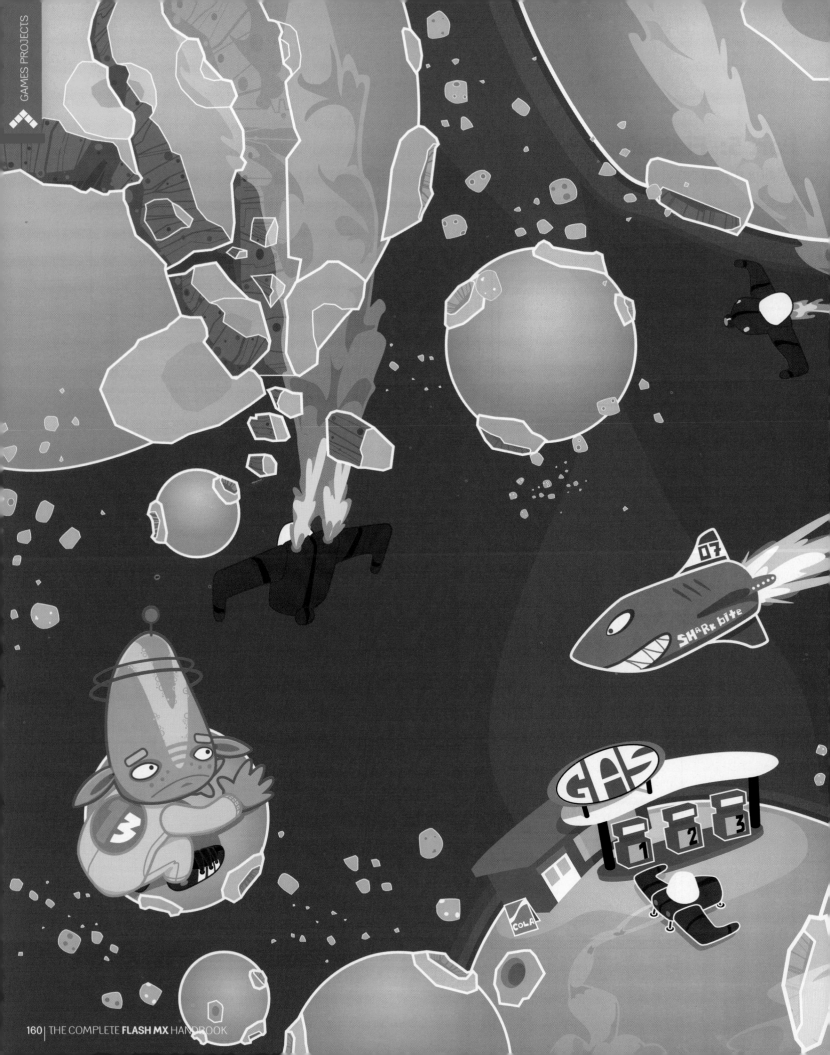

Illustration: BrownJames [t] 0121 350 8561
[e] jimmyjames@btinternet.com [w] www.brownjames.co.uk

Recreate a classic arcade shooter

Use Flash MX to make an arcade space combat game featuring floating rocks and a spaceship built to destroy them…

Expertise by Gary Rosenzweig. Gary is the founder and Chief Engineer at CleverMedia [w] http://clevermedia.com/, a company that specialises in Flash and Shockwave games. His latest book is called Flash MX ActionScript for Fun and Games. You can find out about Gary's books and contact him through [w] http://garyrosenzweig.com/.

Files on disc
The files needed to support this tutorial can be found in the Tutorial\gm_rocks folder on the cover CD.

With Flash MX's improved speed and new scripting features, it's now easier than ever to create arcade games for your Website. Space Rocks is a classic and was one of a genre of arcade games that dominated in the early 1980s and still manages to entertain a large number of players today.

The game features a small ship placed in the middle of a large field of floating rocks. The rocks whizz around the screen at various speeds — they wrap from one side of the screen to the other so they're never very far away.

A lone ship stands against these rocks. The player controls the ship's rotation and can thrust the vessel forward to avoid the rocks. The ship can also fire an endless amount of bullets to combat the rocks. The larger rocks break into smaller pieces, and eventually disappear completely.

To make a game like Space Rocks, you need Flash MX, the latest version of Macromedia's popular Web development tool. You also need to be familiar with the application because you'll be using some of its new scripting features during this tutorial. >

Part 1: Create the games arena

The first thing you need to do is create your game intro screen...

Starry skies

If you want to create a more interesting background than the plain black one used here, you can make a new layer in the main timeline and fill it with little dots to represent stars. Make sure these dots are very small, so they won't be confused with the rocks.

1 Open Flash MX. Select the first frame in the main timeline and use the Property Inspector to name the frame 'intro'. Save the movie as spacerocks.fla and remember to save after each step.

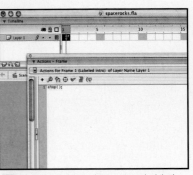

2 Press F9 to bring up the script panel while the first frame is selected. Enter the simple script stop(); to get the movie to pause on this frame when it starts. Without this script, the movie would play through all the frames we are about to create as if it were an animation, rather than a game.

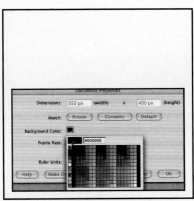

3 Open the movie Properties dialog by choosing Modify>Document. Click on the Background Colour chip and change it to black.

4 By using text and graphics of your own choice, draw on this first frame to create a title graphic and introduction. Later, you can add instructions and other content to this frame.

5 Create a button graphic on the stage. Select it and use F8 to convert it to a button. Name it anything you like. Make sure you select Button in the Convert to Symbol dialog box.

6 With the button selected, press F9 to create a script for it. Type in the simple script shown and close the script window. When the user presses this button, the movie will advance to the 'play' frame.

Part 2: Design your space rocks

Make the rocks that you'll destroy later...

More rocks

You can create more than three rocks if you want more variety. Just change the line in the code where Math.Random is multiplied by 3. For instance, if you have five rocks, change the multiplier to 5. Be sure to name the rocks 'Rock1', 'Rock2', and so on when creating the Library elements.

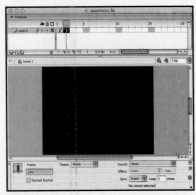

1 Select the second frame in the main timeline. Press F7 to insert a new keyframe there. Use the Property Inspector to name this frame 'play'.

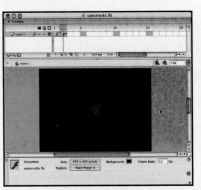

2 In the middle of the screen, draw a rock. Make it about 60 pixels in diameter. Use whatever style you wish, from hand-drawn vector graphics to full-rendered rocks imported from a 3D program.

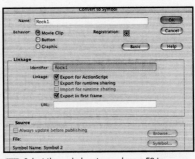

3 Select the rock drawing and press F8 to convert it into a movie clip. Make sure you select Movie Clip as the symbol's Behaviour. Name it Rock1. Also check the Export for ActionScript box. This will ensure that the movie clip is available to your code after the movie has been saved as a compressed Flash file.

Faster rocks

The rocks are initialised to move at a speed of four times a random number between –.5 and .5. So the speed can be between –2 and 2 in both horizontal and vertical directions. To change the potential speed of the rocks, increase or decrease the value by 4. For instance, to speed them up an average of 50 per cent, change this number to 6.

Smooth running

The speed of this game is somewhat independent of the framerate of the movie. This is because the setInterval command is used to make steps 50 milliseconds regardless of the framerate. However, you'll probably want to increase the framerate to some decent rate, like 30fps, to ensure smooth play.

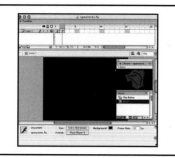

4 Delete the movie clip from the stage. It should remain in the Library as 'Rock1' even though it's no longer on the stage anywhere. Because you selected Export for ActionScript when creating the movie clip, it'll still be included in the compressed Flash file and we can reference it with our ActionScript code.

5 Create two other rocks named 'Rock2' and 'Rock3' by repeating steps 1-3 of Part 2. Make sure you check the Export for ActionScript box for both, and delete both from the stage.

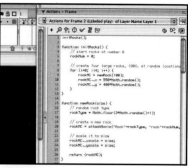

6 Select the second frame in the timeline and press F9 to open the script window. Add the script shown to the frame. These two functions will create four rocks in random positions on the screen. Test the movie by choosing Control>Test Movie. You should see four rocks appear at random locations.

7 Open the frame script again and add the new code as shown in the selected area. This adds the properties dx and dy to the movie clips. This is the horizontal and vertical speed of the rock. The setInterval command will call the function moveRocks every 50 milliseconds to move the rocks that amount.

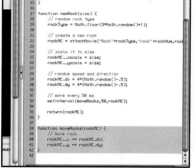

8 Add a new function – moveRocks. The moveRocks function will move a rock horizontally and vertically according to its dx and dy properties. Test the movie again to see how the rocks move.

9 Add the new code to the moveRocks function. This will check the rock's new location against the edges of the screen and wrap it around to the other side if necessary. It uses the edges of the screen plus 10 pixels to make the wrap a little smoother. Test the movie again to see the rocks wrap.

Part 3: Creating the ship

Build a spaceship and make it move…

1 At the middle of the screen, draw a small spaceship. Make sure that the front of the spaceship is pointing up.

2 Select the ship and press F8 to convert it to a movie clip. Make sure you select Movie Clip as its behaviour. Name it Ship.

3 Leave this movie clip on the stage. Select it and use the Property Inspector to name this instance of the movie clip 'ship'. ❯

Creating the ship continued...

Double speed

To make the ship rotate faster or slower, alter the amount by which the _rotation property is changed. For instance, to double the speed of rotation, change the number to 10 instead of 5.

```
35      return(rockMC);
36  }
37
38  function moveRocks(rockMC) {
39      // move rock
40      rockMC._x += rockMC.dx;
41      rockMC._y += rockMC.dy;
42
43      // wrap around screen
44      if (rockMC._x > 550) rockMC._x -= 570;
45      if (rockMC._x < -10) rockMC._x += 570;
46      if (rockMC._y > 410) rockMC._y -= 420;
47      if (rockMC._y < -10) rockMC._y += 420;
48  }
49
50  function initShip() {
51      // start still
52      ship.dx = 0;
53      ship.dy = 0;
54
55      // move every 50 ms
56      setInterval(moveShip,50);
57  }
58
```

4 Add the initShip function. This sets the velocity of the ship, dx and dy, to 0 since the ship should start off standing still. The setInterval command will make sure that moveShip gets called once every 50 milliseconds to move the ship. Add the call to initShip(); right under the call to initRocks(); at the start of the script.

```
56      setInterval(moveShip,50);
57  }
58
59
60  function moveShip() {
61      // rotate ship left and right
62      if (Key.isDown(Key.LEFT)) {
63          ship._rotation -= 5;
64      }
65      if (Key.isDown(Key.RIGHT)) {
66          ship._rotation += 5;
67      }
68
69      // thrust forward
70      if (Key.isDown(Key.UP)) {
71          shipAngle = 2.0*Math.PI*(ship._rotation-90)/360.0;
72          ship.dx += Math.cos(shipAngle);
73          ship.dy += Math.sin(shipAngle);
74      }
75
76      // move ship
77      ship._x += ship.dx;
78      ship._y += ship.dy;
79
```

5 The moveShip function first checks the left and right arrow keys and rotates the ship by changing its _rotation property. It then checks the up arrow and thrusts the ship forward if it's pressed. It does this by using Math.cos and Math.sin to convert the rotation of the ship into x and y components. It then moves the ship according to dx and dy.

```
57  }
58
59
60  function moveShip() {
61      // rotate ship left and right
62      if (Key.isDown(Key.LEFT)) {
63          ship._rotation -= 5;
64      }
65      if (Key.isDown(Key.RIGHT)) {
66          ship._rotation += 5;
67      }
68
69      // thrust forward
70      if (Key.isDown(Key.UP)) {
71          shipAngle = 2.0*Math.PI*(ship._rotation-90)/360.0;
72          ship.dx += Math.cos(shipAngle);
73          ship.dy += Math.sin(shipAngle);
74      }
75
76      // move ship
77      ship._x += ship.dx;
78      ship._y += ship.dy;
79
80      // wrap around screen
81      if (ship._x > 550) ship._x -= 550;
82      if (ship._x < 0) ship._x += 550;
83      if (ship._y > 400) ship._y -= 400;
84      if (ship._y < 0) ship._y += 400;
85  }
86
```

6 Add the four lines of code shown above so that the ship will also wrap around the four edges of the screen.

Part 4: Firing bullets and destroying rocks

Enter the code that will enable the all-important bullet-firing function...

Skipping bullets

Notice the number 10 is used for the speed of the bullets. You can increase or decrease this number to speed up, or slow down, the bullets. However, if you speed it up too much, the bullet will appear to skip across the screen. In addition, this skipping will mean that it might skip right over a rock and miss it.

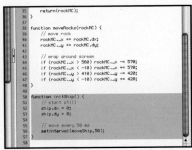

1 Create a small circle on the stage to act as the bullets which the ship will fire. Make the dot only a few pixels in diameter.

2 Select the dot and press F8 to convert it to a symbol. Give it a Movie Clip Behaviour. Name it Bullet and select Export for ActionScript.

3 Delete the bullet from the stage. This will leave it in the Library. We can refer to this Library member as 'bullet' in our code.

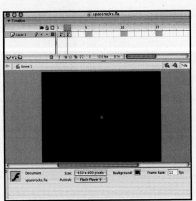

```
1   initRocks();
2   initShip();
3
4   // listen for key presses
5   spacebarListener = new Object();
6   spacebarListener.onKeyDown = fireBullet;
7   Key.addListener(spacebarListener);
8
9   function initRocks() {
10      // start rocks at number 0
11      rockNum = 0;
12
13      // create four large rocks, 100%, at random locations
14      for (i=0; i<4; i++) {
15          rockMC = newRock(100);
16          rockMC._x = 550*Math.random();
17          rockMC._y = 400*Math.random();
18      }
19  }
20
21  function newRock(size) {
22      // random rock type
23      rockType = Math.floor(3*Math.random()+1);
24
25      // create a new rock
26      rockMC = attachMovie("Rock"+rockType, "rock"+rockNum,
27
28      // scale it to size
29      rockMC._xscale = size;
30      rockMC._yscale = size;
```

4 Add the code shown to the very beginning of the script. This makes the movie listen for key presses and pass them on to the fireBullet function.

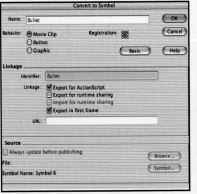

```
81      ship._x += ship.dx;
82      ship._y += ship.dy;
83
84      // wrap around screen
85      if (ship._x > 550) ship._x -= 550;
86      if (ship._x < 0) ship._x += 550;
87      if (ship._y > 400) ship._y -= 400;
88      if (ship._y < 0) ship._y += 400;
89  }
90
91
92
93  function fireBullet() {
94      if (Key.getAscii() == 32) {
95
96          // create new bullet at level 1000+bulletNum
97          bulletMC = attachMovie("Bullet","bullet"+bulletNum,1000+bulletNum++);
98
99          // start at center of ship
100         bulletMC._x = ship._x;
101         bulletMC._y = ship._y;
102
103         // direction of ship
104         shipAngle = 2*Math.PI*(ship._rotation-90)/360;
105         bulletMC.dx = Math.cos(shipAngle);
106         bulletMC.dy = Math.sin(shipAngle);
107
108         // attach movement function
109         bulletMC.moveBullet = moveBulletFunction;
110         setInterval(bulletMC,"moveBullet",50,bulletMC);
111     }
112 }
```

5 Add the fireBullet function. This function is called whenever a key is pressed, but we only want to perform an action when the spacebar is pressed. It will create a new movie clip, assign it a dx and dy according to the ship's orientation, and set up moveBulletFunction to be called from inside the new movie clip every 50 milliseconds.

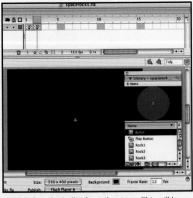

```
86      // wrap around screen
87      if (ship._x > 550) ship._x -= 550;
88      if (ship._x < 0) ship._x += 550;
89      if (ship._y > 400) ship._y -= 400;
90      if (ship._y < 0) ship._y += 400;
91  }
92
93  function fireBullet() {
94      if (Key.getAscii() == 32) {
95
96          // create new bullet at level 1000+bulletNum
97          bulletMC = attachMovie("Bullet","bullet"+bulletNum,1000+bulletNum++);
98
99          // start at center of ship
100         bulletMC._x = ship._x;
101         bulletMC._y = ship._y;
102
103         // direction of ship
104         shipAngle = 2*Math.PI*(ship._rotation-90)/360;
105         bulletMC.dx = Math.cos(shipAngle);
106         bulletMC.dy = Math.sin(shipAngle);
107
108         // attach movement function
109         bulletMC.moveBullet = moveBulletFunction;
110         setInterval(bulletMC,"moveBullet",50,bulletMC);
111     }
112 }
113
114 function moveBulletFunction() {
115     // move bullet
116     bulletSpeed = 10.0;
117     this._x += bulletSpeed*this.dx;
118     this._y += bulletSpeed*this.dy;
119 }
```

6 The moveBulletFunction will push the bullet along according to its own dx and dy properties.

Multiple lives

You may want to give the player multiple chances, or lives, so they can get hit by a rock three times before the game is over. This gets tricky as you need to reset the ship and wait for all rocks to clear the centre area before resuming the game. It'll add quite a bit more code to the game, but expert ActionScript programmers should be able to do it.

```
88  }
89  function fireBullet() {
90      if (Key.getAscii() == 32) {
91          // create new bullet at level 1000+bulletNum
92          bulletMC = attachMovie("Bullet", "bullet"+bulletNum, 1000+bullet
93          // start at center of ship
94          bulletMC._x = ship._x;
95          bulletMC._y = ship._y;
96          // direction of ship
97          shipAngle = 2*Math.PI*(ship._rotation-90)/360;
98          bulletMC.dx = Math.cos(shipAngle);
99          bulletMC.dy = Math.sin(shipAngle);
100         // attach movement function
101         bulletMC.moveBullet = moveBulletFunction;
102         setInterval(bulletMC, "moveBullet", 50, bulletMC);
103     }
104 }
105
106 function moveBulletFunction() {
107     // move bullet
108     bulletSpeed = 10.0;
109     this._x += bulletSpeed*this.dx;
110     this._y += bulletSpeed*this.dy;
111
112     // see if reached end of screen
113     if (this._x > 550) this.removeMovieClip();
114     if (this._x < 0) this.removeMovieClip();
115     if (this._y > 400) this.removeMovieClip();
116     if (this._y < 0) this.removeMovieClip();
117 }
118
```

7 This new section of code tests to see if the bullet has reached the edge of the screen. It will then remove itself. So bullets won't wrap, but instead only travel until they hit the edge of the screen.

```
4   // listen for key presses
5   spacebarListener = new Object();
6   spacebarListener.onKeyDown = fireBullet;
7   Key.addListener(spacebarListener);
8
9   function initRocks() {
10      rocksArray = new Array();
11
12      // start rocks at number 0
13      rockNum = 0;
14
15      // create four large rocks, 100%, at random locations
16      for (i=0; i<4; i++) {
17          rockMC = newRock(100);
18          rockMC._x = 550*Math.random();
19          rockMC._y = 400*Math.random();
20      }
21  }
22
23  function newRock(size) {
24      // random rock type
25      rockType = Math.floor(3*Math.random()+1);
26
27      // create a new rock
28      rockMC = attachMovie("Rock"+rockType, "rock"+rockNum,
29      // scale it to size
```

8 To determine if a bullet and a rock meet, you first have to start keeping tabs on the rocks. Right now they're all independent objects. You need to create an array and store a reference to each rock in the array.

```
23  function newRock(size) {
24      // random rock type
25      rockType = Math.floor(3*Math.random()+1);
26
27      // create a new rock
28      rockMC = attachMovie("Rock"+rockType, "rock"+rockNum,
29
30      // scale it to size
31      rockMC._xscale = size;
32      rockMC._yscale = size;
33
34      // random speed and direction
35      rockMC.dx = 4*(Math.random()-.5);
36      rockMC.dy = 4*(Math.random()-.5);
37
38      // move every 50 ms
39      setInterval(moveRocks,50,rockMC);
40
41      // store in array
42      rocksArray.push(rockMC);
43
44      return (rockMC);
45  }
46
47  function moveRocks(rockMC) {
48      // move rock
49      rockMC._x += rockMC.dx;
50      rockMC._y += rockMC.dy;
51
52      // wrap around screen
53      if (rockMC._x>550) rockMC._x = 570;
```

9 The above code will add each rock to the array as it's created.

```
115 function moveBulletFunction() {
116     // move bullet
117     bulletSpeed = 10.0;
118     this._x += bulletSpeed*this.dx;
119     this._y += bulletSpeed*this.dy;
120
121     // see if reached end of screen
122     if (this._x > 550) this.removeMovieClip();
123     if (this._x < 0) this.removeMovieClip();
124     if (this._y > 400) this.removeMovieClip();
125     if (this._y < 0) this.removeMovieClip();
126
127     // loop through rocks to see if bullet hit any
128     for (var i = _root.rocksArray.length-1; i>=0; i--) {
129         if (_root.rocksArray[i].hitTest(this._x, this._y)) {
130
131             // remove bullet
132             this.removeMovieClip();
133
134             // deal with rock destruction
135             _root.hitRock(_root.rocksArray[i]);
136
137             // remove rock from array
138             _root.rocksArray.splice(i, 1);
139         }
140     }
141 }
```

10 This code, added to the moveBulletFunction function will check each rock in the array to see if the bullet has collided with it. If so, the bullet removes itself, it calls the hitRock function to let the rock deal with its own destruction, and the rock is removed from the array.

```
136             // remove rock from array
137             _root.rocksArray.splice(i, 1);
138         }
139     }
140 }
141 }
142
143 function hitRock(rockMC) {
144     if (rockMC._xscale > 25) {
145         // if rock is large enough, split in two
146         for (var i=0; i<2;i++) {
147             // new rocks are half the size
148             // starting at old location
149             newRockMC = newRock(rockMC._xscale/2);
150             newRockMC._x = rockMC._x;
151             newRockMC._y = rockMC._y;
152         }
153     }
154
155     // remove old rock
156     rockMC.removeMovieClip();
157 }
158
```

11 The hitRock function will check the rock's scale. If it's greater than 25 per cent, it'll create two new rocks at half the original rock's scale. So a rock at 100 per cent will split to two 50 per cent rocks; a rock at 50 per cent will split into two 25 per cent rocks; and a 25 per cent rock will just disappear. The old rock movie clip will be removed. You can test the movie now to see the bullets in action.

```
83      // move ship
84      ship._x += ship.dx;
85      ship._y += ship.dy;
86
87      // wrap around screen
88      if (ship._x > 550) ship._x -= 550;
89      if (ship._x < 0) ship._x += 550;
90      if (ship._y > 400) ship._y -= 400;
91      if (ship._y < 0) ship._y += 400;
92
93      // see if ship hit rock
94      for(var i in rocksArray) {
95          if (rocksArray[i].hitTest(ship._x,ship._y)) {
96              gotoAndStop("lose");
97          }
98      }
99  }
100
101 function fireBullet() {
102     if (Key.getAscii() == 32) {
103         // create new bullet at level 1000+bulletNum
104         bulletMC = attachMovie("Bullet", "bullet"+bulletNum,
105
106         // start at center of ship
107         bulletMC._x = ship._x;
108         bulletMC._y = ship._y;
109
110         // direction of ship
111
```

12 The new code added to moveShip will loop through the array of rocks and check to see if any is too close to the ship. If so, the movie jumps to the "lose" frame.

Part 5: Prepare to die

Making sure the player doesn't get killed immediately…

```
132         if (this._y < 0) this.removeMovieClip();
133
134     // loop through rocks to see if bullet hit any
135     for (var i = _root.rocksArray.length-1; i>=0; i--) {
136         if (_root.rocksArray[i].hitTest(this._x, this._y)) {
137
138             // remove bullet
139             this.removeMovieClip();
140
141             // deal with rock destruction
142             _root.hitRock(_root.rocksArray[i]);
143
144             // remove rock from array
145             _root.rocksArray.splice(i, 1);
146
147             // see if all rocks are gone
148             if (_root.rocksArray.length == 0) {
149                 gotoAndStop("win");
150             }
151         }
152     }
153 }
154
155 function hitRock(rockMC) {
156     if (rockMC._xscale > 25) {
157         // if rock is large enough, split in two
```

1 This new code added to the moveBulletFunction function will check to see if there are any rocks left in the array. If not, then the player has destroyed them all. The game jumps to the "win" frame.

```
1   initRocks();
2   initShip();
3
4   // listen for key presses
5   spacebarListener = new Object();
6   spacebarListener.onKeyDown = fireBullet;
7   Key.addListener(spacebarListener);
8
9   // start time for game
10  gameStartTime = getTimer();
11
12  function initRocks() {
13      rocksArray = new Array();
14
15      // start rocks at number 0
16      rockNum = 0;
17
18      // create four large rocks, 100%, at random locations
19      for (i=0; i<4; i++) {
20          rockMC = newRock(100);
21          rockMC._x = 550*Math.random();
22          rockMC._y = 400*Math.random();
23      }
24  }
25
26  function newRock(size) {
27      // random rock type
28      rockType = Math.floor(3*Math.random()+1);
29
30      // create a new rock
```

2 You need to avoid the case where the game starts with a rock already on top of the ship because this gives the player no hope of survival. So record the time that the game started.

```
70  function moveShip() {
71      // rotate ship left and right
72      if (Key.isDown(Key.LEFT)) {
73          ship._rotation -= 5;
74      }
75      if (Key.isDown(Key.RIGHT)) {
76          ship._rotation += 5;
77      }
78
79      // thrust forward
80      if (Key.isDown(Key.UP)) {
81          shipAngle = 2.0*Math.PI*(ship._rotation-90)/360.0;
82          ship.dx += Math.cos(shipAngle);
83          ship.dy += Math.sin(shipAngle);
84      }
85
86      // move ship
87      ship._x += ship.dx;
88      ship._y += ship.dy;
89
90      // wrap around screen
91      if (ship._x > 550) ship._x -= 550;
92      if (ship._x < 0) ship._x += 550;
93      if (ship._y > 400) ship._y -= 400;
94      if (ship._y < 0) ship._y += 400;
95
96      // see if ship hit rock
97      if (getTimer() - gameStartTime > 3000) {
98          for(var i in rocksArray) {
99              if (rocksArray[i].hitTest(ship._x,ship._y)) {
100                 gotoAndStop("lose");
```

3 You need to make sure that the game has been going on for at least three seconds before allowing the player to die. ❯

Part 6: Game over screen and score card

Adding animated thrusters, scoring and closing screens…

Additional frames

You can add a lot more than three frames if you want to. As long as no scripts are placed in any of these new frames, the movie clip will animate to the end and loop back to frame 1.

Multiple levels

You may choose to create a game with multiple levels. This can get tricky, but it basically comes down to not resetting the score after a win, and also increasing the speed or number of rocks when the new level begins. This will require expert ActionScript skills.

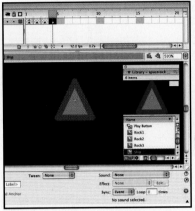

1 Open the Library panel and double-click on the Ship movie clip. Select the second frame and press F6 to duplicate the first keyframe there. Do this three times to create frame 2, 3 and 4.

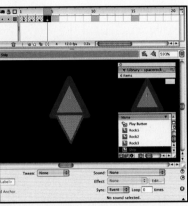

2 Go to each of the frames 2, 3 and 4, and add flames to the bottom of the ship. Each of these three frames should have differently shaped flames. When the thrusters fire, the ship will animate between frames 2, 3 and 4 very quickly.

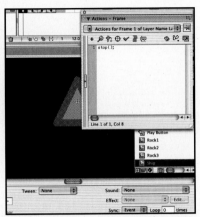

3 Choose the first frame and press F9 to bring up the script panel. Add the 'stop();' script – without this, the ship movie clip will continuously animate from the very start.

4 Add this code to the moveShip function. This checks to see whether the ship is already animating, and will only jump to frame 2 if it's not. Once on frame 2, the animation will automatically continue to frames 3 and 4 and then back to 1. At that point, if the up arrow is still down, the animation will start again.

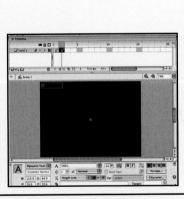

5 Use the Text tool to create a text area at the top-left side of the screen. Start this area with the number 0. Use the Property Inspector to set its type to Dynamic Text and its 'Var' to 'score'.

6 Add this code to start the score of the game at 0. The variable 'score' and the text field created in the previous step are linked, so any changes to the variable score will be immediately shown in the text field.

7 In the hitRock function, award the player ten points each time a rock has been hit.

8 Back in the main timeline, select the third frame and press F7 to create a new keyframe there. Use the Property Inspector to name this frame 'win'. Create graphics for this 'win' frame. We re-used the graphics from the first frame but with some additional text. Also include the Play button so that the user can start a new game.

9 Now select the fourth frame in the main timeline and press F7 to create a new keyframe there. Name this frame 'lose' and add graphics to it. Include the Play button again so the user can start a new game.

SET YOURSELF FREE

Save time, hassle and money with open source software. We show you how to kit out your PC with the best the Net has to offer.

ONLY IN ISSUE 109 OF .net ON SALE NOW

.net ON SALE NOW!
www.netmag.co.uk

IN AMAZING MONOCOLOR

Illustration: Pete Draper [w] www.xenomorphic.co.uk

UP TO 2 PLAYER TERROR!

Space Invaders

With the Flash games market thriving like never before, we're going back in time to learn from an old classic and revive it in 46 steps!

Tutorial and code by Niklas Alvaeus
[e] helloniklas@yahoo.com
[w] www.helloniklas.com
Graphics and animation by Suman Joshi
[e] suman@zoom.co.uk

Files on disc

The files that support this tutorial can be found in the Tutorial\gm_space folder on the Cover CD.

Let's see what we can learn from recreating the mother of all space games in the modern environment of Flash MX. The concept is simple — evil aliens move faster and faster down the screen towards a defending ground ship. However, programming Space Invaders will take you through some of the most essential development techniques that you'll come to use, whatever action game you want to create. We'll show you how to clone a single alien into a full armada of evil shooting creatures; how to detect collisions between different objects and time them with explosions and sounds; how to add user key control; and how to count scores. We'll finish it all off by setting up a score board.

To follow this tutorial you'll need to have a good understanding of how to use the Flash MX environment and at least a basic understanding of ActionScripting using dotted syntax. If, up until now, you've only briefly played around with ActionScript and have never used it in Expert mode, you should prepare yourself for a bumpy ride. Still, these could be your first vital steps into the powerful world of ActionScripting.

Before starting with the 45 steps below, have a good look at the finished product which is supplied on the CD. Play through the game until you're familiar with all the different events that occur in it, as well as all the different objects that exist and how they behave. Happy reading! >

Part 1: Setting up the graphics

Create all the explosions, aliens and spaceship images you'll need…

Storing your ActionScripts and frame labels

It's good practice to keep your frame labels on their own layer, separate from code and graphics, and let it stay on top of all the other layers. Separating your ActionScripts over different layers will also enhance the readability of the code and bring a clear structure to the build of the game.

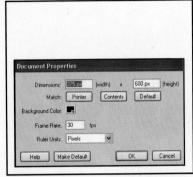

1 To start with, you'll need to launch Flash MX and create a new document. Begin by modifying its basic properties (Modify>Document). Change the dimensions to 375 pixels width and 600 pixels height. Now change the background colour to black and set the frame rate to 30 fps. Finally, click OK.

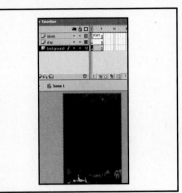

2 Insert two new layers. Name the top one Labels, the bottom one Background and the middle one Ship. With the Background layer selected, import a bitmap and place it on stage at position 0, 0. Click on the first frame in the Labels layer and set the frame label name to "start".

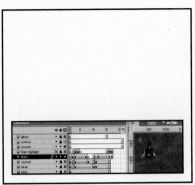

3 Create a new movie clip (Ctrl+F8) and name it mcShip. This clip will hold the graphics for the defending spaceship. Add layers for labels, actions, sounds and whatever other layers you'll need for the graphics. The ship itself will have three states: one when it's doing nothing, one when it's shooting and one when it's dying.

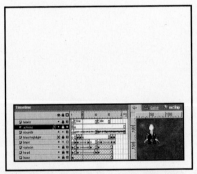

4 Inside mcShip create frame labels called "fire" and "die" on the Labels layer. Fill the frames under label "fire" with animations and sounds for the spaceship shooting, and the frames under label "die" with animations and sounds for the spaceship dying. Leave the first frame for its normal state. Create a keyframe on this first frame on the Actions layer and put the code stop() on it.

5 Go back to the main timeline and select the Ship layer. Drag the new movie clip of the ship onto the stage. Select the movie clip and give it the instance name mcShip. The space ship is now ready for action but leave it there for now.

6 Create another movie clip (Ctrl+F8) called mcAlien1. Set it up with two layers, one called Actions and one called Graphics. This movie clip will have two frames to create the aliens' stepping animation that is the trademark of the classic Space Invaders game, the first frame showing first position and the second the other position. Put the code stop() in the first frame on the Actions layer to prevent the clip from looping.

7 Go back to the main timeline and create another layer called gfx. With the gfx layer selected, drag out the movie clip mcAlien1 from the library and onto the stage. Select the movie clip and convert it into a second nested movie clip by pressing F8. Call it mcAlienA. Double click on the new movie clip mcAlienA to get into its timeline.

8 Like the ship we created in step 3, this alien will also need three states: one normal, one when it's been hit and one when it's dead. Create new layers for labels, actions, sounds and explosions. Leave the mcAlien1 on its own layer called Alien. Select mcAlien1 and give it the instance name Alien. We will need to reference this movie clip later on to animate between the two frames that reside in it.

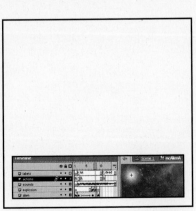

9 Create a tween of the alien exploding, starting from the frame labelled "hit". Add the sound starting from the same frame. Leave the frames empty under the frame labelled "dead". Add the code play() on the Actions layer under the "hit" frame. Add a stop() under the "dead" frame.

Masking bitmaps

Converting the vector graphics into bitmaps can greatly increase the speed of the game. Simply take a screen grab of your objects in Flash, crop them down in Photoshop and save them as .gifs or .png files with a transparent background. Import them back into Flash and replace your vector graphics with the bitmap. Sometimes you get a smoother result by putting a mask around the imported bitmap instead of using the transparency in the image.

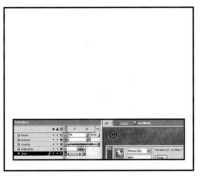

10 Repeat the process from step 6 two more times, creating a movie clip, mcAlien2, that resides inside a movie clip called mcAlienB and a third alien called mcAlien3 that resides inside mcAlienC. Don't forget to set the instance name of all of them to Alien. Since they all sit inside different movie clips they will have a unique reference path, although they all have the instance name Alien.

11 You should now have three aliens sitting on the layer called gfx on the main timeline. Select each one of them and give them the instance names of mcAlienA, mcAlienB and mcAlienC respectively. Note that the instance name doesn't have to be the same as that of the symbol, but it makes it easier to keep track of things.

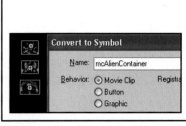

12 Select all three aliens and press F8 (Insert> Convert to Symbol). Select Movie Clip and type the name mcAlienContainer. We now have a single movie clip on the stage called mcAlienContainer which contains all three aliens. This will make it more efficient later on when we will animate all the aliens moving across the stage as we will just have to change the properties of mcAlienContainer to make all the movie clips inside it move. Select the movie clip mcAlienContainer and set its instance name to mcAlienContainer.

13 Create a new movie clip and name it mcAlienShot. Put some graphics resembling a bullet on its first frame. Drag it out to the main timeline on the gfx layer. Select it and give it the instance name of mcAlienShot.

14 Create another movie clip and name it mcShipShot. Inside, create layers for labels, actions, sounds, explosions and layers for the graphics. We use a masked bitmap for this. Put the graphics of the bullet itself on the first frame.

15 Create a label named Explosion on the second keyframe on the layer Labels. Put a small explosion on this key frame. Add the code stop() on the first frame on the Actions layer, play() on the frame labelled Explode and another stop() on the last frame.

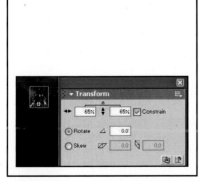

16 Go back to the main timeline and create a new layer called Lives. Select your ship mcShip and press Ctrl+C to copy it. Select the layer Lives you just created and press Ctrl+V to paste in a copy of the ship. With the copied ship selected, press Ctrl+T to bring up the transform palette. Change the scale to about 65 per cent with the Constrain box ticked.

17 Make two more copies of the scaled down copy of the ship and place them next to each other towards the top right corner of the stage. Give them the instance names of mcLife1, mcLife2 and mcLife3 respectively.

18 Create a new layer on the main timeline called Outlines and another one called Score. Draw a grid on the layer Outlines. Select the Score layer and type the text "Score", followed by an empty text box. Select the empty text box and make sure it's set to Dynamic text. Set its Var property to Score. ➤

Part 2: Creating the game and high score table

Animate your images as you recreate the classic alien attack…

Accessing movie clip properties

To access a movie clip's properties dynamically with ActionScripting, use the _root["myclip" + i]_x; instead of the older myClip = eval("_root.myclip" + i); myClip._x; statement. Using the older eval-style statements can, in certain circumstances, cause problems in Flash MX, and it's much more hassle anyway.

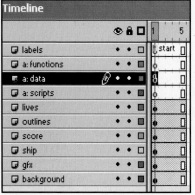

1 Select the mcShip movie clip. Press F9 to bring up the Actions panel and add an onClipEvent(enterFrame). The code inside the brackets will run as frequently as the frame rate of the movie. Check if the right arrow key is pressed and that the x position of the movie clip mcShip is less than 365 to prevent it going off stage. If it does, we increase the x position of mcShip by four pixels. If the left arrow key is pressed and the position is more than 10, decrease the x position. We've now got key control of mcShip.

2 Create three new layers on the main timeline called a: functions, a: data and a: scripts. These layers will hold functions, data and scripts calling the functions. Select the first keyframe on the a: data layer and press F9 to open the Actions panel.

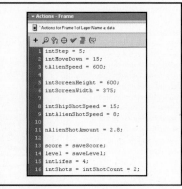

3 Initialise the variables we will use. Place the a: scripts layer beneath the a: data and a: functions layers to make sure the functions and data are loaded before we make any use of them from the a: script layer. Select the first frame on the layer a: functions. We'll keep our functions here.

4 Add a function called fCreateAliens() which will duplicate the three aliens (mcAlienA, mcAlienB and mcAlienC) into a whole armada of 49 aliens with the instance names mcAlien1, mcAlien2, mcAlien3 and so on, up to mcAlien49. They will all reside in the movie clip mcAlienContainer, so their full reference path is mcAlienContainer.mcAlien1, mcAlienContainer.mcAlien2 and so on. Save a reference to each one of them inside an array called arrAliens. Set a variable called intNumber in every one of them saying which one of the 49 aliens they actually are.

5 Position the mcAlienContainer towards the top left of the stage and hide the movie clips of our original aliens by putting them far off the stage.

6 Click on the first frame on the a: scripts layer and add a call to the fCreateAliens function. Put a stop() afterwards to halt the play head on the first frame. Running the Flash file should produce a group of 49 aliens sitting at the top of the stage.

7 Create a new movie clip (Ctrl+F8) and name it mcScreenStop. Draw a solid shape about 20 pixels wide and as high as the whole stage (600 pixels) on its first frame. Go back to the main timeline and drag two instances of the new movie clip out on the stage. Give them the instance name of mcBorderLeft and mcBorderRight and put them just outside the edges of the stage.

8 Click on the first frame in the a: functions layer and press F9 to bring up the Actions panel. Add a new function called fStep(). Loop through all the aliens stored in the array arrAliens and check what frame the movie clip alien is on (see step 8 in part 1). Change the frame of the movie clip alien to create the stepping animation.

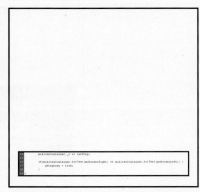

9 Change the x position of all the aliens by adding the variable intStep to the x position of movie clip mcAlienContainer. Check if mcAlienContainer reached either side of the screen by seeing if it has collided with mcBorderRight or mcBorderLeft. Set the variable nStepDown to true if this has happened.

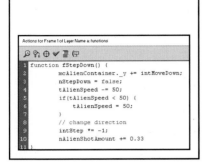

```
Actions for Frame 1 of Layer Name a: functions

1  function fStepDown() {
2      mcAlienContainer._y += intMoveDown;
3      nStepDown = false;
4      tAlienSpeed -= 50;
5      if(tAlienSpeed < 50) {
6          tAlienSpeed = 50;
7      }
8      // change direction
9      intStep *= -1;
10     nAlienShotAmount += 0.33
11 }
```

10 Add another function called fStepDown() that moves the mcAlienContainer downwards by the value in intMoveDown every time they reach either side of the screen. Negate the value in intStep to make the aliens move in the opposite direction next time the function fStep() is called. Decrease the value in tAlienSpeed, making the aliens gradually move faster and faster every time they turn.

11 Create a new movie clip (Ctrl+F8) and name it mcController. Exit the clip and go back to the main timeline. Drag the movie clip out on the stage. Select it and press F9 to bring up the Actions panel.

```
1  onClipEvent(load) {
2      tThen = getTimer();
3      tThen2 = getTimer();
4  }
5
6  onClipEvent(enterFrame) {
7      if(getTimer() - tThen > _root.tAlienSpeed
8          if(_root.nStepDown) {
9              _root.fStepDown();
10         }
11         else {
12             _root.fStep();
13         }
14         tThen = getTimer();
15     }
16 }
```

12 Add an onClipEvent(load) and set the variables tThen and tThen2 to the current time. Add an onClipEvent(enterFrame). Check if the current time minus tThen is greater than the value in _root.tAlienSpeed. If so, call the function fStepDown or fStep, depending on the state of nStepDown. This will make the aliens step sideways with an interval of _root.tAlienSpeed and step downwards when they reach the end of either side of the stage. Reset tThen to the current time again.

13 Go back to the main timeline and select the first frame on layer a: functions. Add a function called fShipShot(). Duplicate mcShipShot into a new movie clip with the name mcShipShot, plus the variable intShotCount. This will create movie clips which alternate their names between mcShipShot1 and mcShipShot2 every time the ship is shooting, permitting more than one duplicate on screen at the same time. Set its position to line up with the ship.

14 Select mcShip and press F9 to bring up the Actions panel. Add an onClipEvent(load) and set the variable tShotShipTime to the current time. In the onClipEvent(enterFrame) add a check for the Space key and go to frame "fire" if one second (1000ms) has passed since the last time Space was pressed. Add a call to a function called _root.fAlienShot() that will let the aliens shoot back when they're being shot at.

```
_root.fShipDead();
stop();
```

15 Double click on the mcShip and add a call to _root.fShipShot() on the Actions layer under the label "fire". This will time the ship's fire animation and sound with the function that triggers the mcShipShot movie clip. Also add a call to _root.fShipDead() on the last frame.

```
Actions for mcShipShot (mcShipShot)

1  onClipEvent(enterFrame) {
2      if(_name != "mcShipShot") {
3          _y -= _root.intShipShotSpeed;
4          if(_y < 0) {
5              this.removeMovieClip();
6          }
7      }
8  }
```

16 Go back to the main timeline and select mcShipShot. Press F9 to bring up the Actions panel. Add an onClipEvent(enterFrame). Check that the name of this movie clip is not mcShipShot as the code here only should affect duplicates of mcShipShot and not the original movie clip. Move it upwards on the screen by decreasing its y position with _root.intShipShotSpeed. Remove the movie clip if it goes off stage.

17 Select mcAlienShot. Add similar code here as in mcShipShot but let it move downwards. Check if it hits mcShip and tell mcShip to die if it does. Also, check if it hits one of the duplicates of mcShipShot and tell it to explode if it does.

```
Actions for Frame 1 of Layer Name a: functions

32 function fShipDead() {
33     intLifes--;
34     if(intLifes <= 0) {
35         gotoAndStop("gameOver");
36     }
37     else {
38         _root["mcLife" + intLifes]._alpha = 30;
39         mcShip.gotoAndStop(1);
40     }
41 }
```

18 Go back to the main timeline and select the first frame on a: functions. Add a function called fShipDead(). Decrease the variable intLifes and go to a frame labelled "gameOver" if all lives are gone. If there are lives left, fade out one of the duplicate mcLifes by changing its alpha value (see step 17 in part 1). Reset mcShip to its first frame. ▶

Speeding up sound effects and music

If you end up using a lot of sounds with MP3 compression you may find that it take an awful lot of time to publish your movie. Changing the MP3 compression to "fast" in the publish settings (File>Publish Settings) is a good way to temporarily override the more time-consuming "best" setting on your sound clips without having to restore all your individual settings.

19 Add another function called fAlienShot() that takes the parameter amount. Randomly pick one of the aliens from the array arrAliens. Position a duplicate of mcAlienShot at the picked alien's position. Repeat this for as many times as the value in variable amount, creating new duplicates of mcAlienShot every time.

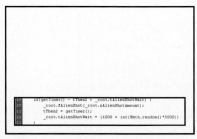

20 Select the movie clip mcController created in step 11. Add a new if statement that triggers the _root.fAlienShot() at intervals of _root.tAlienShotWait. Send in the parameter _root.nAlienShotAmount to tell it how many alien shots to generate. This gets increased by a third every time fStepDown() runs, making one more alien shot every third time the aliens steps downwards on the stage (see step 12).

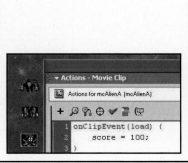

21 Double click on the movie clip mcAlienContainer on the stage. Select the movie clip mcAlienA that resides inside it and press F9 to bring up the Actions panel. Add an onClipEvent(load) and set the variable score to 100.

22 Add an onClipEvent(enterFrame) after the onClipEvent(load). Check if any of the duplicates of mcShipShot (see step 13) has hit this alien. If so, loop through the array arrAliens to find this alien's position in the array, remove it from the array and break out of the loop. This will prevent the dead alien from being triggered by fAlienShot() (see step 19). Tell the alien to go to frame "hit" and remove the duplicate of mcShipShot that has hit it.

23 Double click on the movie clip mcAlienA to go into its timeline. Add a key frame on the Actions layer under the frame label "dead". Add the variable score set up in step 21 to the variable _root.score which is mirrored on the stage (see step 18). Check how many aliens are left in the array arrAliens. If none are left, call the function _root.fLevelDone(). Remove the movie clip. Repeat the process from step 21 with mcAlienB and mcAlienC but give them different score values.

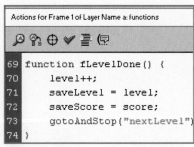

24 Go back to the main timeline and select the first frame on the a: functions layer. Add the function fLevelDone(). Increase the variable level and store the variables score and level in a pair of new variables. Insert a gotoAndStop frame label called "nextLevel". Create two new frame labels on the main timeline called "nextLevel" and "gameOver".

25 Create a keyframe under the frame label "nextLevel". Put a button that jumps back to the label "start" when pressed. Create another keyframe under the frame label "gameOver" and put a button here with code to check if the current score is higher than the lowest score in the high score list. Go to a frame labelled "newHigh" in a new scene called Highscore if there's a new high score. Otherwise go to a label called "highScore".

26 Insert a new scene (Insert>Scene) and name it Highscore. Create layers for labels, a: scripts, text and for any graphics you want. Create two keyframes and label them "newHigh" and "highScore". Under the frame labelled "newHigh" put a stop(). On the a: scripts layer add an input text field with the Var field set to newname. Now add a button that goes to the frame labelled highScore when pressed.

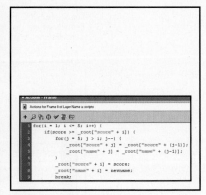

27 Under the frame labelled "highScore" put five dynamic text fields in two columns named name1 to name5 and score1 to score5. Add a script to the frame in the a: script layer that checks which position in the list the new score has. Move down the other high scores from that position, leaving the bottom one to go off the list and add the new one to its position in the list. Add a "play again" button that jumps to label "start" in the scene where the game is. Finally, add a new scene called "intro" that comes before the game starts. Initialise the variables score1 – score5 and name1 – name6 here.

Internet WOrks

Business without boundaries

NEWLOOK NEWDIRECTION NEWIDEAS

- AUTHORITATIVE ANALYSIS
- INSIDER STRATEGIES
- PRACTICAL SOLUTIONS
- ESSENTIAL LEGAL AID

PLUS
Expert advice from key industry players

MAKE MORE ON YOUR BOTTOM LINE!

ON SALE TUESDAY 18 MARCH 2003 ONLY £3.99

"Don't let the technology drive the business, but let the business needs and those of customers determine the way technology is exploited"

STEPHEN TIMMS MINISTER OF STATE FOR E-COMMERCE

NEW LOOK MAGAZINE!

Internet WOrks

www.iwks.com

Business without boundaries

REVEALED!
THE TRUTH BEHIND THE GOVERNMENT PROMISES FOR E-COMMERCE

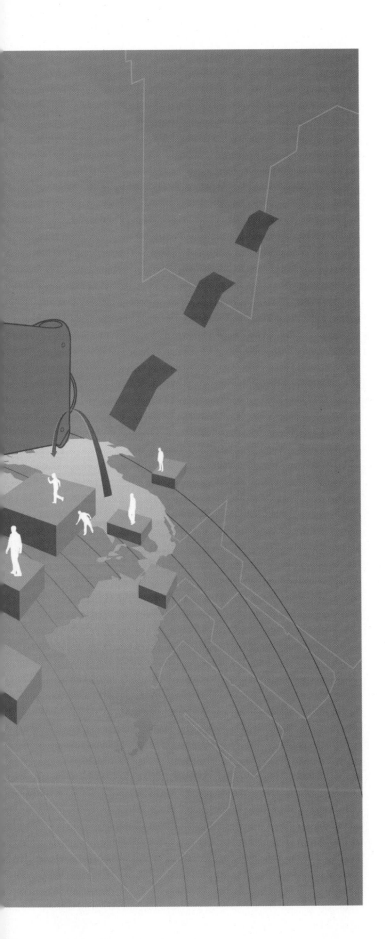

Game techniques

Developing Flash games helps you fine-tune many techniques that you can use elsewhere – creating pre-loaders for large files or projects for Pocket PCs, for example

100000

80000

60000

40000

20000   ACTION

0

1UP

```
MovieClip.prototype.shootBullet = function() {
    if (_root.bulletOnScreen == false) {
        _root.attachMovie("bullets", "liveBullet", 1);
        currentBullet = _root["liveBullet"];
        currentBullet._x = this._x;
        currentBullet._y = this._y;
        currentBullet._rotation = this._rotation;
        _root.bulletOnScreen = true;
```

Five essential ActionScript commands for gaming

When it comes to games and interactivity, ActionScript is the prime component for success. We're going to briefly step through five essential ActionScript structures for games programming and compile them all into a simple Asteroids-style game…

1 Keyboard control
Detecting and acting on the player's keyboard inputs.

3 Moving sprites
Making the bullets fly in the direction in which you fired them.

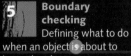
5 Boundary checking
Defining what to do when an object is about to leave the play area.

All of these structures are described in a modular

2 Creating assets
Taking your sprites from the Library and into the game world proper.

4 Detecting collisions
Reacting to two objects coming into contact.

fashion. This means that you can use them in the Asteroids-style game which we've provided code for in this feature, or you can take the structures out and plug them into any other games that you create. ❯

Expertise provided by Kristian Besley and Ben Renow-Clarke.
[e] ken@pinderkaas.com or [w] www.pinderkaas.com

Files on disc
The files needed to support this tutorial can be found in the Tutorial\feat_action folder on the cover CD.

Illustration: Magictorch [w] www.magictorch.com

Preparing the asteroids movie

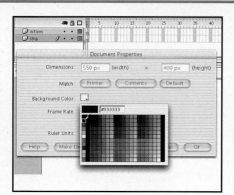

1 In a new movie, insert a new layer on the main timeline and rename the layers to Actions and Ship. Then choose Modify>Document and change the background colour to dark grey (#333333).

2 The next step is to draw a simple spaceship on the Ship layer and convert it into a movie clip symbol. Give your spaceship the name Ship and give it a central registration point.

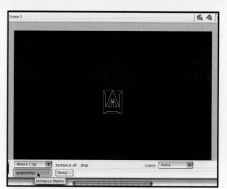

3 Finally, simply select the Ship movie clip on the main stage and give it the instance name of Spaceship. Believe it or not, we've now prepared our entire movie for the asteroids!

1. Keyboard control: Listeners 01_keyListener.fla

Every game needs to detect some kind of input from the player, and the most common computer input device is the keyboard. Flash MX introduced keyboard Listeners for detecting input, which are far more efficient and processor-friendly than the old methods because they don't require a loop to check every frame. In the Asteroids game, the motion is limited to simple left and right rotation only.

All of the code in this exercise will be on the same frame, so select frame 1 of the Actions layer and enter the following code:

```
MovieClip.prototype.keyboardControl = function(toMove, rotSpeed) {
kbdGet = new Object();
kbdGet.onKeyDown = function() {
    if (Key.isDown(Key.SPACE)) {
        trace ("Fire!");
    }
    if (Key.isDown(Key.RIGHT)) {
        toMove._rotation += rotSpeed;
    }
if (Key.isDown(Key.LEFT)) {
        toMove._rotation -= rotSpeed;
    }
}
```

```
Key.addListener(kbdGet);
};

//initialisation
keyboardControl (spaceship, 20);
```

This code defines a method called keyboardControl that checks for input. When either cursor key is pressed the ship is rotated while a spacebar press displays "Fire!".

2. Attaching from the Library

02_attachMovie.fla

Whether it's another enemy or another weapon to defeat it with, creating new items is an essential part of all games.

Before attaching a bullet, you need to draw one. Create a new movie clip symbol called Bullet and draw a bullet inside it. Centre it on the stage and then return to the main timeline.

The Bullet movie clip now needs a Linkage name. Right-click on it in the Library and select Linkage. Tick the Export for ActionScript box and enter bullets as the Identifier, then click OK.

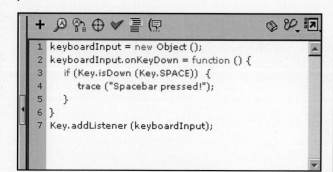

```
1  keyboardInput = new Object ();
2  keyboardInput.onKeyDown = function () {
3      if (Key.isDown (Key.SPACE)) {
4          trace ("Spacebar pressed!");
5      }
6  }
7  Key.addListener (keyboardInput);
```

Here is a typical script to send a message to the Output window when the spacebar is hit. Some example movement types are included on the CD.

Add elements dynamically from the Library using attachMovie.

Back in frame 1 of the Actions layer, add the following code before everything else:

```
MovieClip.prototype.shootBullet = function() {
    if (_root.bulletOnScreen == false) {
        _root.attachMovie("bullets", "liveBullet", 1);
        currentBullet = _root["liveBullet"];
        currentBullet._x = this._x;
        currentBullet._y = this._y;
        currentBullet._rotation = this._rotation;
        _root.bulletOnScreen = true;
    }
}
```

This part of the method attaches a copy of the Bullet movie clip from the library, giving it the instance name liveBullet. The bullet is then positioned in the same place as the calling object.

In the keyboardControl method, change the code for the spacebar to:

```
if (Key.isDown(Key.SPACE)) {
    toMove.shootBullet ();
}
```

This will change the spacebar so it fires a bullet.

Add the following line of code to the very end of the script:

```
bulletOnScreen=false;
```

The bulletOnScreen variable is used to limit the number of bullets which appear on screen at any time to one.

Test the movie, and when you press the spacebar you'll see the bullet appear and mimic the ship's x, y and rotation.

3. Changing movie clip Properties: moving sprites 03_moveBullet.fla

Now that the bullet is on screen it needs to move a little, and a few additions to the shootBullet method will take care of this. Before we do this, look at the screen on the right. This shows the standard syntax to set the x and y properties of an object so that it moves consistently.

Remove the last two braces from the shootBullet method and add the following code:

```
currentBullet.calculateSpeed (_root.bulletSpeed);
currentBullet.onEnterFrame = function() {
        currentBullet._y -= currentBullet.yadd;
        currentBullet._x += currentBullet.xadd;
        if ((currentBullet._x>_root.stageWidth) ||
(currentBullet._x<0) || (currentBullet._y>_root.stageHeight) ||
(currentBullet._y<0) {
            currentBullet.removeMovieClip();
            _root.bulletOnScreen = false;
        }
    }
}
```

This part of the method does two things — it moves the bullet and it also checks to see if it is still on the screen.

The calculateSpeed method called in the shootBullet method uses a little math to calculate the x and y speed according to its angle, filling the variables xadd and yadd with the results. These are then used in the shootBullet function to move the bullet according to its current position.

```
MovieClip.prototype.calculateSpeed = function(velocity) {
    this.xadd = velocity*Math.sin(this._rotation*(Math.PI/180));
    this.yadd = velocity*Math.cos(this._rotation*(Math.PI/180));
};
```

Add these variables to the very end of the code and then test the movie:

```
_root.bulletSpeed = 10;
_root.stageWidth = 550;
_root.stageHeight = 400;
```

This time the bullet speeds off and allows you to shoot again when it has left the edge of the screen.

As a quick note here, object._y += 2 is just a shorthand way of representing object._y = object.y + 2, and the same goes for -= in the opposite direction.

4. Collision detection with hitTest

04_checkCollision.fla

The simplest method of detecting collisions in Flash involves using the bounding boxes that Flash places around all shapes. Unfortunately, what this means is that, in Flash's eyes, all your circles become squares.

Insert two new layers, one called Text and one called Asteroid. On the Asteroid layer draw a large rock, making it more square than circular so that it will work satisfactorily with our collision detection method. Convert it to a movie clip of the same name with a central registration point and give it an instance name of Asteroid.

Now create a dynamic text box on the text layer and give it the instance name of scoreText. This text box will be used to keep score every time one of the ship's bullets hits an asteroid. The

Detect object collision with the standard Flash method, hitTest.

value of this textbox is set using the following code:

scoreText.text = 50;

The next function is used to increment the score. Insert this script at the very start of the code:

```
keepScore = function (addScore) {
    _root.totalScore += addScore;
    _root.scoreText.text = "Score: "+_root.totalScore;
};
```

Now add the code below. The checkCollision method performs a

hitTest with the parameters sent to it. If true, it tells it which function to perform. The enterFrame code for the asteroid simply runs hitFunction when there is a hit, making sure that the score is incremented.

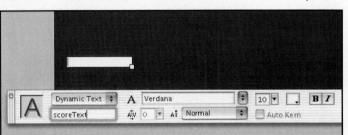

```
MovieClip.prototype.checkCollision = function(toHit,
functionToRun) {
    if (this.hitTest(toHit)) {
        functionToRun(this);
    }
}
hitFunction = function () {
        trace ("the bullet hit the
asteroid!");
    keepScore (100);
}
asteroid.onEnterFrame = function () {

    this.checkCollision(_root.liveBullet,
hitFunction);
}
```

5. Boundary Checking: if statements 05_asteroidMovement.fla

A static asteroid isn't much threat to the galaxy so you need to make it really hurtle through space. In this Flash file, however, the galaxy is only 550 x 400 pixels, so fast-moving asteroids would rapidly disappear. To counteract this, we can make the asteroids bounce off the sides of the screen or loop over to the other side. The most basic syntax for each method is found in the screens shown on the left.

We're using the looping syntax for our game, which means you need a method to move the asteroids and to provide the checking. The way in which we do this is by removing the entire asteroid.onEnterFrame function and adding the following code before everything else:

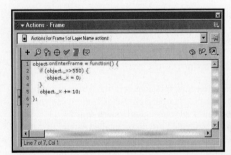

Looping syntax: exit stage left, enter stage right, exit left…

```
MovieClip.prototype.randomMovement =
function(speed) {
    this._rotation = random(360);
    this.calculateSpeed (speed);

    this.onEnterFrame = function() {
        this._y -= this.yadd;
        this._x += this.xadd;
        if (this._y>stageHeight) {
            this._y = 0;
        }
        if (this._y<0) {
            this._y = stageHeight;
        }
        if (this._x>stageWidth) {
            this._x = 0;
        }
        if (this._x<0) {
            this._x = stageWidth;
        }
```

```
    this.checkCollision(_root.liveBullet,
hitFunction);
    }
}
```

This function uses the calculateSpeed method to give the asteroid a direction based on an initial random rotation. The asteroid is moved and the boundaries are checked each frame. The checkCollision code is run to see if it has collided with a bullet.

Add the following at the end of all the code to move the asteroid at a speed of 2.

asteroid.randomMovement (2);

Now run the movie and aim at the asteroid!

You can take a look at asteroids.fla on our cover CD to see the final code that is required to complete the game. And that's it! You've created a classic game using techniques that can be applied elsewhere.

Bouncing syntax: *= -1 here reverses the previous value (from 5 to -5 back to 5).

The finished thing, in all its retro arcade glory. The techniques shown in this tutorial are modular and so they can also be applied to a number of other games. Use them to experiment…

Illustration: Thomas Brodahl [w] www.surfstation.lu [w] www.xtrapop.com

Create a games preloader

Preloaders are essential to let your users know how much of your file has still to load. Here's how you create them…

F lash games tend to be bloated beasts, what with all the sound and data involved. With broadband connections becoming more common, game developers are starting to enjoy the luxury of making even more impressive games that take advantage of these bigger pipes. However, as the majority of UK home Web users are still squeezing data through 56k modems, even a 200k file can turn into a headache.

By adding a preloader to the beginning of your movie you not only provide users with some idea of how long it will take before they can start playing your game but there's also the opportunity to embed information such as game instructions, credits or even a mini game to play while the user waits for the entertainment to start.

Most of the requirements for a preloader are provided through ActionScript, and while you don't need to be a master coder to put the basic method in place, a little understanding of ActionScript syntax is a bonus.

Over the following pages we show you how to make a more effective preloader that recognises the amount of data downloaded and intelligently compares this with the total left, providing a progressive and graphical method of showing the user exactly how much more is still to come.

There is a method of gauging the amount of content downloaded using the Timeline properties of _framesloaded and _totalframes but we're going to use a method that compares the getBytesLoaded() with getBytesTotal(). This is more accurate as individual frame data content is often not evenly spread, while the data equivalent provides a smooth and more progressive load rate, giving the viewer a better idea of when the download will be complete.

As well as the familiar filling bar method, we've added a bit more script to numerically show the percentage of the file downloaded. We don't have space here but you can see how you might embed other information to play back while the file is downloading using regular Flash tools and methods.

All the script that controls the preloader is actually held in a single frame, making this an efficient method not only for developing the original feature but also for minimising any additional weight onto the final size of the delivered file. After all, we don't want to preload the preloader…

Expertise provided by Chris Schmidt. You can contact Chris at [e] chris@track5.co.uk or [w] www.track5.co.uk

Files on disc
The files needed to support this tutorial can be found in the Tutorial\tech_preload folder on the cover CD.

Part 1: Visual reference

Before you jump into the code you need to get your visual elements established…

Original ideas

We've used the filling bar idea here as a generic container that is easily recognisable for most users downloading any kind of information. However, Flash enables you to use any kind of graphical object as a reference to your file's download status so feel free to play around with other ideas that may be more suitable for your game's theme or design.

1 Draw a long rectangle with the stroke and fill being the same colour. Select the border alone and turn this into a graphic symbol called 'container'. This will become the outline of the percentage bar that defines the extent of the expected download.

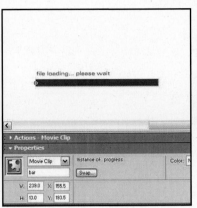

2 Next, select the rectangle's fill and convert to a movie clip, making sure the registration point is at its far left edge. Give this an instance name of 'bar' (without the quotes) in the property inspector so we can reference this through the code later on.

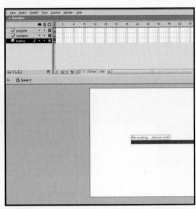

3 With the essential components in place we can now arrange the rest of our layout. We've placed the container and progress symbols on separate layers here and added a little text to make the preloader obvious.

Part 2: Adding the code

Keeping the code simple reduces the download and gets the preloader operating smoothly…

Something for nothing

There's obviously no point creating a preloader if there's nothing to anticipate. If you don't have a suitably large .FLA file in existence, create one using heavy graphics or sound files. Similarly, you won't get the full benefit by running the preloader on files stored locally on either your own computer or a local network as the file will almost certainly load instantly. For the most realistic results, load the completed .SWF file onto a remote server.

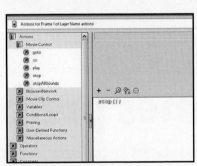

1 Create a new layer at the top of the stack and call this Actions. Select the first frame and insert a Stop action to restrict the movie from playback until the following preloader code criteria has been met.

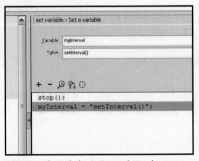

2 Now, through the Actions palette, choose Actions>Variables>Set Variable and enter a name to identify a setInterval action in the Variable field. In the Value field, choose Actions>Miscellaneous Actions>setInterval.

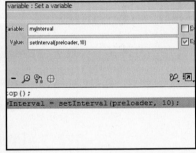

3 Enter the name of a function between the parenthesis of the setInterval action, as shown in the screen above, followed by the interval 10. Now click the expression box. This calls the functions every 10 milliseconds.

Detecting frames

You can easily modify the code here to show the progressive rate that your movie frames are loading in preference to data, as we have here. Simply replace the contents of the Condition field with _framesloaded and _totalframes in place of getBytesLoaded and getBytesTotal respectively, and replace the similar commands in the last statement of the function.

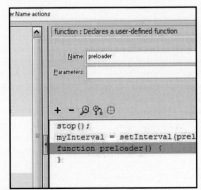

4 To set the actual function, choose Actions>User-Defined Functions>Function and, in the Name Field, enter the name you gave to your function in the setInterval action.

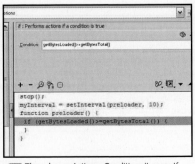

5 Then choose Actions>Conditions/Loops>If and enter the following code into the Condition field: **getBytesLoaded()>=getBytesTotal()** Alternatively, these methods can also be retrieved by choosing Objects>Movie>Movie Clip>Methods if you're not completely confident about entering the code directly.

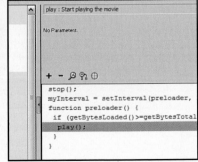

6 The previous step configured the code that compares the amount of data downloaded with the total expected. When this has been met we need to instruct the function on what to do next by adding the Play control via Actions>Movie Control>Play.

Other uses

The more obvious use of the kind of preloader we've created here would be for a data intensive Flash-driven Website. With such simple code already created, you could easily cut and paste the ActionScript before any areas of your site that may require the end user to wait until the download has completed.

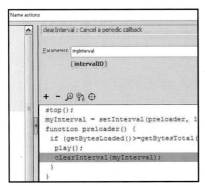

1 After all the data has been received we no longer need the setInterval action so we can remove this by choosing Actions>Miscellaneous Actions>clearInterval and entering the name you used to identify the setInterval action earlier.

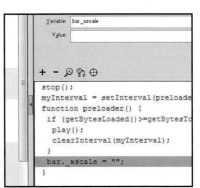

2 The final part is to define the statement that dynamically changes the width of your visual movie clip. Select the closing brace of the If statement and choose Actions>Variables>Set Variables, entering **bar._xscale** as the variable.

3 Enter the code shown above as the value, making sure to check the expression checkbox. To test the function, create a second frame and import a substantial graphic file to affect the preloader, then upload to a remote server and view to see the preloader in action.

Part 3: Adding a numeric display

Using a dynamic text field to create a text alternative to complement the graphic approach…

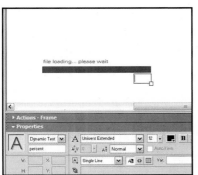

1 Continuing from the previous stage, select the Text tool and drag a text field onto the stage. Give this the name of 'myTextField' in the property inspector so we can target this from the code, as we did with the progress bar previously.

2 Return to the first frame of the Actions layer and expand the Actions palette if necessary to view the code we created previously.

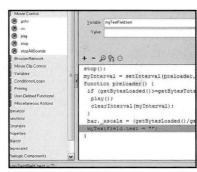

3 Select the last line in the function statement and choose Actions>Variables>Set Variables to create a new line requesting the variable and value attributes. Enter **myTextField.text** as the variable. This refers to the text object which we named in the first step.

4 Enter the value code as shown above, making sure to define this as an expression using the checkbox to the right of the value field. Your code should now be complete and ready to run.

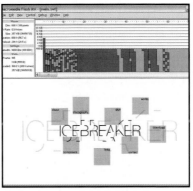

5 You can use Flash's Bandwidth Profiler to see how data is distributed throughout your Flash movie when in test mode. First preview the movie through Control>Test Movie and then toggle the profiler on and off via View>Bandwidth Profiler.

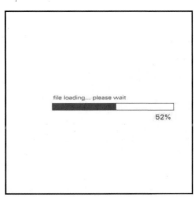

6 The final result should provide a preloader that shows a consistent load rate and which provides the end user with some clear indication as to when the complete file will be available using their connection speed.

Illustration: Magictorch [w] www.magictorch.com

Adding sound to Flash games

Tired of seeing audio clips tacked clumsily onto Flash files? Our tutorial uses new MX capabilities to develop sound as an inherent part of gameplay…

Expertise provided by Jerome Turner. Jerome is a Friends Of Ed author and has worked on several books including Foundation iMovie 2, Foundation Dreamweaver MX and Flash MX Studio.
[w] www.jerometurner.co.uk,
[e] info@jerometurner.co.uk.

Files on disc
The files that accompany this tutorial can be found in the Tutorial\tech_sound folder on the cover CD.

ost Flash designers will have used sound in their work somewhere along the line, but what happens once you tire of simply dragging various 'pings' and 'bongs' onto your buttons? In the same way that sound recordists in film often lose out to the cameraman in terms of recognition for their work, the potential of audio on the Web is often neglected.

We start by showing you how sound can be recorded and prepared before importing to Flash. Then we take a look at how clips work as part of a Flash movie to be manipulated using ActionScript.

The game itself approaches the use of sound from a new angle. Richard The Cat started off as a generic maze hide-and-seek game (CD file soundtut_01.fla) but this tutorial shows you how to develop the idea with ActionScript to incorporate sound as an intrinsic part of the game-playing strategy. When was the last time you played a Flash game that required the use of two of your senses?

Maybe the next version of Flash will have smellovision but for now we start with the game as a half-finished fla, ready to be beefed up by adding our audio files.

Part 1: Creating sound files

The first thing to do is record a demonic laugh…

No program?

If you don't have a sound editing package like Sound Edit or Peak to create your own sound files, you'll find all the sounds used in this tutorial on our cover CD in the Tutorial\tech_sound folder.

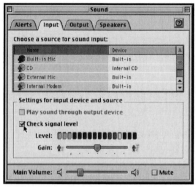

1 Make sure your computer's sound input is set to record using a plugged-in or built-in microphone, depending on what's available to you, then open your sound application.

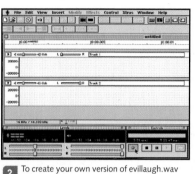

2 To create your own version of evillaugh.wav (which can be found on the cover CD), start a new file, click Record (Window>Controls) and laugh demonically into your microphone. Hit Stop when you've finished but remember not to get too carried away – the longer the sound, the larger the file is going to be in Flash.

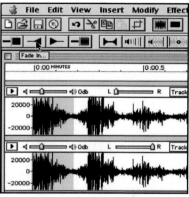

3 Select any 'silent' areas at either end of your recording and trim them. It the sound starts or ends too harshly, cover this area and Fade In or Out.

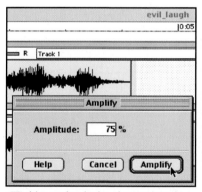

4 If the waveform has lots of contrast between loud and quiet areas, use a 'normalising' effect to centre the volume and then amplify the sound to around three quarters of the maximum level.

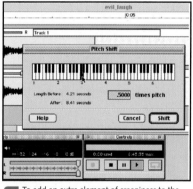

5 To add an extra element of creepiness to the sound, change the pitch or duration to slow down the laughter, then Save As either a WAV or AIFF file for use in Flash.

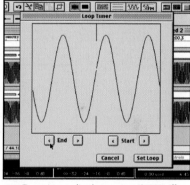

6 To create soundtrack.wav, open JS1010.aiff from the Sound Library files and trim a short looping sequence. Ensure the playback controls are looping, Copy and Paste into a new file and Save.

Part 2: Sound Objects in Flash MX

Make a meowing Sound Object…

1 Start by opening the soundtut_01.fla in Flash MX and read through the comments to guide you through the ActionScript on Frame 1. This is the location for all the code, so Pin the script to make sure the Actions window is always open on this frame.

2 Go to File>Import to Library and select catsound.aif, jingle.aif (also available from the Sound Library) and evillaugh.wav. You will see them listed in the Library panel where they can also be played back and renamed if necessary.

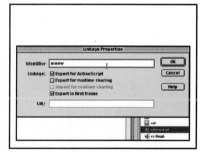

3 ActionScript can refer to sound files in the Library without placing them on the stage, but to do this we need to give each one a Linkage Identifier. Select the catsound.wav file and then Linkage from the Library's drop-down menu. Tick Export for ActionScript and name the Identifier. Repeat for each file. ⟩

Sound Objects in Flash MX continued...

Sound objects

Using Linkage Identifiers, rather than dragging clips onto the stage, means that your work area is more accessible and uncluttered. However, as Sound Objects can seem quite abstract (you can't see them) you might like to think of them as drawers with each one containing a sound file from the Library. Any change or reference to the Sound Object is like opening a drawer and amending the file inside.

```
9   //
10  //This displays the intro.
11  intro.gotoAndStop(1);
12  catDetect = new Sound();
13  catDetect.attachSound("meow");
14  win = new Sound();
15  win.attachSound("jingle");
16  lose = new Sound();
17  lose.attachSound("dead");
18  //This creates a new Object used to
19  //and plays all the rest of the act
```

4 After the first line of ActionScript (Line11), add the commands shown. This creates a Sound Object called catDetect and attaches the audio file via its Identifier "meow". Repeat to make Sound Objects 'win' and 'lose', which will wait here until they're 'called' later in the script.

```
20  start = new Object();
21  start.onKeyDown = function() {
22      if (Key.isDown(Key.SPACE)) {
23          intro.gotoAndStop(2);
24          restartText = "HIT SPACE TO RESTART";
25          statusText = " ";
26          //This initializes the cat and man positio
27          //Note the cat is placed ON TOP of the maz
28          man._visible = true;
29          cat._visible = true;
30          man._x = 10;
31          man._y = 410;
32          cat._x = 10;
33          cat._y = 390;
34          catDetect.start(0, 9999);
35          //This registers the time in milliseconds
36          startTime = getTimer();
37          //All the remaining code loops until the g
38          //been restarted by hitting SPACE.
39          _root.onEnterFrame = function() {
40              // MOVING THE MAN
```

5 Pressing the space bar starts the game. The player then needs to hear the cat meowing, so apply a 'start' command to the catDetect object (line 34). The two parameters (0, 999) specify the point at which the sound should start playing, in seconds, and the number of times it should loop.

```
25          cat._y = 390;
26          //The cat sound is stopped
27          // This avoids the sound be
28          //due to it's repeated loop
29          catDetect.stop();
30          catDetect.start(0, 9999);
31          //This registers the time i
32          startTime = getTimer();
```

6 However, if the space bar has been pressed to restart the game for any reason, catDetect will also start again, on top of the last time it was called, so we check the sound isn't playing each time with a stop command (line 29) placed before the start.

Part 3: Incorporating sound into gameplay

The mathematics of getting your sounds into the game...

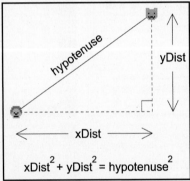

$$xDist^2 + yDist^2 = hypotenuse^2$$

1 Our first instance of incorporating a sound into the gameplay comes in the form of the cat meowing – the closer the man is to the cat, the louder the sound. We need to use Pythagoras' theorem to work out the distance of the man to the cat.

```
68  //starting the loop here.
69  if (maze.hitTest(cat._x, cat._y, true)) {
70      cat._x = 10+(Math.round(Math.random()*19)*20);
71      cat._y = 10+(Math.round(Math.random()*19)*20);
72  }
73  // This calculates the distance from the man to the
74  // in terms of it being the hypotenuse of a right an
75  // triangle given the rule that
76  //xDist squared + yDist squared equals hyp squared.
77  xDist = cat._x-man._x;
78  yDist = cat._y-man._y;
79  hyp = Math.sqrt((xDist*xDist)+(yDist*yDist));
80  // This checks to see if the man has 'found' the cat
81  // and deletes the looping gameplay.
82  if ((man._x == cat._x) && (man._y == cat._y)) {
83      statusText = "YOU FOUND RICHARD!";
84      restartText = "HIT SPACE TO PLAY AGAIN";
```

2 In ActionScript terms the same rule looks like the above. In line 77 xDist is worked out by taking the man's x position from the cat's, and the same applies to yDist. The hypotenuse is found in line 79 using Math.sqrt to find the square root of our equation.

```
77  xDist = cat._x-man._x;
78  yDist = cat._y-man._y;
79  hyp = Math.sqrt((xDist*xDist)+(yDist*yDist));
80  // This checks to see if the man has 'found' t
81  // and deletes the looping gameplay.
82  if (hyp==0) {
83      statusText = "YOU FOUND RICHARD!";
84      restartText = "HIT SPACE TO PLAY AGAIN";
85      cat._visible = true;
86      man._visible = false;
87      delete this.onEnterFrame;
88  }
89  //This compares the start value of the timer t
```

3 In our original code for the game we had to use the man's x position and y position against the cat's values to check for a 'hit' (see line 82 in previous screenshot) but now we can check the hyp value instead (line 82 here) so change it accordingly.

```
78  yDist = cat._y-man._y;
79  hyp = Math.sqrt((xDist*xDist)+(yDist*yDist));
80  // This checks to see if the man has 'found' the cat
81  // and deletes the looping gameplay.
82  if (hyp = 0) {
83      statusText = "YOU FOUND RICHARD!";
84      restartText = "HIT SPACE TO PLAY AGAIN";
85      cat._visible = true;
86      man._visible = false;
87      catDetect.stop();
88      win.setVolume(100);
89      win.start(0, 1);
90      delete this.onEnterFrame;
91  }
92  //This compares the start value of the timer to the c
```

4 In addition to the events that take place on finding the cat, add the lines 87-89. As the cat has been found, he can stop calling out for help. The volume for our win sound needs a parameter from 0-100, then start the sound as usual, looping it just once.

```
80  // This checks to see if the man has 'found' the
81  // and deletes the looping gameplay.
82  if (hyp = 0) {
83      statusText = "YOU FOUND RICHARD!";
84      restartText = "HIT SPACE TO PLAY AGAIN";
85      cat._visible = true;
86      man._visible = false;
87      catDetect.stop();
88      win.setVolume(100);
89      win.start(0, 1);
90      delete this.onEnterFrame;
91  }
92  if (hyp<300) {
93      meowVol = 100-(hyp/3);
94  } else {
95      meowVol = 0;
96  }
97  //This compares the start value of the timer to
```

5 Next add the following 'if' statement which translates hyp into meowVol, a value between 0 and 100 to set catDetects volume. If hyp was larger than 300, the equation in line 93 would return a negative value so line 95 makes sure it can't drop below 0.

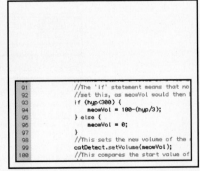

```
91  //The 'if' statement means that no
92  //set this, as meowVol would then
93  if (hyp<300) {
94      meowVol = 100-(hyp/3);
95  } else {
96      meowVol = 0;
97  }
98  //This sets the new volume of the
99  catDetect.setVolume(meowVol);
100 //This compares the start value of
```

6 Finally, after all the maths, we have a value that can be used to setVolume of catDetect. As this section of the code loops from the moment the space bar is pressed, the cat meow's volume repeatedly updates to always tell you how close you are to the cat.

Compress in MX

As most Flash games are aimed at the Web, MX allows us to compress the audio files used in order to keep file size down. Select your sound in the Library and choose new Compressions via the Properties panel. Think carefully about where you can sacrifice sound quality though, and try exporting with different settings to compare quality over file size.

7 The game is already set to end if the player runs out of time, but as they've spent all that time looking, add line 109 to show them where he was hidden. Also stop the catDetect sound as before. Finally setVolume and start the lose sound object to play it once.

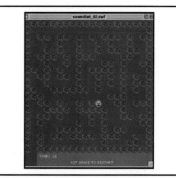

8 Now test your fla and marvel at how much more the use of those sounds has brought to your game. If there are any problems, check your finished file's code against soundtut_02.fla, using the comments as a guide.

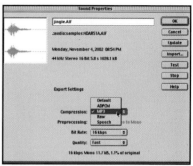

9 If the exported .swf is too large for your intended Web audience, don't forget you can compress the audio files used in Flash. In the Library select a sound, choose Properties from the drop-down, change the Compression type and click Update. Test again to note the difference in file size.

Part 4: **Controlling sound**

Create a soundtrack that plays throughout the game…

Using independent sounds

If you create a Sound Object without specifying a movie clip for its parameter, any methods used on it will affect the global sounds of the fla. Although this won't be problematic where one sound follows another, if more than one sound is playing at the same time with different volume or pan settings, parameters will need to be specified in the Sound Object. For example:

    _root.createEmptyMovie
    Clip("mc",1);

    mySound = new Sound (mc);

    mysound.setPan(20);

No preload

If you're thinking this game could do with a preloader, then think again. To start with, the file itself isn't that large but, more to the point, any file attached using an Identifier (rather than appearing on the stage) loads up before Frame 1 of your movie. So if you did include a preloader on Frame 1, all the sound would have already loaded up anyway so it becomes useless.

```
1  //This displays the intro.
2  intro.gotoAndStop(1);
3  //This creates sound Objects, attaches a sound
4  //using the Linkage names and initializes the
5  catDetect = new Sound();
6  catDetect.attachSound("meow");
7  win = new Sound();
8  win.attachSound("jingle");
9  lose = new Sound();
10 lose.attachSound("dead");
11 _root.createEmptyMovieClip("musicMC", 1);
12 musicTrack = new Sound(musicMC);
13 musicTrack.attachSound("track");
14 //This creates a new Object used to check if $
```

1 Although it's not particularly helpful in the cat game (where we need to listen for the meows), we'll finish by creating a soundtrack that plays during gameplay. Import the soundtrack.aif with the Identifier track. This sound will be controlled independently of the global sound, so specify it to a new Movie Clip (lines 11-13).

```
1  //This displays the intro.
2  intro.gotoAndStop(1);
3  //This creates sound Objects, attaches a sound
4  //using the Linkage names and initializes the v
5  _root.createEmptyMovieClip("catMC", 2);
6  catDetect = new Sound(catMC);
7  catDetect.attachSound("meow");     I
8  win = new Sound();
9  win.attachSound("jingle");
10 lose = new Sound();
11 lose.attachSound("dead");
12 _root.createEmptyMovieClip("musicMC", 1);
13 musicTrack = new Sound(musicMC);
14 musicTrack.attachSound("track");
15 //This creates a new Object used to check if $$
```

2 As catDetect will be playing at the same time, it also needs to be specified to its own new Movie Clip to distinguish it. Otherwise any command sent to catDetect (such as setVolume) will affect all sounds. Note the second parameter, positioning this empty movie clip on level 2.

```
17 start = new Object();
18 start.onKeyDown = function() {
19    if (Key.isDown(Key.SPACE)) {
20       intro.gotoAndStop(2);
21       restartText = "HIT SPACE TO RESTART";
22       //This initializes the cat and man po
23       //Note the cat is placed ON TOP of th
24       man._visible = true;
25       cat._visible = false;
26       man._x = 10;
27       man._y = 410;
28       cat._x = 10;
29       cat._y = 390;
30       //The music stops here and the cat so
31       //started. This avoids the sound bein
32       //due to it's repeated looping on eac
33       catDetect.stop();
34       catDetect.start(0, 9999);
35       musicTrack.stop();
36       musicTrack.start(0, 9999);
37       //This registers the time in millisec
```

3 As before with catDetect, place a stop then start after if (Key.isDown(Key.SPACE)) statement to initialise the music at the start of the game. Again, this ensures that the music doesn't overlap itself each time the game restarts.

```
97        if (hyp<300) {
98           meowVol = 100-(hyp/3);
99        } else {
100          meowVol = 0;
101       }
102       //creates a draggable slider
103       slider.onPress=function(){
104          this.startDrag(0, 50,430,100,430);
105       }
106       slider.onRelease=function(){
107          stopDrag();
108       }
109       //This sets the new volume of the cat m
110
```

4 Next draw a small square movie clip on the stage, with the instance name slider. Place it on the left end of a 50 pixel horizontal line and add the following script to create a draggable slider.

```
101       }
102       //creates a draggable slider
103       slider.onPress = function() {
104          this.startDrag(0, 50, 430, 100, 430);
105       };
106       slider.onRelease = function() {
107          stopDrag();
108       };
109       musicVol = (slider._x-50)*2;
110       //This sets the new volume of the cat meow to
111       catDetect.setVolume(meowVol);
112       musicTrack.setVolume(musicVol);
113       //This compares the start value of the timer
```

5 Then create a variable from the slider's x position, which returns a number between 0 and 100 for musicVol (in line 109). Use setVolume to update the volume of the music as set by the player. Finally stop() the music in the if(hyp==0) and if (showTime<=0) statements, as we did earlier with catDetect.

6 The final file can be found on the CD as soundtut_03.fla, but consider other ideas that could be applied to your own games. Remember we've only touched on a few uses of Sound Objects – there's a lot more to work with in the Objects> Sound section of the Reference panel.

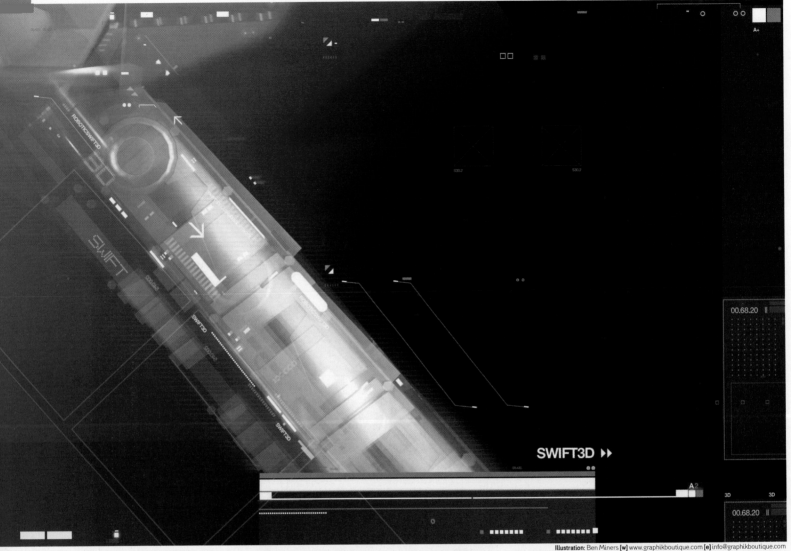

Illustration: Ben Miners [w] www.graphikboutique.com [e] info@graphikboutique.com

Create a 3D game character

3D can be a part of Flash thanks to the surprisingly powerful Web-friendly Swift 3D…

Expertise provided by George Cairns. George is a high-end user of the professional 3D application *Maya* but is impressed by *Swift 3D*'s Web-friendly render options. Contact George at [e] george@georgecairns.com, [w] www.georgecairns.com.

Files on disc
The files needed to support this tutorial can be found in the Tutorial\tech_3D folder on the cover CD.

Now in its third incarnation, Swift 3D is a relatively inexpensive tool that can be used to create 3D objects and characters for Flash. The cool thing about Swift 3D is that you can produce Flash 3D animations that take up relatively little file space. Swift 3D animations can also be imported into Flash as editable layers. This tutorial shows you how to build a fearsome robotic adversary to liven up a Flash game and gets those with a knowledge of Swift 3D using some of the new tools and features in version 3. The new Hierarchy Editor in particular enables us to animate our droid to display menacing claw-waving action. The novice should embrace this opportunity for a fun introduction to the great world of 3D.

Swift 3D v3 also boasts some powerful new raster rendering options, that enable you to add complex texture maps to your character. However, as our robot is destined for a Flash game, we want the finished file size to be as small as possible so we're going to stick to vector rendering, which is something Swift 3D excels at.

We've chosen a robotic game character because its angular surfaces will suit the vector style renderings favoured by Flash. Have fun!

Part 1: Getting started

Let's get up to speed with the updated Swift 3D interface…

Changing views

You can toggle between seeing one main window and two smaller ones using the 'Show Secondary camera' icon at the top. The view on the left is the one that goes to full screen. Do keep an eye on your scene from more than one viewpoint from time to time.

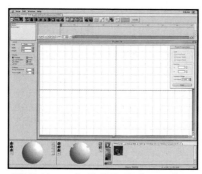

1 Start by opening Swift 3D. The layout will arrange itself to fill your monitor. It's fully customisable so you can hide various windows depending on the amount of desk space you have. Leave everything on display so you'll become aware of what each window does as you're working through this tutorial.

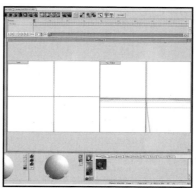

2 When working in 3D space you may think that your 3D objects are sitting on top of each other, only to later discover that they're miles apart! Using two windows – for example, front and top – will help to avoid unhappy surprises later on.

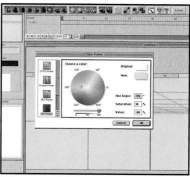

3 You can change the Background Colour of your scene using the Environment options in the Properties toolbar. However, as we're making a robot to be exported to Flash, the Background Colour will be overridden by Flash. Only change it if you find a particular colour easier on the eye.

Part 2: Get Modelling

We'll use Swift 3D v3's improved Extrusion and Lathe Tools to create our droid's components…

Adjusting values

You can change the value of an object's property in several ways. You can either type a new value into the channel box next to the property – Bevel Depth, for example – or you can place the mouse between the up and down arrow next to the channel you want to edit and click-drag to adjust the value interactively.

Ball control

Set the rotation increment of the Rotation Trackball to five degrees. Click the Lock Horizontal icon so the view doesn't rotate out of control. As you click-drag on the Trackball, the Perspective view will rotate and the bevelled shape will disappear out of shot. Now left-click with the mouse to track in the Perspective view until you can see the extruded shape from a new angle.

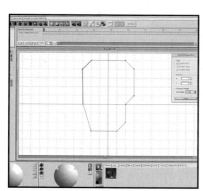

1 Click in the Front view to make it active. Click on the Extrusion Editor Tab at the top of the interface. Draw the profile of the droid's torso by clicking the mouse to place a series of points. Make the last point finish in the same place as the first.

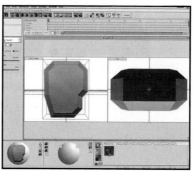

2 Now click on the Scene Editor tab. You'll see that the curve you've drawn has been extruded into a solid 3D shape. Lose the sharp edges of the extrusion. Choose the Bevel option from the Properties toolbar and set the Style to Beveled. Set the Depth of the bevelled edge to 0.02.

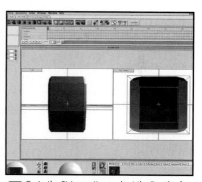

3 Go to the Sizing option and set the Depth of the object to 0.3. View it from different angles by clicking on the tabs in the top left of the view windows. Zoom out by holding right-click and dragging the mouse. Alternatively, control-click if you're using a Mac.

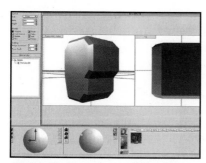

4 Select the Perspective view. Click anywhere in the view window, but not on the object. On the Rotation Trackball at the bottom left of the interface you'll see two arrows appear. Click and drag the ball to rotate the perspective view to see the extruded shape from a more suitable angle. (See 'Ball control'.)

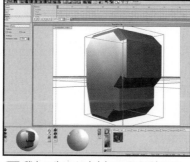

5 Click on the extruded shape. Go to Object in the Properties Toolbar. Label the shape Torso. It's good practice to label your components. As your scene develops you'll get confused trying to differentiate between the many shapes you have if they aren't named sensibly.

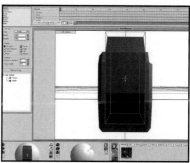

6 Use the Extrusion Editor to draw the outline of a robotic-looking head. Return to the Scene Editor and you'll see that the head shape is overlapping the torso. New shapes are always placed at the centre of 3D space so they need to be moved. Label the new shape Head.

Part 3: Heads up

Learn how to adjust the position and size of the objects you create…

Selecting shapes made easy

One way of selecting shapes is to use the new Hierarchy option. If this isn't showing in the Properties toolbar, click on View from the top menu bar and select Hierarchy. In the Hierarchy window, select a shape by clicking on its label.

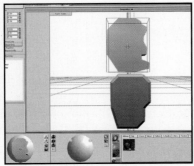

1 Click on the head to select it. Click-drag upwards to position the head above the torso. If the view moves instead of the object, check that the Camera Pan Mode is turned off under Edit. Shift-click to constrain the object's movement in the direction you want to drag it.

2 Scale down the head using Edit>Scaling Mode. Interactively click-drag to scale the object in the x, y and z-axis. Fine-tune the head's position using the Position option in the Properties toolbar. Place it above the body. Bevel the head just like you did with the torso.

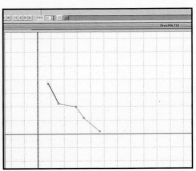

3 To create a neck, go to the Lathe Editor and draw a profile like this. To adjust points once you've drawn them, use the Select tool (the little blue arrow). The Lathe Editor creates a solid shape by rotating the curve you've drawn through 360 degrees around the green y-axis.

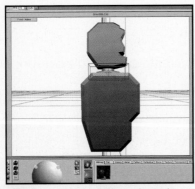

4 Go back to the Scene Editor and move the lathed object up in the y-axis so that it rests between the head and torso. Scale it to an appropriate size using Edit>Scale Mode. Label the lathed object Neck in the Object window.

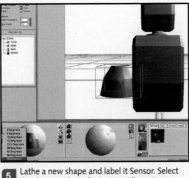

5 Lathe a new shape and label it Sensor. Select the shape in the Left view. You'll see it appear on the Rotation Trackball. Click on the Rotation Increment icon and set it to 90 degrees. Click on the Lock Spin icon. Drag the Trackball and watch the sensor rotate. Scale and position it to fit on the side of the head.

6 Select the sensor shape. Go to Edit>Copy, then Edit>Paste. Use the Rotation Trackball to rotate the duplicated through sensor 180 degrees. Drag it into position on the opposite side of your robot's head.

Part 4: Linking the components

We can give our killer robot moving parts by linking them together in a specific order…

Parent/child relationships

The Hierarchy window is where you link shapes together in a logical way. Drag the Head Group icon onto the Neck icon. The head group becomes part of the neck. When the neck is rotated, the head group rotates with it. The head group has become a child of the neck. By linking up your model in a logical way you can animate its components more easily later. Parent/child relationships are a universal technique that are used in all decent 3D applications.

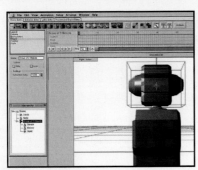

1 Shift-click to select the head and both sensors. From the top menu choose Arrange>Group. Notice that a Group icon appears in the Hierarchy window containing both the head and sensors. They can now be moved as one by click-dragging them in a view window or rotated using the Trackball. Name the group Head Group.

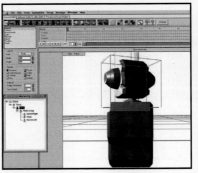

2 Drag the Neck label onto the Torso label in the Hierarchy window (see 'Parent/child relationships'). Now when you move or rotate the torso, the neck and head Group will move with it. You can still make the neck (the child) rotate independently of the torso (its parent).

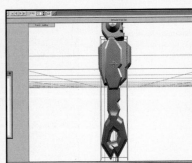

3 Build the upper part of the arm using the Extrusion Editor, then bevel it. Copy the upper arm and scale it down to make a forearm. Add an extruded claw. Position the parts as shown. In the Hierarchy window drag the claw to the forearm and then drag the forearm to the shoulder in order to link them together.

Part 4: Linking the components continued...

Navigating in 3D Space

You can zoom in and out of a view. On the PC, right-click and drag down to zoom out of a window and up to zoom in. On a Mac, hold control and drag, unless you have a three-button mouse which will let you navigate in the same way as a PC user.

1 Each component has a pivot point icon that appears at its centre. The object rotates round this point. Select the shoulder. Go to the Position window. Click on Move Pivot Only. Re-position the pivot point as shown. Select the forearm and move its pivot point to where the elbow should be.

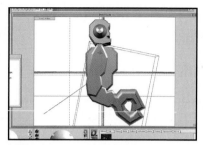

2 Move the claw's pivot point to the wrist. Now when you rotate the shoulder, the forearm and the claw will move with it because of the hierarchical links. If you just rotate the forearm then only the claw moves too. If you click on the claw, it rotates on its own without affecting any of the objects further up the chain.

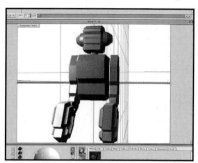

3 Select the Right Arm Group in the Hierarchy window. Go to Edit>Copy from the top menu bar. Then select Edit>Paste. Holding Shift, drag the new Arm Group horizontally until it's positioned on the opposite side of the droid.

Part 5: Texture time

Swift 3D v3 has lots of smart new textures to play with...

Adding texture

Swift 3D v3 sees dramatic improvements on the texture front. Although we could add Photorealistic textures to our character, we want to keep the file size as small as possible. As it's destined for a Flash game we also want it to scale smoothly so we're going to stick with texturing and rendering with Vector-based colours for this project.

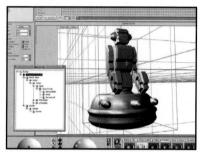

1 Finish off the droid by adding an extruded abdomen and a lathed hover base. Top it off by lathing some menacing missiles. Choose Edit>Select All, then Arrange>Group. You'll see a new Group Icon appear in the Hierarchy Editor. You can now select and move the whole robot by clicking on this.

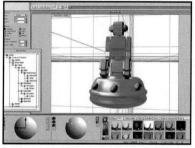

2 Choose a reflective texture from the Material Palette. Drag the material to various parts of your Droid. Drag the texture to the bevelled surfaces too. These can be textured independently, if desired, with other colour styles. As you move the mouse over a texture, make sure a label pops up to say it's a Vector texture.

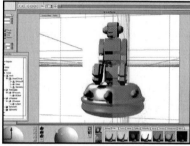

3 Click on the Render Window icon. If you change one component, save rendering time by using the Render Rectangle icon to choose specific areas of the scene to re-render. To make sure the lights are going to glint off that lovely reflective surface, use the Light Trackball to position them high in the scene.

Part 6: Animate and render

You can make any part of the robot animate over time using keyframe animation...

Keyframing

Keyframe animation is a powerful tool. You use it to set the position of an object at the sequence's start time, then you set a new position for the object at the end of the sequence. The software then calculates all the positions the object needs to go through to get from start position to finish. In Swift 3D v3 you'll see a green line appear in the Timeline, which indicates the presence of keyframes for an object's particular attribute; for example, Rotation.

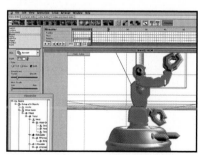

1 Select the Right Shoulder Group from the Front view. Click on Animate. In the Rotation Trackball set the Rotation Increment to 90 degrees. Click Lock Spin. In the Timeline go to frame 20. Rotate the arm upwards 90 Degrees. A keyframe is set. Go to frame 40. Rotate the arm back to its starting position. Another key is set. Hit Play to preview the movement.

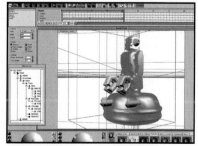

2 Set keyframes for the robot's whole movement. At frame 40, keyframe each component to be where it was at frame one. Use the Trackball's incremental move option to do this accurately. Now the animation for every component will start and end at the same position, allowing you to loop it in Flash. Turn off Animate and position the Perspective view for the final render.

3 Go to the Preview and Export Editor. Set Output options to Vector. Set Target File Type to the new Swift 3D Flash Importer (SWFT). Click Generate All Frames. Click Export All Frames. You can now import the animation into Flash MX. Experiment with the Swift 3D settings. The more colours, detail and reflections you choose, the bigger the finished file will be. Check out our fully scaleable Droid. SWF render on the CD.

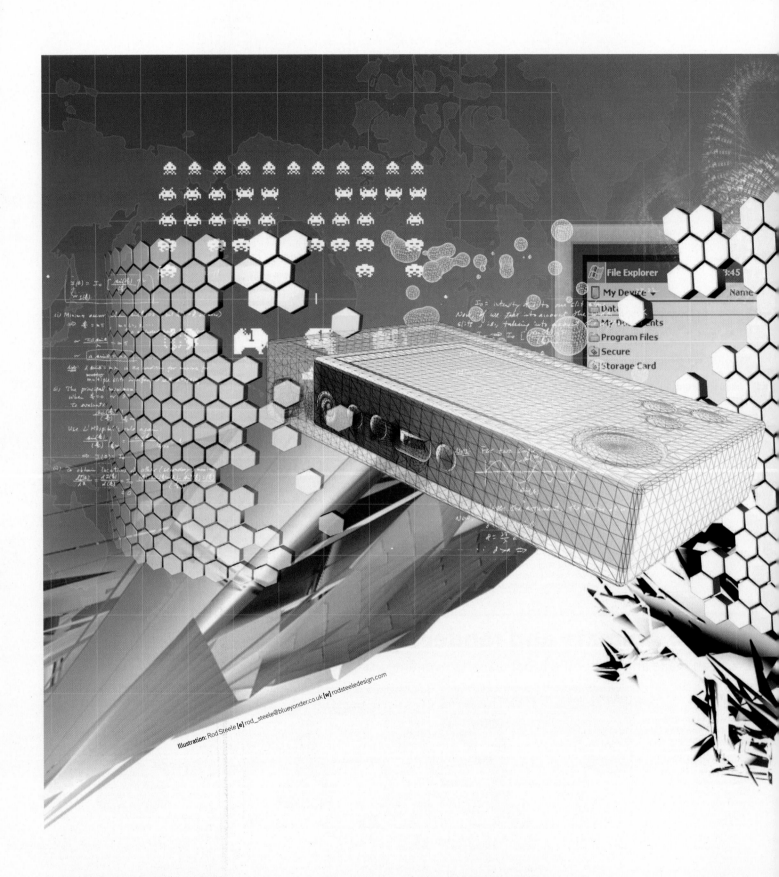

Illustration: Rod Steele [e] rod_steele@blueyonder.co.uk [w] rodsteeledesign.com

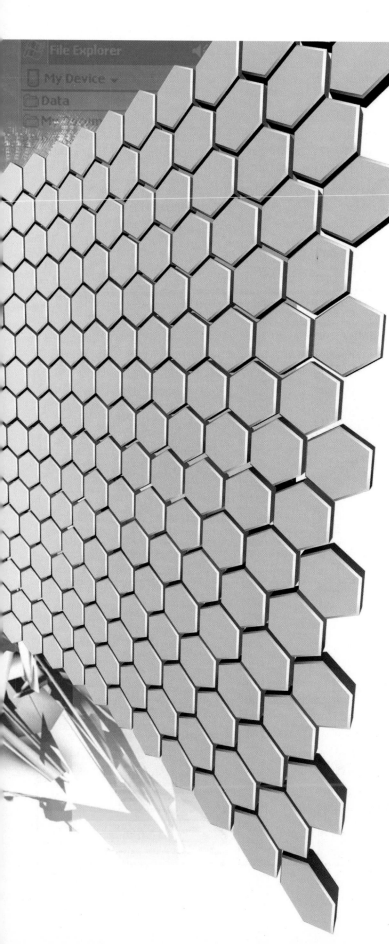

Flash gaming for Pocket PCs

Learn how to develop pocket-sized games that really perform. We explain how to deal with the foibles of the format and walk you through the development of a Pong clone…

The release of Macromedia's Flash 4 Player came at the right time when portable computing was becoming more affordable, powerful and popular.

In this tutorial, we're going to write a version of the classic bat and ball game, Pong, for the Pocket PC. We also look at movie settings and fonts and file sizes needed in developing for this platform.

The Flash 4 Player, and its successor the Flash 5 Player, can be used on all PPC (Pocket PC) platforms, which opens up a new format for Flash developers. Sadly, the combination of low CPU power and numerous inconsistencies between portable and desktop players has deterred a lot of developers.

However, despite these drawbacks, the format is still exciting. By following some simple pointers and getting used to the capabilities of the PPC, fun, high-performance Flash movies can be developed quickly and easily.

This tutorial is written in Flash 5 but you can follow the same techniques using Flash MX. ➤

Expertise for this tutorial was provided by Chi Dire, [e] chi.dire@btclick.com and Web game developer and ex-console programmer Scott Lamb of SpacehopperStudios.com, [w] www.spacehopperstudios.com.

Files on disc
ActionScript from the movie can be found in the Tutorial\Handheld folder on the cover CD.

Part 1: Getting started

Creating a Flash movie for your handheld is easy, use the files in the Tutorial\Handheld folder on the cover CD to help you…

Version confusion

Macromedia has only released a Flash 5 Player for the Casio Cassiopeia. All other PPC platforms can only run Flash 4 movies. It makes sense to stay with version 4 to ensure your movie can run on all devices.

Frame rate

The frame rate you can achieve on a PPC is usually very low. A movie with a lot of ActionScript and complex graphics might run as slowly as 4fps. Even simple movies are unlikely to run much faster than 10fps. As with desktop platforms, the power of the different PPCs varies.

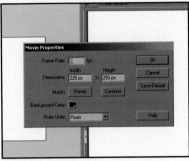

1 First, create a new Flash movie. Right-click the stage and set the dimensions to 225x250 pixels. This is a typical resolution for Pocket PC devices. Also set the background colour to black and the frame rate to 10fps.

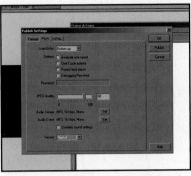

2 Next, select File>Publish Settings>Flash, and select Flash 4. All but one PPC only run Flash 4 only, so if you're using the Flash 5 editor, you must do this for your movie to run correctly.

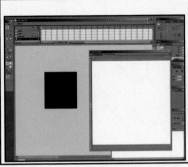

3 Add four layers. Organising your layers is important, especially as the movie will feature a lot of ActionScript. We'll keep ActionScript, labels and graphics separate where possible.

4 Add seven keyframes, a suitable space apart (five or ten frames). Label these frames splash, start, init, game, pause, win and lose. These will be the main sections of our game.

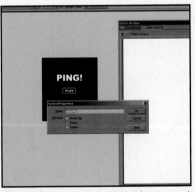

5 Add a splash graphic on the Interface layer and a simple button to take the user from the splash screen into the game.

6 Next, add the first piece of code to the movie, which is on the cover CD. We will use Expert Mode to edit the script. The Play button uses an on(release) event to jump to the start label.

Part 2: The bat and ball

We now need a bat and ball to play our game…

Code required

All code required for this tutorial is on the cover CD in the Tutorial\Handheld folder. Unless stated otherwise the code can be found in the code subfolder.

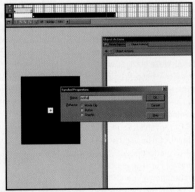

1 Create a white square of 20x20 pixels on the game layer. Make this keyframe run from the start label to the end of the pause label. Select the square and create a new symbol called mcBall.

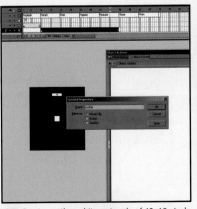

2 Create another white rectangle of 40x10 pixels in the same keyframe. Hit F8 and convert this to a symbol named mcBat.

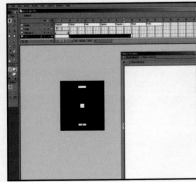

3 Copy and paste the bat symbol so that we now have two balls and a bat. Align all three symbols to the centre of the stage. Set the top bat's Y value to 30, the ball's Y to 125 and the lower bat to 220.

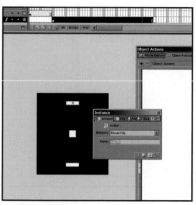

4 Select the top bat and set its name in the Instance panel to batCPU. Set the ball's instance name to ball and the lower bat's name to batPlayer. We now have our clips to manipulate.

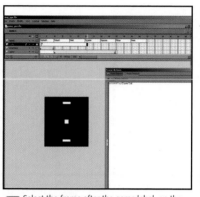

5 Select the frame after the game label, on the code layer. Add the command to **gotoAndPlay("game");** - this is our main game loop. Publish your movie now, and check that you have a splash screen and a (static) game loop.

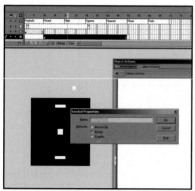

6 Create another small white box off-stage, in the same keyframe as the bats and ball. Convert this square into a button called buttonKeyTest. This will be used to register key presses, and is not to be seen on the stage.

Part 3: **Setting up the variables**

Adding a momentum effect to the bat and ball…

PPC Resources

The official Macromedia PPC development homepage can be found at [w] www.macromedia. com/software/flashplayer/ pocketpc. This includes an FAQ, the Flash player for supported devices, a development guide and example movies.

Fonts and file size

When using text, remember that file size is paramount for PPC development. Dynamic text fields should use Tahoma, as this is a standard PPC font and will be reproduced well.

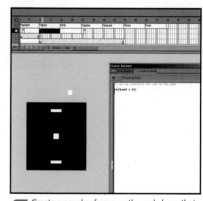

1 Create a new keyframe on the code layer that lasts from start to init. This is where we will set up all the variables to use throughout the movie. Add the ActionScript **batSpeed = 10;**

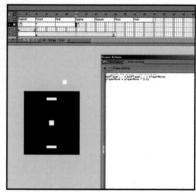

2 Add a new keyframe on the code layer on the same frame as the game label. Add the code to update the player's bat position which is on the CD in the game.txt file to add a momentum effect.

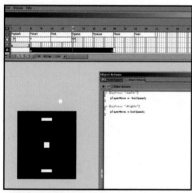

3 Select the dummy button and these two functions. This uses the value set in the start block and connects it to the variable we used in the game update loop. The code required is on the CD.

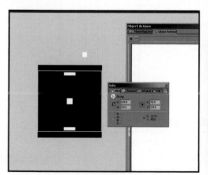

4 Create a white box to the dimensions and position shown in a new keyframe on the Interface layer. Delete the fill from this box and group it. This frame indicates the game's play area.

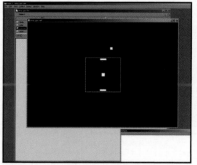

5 Publish the movie now. Click on the Play button, to see the basis of the game. After about a second, pressing the left and right cursor keys will move the lower bat.

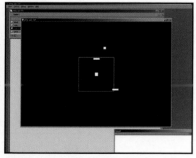

6 The control of the bat will require repeated key presses, as Flash 4 can't detect key releases. It's also possible to move the bat right off the game screen because we haven't written any collision code yet.

Part 4: Adding the text

Use the provided code to add text to your game…

Button issues

Pocket PCs use a stylus rather than a mouse, so buttons work differently to normal Flash movies. Rollover frames in buttons do not work at all, and mouse–down frames are only shown for one frame, when the button is released.

Test, test, test

Be sure to test your movie on an actual PPC regularly. You can tell how well your movie will really run and avoid over complicating your movies.

1 Add the code from start.txt in the Tutotial\Handheld folder on the cover CD to the ActionScript that's in the start block. This is a long list of useful definitions needed for the game.

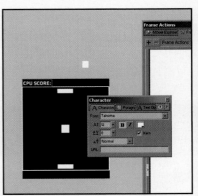

2 Add a piece of static text as shown. As it will be followed by a piece of dynamic text, select Tahoma as the font. Make the text bold and 12 points to make sure it will be legible on the PPC.

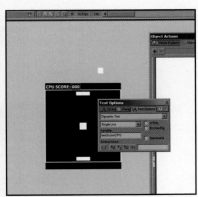

3 Insert a piece of dynamic text, aligned with CPU SCORE. Give this the variable name textScoreCPU, uncheck Selectable and use the same font and size as before.

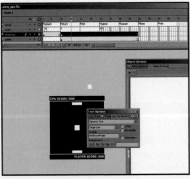

4 Duplicate both text fields in the lower-right corner of the stage. The new static field should read PLAYER SCORE: and set the variable name of the second dynamic field to textScorePlayer.

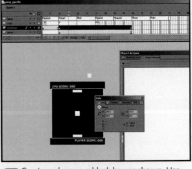

5 Create and group a black box as shown. Use Modify>Arrange>Send To Back to place this behind the text. Duplicate this box, set the Y coordinate to 244 and send it to the back. These blocks act as a quick and simple mask.

6 Insert the script from the CD to the code layer beneath the init label. Whenever this is run, it will pick a random direction for both the X and Y axis of the ball's movement.

Part 5: Updating and checking the movie

Perform these easy tests to make sure that everything is in order…

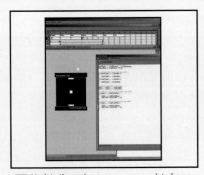

1 Update the code on your game update frame. The code required is in the game.txt file in the Tutorial\Handheld folder on the cover CD. At this point you should use the code to update the player's bat position, collide the player with the walls, update the ball's positon, test for collision with the right wall, and test for collison for the left wall.

2 These tests check if the ball is at a suitable height for a collision with either bat. Another test is made in the X axis. The ball is given more speed if it hits the edge of the bat. We need to add the code to update the player's bat, collide the player with the walls, collide with the player, collide with the CPU, update the ball's position, test for collision with the right and left walls.

3 Now we add some life to the CPU player. The script moves the AI player to seek the ball and uses the same tests we added for the player's bat to collide the bat with the left and right walls.

More than meets the eye

Running Flash 4 movies on your desktop computer (which is likely to have the Flash 5 Player) can be very deceptive. Many Flash 5 Action Script commands will execute in a Flash 4 movie run on the latest player, but will not execute on the PPC. Test any new code on the PPC as often as possible.

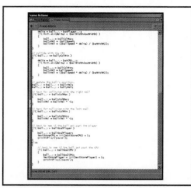

4 The last addition to the game loop is a test to see if a goal has been scored. We need the code from game.txt titled to check if ball has got past player and check if ball has got past CPU. This is added after the other code. If the ball has slipped past either player, it jumps to the pause frame.

5 Create a new keyframe at the end of the pause block and add the code for this step from the CD. When the end of the pause is reached, the script will either initialise another round or jump to the appropriate end frame.

6 Now we need to reset everything at the start of each round. Add the code from the init.txt file in the Tutorial\Handheld folder on the CD to the init section. The last three lines speed up the action from one round to the next.

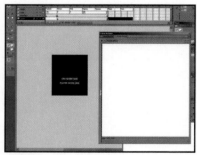

7 Take a copy of the text fields from the main game section and place them in a new keyframe on the game layer, running from lose to win. At the end of a game, this will show you the final score.

8 Insert a new keyframe that runs the length of the lose label. Add some suitably abrasive static text to be shown above the final scores.

9 Next, add a similar range of frames for the win section with some congratulations.

Part 6: The finishing touches

The final steps to complete your Flash movie…

Quality

The Pocket PC Flash 4 player is only capable of running at medium quality. Even if you set your movie to high quality, it won't perform that way. Unexpected jaggies and a lack of anti-aliasing can be an unpleasant surprise the first time you test your movie on a PPC.

1 To make the game flow correctly is a button to take you back to the splash screen. Like the score text, this button is common to both the win and lose sections. Add this, then save and publish your movie.

2 Internet Explorer for the PPC uses different HTML to embed Flash movies. The code above is the simplest template that will work on a PPC. Replace all references to the SWF file with your own filename. The code, ping_ppc.fla is on the cover CD

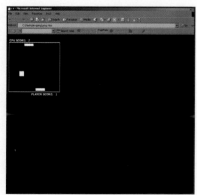

3 Your finished game should now run on both your desktop computer and a PPC. Make sure you copy the Flash and HTM files to your PPC and install the Flash Player to test your game.

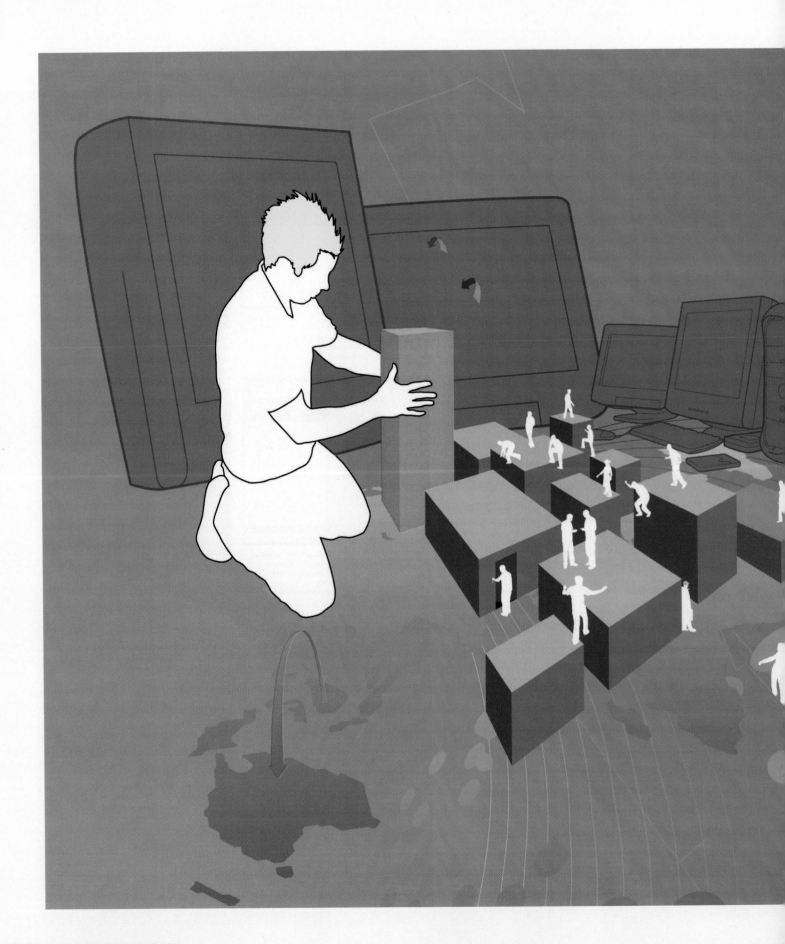

Q&A

Stuck with a tricky Flash MX problem? Maybe we can help. Over the next few pages, our experts sort out some common Flash conundrums

Q&A
Masked effects and Flash

"I've designed a site using masked effects in Photoshop and I'd like to animate elements in Flash using a similar technique. How do I do this?"

Masks are a common feature when working in Photoshop and the same concept can be used in Flash. The technique requires the original image layer plus a masking layer revealing areas of the image below. You might find masks in Flash, for example, being used to give the illusion of a spotlight moving across a larger background image.

Of course, when using Flash, the results achieved can be much more complex than such a simple effect. Animation can be applied not only to the mask but also the masked layer and, by using movie clips, even more complex effects are possible such as multiple masks, masks moving along motion guides or even dynamically generated masks that respond to a users' actions.

Inserting layers above or below masks can also provide extra options. Returning to the spotlight mask idea, you can introduce a third layer in between your existing background and mask, copying the mask shape, which is then filled with a radial gradient of a transparent centre to an opaque perimeter the same colour as the stage.

The result is a softer-edged mask effect than the hard clinical vector lines usually associated with Flash designs.

Channel 4

Masks are used in Flash to create transitional effects when changing backgrounds — think of the Channel 4 vertical stripe effect

Multiple masks

Although a single mask can affect multiple layers, it is impossible to apply more than one mask to a layer. If you need to achieve this, to have two independent moving spotlights for example, you'll need to animate these on separate layers within a movie clip that can then be placed within the mask layer. Using this technique not only makes multiple masks possible, it provides a method of forcing a mask to follow a motion path.

Setting up an updateable SWF file

1 Open a new Flash file and create or import a background image into layer 1, name this Background. A mask layer affects the layer below it, so create a new layer above your background and name it Mask.

2 Right-click (PC) or Ctrl-click (Mac) the top mask layer in the timeline to access the Contextual menu, then choose Mask to change the behaviour of the layer.

3 The layer is then converted and linked to the now indented layer immediately below, indicating its relationship to the mask. Both layers have their identifying icons, also converted to reflect their new roles.

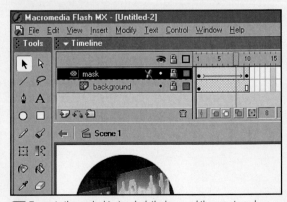

4 To create the mask object, unlock the layer and then create and animate a simple object moving across the background. Once complete, lock both layers and run the animation to see your mask in action.

Rotoscoping and video

"I'd really like to rotoscope my video files – how can I do this using Macromedia's Flash?"

Rotoscoping is a traditional animator's technique. Pre-dating motion capture technology, it describes the tracing by hand of live-motion film, frame-by-frame, to facilitate more natural movement in animation. The process is named after the machine that originally projected the film onto the animation board.

With the improved direct support for video files, Flash MX is an ideal environment for re-creating such an effect – although the procedure is a lengthy one, the results can lead to incredibly natural animation at a fraction of the file size of the original video clip.

First, you need to import a video clip into Flash and lock the layer that contains it, minimising any unwanted movement to the original tracing layer. Add a new layer above this and use Flash's drawing tools to trace around the object in the first frame. If you're using the Pencil tool, remember to set the mode to Smooth or Ink to reduce the risk of any unwanted modification to your strokes.

Now continue adding keyframes, tracing around the moving object until the sequence is complete. Keep the trace simple and use Flash's Onion Skinning feature to improve your understanding of where the motion is coming from and going to. Also, depending on the background composition, use the Show Layers As Outlines option or reduce the opacity of the original video to help distinguish your trace from the background.

When you've finished, and before you delete the layer containing the original video, it's worth hiding this and previewing the animation; you'll soon notice any potential errors and be able to make final amendments before losing the video clip completely.

It takes time but rotoscoping is a labour-intensive process. However, the results speak for themselves. A simple outline provides effective results with minimal file size requirements. If you have more time, and the output media supports it, you can make the conversion as detailed as you like.

Video to vector

If the process of hand-drawing each individual frame sounds too tedious, or the length of video is too long to make this practical, you might consider an alternative option, namely Wildform's video-to-SWF conversion software, Flix. The current Pro version has a useful tool that converts a standard video clip to SWF, while also breaking down the bitmap content into vector objects.

The Flix Vectorise feature enables you to configure the conversion by removing right angles, jagged edges or fitting curves and straight lines to variable degrees. There are also some intriguing colour options which can flatten results, leading to some unusual posterised

effects. Another useful feature is Flix's ability to edit the original video for better control over input and output.

You can then import the resulting SWF into Flash, to incorporate it into a larger project, or for editing further using the superior controls available through Macromedia's excellent vector tool.

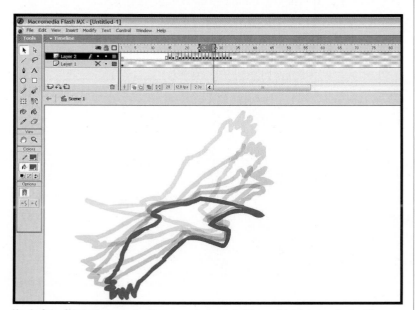

The original video is hand-traced frame-by-frame to capture the natural movement of the flying bird.

Use the Onion Skinning feature to view frames around your selected frame – this helps you understand the lateral movement of your image.

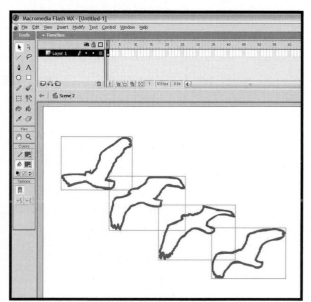

The resulting outlines produce efficient results, with a natural motion that would be virtually impossible to re-create by hand.

Dynamically loading copy

"How can I dynamically load copy from an external text
file into an SWF file – say, to update site data?"

Updating

This approach enables the site
designer to create the shell of a
site for clients — who can then
update their site by amending a
simple text file

With Flash MX's improved scripting
capabilities, this particular
feature becomes much more
manageable through the use of
the LoadVariables action. In the FLA file, you
can specify basic text attributes, such as font
size and colour, for a dynamic text field that
pulls in content from a specified text file.

The advantages of this method are many:
revising existing Flash content needn't be
overly complicated — after all, even the
biggest technophobe should be able to
change the copy of a text file. This approach
enables the site designer to create the shell
of a site for clients, who can then update their
own details by amending a simple text file.

The text file that will load into the dynamic
text field includes the actual text that will be
rendered, as well as the opening variable:
textField=. When you change the text file,
make sure this variable is left in place. By
giving the Var text box the same name, you're
naming the variable the movie should load.

In our walkthrough example, we've
specified the _sans font, because this is a
device font that's appropriate for multiple
computer platforms. The purpose of using
dynamic text is to be able to change the text
file feeding the content as necessary. If we
weren't using a device font then we would
have to embed the required font into the SWF,
increasing its file size and complexity.

The loadVariables action includes the
parameter to specify the path to the variable
text which, in this case, needs to be in the
same folder as the hosting SWF. However, if
the file is stored elsewhere, you need to
amend this to a relative or absolute location.

We don't have enough space here to go
into formatting or creating scroll attributes,
but at least the technique outlined below will
help you create Flash elements which you
can then dynamically load into your SWF file.

To get started with a possible scenario for
a band's gig page, grab hold of the Cover CD
and copy the movie.fla and copy.txt files from
the folder Tutorial\QA_Flash. Open the Flash
file and follow the steps below.

Setting up an updateable SWF file

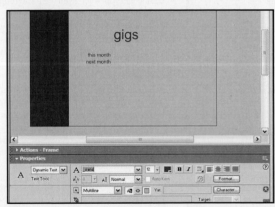

1 Open movie.fla, select the copy layer and choose the Text tool. Select
Dynamic Text, choose _sans as the font, set the point size to 12, the
Text (fill) colour to 666666 and select the Multiline option for the Line Type.

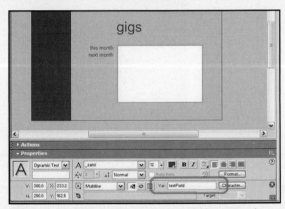

2 On the stage, drag the cursor to create a text field approximately
300x200 pixels in size, as shown above. Back in the Property
Inspector, type textField in the Var text box.

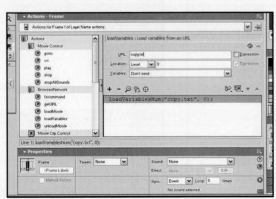

3 Open Window>Actions if this isn't already available, and select the
Actions layer in the timeline. In Normal mode, choose
Actions>Browser/Network and double-click loadVariables. Type copy.txt
in the URL text box.

4 Save the movie, then choose Control>Test Movie to see the results
and generate the SWF file. Close the SWF file, amend the copy.txt
file, then open the SWF again to see your new changes in place.

Sound advice

"Is it possible to modify sounds in Flash to create more realistic sound effects?"

Creating and editing sound clips is an art often beyond the realm of your average graphic designer — the complexities of envelopes, balance and filters are as alien as the pointy brackets that fill the upper portions of their Dreamweaver screens. However, even the most tone-deaf pixel-pusher has some idea of controlling sound events through the most basic volume and panning controls.

With the latest MX version, Flash offers a number of ways to control your sound clips through the ActionScript-powered Sound object. This is ideal if you need to control when a sound plays, change its volume or determine the sound's stereo position.

To create a global Sound object, select the first frame of your main timeline and open the Actions panel. Choose Actions>Variables> Set Variable and enter an appropriate name for your clip in the Variable field. Click the Value field and choose Objects> Movie>Sound >New Sound and check the Expression checkbox.

Although you can reference an external MP3 file, we're assuming that you're importing a sound file into Flash that you want to associate with the new object. To do this, choose File>Import, locate the necessary file and select this from your Flash library. Choose Linkage from the Options menu.

In the dialog box that appears, check Export for ActionScript and accept the other options that come up. Enter a name in the Identifier field and click OK. We can now reference the file through this unique identifier from the Sound object we created earlier.

Access the code to this, select the new Sound() statement and choose Objects> Movie>Sound>Methods>attachSound. Next, enter the name of your Sound object in the Object field and then the identifier within quotes in the Parameters field.

With the Sound object defined, you can now modify your sound's volume and balance through the setVolume() and setPan() methods respectively. The setVolume() method is set by a parameter value of between 0 (silence) and 100 (maximum volume), while the setPan() method offers a range of −100 to 100 for the full range between left and right speakers.

Volume control

With the sound object defined, you can now modify the volume and balance of your sound through the setvolume() and setpan() methods respectively

Creating the sound object

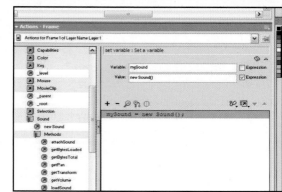

1 Creating a Sound object is as simple as defining a new variable and assigning the new Sound() value as an expression. This can reference an imported sound file or an MP3 file, held outside the hosting SWF file.

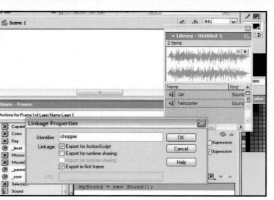

2 With a sound file imported, we can define the Flash library instances' linkage properties, which determine the available attributes that are permitted, and give it a more recognisable name.

3 Using the identifier provided through the linkage definition, we can now associate the sound file with the Sound object. Put the parameter name in quote marks so Flash recognises it as a literal name.

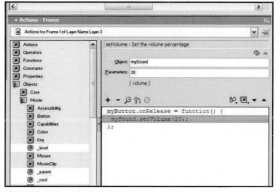

4 With the Sound object defined, you can now modify the sound to suit your Flash movie. Here we're tweaking the setVolume() parameters; setPan() uses the same syntax, but its values range from −100 to 100.

Online games

"I'm interested in using Flash to develop online games. How can I make objects react depending on their relative positions?"

Point and movie clip collision

For more precise collision detection (namely with a movie clip's X-Y coordinates), continue with the file we created and select the first frame of the root timeline. Select the if statement and change the expression field to read: rock.hitTest (ship._x, ship._y, true)

The hitTest method now compares the X and Y positions of the ship movie clip with the location of the rock clip.

This technique tests whether the registration point of our ship movie clip comes into contact with any part of the rock clip.

Using this method, you can refine your collision detection still further. This is great when you're using irregular shapes — here, for instance, it enables our draggable ship to venture within the boundaries of the rock without automatically triggering a collision.

The secret behind such a requirement is collision detection. This is found extensively in game design and requires only a relatively short amount of coding that you can apply to all kinds of situations within Flash.

Obviously, games provide the most clear examples of collision detection, from the basic bat-and-ball principle behind Pong to the multi-car pile-ups associated with GTA Vice City, although you could also apply the same idea to Flash-based shopping carts, which enable customers to drag-and-drop items directly through your site's interface. Remember, it's the act of moving objects around a browser that gives the user a feeling of interaction and, as such, collision detection is only possible through the draggable movie clip object. The movie clip supports the crucial hitTest() method (which you can use to check whether the bounding boxes of an object intersect) or the more point-specific method (which uses defined X-Y co-ordinates via the shapeflag parameter).

To detect such an intersection, you need two named movie clips, at least one of which must have actions assigned to make it draggable. If you're unsure how to do this, open and check out the code to our example file collide.fla on the CD.

Select the last line in the script pane and choose Objects>Movie>Movie Clip>Events>onEnterFrame, entering _root in the Object field. This creates an appropriate event handler at the same frame rate of the movie that's best suited for checking the hitTest condition. Now choose

Actions>Conditions/Loops>if and enter the name of the draggable movie clip. Choose Objects>Movie>Movie Clip>Methods>hitTest and enter the path of the stationary movie clip within the brackets. Follow this with two equals signs and the word true.

That's all you need to configure the actual collision detection. Now you can create whatever results occur when the criteria is met (explosion graphic, points, etc). Otherwise, there'll be little to indicate that the hitTest() has been detected.

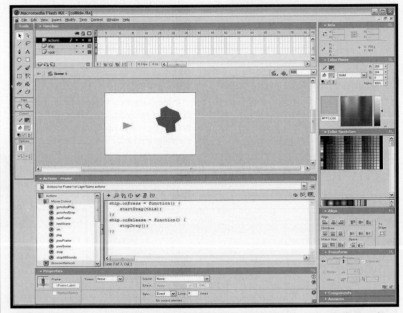

Taking a simple Asteroids idea, we've created two named movie clips and assigned basic drag attributes to the spaceship, so we can manually move it around the screen.

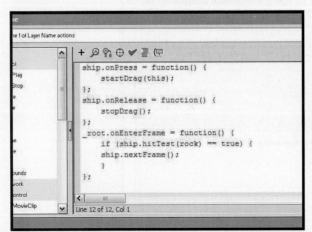

The addition of the hitTest function enables us to recognise when the two clips intersect. We've also added the ship.nextFrame() response, so we get some visual indication when the collision occurs.

```
ship.onPress = function() {
    startDrag(this);
};
ship.onRelease = function() {
    stopDrag();
};
_root.onEnterFrame = function() {
    if (ship.hitTest(rock) == true) {
        ship.nextFrame();
    }
};
```

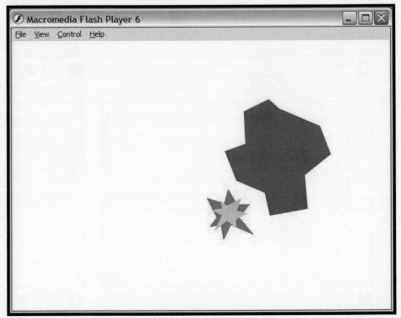

With our basic detection, the boundaries of the two movie clips determine the collision. Modify the code as described in the boxout to improve on this when detecting such actions between irregular shapes.

Scrolling text boxes

"How can I create a scrolling text box without delving into overly complex ActionScripting?"

sing Flash 5, creating such a feature would indeed have involved lengthy and tedious coding. While Flash MX offers even more complex and flexible coding capabilities, there have also been numerous simplifications to the creation of such standard User Interface (UI) elements — through the new Components panel.

Components operate rather like templates, providing objects (including scrollbars), check boxes, list boxes, radio buttons, scroll panes, combination boxes and push buttons that you can simply drag and drop into place within your Flash movie. Each component has its own particular range of parameters, available as a separate tab from within the

Properties Inspector, from where you can configure their available options and handlers.

If you follow the four simple steps outlined below, you'll soon see how such a previously complex task of creating a scrolling text box has been simplified for even the most code-shy Flash designer. If you need to further adapt the appearance of such a feature, you can easily edit the generated movie clip items that have been created in a dedicated folder within your library to match your final project design or functionality.

The strength behind components is their generalised purpose. They have been created to be as generic as possible, enabling you to configure their parameters to suit your

particular purpose while only imposing the limitations of your chosen object. If you need more specific information on a particular component's parameters, the Flash Help files and ActionScript Dictionary provide more detailed advice than we have space for here.

Once you're familiar with the way components work, you can go on to create your own customised components for use with future projects.

Alternatively, if you're not too confident with the coding of such elements, you may want to search around for similar features from Macromedia or other third-party developers that you can simply add into Flash through the Macromedia Extensions Manager software.

Components

Components operate rather like templates, providing you with objects that you can drag and drop into place within your flash movie

The scrollbar component

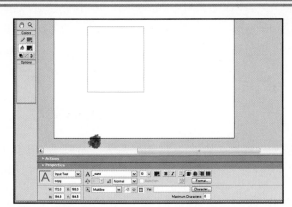

1 Select the Text tool and set its properties to Input Text and Multiline. Activate the borders and set the font properties to suit your final design, before dragging a text field onto your stage. Give this a unique name within the Properties Inspector.

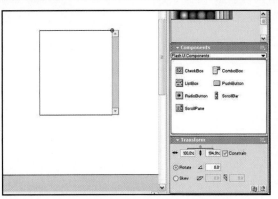

2 In the Components panel (Windows>Components), select the ScrollBar object and drag it onto the stage. Now release it towards the right-hand side, inside the text box. The component will automatically snap and scale itself to the right of your text field.

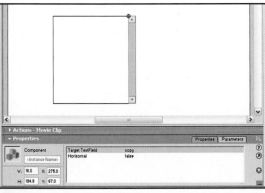

3 With the scrollbar selected, click the Parameters tab in the Properties Inspector. Scrollbars options are limited, but notice how the Target TextField has been automatically named.

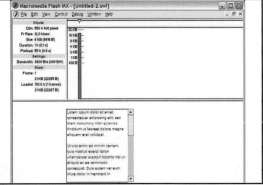

4 With your component in place, you can now test your movie. Enter text in the field until it exceeds the area; you'll notice how the scrollbars are created and adapt to contain the extra content.

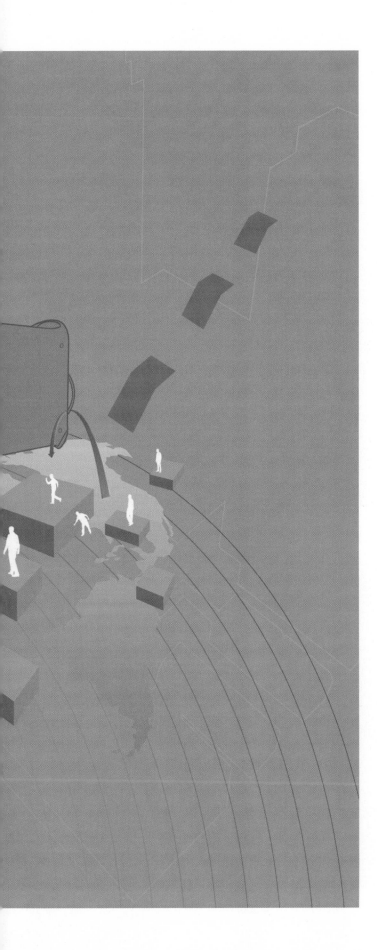

Gallery

In need of some inspiration? Then browse through the following pages where we look at cutting-edge Flash work – from corporate Web pages through to experimental sites…

Flash gallery

Looking for inspiration? We check out a range of Flash sites from corporate destinations to experimental sites…

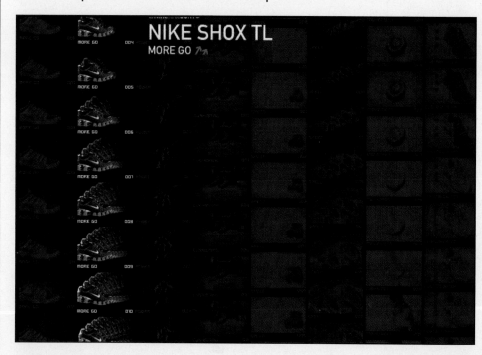

Nike, corporate site
www.nike.com/nikelab/

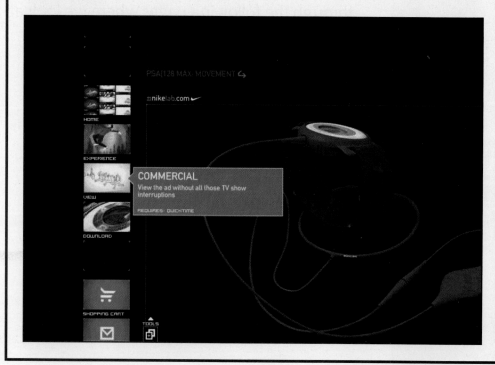

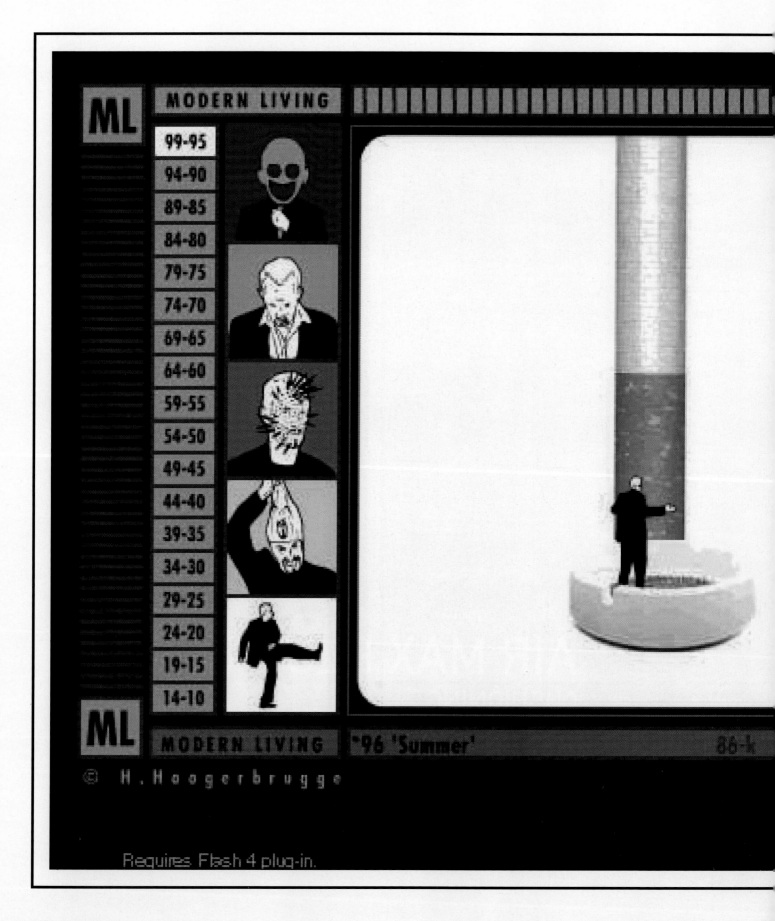

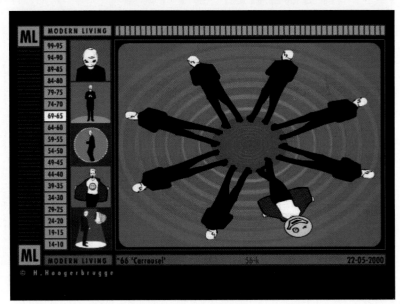

Modern Living, experimental site from the Netherlands by H Hoogerbrugge
www.hoogerbrugge.com

THE COMPLETE **FLASH MX** HANDBOOK | 213

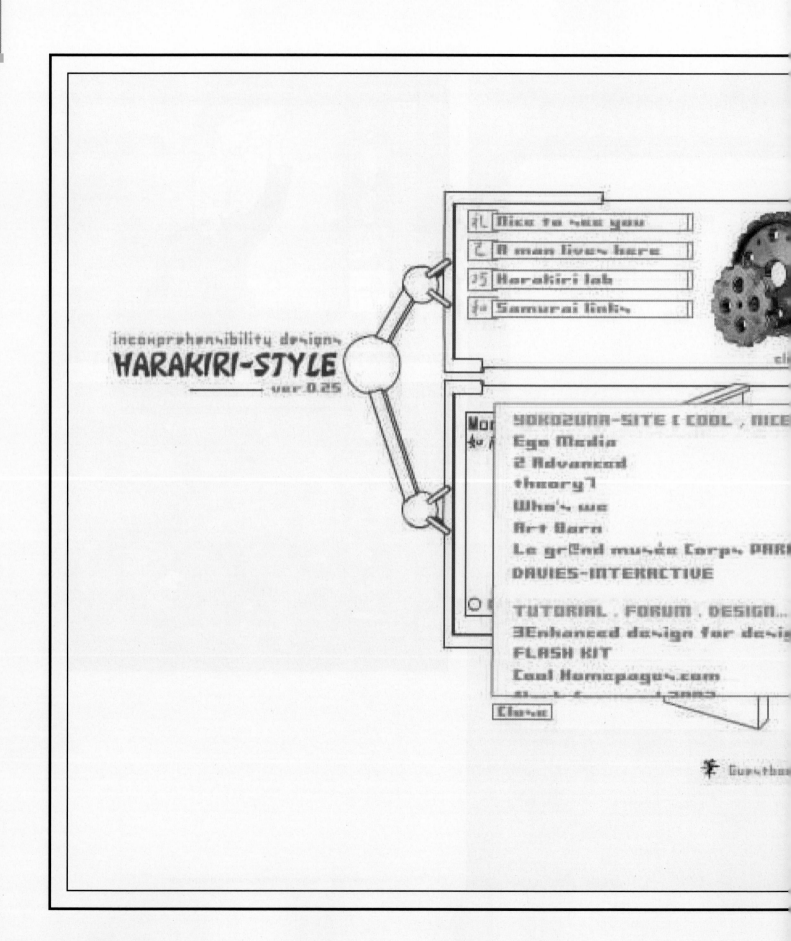

Harakiri Style, 3D animation from Japan
www.harakiri-style.com

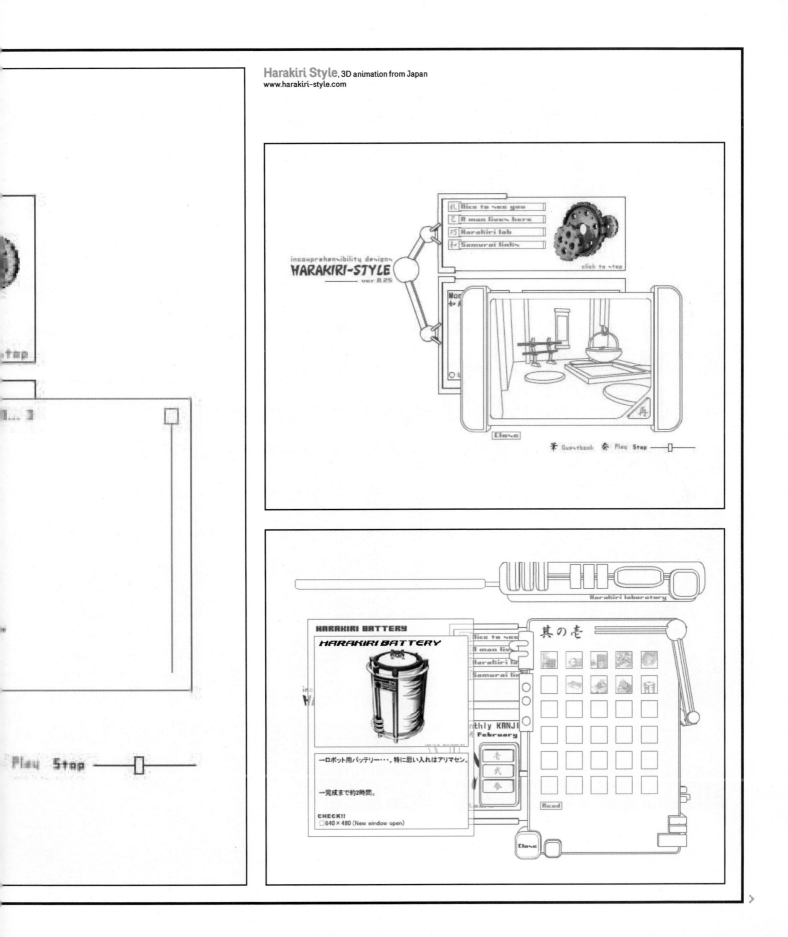

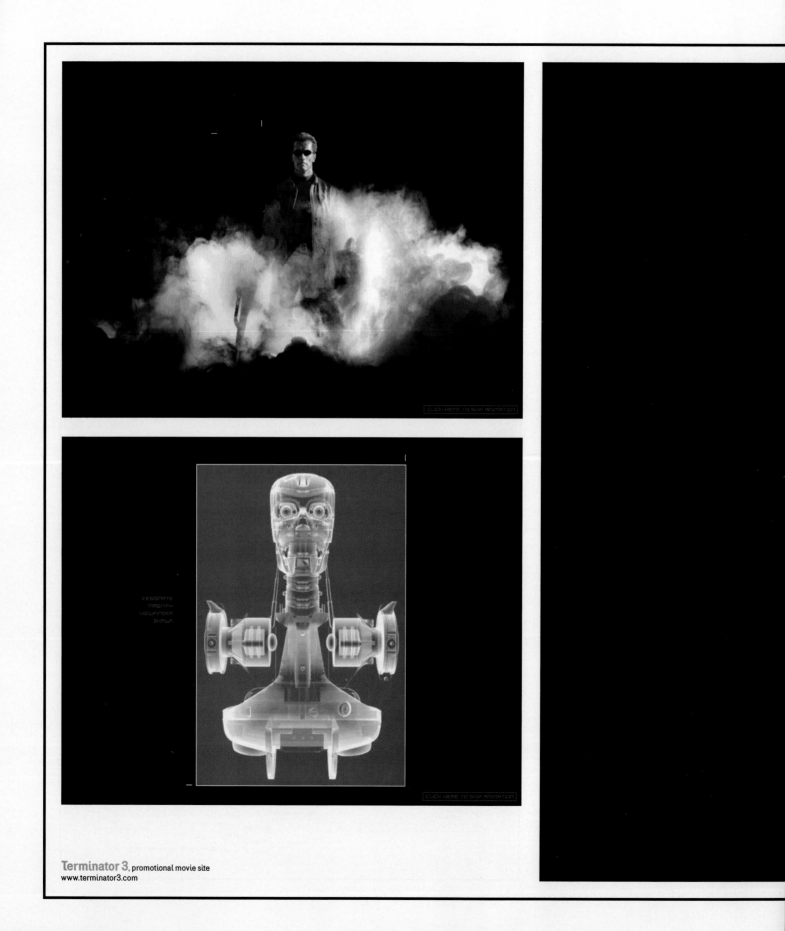

Terminator 3, promotional movie site
www.terminator3.com

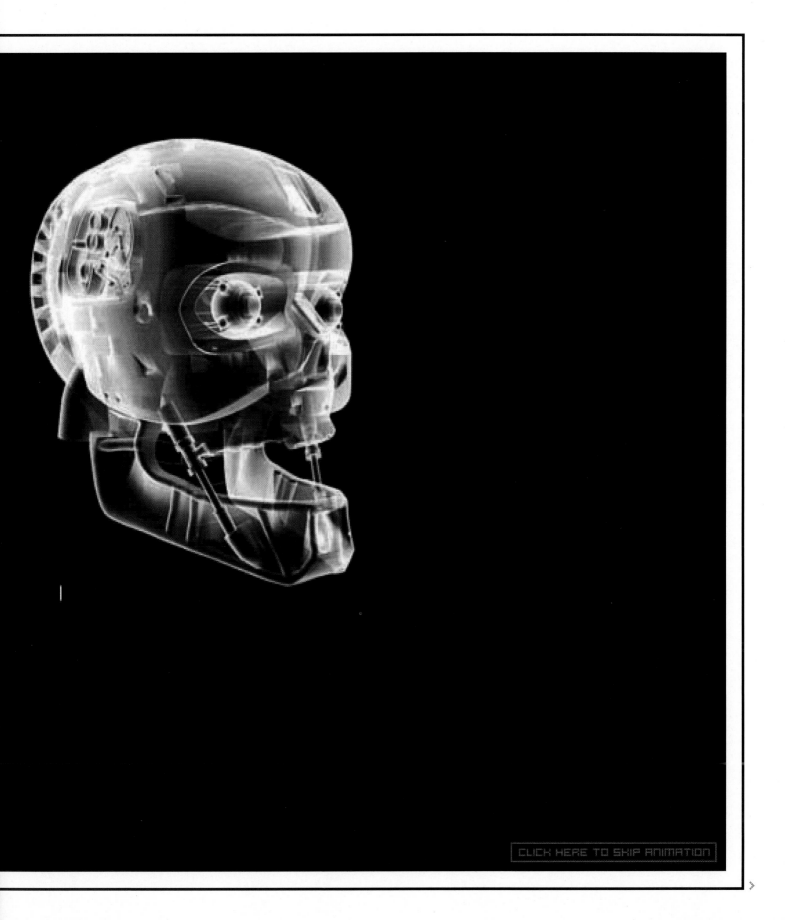

CLICK HERE TO SKIP ANIMATION

Conceptual Integration, experimental site, design company
www.conceptualintegration.com/

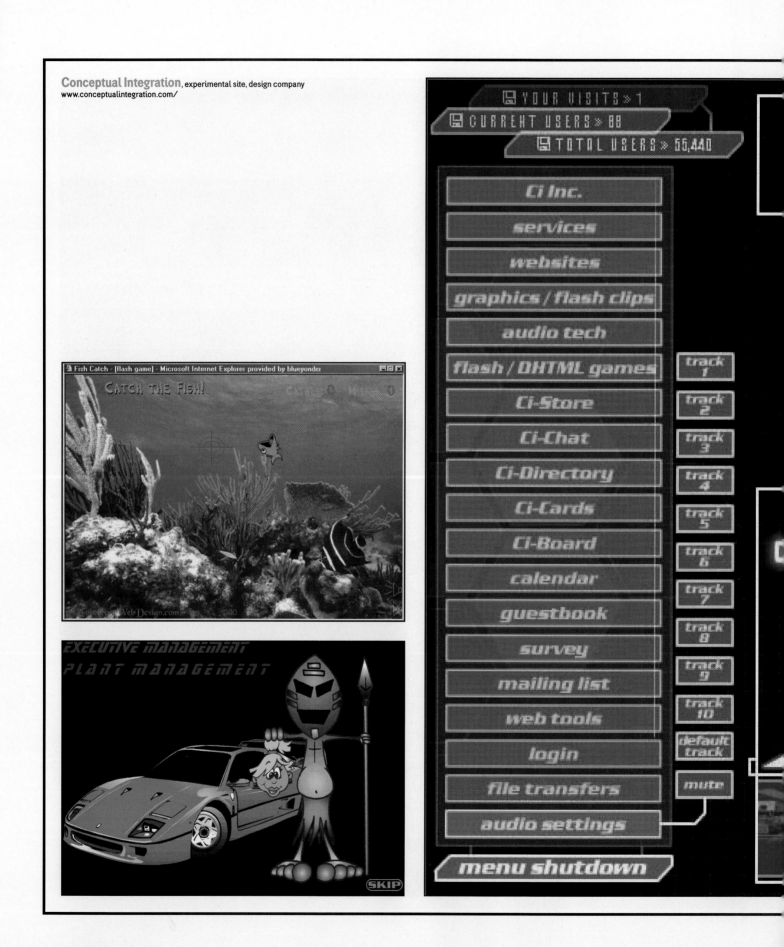

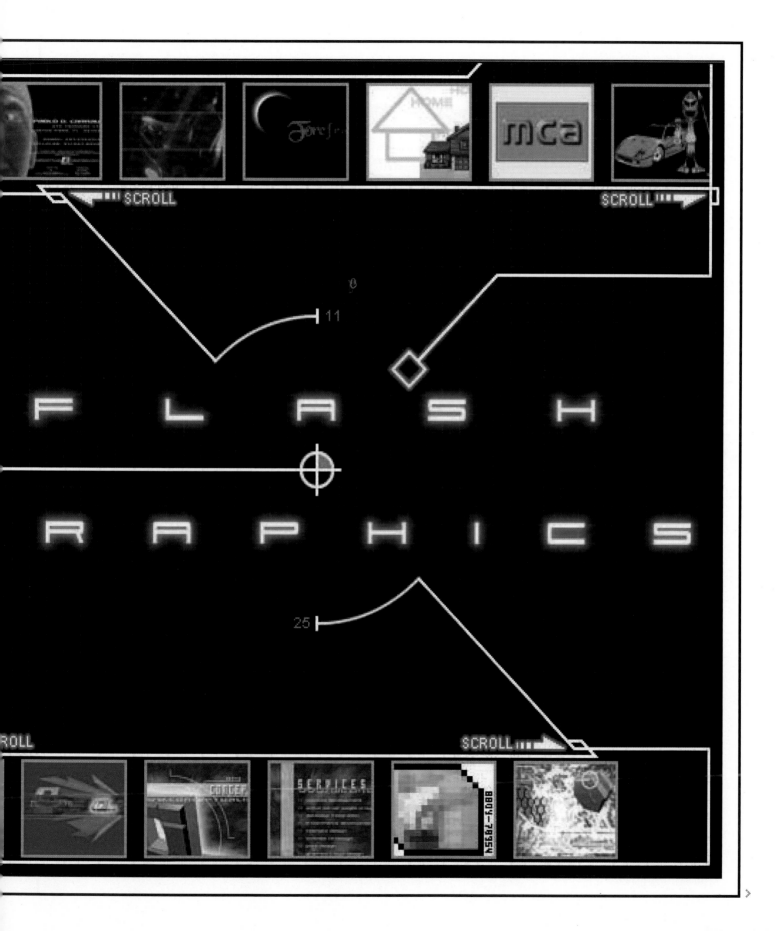

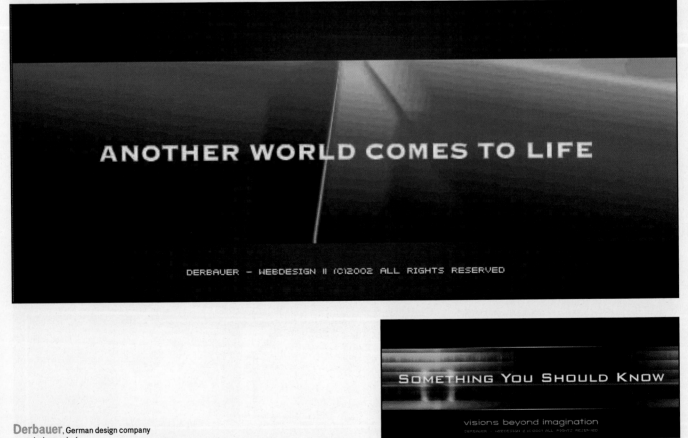

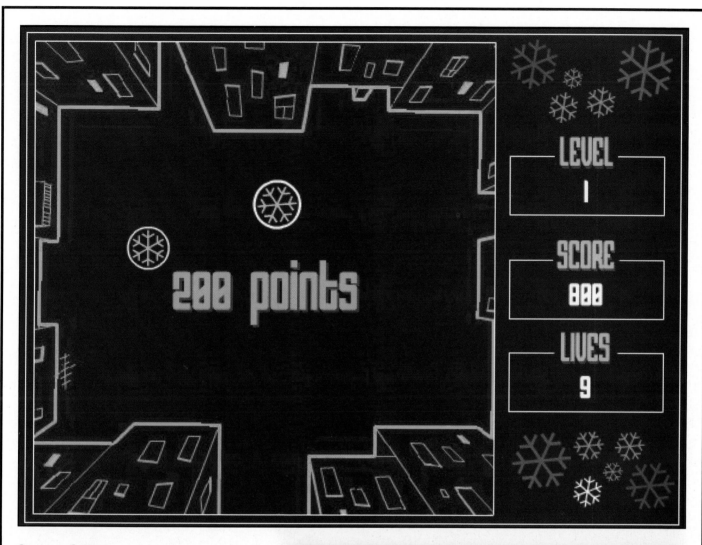

Cartoons Online, Flash cartoons and games
http://cartoons-online.com

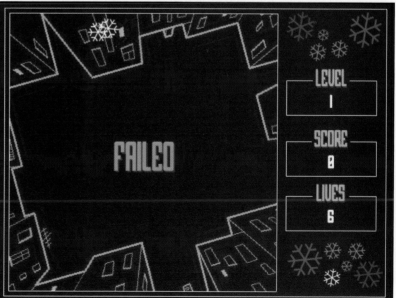

Sumo Panda

He is Rebecca's best fighter at the Fursvalley Dojo. His only concern is to keep his undefeated status and to bring honor to his family and to Fursvalley. Year after year he ensures Fursvalley's defeat of Toyshaven in the martial arts tournaments. He has heard that Tedi, Toyshaven's top fighter, has been training very hard this time around and will be difficult to beat. Sumo Panda is unconcerned. He is undefeated after all.

movie | characters | artwork | story | message board | free stuff
store | games | awards | credits | contact

Floating Pear Productions © 2003

Frozen Fury

48%

Frozen Fury

Tedi Online, animation/cartoon site
www.tedionline.com

YOU DESIRE.

ONLINE STRATEGIC MARKETING
FILM, GAME, TV, NEW MEDIA
INTERACTIVE CD ROM – KIO

COMP

All Media Studios, design company
www.allmediastudios.com

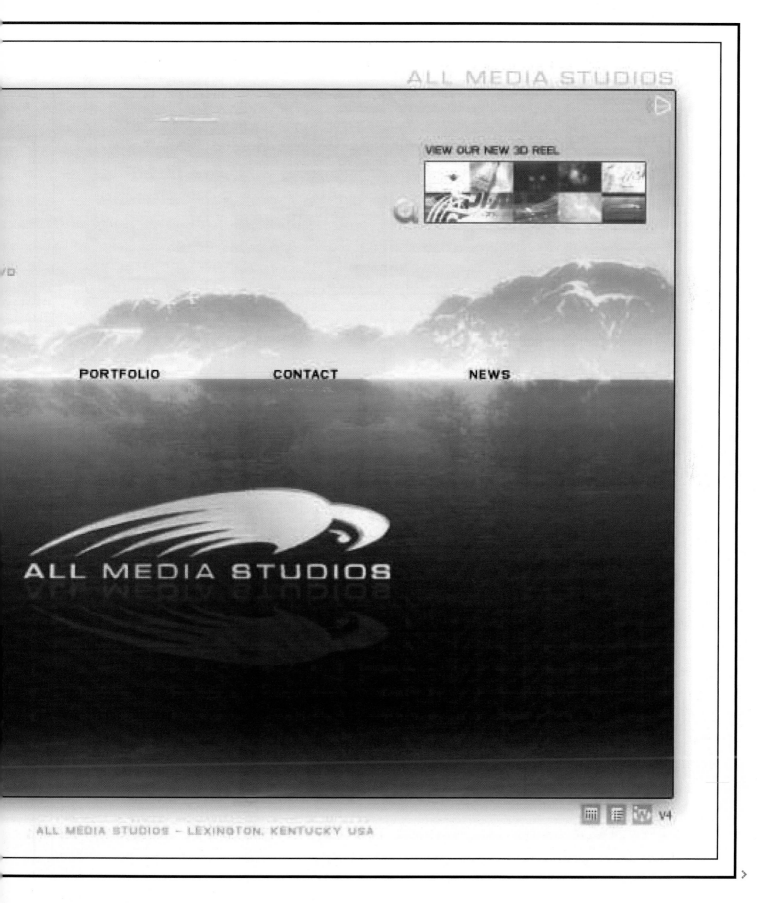

ALL MEDIA STUDIOS

VIEW OUR NEW 3D REEL

PORTFOLIO   CONTACT   NEWS

ALL MEDIA STUDIOS

V4

ALL MEDIA STUDIOS – LEXINGTON, KENTUCKY USA

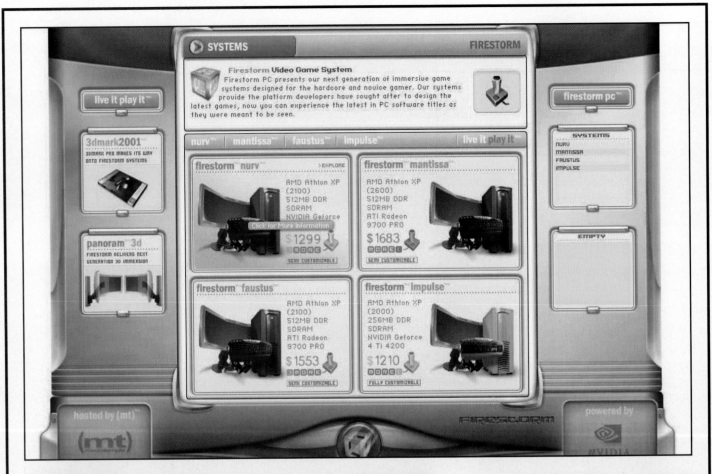

Firestorm PC, corporate site
www.firestormpc.com

Arctic Cat, corporate site
www.arcticcat.com

Supergrass, rock 'n' roll band's site
www.supergrass.com

SUPERGRASS'R'US
Open 34 hours, 8 days a week, this giant
Supergrass retail park is ready to accept
your hard earned cash in exchange
for T-shirts, socks, iron board covers and
anything else that sits still long enough to
stick a Supergrass logo on.

So stop being silly and come on in today
and buy loads of stuff, you know you
want it.

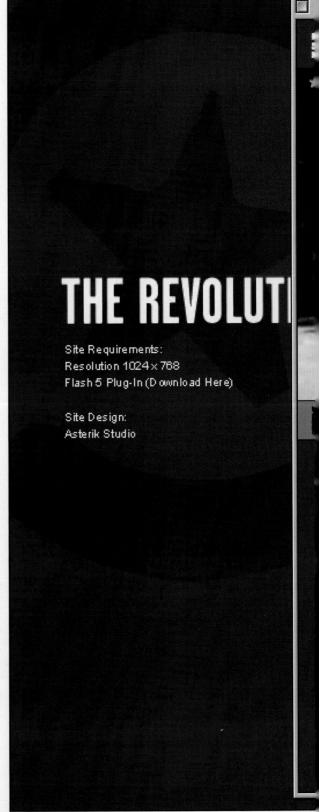

Site Requirements:
Resolution 1024 x 768
Flash 5 Plug-In (Download Here)

Site Design:
Asterik Studio

The Revolution Smile, up and coming rock band
www.therevolutionsmile.com

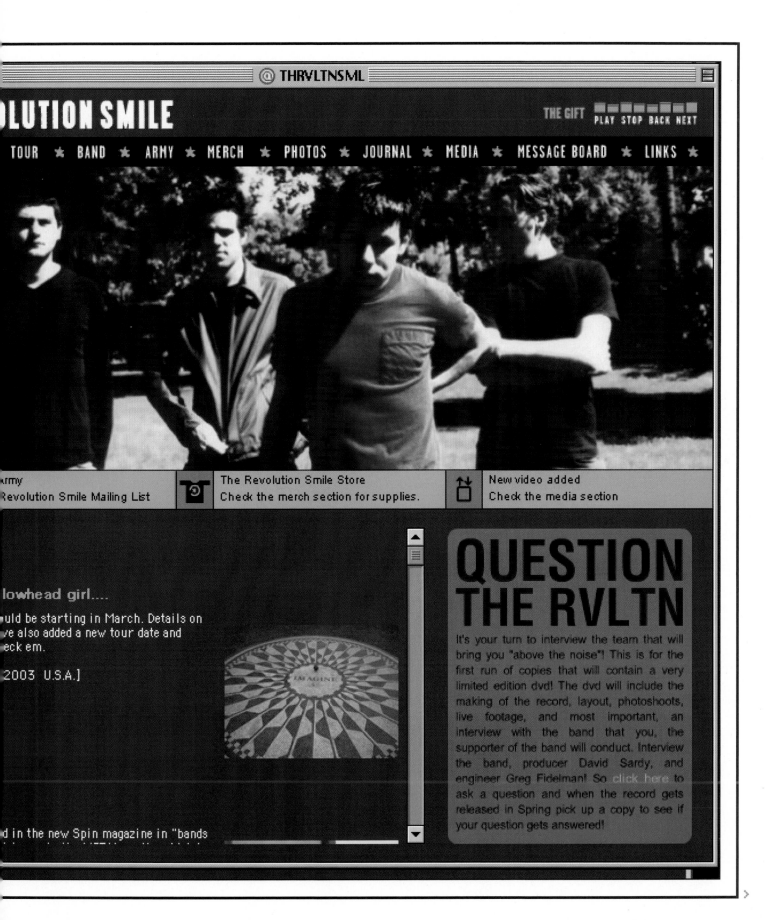

I Want My Flash TV, short films site
www.iwantmyflashtv.com/

For an overview of what's going on in the world of Flash sites, I Want My Flash TV is an excellent resource, packed with state-of-the-art animation from a variety of different agencies and Flash artists.

For more sites:
www.bestflashanimationsite.com/flasharchive.php?cat=4

For another excellent selection of Flash sites, check out
Macromedia's home pages at www.macromedia.com. The
company regularly highlights the work of Flash designers and
keeps an archive of sites that are worth checking out.

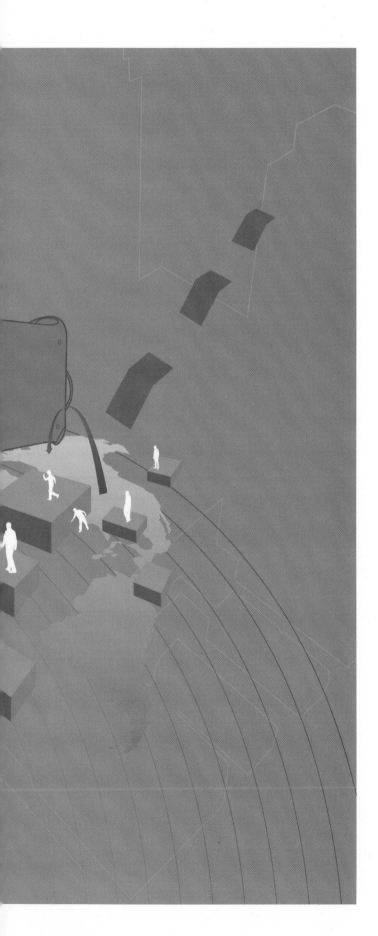

Reviews

An in-depth look at some of the other programs that make up Macromedia's MX family. Plus a selection of books to improve your Web-building skills

Dreamweaver MX

Dreamweaver retains its crown as the best Web authoring package…

Price

£351
(upgrade £175)

Company

Computers Unlimited

Telephone

020 8200 8282

Website

www.macromedia.com

Features

- Drag-and-drop Web authoring
- Web application development
- Improved coding environment
- ColdFusion-optimised
- Support for PHP, JSP, ASP.net and ColdFusion
- Macromedia MX interface
- Extensive reference materials
- Tag editors and inspectors
- Tag completion
- New Insert panel

System

PC: 300MHz Pentium II • 96MB RAM • 275MB hard disk space • Win 98/2000/ME/NT4/XP

Mac: PowerPC • 96MB RAM • 275MB hard disk space • OS 9.1 or OS X 10.1

Try the preview
Take Dreamweaver MX for a test drive with our Cover CD.

Perhaps you should sit down before you read on… the default package in Dreamweaver MX boasts all the power of Dreamweaver UltraDev. That's right, the standard Dreamweaver package is now a Web application development environment. It can produce database-powered Websites using the Active Server Pages protocol, ColdFusion and, at last, PHP. Excited?

What's more, the new interface has not merely been tweaked — it has a look and feel that's been redesigned from the ground up.

Even if you're new to Web design, you probably know that Dreamweaver is the designer's choice Web authoring application. It outsells all its rivals except Microsoft's FrontPage, which appeals more to corporate users and is bundled in with the company's ubiquitous Office suite of products. From version 1.0, Dreamweaver has had visual layout capabilities that few other products have competed with. Over time, Macromedia has introduced upgrades to this original model, bringing in Roundtrip Code and Layout Tables, integrating CSS editing features and improving the manual coding features. The standard drag-and-drop metaphor has changed little.

Dreamweaver's key tools have always been within the Objects panel, where you could find page elements and the Property Inspector that enabled you to change the parameters of those elements in your page. The combination was simple and effective — the foundation of Dreamweaver — so the disappearance of the Objects panel in Dreamweaver MX may surprise you.

The panel hasn't gone altogether; it has been revamped and renamed. When you launch Dreamweaver MX you'll wonder where it is. Look at the top of the screen, just below the standard menu bar, and you'll find a tabbed, horizontal sub menu. Look under the Window menu and you'll see that this is called the Insert menu; presumably because not all the elements you can access from here are objects.

Most of the tab names are familiar, a couple are new and some have been

The new Insert menu is part of a wider interface overhaul, with a nod to the style of Flash MX

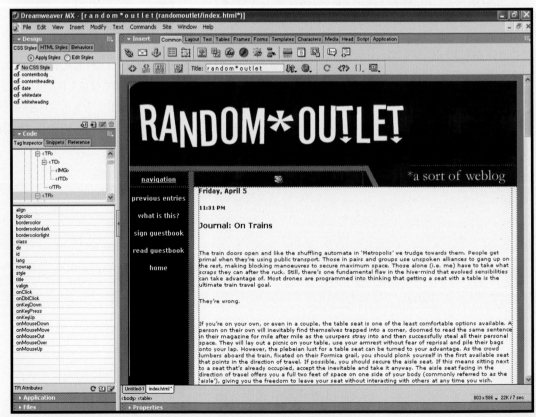

Macromedia Dreamweaver gets the MX treatment in this latest version, with Panel Groups that enable you to organise frequently used windows, dockable panels and new layouts.

moved from other parts of the Interface. You'll find the default sets of Common HTML objects here: Head, Forms, Frames and Characters. There's now a separate tab for Layout controls that includes access to the Table and Layers objects in standard view, and Layout Tables and Cells in Layout View. Oddly, there's also a separate Tables tab with which you can define a table through a dialogue, whether you're in Standard or Layout mode.

Some of the tabs, such as Applications and Templates, are there to service features that deserve their own explanation. The Script tab gives you access to the JavaScript editing window which was once hidden in the Invisibles section, and also has the Server Side Include object that was so easy to overlook when it was located alongside Common elements.

Overhaul

The new Insert menu is part of a much wider interface overhaul. This is Dreamweaver MX, not Dreamweaver 5, and the interface that first debuted in Flash MX is evident here. You get dockable panels, rollup–style panel-hiding features and the ability to float any window.

The main panels are arranged into Panel Groups, tabbed collections of related panels. Although you can't create your own, you can rename the existing groups. You can tear individual panels from a group or add them to another group. This gives you a great deal of control over how the workspace looks, so you can tailor it to the task in hand. Unlike Flash, however, there's no feature that enables you to save Panel layouts. This omission seems unusual, considering that the facility is built into the software.

Site development tools

Although Dreamweaver MX is a much more complex tool than its predecessors, it compensates for this with a streamlined development process…

1 Creating a new site has been made much easier for beginners. Choosing New Site from the Site menu launches a Wizard based set-up. If you're a more advanced user, you can still create sites in the usual way – where you'll find some new options.

2 As well as Remote and Local servers, you can now specify a 'testing' server. This is an inspired idea for application development, enabling you to set up paths for publication to the remote server at development time while testing the functions of your site locally.

3 When your site is set up you can start to add pages. Going to File>New opens a revamped dialogue with a list of document types, from basic HTML pages, through dynamic documents with scripting options to layout templates.

4 Dreamweaver has been XML-savvy since version 3, when the code base was shifted to a model that could be customised using XML and JavaScript. Now it can write XML documents. Take a step in this direction by ticking 'Make XHTML Compliant' in the document dialog.

5 If you need to rapidly develop layouts you'll appreciate Image Place Holders. Insert them into pages just as you would place regular images. The main difference is that you do not need to associate them with a file. It is ideal for templates.

6 There are now several ways to directly edit Tag attributes. You can use the Property Inspector, the Tag Inspector, edit manually in code view or right-click (Ctrl-click on the Mac) to open a Tag Editor. You've never had it so good.

If you go to Edit>Preferences, then click on Change Workspace, you can choose to work with a standard Dreamweaver MX layout or a Homesite/Coder-style layout. You can also choose to work with a Dreamweaver 4-type windowed workspace. In this mode, the tabbed Insert panel reverts to being a vertical toolbar, and all Windows are free- floating. On the Mac version, windows are always free–floating, in Windows the MX interface is contained within a larger Window.

The philosophy behind the MX interface acknowledges that Macromedia's Web range is now mature. It has been through several revisions and had lots of functionality built in along the way. The interface enables the continual addition of new

Based on UltraDev

The most significant change in the Dreamweaver product line is that MX is based on Dreamweaver UltraDev. Formerly a separate package with all Dreamweaver's layout power and the ability to build database driven dynamic Web sites, the new version has a solid foundation to build on.

Macromedia acquired the ColdFusion application server from Allaire last year, and MX is well optimised for it. In turn, the ColdFusion server has had a major revamp to make it a cross-platform, Java–based solution to Web app development. This doesn't mean Dreamweaver MX doesn't cater for other languages or protocols; it now supports PHP scripting and ASP.net.

Many of the features covered in this review have been brought in with dynamic scripting in mind. The Tag Chooser includes ASP, PHP and CFML (ColdFusion Mark–Up Language) libraries, the New Document dialogue has a collection of dynamic templates for use with Web application development.

Also, application 'objects' can now be inserted into pages from the Insert menu, allowing you to visually build dynamically driven pages.

You'll also find that the Reference panel has been updated to reflect the changes to the package, with full coverage of ASP, JSP and CFML scripting. A PHP guide would have been welcome too, and we can only assume that one will soon be available from the Dreamweaver Exchange.

There are some differences between the Mac and Windows versions. Some features of the MX interface rely on Windows MDI functionality, so the Mac's panel docking abilities are less pronounced.

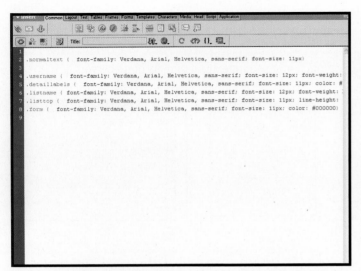

There's no need to exit the package to manually edit external style sheets, now. There's support for a variety of document types directly within Dreamweaver.

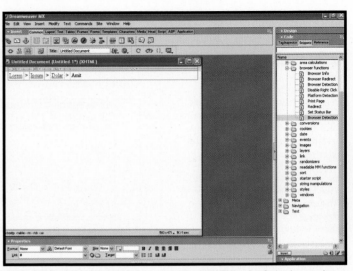

Another idea from HomeSite, code Snippets are ready-made HTML or JavaScript elements that can be dropped directly into your pages and edited as required.

primary functions and features without cluttering up the screen. The package boasts some significant additions but, if anything, it looks more streamlined than its predecessors.

Among the new panels, you'll find the Site panel. This incorporates all the features of the old site view, but you can now see it alongside the page

you're working on, docked with the other panels. If you prefer, you can tear the panel from its dock and open it into a full window.

If you're a Dreamweaver veteran, you'll be relieved that you can now access your computer's desktop from the Local View of the Site panel; no more switching to the Finder or

Windows Explorer to drag in assets you forgot to add. The Site panel shares a Panel group with the Assets panel, which now includes a tab for access to Templates.

Dreamweaver has traditionally taken a blank canvas approach to Web design; clicking on File> New simply opened a new HTML document. Now,

the New document dialogue reflects the complexity of the package, giving you the option of creating a series of document types, from basic HTML pages to Library items, CSS style sheets, scripts or pages that contain dynamic content.

Templates

Move down the list a bit and you'll find that Dreamweaver MX does something previous versions have never done: it gives you ready-made templates to base your site on. Forget the garish layouts that FrontPage and NetObjects Fusion can be guilty of, these templates are barebone layouts, for customising by designers. You won't find wooden buttons or chrome logos, just plain HTML and JavaScript information designs.

Templates have been a mainstay of Dreamweaver since version 3 — now they've had an overhaul to make them more suitable for use with dynamic data. To make a template editable, you select an area to create an editable region. These regions can now be set to repeat or be flagged as optional.

Repeatable regions enable content providers to add multiple items to a document, a list or a series of articles, while maintaining the same basic layout imposed by the designer. Optional regions are areas of content that can be turned off by the author. You can also configure a template so that only specific tag parameters can be edited — enabling you to let a source image be changed while leaving its dimensions fixed, for example.

Dreamweaver has always been a visual design environment. So little was

The big news is that UltraDev and Dreamweaver are no longer separate product lines. Dreamweaver MX continues from Dreamweaver Ultradev 4 rather than the plain version. That's reason enough for anyone to upgrade.

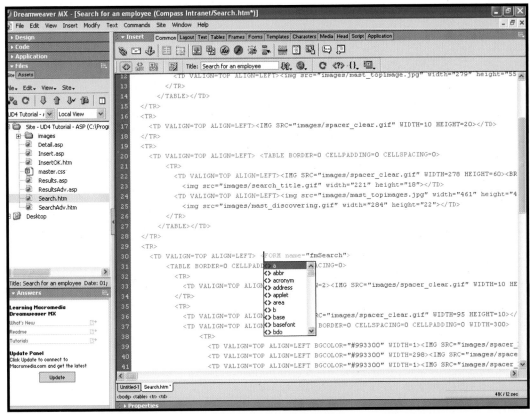

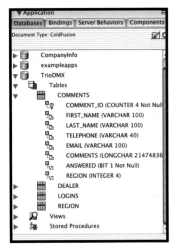

Database connectivity has been expanded to include PHP and MySQL support. This means Mac users can develop Web apps in Dreamweaver direct from their desktops, for the first time.

Incorporating the best features from HomeSite, Dreamweaver's code editing capabilities finally match its visual layout features.

wrong with the original authoring tools that they've remained relatively unchanged from version one. The package's coding tools have undergone a gradual evolution though, and in this version they reach a peak.

The program can now be launched with a special code editing layout, using familiar tools such as the Site panel to work with the code directly. The code view that debuted in Dreamweaver 4 is now a multi-purpose

coding environment: you can edit HTML, tweak your ASP scripts, write ColdFusion from scratch and develop CSS Style Sheets manually. This is made far easier by the new Tag Chooser panel. In common with HTML crunching tools such as HomeSite, this enables you to apply tags directly to the content in your page.

Used in tandem with the new Tag Inspector panel that allows you to edit code parameters directly, Dreamweaver is now every bit as good at code processing as it is with drag-and-drop capabilities. The Tag

Inspector/Chooser combo doesn't stop at HTML, either. The Chooser has a library of ASP, ColdFusion, WML, Jrun, JSP and PHP tags too, making for a truly integrated coding platform.

The wait for the new Dreamweaver has been worth it. This version retains all the superlative features that first made the package so attractive to Web designers. Macromedia has not touched most of the best features — it has, instead, enhanced the aspects of the program that needed it, to provide a visual editor that's now every bit as competent with code as with layouts.

As a designer, the changes to the template system and comprehensive interface updates will be the first aspects you'll notice. In the long term, these development features may be the catalyst that get you building the dynamic Websites you always thought you needed someone else for. Dreamweaver MX is the complete Web building package.

> ## Dreamweaver is now every bit as good at code processing as it is with drag-and-drop functions

HomeSite+

When Macromedia acquired Allaire's ColdFusion, it also got HomeSite, the HTML coding package that shipped with previous versions of Dreamweaver. With all the enhancements to the coding tools in Dreamweaver MX, you might think that HomeSite would be the first casualty of the

overhaul, especially as many of those features were inspired by HomeSite in the first place.

However, HomeSite is back in the Windows version of Dreamweaver MX, and it's bigger than ever. HomeSite + is an amalgamation of the original HomeSite HTML editor and ColdFusion Studio, Allaire's

scripting tool for the ColdFusion Application Server.

With closer integration between Dreamweaver and HomeSite, it's possible to switch between the two as you work. It's hard to see what benefit the tool presents to anyone but hardcore ColdFusion Studio coders reluctant to switch app.

This point is probably what explains its inclusion; like the option to switch to a Dreamweaver 4–style interface, HomeSite+ will placate more stubborn coders who'd rather have a scripting environment stripped of the bells and whistles offered by Dreamweaver.

Verdict

Speed	
Value for money	
Ease of use	
Documentation	

For: *Integration of UltraDev into Dreamweaver product line • Coding enhancements • MX interface*

Against: *No HomeSite+ in the Mac OS X version*

Fireworks MX

A jump to v6 for the streamlined Web graphics app with an all-in-one toolset…

Price

£257 (upgrade £128, MX Studio £692)

Company

Computers Unlimited

Telephone

020 8200 8282

Website

www.macromedia.com

Features

• Interactive and animated Web graphics

• Vector, bitmap & HTML toolset

• MX-style reduced interface

• Improved bitmap tools

• Live, editable bitmap effects

• Library, symbols & instances

• Slicing, image swaps and imagemaps

• Pop-up menu creator

• Tweening

• Data-driven graphics

System

PC: 300MHz PII • Win 98/2000/ NT/ME/XP • 98MB RAM • 275MB HD space

Mac: PowerMac G3 • 96MB RAM • 275MB HD space • OS 9.1/OS X 10.1

 Try the preview
You can try out Fireworks MX with our Cover CD.

Long the underdog in Web graphics production Macromedia's Fireworks is an extremely adaptable and somewhat undervalued asset to the interactive designer. Its forte is the seamless combination of vector and bitmap tools dedicated to design at 72dpi/RGB, and presented through an incredibly easy workflow. It offers editable vector drawing, bitmap paint and effects, one-click DHTML behaviours and superb optimisation output. The application is also stable, fast and refreshingly bug-free.

Fireworks MX is part of Macromedia's pan-application, empire-building ploy, taking a sneaky leap from version 4 to version 6. It's open to debate whether the new features merit this but there's easily enough here to justify the price rise.

The most obvious change is the MX interface. All the object properties and tool options are compounded into a

In Fireworks MX, you can now apply and edit text directly on the canvas.

Live bitmap effects are quick to apply and edit. Creating buttons is a breeze.

single, context-sensitive Property Inspector that you can move around.

This is a masterstroke in usability, as it replaces the old Object, Fill, Stroke, Effects, Options and Info palettes, puts text options at your fingertips, and saves considerable screen real estate.

The remaining palettes — Layers, Frames, Behaviours and more — use MM's funky new docking mechanism. The toolbox has been re-arranged to group tools according to what they do:

Selections, Bitmaps, Vectors, Web-stuff or Colours.

Fireworks MX has as much kick under its bonnet as it has panache on the catwalk. There are no changes in behaviour as you move between vectors and bitmaps — the two media now work as one with no mode change.

To paint a bitmap stroke, you use the new bitmap Paint or Pencil tool; to draw a vector you use the Bézier Pen or Vector Path tool. Either way, the same

The combination of editable vectors with aliased bitmap preview makes Fireworks great for Web design: you can always see what you'll get and edit it.

tool options apply: choose one of 48 predefined, pressure-sensitive brush strokes or create your own, add colour, thickness, softness and texture, then indulge in transparency and effects.

In particular, Fireworks includes about 50 on–board effects and filters including shadows, bevels, Photoshop-style Brightness/Contrast and Curves and so on, which remain editable at all times, even on bitmap objects. This Live Effects engine also supports the Photoshop plug-in format.

One-click tricks

The bitmap tools resemble those in Photoshop — Marquees, Wands, and so on — while Blur, Sharpen, Dodge, Burn and Smudge for photo style work make their debut. A new Select menu complements these with one–click marching ant operations, such as contracting and bordering a marquee.

Vectors that look like bitmaps have always been a Fireworks strength, combining scaleability and editability with pixel-level precision, aliasing control and native bitmap preview and output. It smells like a paint stroke, it works like a path.

Squares, rectangles, circles and oddball shapes are easy to create, change and resize using path operations that match those in Illustrator, while gradients and bitmap texturing open the way for less flat-colour artwork, for a more natural look.

The same methods apply text in Fireworks, which is more intuitive than in Photoshop. You can now apply it directly to the canvas, without a separate text editor. All the text options have moved to the Property Inspector — you'll find new paragraph controls and a Dreamweaver/Flash-style space for giving your text container a name. This

Symbols, buttons and menus

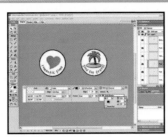

1 Design in Fireworks is as simple as drawing, reshaping and colouring objects, applying textures and effects, and importing existing bitmap or vector files. You can work seamlessly between formats.

2 Fireworks uses symbols which, like Flash, enable you to have common graphical elements which all update when you change the master copy – a big time saver as you evolve the look of a Website.

3 Rollover buttons with complex interactions are a doodle to create using the Button Editor window, which pops up when you create a new button type symbol. The tabs at the top offer on-click access to the different button states.

4 You can now apply different text and URLs to different instances of a symbol; when you change the master symbol, it's just the graphics and styling that update across all instances.

5 Using the Modify>Pop-up Menu command, you can easily insert sophisticated customisable DHTML menus. The code that drives them in the Web page is created on the fly, when you export your document.

6 Using the Quick Launch menu, you can instantly launch and transfer the export HTML to Dreamweaver, which fully interprets the Fireworks code; or you can continue to manipulate and refine the interface features and layout.

opens the way for generating images based on an external data source, using the new data-driven Graphics Wizard in the Commands menu.

Workflow

Fireworks 4 introduced fantastic features for creating buttons, interactivity and animation, while slicing and world-class optimisation had been established in the app for some time. These remain broadly the same, and the diversity of import/export formats continues to impress; there's everything from Photoshop and Illustrator to WBMP and SWF.

A few new toys in the Behaviours palette would have been welcome — such as pop-up windows or show/hide layers — although the popular Pop-up Menu creator from the previous release has been improved to offer tighter controls and better integration with Dreamweaver.

Such workflow-oriented integration has become Macromedia's byword over the last year or so, as evidenced by the Quick Export menu at the top-right of your Canvas, where you can deliver your work directly to Dreamweaver, Flash, FreeHand and so on. A new Sitespring plugs you straight into Macromedia's workgroup server tool — although sadly without WebDAV — while developers can create palette interfaces in Flash for Fireworks JavaScript customisations, exemplified in a new, all-signing Align palette.

In Web design, it really is the simple things that count. The defining issue for any creative software is: how fast can users get from a moment of inspiration to polished creation, without getting tied up technology? For Fireworks MX, Macromedia has heeded this philosophy; rather than pack this already-ideal design app with crass effects and gizmos, the company has focused on making simpler what it's already got. It should help you see your way clearer to a greater Website.

Verdict

Speed	
Value for money	
Ease of use	
Documentation	

For: *Impressive all-in-one toolset • Easy to use • Excellent workflow and integration*

Against: *Not ideal for photos • Reduced text features • SWF export still a bit ropey*

The new interface is efficient on screen space; the Property Inspector dispenses with six palettes.

Director MX

This latest release strengthens the tool's position as a top all-round multimedia application

Price

Mac and PC £1056
(upgrade £175)

Company

Computers Unlimited

Telephone

020 8200 8282

Website

www.macromedia.com

Features

- Multimedia creation for CD-ROM or the Web

- Accessibility behaviours

- Flash MX integration

- Powerful scripting language

- Lingo and Scripting window enhancements

- MPEG-4 support

While Matchware's Mediator may appear to be gaining ground on Macromedia's tool — and is undeniably good value for money — Director is still a multimedia force to be reckoned with. Unfortunately, its considerable benefits are not so immediately apparent as those of its multimedia rival... Take the fact that Director is both PC and Mac compatible, for instance. Whereas Mediator can only export standalone files for PC (.exe), Director (even though you have to buy two copies of the app — one for Mac, one for PC) can create standalone presentations for both platforms. This fact alone should keep the user-base of Macromedia's application suitably populated.

Admittedly, version 9 of Director doesn't immediately impress as the hugest of upgrades. It's surprising, for example, that there are no new additions to the Shockwave 3D tools that made Director 8.5 such a powerful product. But beneath the surface, Director MX looks set to be an upgrade that professional multimedia artists will be itching to get their hands on.

MX-compatible

There's no doubting that Flash MX has taken off in an incredible way — it was one of the big releases of 2002. Many multimedia designers took it on board to perform tasks that Director just wasn't cut out for. However, Director 8.5 wasn't capable of importing Flash Player 6 files (mainly thanks to new ActionScript commands). This has been fixed in Director MX — but, thankfully, Macromedia hasn't stopped there. Tight integration with Flash MX makes Director MX a winner. The Launch and Edit feature does exactly what you'd think — a commonplace system in

The new release of Director enables you to combine Flash movies, MPEG-4 content, communication devices and 3D. In short, the tool is more powerful than ever.

modern applications — enabling you to double-click a SWF file within Director (the app automatically launching Flash MX), edit it, save it and see it updated in Director accordingly. It's a small addition, but one that Flash designers porting work to Shockwave or CD-ROM will adore. It seems that efficiency of working was high on the agenda for Macromedia with this release.

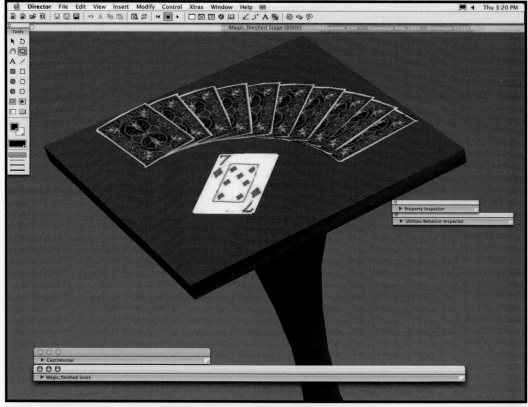

The now familiar MX interface enables you to dock any of Director's palettes at will – making it generally easier to manage the Director interface, hugely reduce screen clutter and improve workflow. Long-term Director users won't know what's hit them.

Further Flash integration includes the ability to control Flash objects on the stage using Lingo, and even the ability to create new Flash objects with Lingo scripts. And why would you want to do this? To save time, we suppose — it basically means you don't need to go back into Flash to create somewhat minor movie elements.

Where Director gets very clever is in the integration of Flash Communication Server MX. Director MX enables you to have direct access to Communication Server MX and Flash Remoting features, without going into the applications themselves. Obviously, you need the applications installed to get this to work — but it gives scope for including communication applications within standalone or Shockwave files. This in itself adds an exciting new dimension to the uses of Director.

Whereas the Flash Communication Server itself provided the tools needed for chatrooms and so on within a Flash Player interface, this combined with Director gives scope for presentations

accessible to everyone has filtered through into Director.

The Accessibility features in Director MX come in the form of behaviours. These work in the same way as any other Director preset behaviour — enabling you to drag and drop behaviours onto sprites from the library. At their most basic, the Accessibility behaviours in Director MX enable you to add text to speech, captioning and tab navigation features to your movies, the latter enabling you to use the keyboard to literally tab between movie items. The Speech Xtra supplied converts text to speech — with voices being the same as specified within the user's OS.

You soon find out, though, that the process of applying Accessibility behaviours to sprites isn't simply a case of dragging and dropping. You need to apply behaviours in a particular order to activate the features (see page 38 for a full tutorial). First, the Target behaviour must be applied in order for the Accessibility behaviours to talk to

Why no OS9?

You may have noticed that Director MX is only available for OS X on the Mac platform. This is certainly a bold move: expecting corporations using Director to migrate to OS X if they wish to build projector files for OS X.

While it may seem common sense, considering the move by Apple to make all new Macs boot only into OS X this year (although some may still boot into OS 9 for publishing houses and education), it is asking a lot from big design firms.

This is our only reservation about Director MX — and it may be a factor in users not choosing to upgrade. The fact you can only create PC projectors with the PC version and Mac projectors with the Mac version, in addition to the OSX constraint, adds up to a huge investment. Time will tell if this strategy works. On the PC, of course, the MX upgrade will work with 98 SE, 2000 and XP.

The process of applying accessibility behaviours to sprites is not simply a case of dragging and dropping

that combine 3D, video and the ability to communicate with others over the Web all at once. And if you look at Director in this way, it all begins to seem very impressive indeed.

Accessibility issue

As certain laws tighten, accessibility is becoming a key issue. Clients have become aware (and, as a result, so have designers) of the needs of disabled viewers. Macromedia is extremely involved in accessibility at the moment, and is working with the RNIB and other charities. This dedication to making the Web, and indeed all presentations,

one another. From here, you assign an Accessibility Group and the Accessibility Item behaviour to each of the sprites you wish to make accessible to impaired browsers. Only after doing this can you begin to apply certain behaviours to certain types of sprite. For example, you could apply a Group Order behaviour to certain objects to enable users to tab through those objects, or a Speak Behaviour which adds user-defined text that will be spoken when the user tabs to or clicks on the designated sprite. It sounds simple enough, but you will need intermediate Lingo knowledge to get everything working properly — we had

to tweak scripts accordingly. On the subject of scripting, Macromedia has thankfully somewhat refined the Director Scripting window, combining it with a Debugger and adding much-needed formatting devices, such as Line Numbering, Auto Colouring, Auto Formatting as well as various new Lingo reference panes and a Scripting Xtras window.

Packed upgrade

Other enhancements to the app include an Answers Panel (like Flash), from which you can get updated tutorials and so on from Macromedia via the Web.

Finally, there's a new QuickTime 6 Xtra, enabling you to take advantage of the new MPEG-4 functionality found in Apple's software. Oh, and, of course, Director has been rejiggled interface-wise to fit in with Macromedia's MX strategy. The more we use this interface, the more intuitive it becomes — particularly if you're up-to-date with other Macromedia products.

So, at first glance, Director MX looks like being a rather timid update. But when you realise the potential of this app for creating multimedia that's genuinely interactive, it really cannot be faulted. Sure, we would've liked to have seen an OS 9 version, but we suspect that certain company politics prevented this. And, yes, it's a little on the pricey side — but then for your cash you get a tool that's capable of creating interactive content for the Web or CD-ROM that's accessible to everybody. And that in itself is no mean feat.

Verdict

Speed	★★★★★
Value for money	★★★★★
Ease of use	★★★★★
Documentation	★★★★★

For: *Impressive all-in-one toolset • Easy to use • Excellent workflow and integration*

Against: *Not ideal for photos • Reduced text features • SWF export still a bit ropey*

The new Scripting window contains a number of new handy features, including Line Numbering, Auto Colouring and Auto Formatting. Borrowed from Flash, these will be a godsend to Director programmers.

The ability to import Flash MX SWF files directly into Director MX, and double-click to edit them in Flash, means that workflow time is significantly reduced.

New Accessibility behaviours within Director MX enable you to make your movies accessible to everyone. Behaviours are drag-and-drop but a knowledge of Lingo is required to make the most out of them.

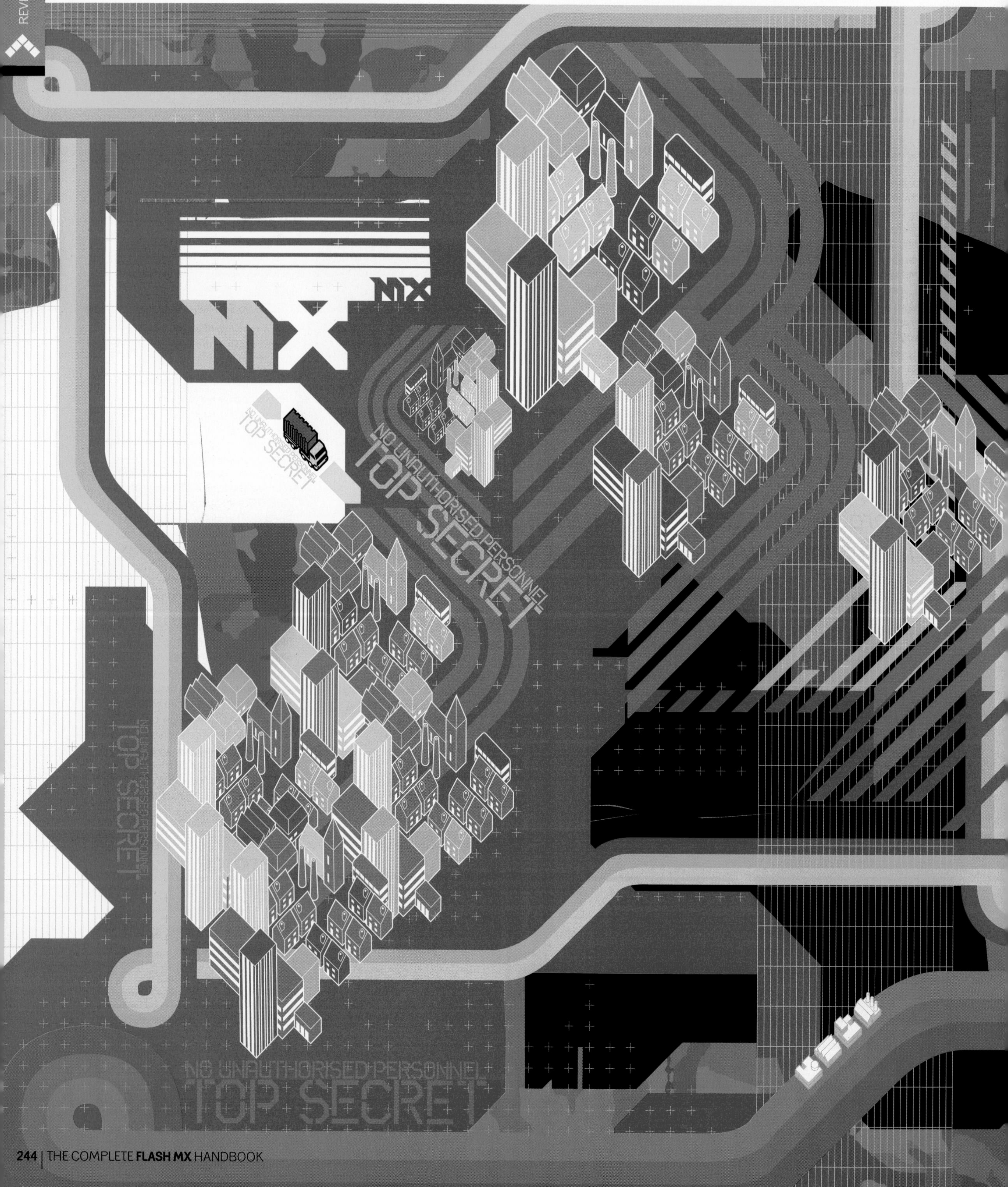
MX
MX
NO UNAUTHORISED PERSONNEL
TOP SECRET
NO UNAUTHORISED PERSONNEL
TOP SECRET
NO UNAUTHORISED PERSONNEL
TOP SECRET
NO UNAUTHORISED PERSONNEL
TOP SECRET

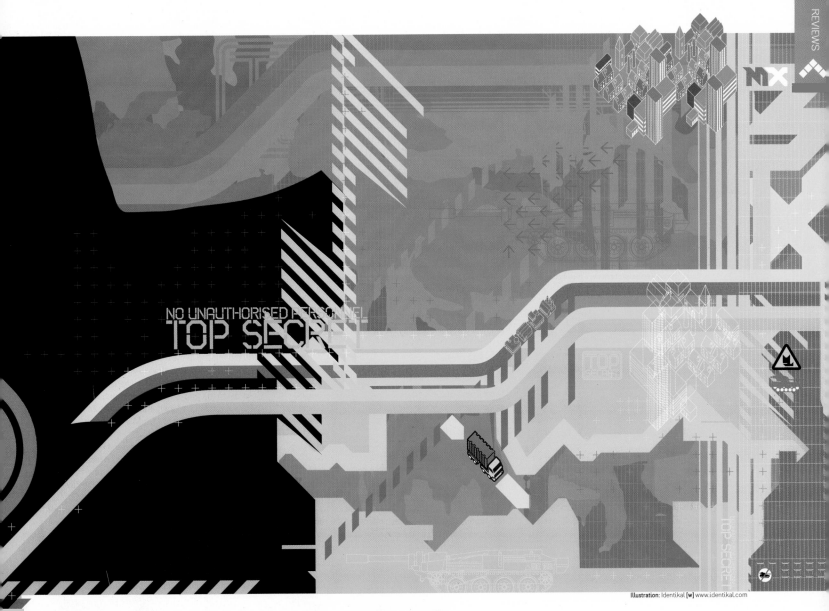

Illustration: Identikal [w] www.identikal.com

Media mogul: Flash Communication Server MX

Macromedia delivers on Flash MX's revolutionary promise with an incredible new server technology...

efore Macromedia launched Flash MX in spring 2002, there was a discreet yet distinct buzz from beta-testers about a raft of new media–rich functions that would revolutionise the Internet.

When MX finally arrived some of us felt a small cloud of disappointment darkening the blue sky of our happiness: many of the media tools about which we'd heard such tantalising rumours were missing.

While Flash MX certainly includes lots of exciting new features and was a major upgrade, it just didn't seem to fulfil the 'revolutionary' promise. But aside from one or two mysterious references to an upcoming product codenamed Tin Can, Macromedia remained mute on the subject.

'Secret' features

Which left matters to those of us who were interested enough to dig on our own. And dig we did. At Flash Forward (a show in San Francisco in 2002) one speaker described how a long list of undocumented objects could be gleaned from Flash Player 6 by opening it in Microsoft Word.

Other investigators cooked up ActionScripts that forced MX to divulge its secrets. Enticingly, entirely

FlashCom server is only available for Microsoft Windows. Client development takes place in Flash MX, available for both PC and Mac.
Server requirements:
Pentium III 500MHz processor or higher (dual Pentium 4 or better recommended) • Windows 2000 Advanced Server or Windows NT 4.0 Server (SP6 or later) • 256MB of available RAM (512MB recommended) • 50MB of available disk space • CD-ROM drive

Expertise provided by Patrick Gardner and Perfect Fools. [e] info@perfectfools.com
[w] www.perfectfools.com

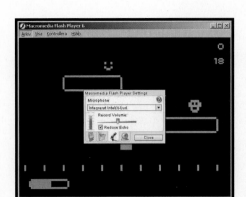

Even before FlashCom arrived developers were testing the exciting 'hidden' objects they discovered in Flash MX. This game uses the microphone. See the tutorial on page 104.

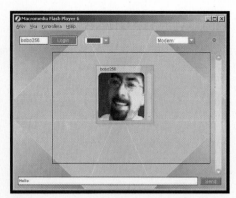

With FlashCom and Flash MX it's easy to create high-level rich-media applications like this video conferencing system. This fully-functional example comes with the FlashCom installation.

new tools like Camera, Microphone and NetConnection began to surface on Flashkit, Ultrashock and the other Flash boards. It turned out that these features were still in Flash Player — they just weren't advertised in the documentation.

Before long, examples were posted that made use of Web cameras and microphones on the user's computer. It was even possible to enable Flash movies on the local computer to share information with each other like never before.

But could you do anything with NetConnection? Could you save the audio or video streams? Or allow another user across the Internet to access them? While nobody knew for sure, the answer to all of these questions seemed to be no, at least for the moment.

In late 2002, with the production release of Tin Can — now dubbed Flash Communication Server MX or FlashCom for short — Macromedia put a resounding end to the guesswork. And with the incredible new features made possible by FlashCom, it may actually be bigger news than Flash MX.

So what is FlashCom?

Flash Communication Server MX enables sharing of streaming video, audio, data and other media elements between users over the Internet. All you need is a browser with Flash Player 6 or higher to enjoy industrial-strength Webchats, multiuser games, video conferencing applications and more. In many ways FlashCom does for Flash what Shockwave Multiuser Server does for Shockwave, but with the addition of rich-media streaming.

Video and audio streams can either be captured in real time via the user's digital camera and microphone or recorded and left on the server for later playback, in the new .flv file format. FlashCom easily scales the same media streams to different users' bandwidth limitations.

The FlashCom package comprises a server software suite as well as additions to Flash MX — many of which, as mentioned above, have actually been in there all along. A FlashCom application consists of a 'client' .swf movie, authored in Flash MX, which uses those once 'secret' objects to communicate with a server-side application, hosted on the FlashCom server. Server-side applications are pure ActionScript, and they control communications between FlashCom and the user or users.

Installing the server is absurdly simple, and that's speaking as a non-techie. It took us about 15 minutes to get it operational, and another ten to give the sample video conferencing application a thorough spin. FlashCom comes complete with an uncomplicated administrative interface and help files that explain everything you need to know to get applications working, both on the server and for the client.

FlashCom's place in the MX family

With the release of the MX generation Macromedia has made a concerted effort to give some sense of order to its burgeoning product line. But between ColdFusion MX and JRun 4, not to mention all of the development environments like Flash MX, Dreamweaver MX and Fireworks MX, it can still get a bit confusing.

So at first blush it's easy to wonder if FlashCom is really necessary, especially given the recent ColdFusion upgrade. The answer: absolutely. FlashCom adds a whole new range of possibilities to the Flash development universe. It augments ColdFusion's ability to deliver dynamic data to the Flash Player with streaming rich-media and the sharing of Flash objects between users.

FlashCom is also designed to integrate smoothly with ColdFusion MX as well as other non-Macromedia products like Microsoft's .Net. It acts as the hub that co-ordinates communication between users and all other application servers or databases.

Power to the people

Starting to sound a little too technical? While FlashCom is a powerful package and certainly has the potential to get esoteric at the higher end of development, Macromedia has worked hard to keep it accessible to a broader audience. Its goal is clearly to make FlashCom attractive to the same non-technical

FlashCom architecture

The ease with which it's possible to get FlashCom up and running belies a robust and highly scalable architecture…

A basic FlashCom application includes a client, created in Flash MX and running in Flash Player, communicating with custom-made server-side applications through Macromedia's Real-Time Messaging Protocol (RTMP). Server-side applications are ActionScripts that are stored in the FlashCom server's applications folder.

FlashCom co-ordinates interaction between the user and the application in use, as well as between users. A Flash-based Administration Console enables real-time monitoring of server activity.

Beyond this simple structure FlashCom is extensible in a number of powerful ways. FlashCom can open its own real-time NetConnections with other FlashCom servers; for example, to create a load-balancing arrangement between high-use servers. It can also use Macromedia Flash Remoting, via the Action Message Format (AMF) over HTTP, to communicate with other application server types including Macromedia ColdFusion MX, Macromedia JRun, Microsoft .NET and J2EE servers. Finally, FlashCom can also connect with other application servers over standard HTTP.

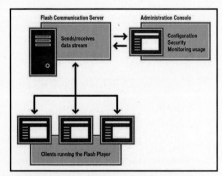

Simple FlashCom architecture. In addition, the FlashCom server can be extended with connections to a number of different application servers using a variety of protocols.

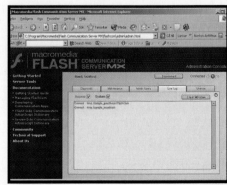

The FlashCom server suite includes a simple management tool through which you control all server activity via (what else?) a Flash interface.

Detailed documentation reveals the 'secret' functions in their full glory. In many cases these objects are even more interesting than we might have hoped.

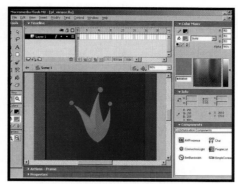

Macromedia offers a new set of Communications Components in a separate, free download. With these components, developing FlashCom apps is that much easier.

developers who have been drawn into doing a bit of ActionScripting by its ease and simplicity.

The FlashCom download includes detailed help files. In addition, the installation upgrades Flash MX by adding a folder called Communications to the Actions Toolbox and updating code-hinting with new hints about the extra objects. Unfortunately, one thing the installation doesn't do is to expand Flash MX's html help files (Using Flash and the ActionScript Dictionary) with the relevant new documentation. When developing FlashCom client movies in Flash MX you'll have to refer to FlashCom's help files for guidance on how to set up your .fla.

But Macromedia has made it even easier. With a new set of Communications Components available in a separate, free download, they've provided the tools you need to get high-level communications applications up and running in no time.

By using pre-formatted components such as Chat, SimpleConnect, SetBandwidth and AVPresence you can build complex applications like video conferencing centres with very few extra lines of ActionScript. Or if you are positively allergic to scripting, you could go a long way simply by taking one of the many fully-functional examples included with the FlashCom installation and modifying the graphics to your needs.

The new features

Whether or not you're an avid ActionScripter, you should check out the objects that come with FlashCom

to get a feel for the new possibilities. On the Flash MX side, they include:

NetConnection

Controls all aspects of the connection between the Flash Player and FlashCom. NetConnection employs Macromedia's proprietary Real-Time Messaging Protocol (RTMP) to provide an efficient, two-way link for streaming video, audio and other data.

NetStream

This enables you to open one or more one-way channel within a NetConnection, to or from the server. Each NetStream contains either video, audio or text data. A typical FlashCom experience might involve multiple NetStreams for each user. Using NetStream, you can choose to record stream data on the server in the .flv file format. With the NetStream.play method it's also possible to display a still image from the beginning of a video stream before the user commits to streaming the full video.

Video

How can Flash Player show video that's not part of the .swf at the time it's created? Thanks to the Video object, a generic container for video streams can be placed on the Stage while building your .fla. The Video object can display a live stream from the user's digital camera or a live or recorded stream from the FlashCom server. FlashCom is not required when using Video objects together with a local camera.

Camera

This provides all the necessary features to capture, adjust and interact with live video through a camera attached to the user's computer. Camera methods such as setMode, setQuality and setKeyFrameInterval make it easy to optimise the video stream for the constraints of the user's uplink to the FlashCom server. As with Video, the Camera object can also be used locally without the presence of FlashCom.

The Camera.activityLevel property, which quantifies the amount of motion detected by the camera, enables interesting interactions based on the contents of the video stream.

For example, you could use this feature to create a home security system with a camera that begins recording as soon as it detects movement.

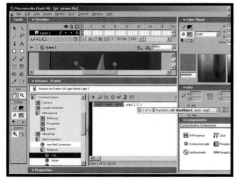

Updates to Flash MX help you get started with FlashCom. A Communications folder is added to the Actions Toolbox along with new code hints.

A global hunt

In the weeks before Flash MX launched, there was word from the beta community about great new media features. When MX arrived without the goods, some folks started digging...

And it wasn't long before they were turning up interesting results. Thanks to Peter Hall and other Flash gurus, ActionScripts exposing Flash MX's hidden objects, as well as sorted lists generated by the scripts, began circulating on many of the Flash boards.

Groups of people with a special interest in these types of tools started trading the shreds of experience they gathered on their forays into the undocumented.

At FlashKit, Steve Ogden (agent vivid) posted another handy script that traced object properties:

```
ASSetPropFlags(_global,null,8,1);
//theTrace = _global;
theTrace = Microphone.get();
for (x in theTrace) {trace(x);}
```

While many succeeded in making simple applications using local features of the new objects, such as sound meters and displays with a local microphone or Web camera, the question that seemed to come up again and again was "Can you save these streams?"

Today all the questions are answered with "Get Flash Communication Server MX."

This ActionScript was posted on Flashcoders Wiki by Peter Hall. When pasted into Flash and tested, it outputs a complete list of Flash objects.

Microphone

Similar to Camera but for capturing audio input through a microphone. As with Camera, the Microphone object has an activityLevel property that facilitates rudimentary interactivity based on the volume of the audio stream. Also like Video and Camera, Microphone can be used locally, independent of FlashCom. For an example of an entirely local interaction using the Microphone object, read Using sound to control moves in Flash on page 104.

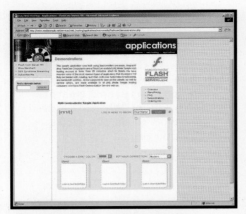

Mediatemple used Macromedia's Communications Components to whip up this chat demo showing off its new FlashCom hosting services.

SharedObject

While it might not be as glamorous as the Video, Camera and Microphone objects, SharedObject may prove to be at least as valuable in the long run. This object makes it possible to save persistent application data on the local machine and quickly share information between users via the FlashCom server.

Local Connection

Enables two or more local Flash movies to communicate without relying on FSCommand or JavaScript, or the FlashCom server for that matter.

On the server-side server, applications written in ActionScript control how FlashCom interacts with corresponding Flash Player clients. The application's scripts are stored as .asc files in FlashCom's applications folder and only activated when the server receives an initial request from the application client. These ActionScripts rely on a new set of objects created specially for FlashCom:

Application

Co-ordinates and stores information relevant to FlashCom's handling of each application instance. Stored information persists only until the application is unloaded from memory (as a default, applications are dumped a maximum of 20 minutes after the last

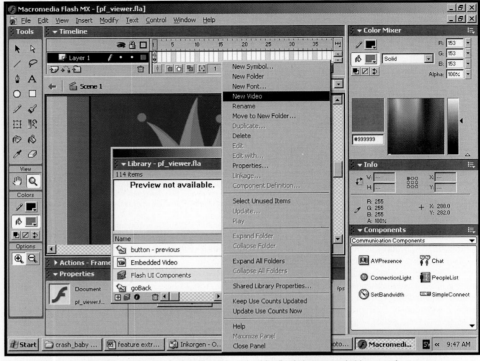

Embedded Video objects enable real-time streaming video without the video first being exported with your .swf.

request to use the application). The Application object manages client connection attempts and enables you to specify functions to be run at application startup or shutdown.

Client

Controls the server end of a NetConnection opened by the Flash Player client. The Client object receives commands from the client and can call methods of the client's NetConnection object. In addition, Client can obtain key information about the user's platform.

NetConnection

This object adds substantially to FlashCom's robustness by enabling the FlashCom server to open NetConnections with other application servers or other copies of FlashCom.

SharedObject

Facilitates interaction with a client's shared objects or between the client and a shared object stored on the server. 'Remote shared objects' can be saved on the server indefinitely, allowing users to view and modify the information they contain, with the changes immediately available to other concurrent users and later users. For example, one remote shared object maintained on the server might contain a high-score list for a multiuser game. As each player's score is recorded, the updated version of the list becomes available to all other list viewers.

Stream

Just as the Client object conducts the server's handling of client-initiated NetConnections, the Stream object is used to guide each stream between server and client. Stream objects are created automatically upon a NetStream request from a client, or launched when needed by a server-side application.

Testing tools

Two more handy additions to Flash MX aid the process of debugging and testing communication applications as you build them. First is the NetConnection Debugger (ND), which you enable within an application through the ActionScript call #include "NetDebug.as". By inserting this line into your movie you allow the ND to track your application's attempts to contact FlashCom. The ND gives detailed feedback on each step of the NetConnection process. Through the ND's Filters panel you can also choose to view limited subsets of the events that occur during a connection.

A second tool, the Communication App Inspector (CAI), monitors what is happening on the server once

With SharedObject you can store application information on the user's computer. The Local Storage dialog allows the user to limit the amount of disk space used.

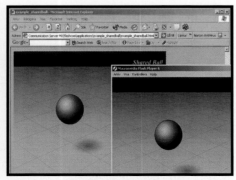

While not as sensational as Camera and Microphone, SharedObjects may prove equally useful. In this example, the ball's movement is synchronised between two Flash clients.

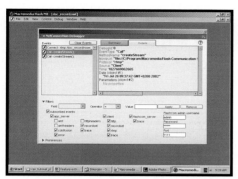

Flash MX's new NetConnection debugger simplifies what might otherwise be a sticky issue: tracking and troubleshooting the client-server connection.

More info about FlashCom

A full, 30-day trial version of Flash Communication Server MX Professional Edition is available for download from [w] www.macromedia.com (yes, that's with the 500 simultaneous connections/10 megabits maximum bandwidth, just to give you a sweet taste of the big-time). More developer resources are available here:

http://www.macromedia.com/go/flashcom_desdev

http://www.macromedia.com/go/Flashcom_resources/

http://www.flashcom.info

an application is running. The CAI provides exhaustive real-time diagnostics about every aspect of the client-server interaction. Included are a list of log messages generated by the server-side application, details about the shared objects and streams in use, and general application status.

Both the ND and the CAI can be found under Flash MX's Window menu.

There's just one catch

As you've probably gathered by now, we're pretty excited about the great possibilities that come with the arrival of FlashCom. Unfortunately, our joy is not entirely unalloyed. If there is one asterisk we have to add to our adoration, it's regarding the price. In short, FlashCom is anything but cheap. While a developer copy runs at £359 (US$499) it comes with just ten simultaneous connections or one megabit of peak bandwidth. Hardly enough to do application testing. The next step is the Professional Edition, with 500 simultaneous users/10 megabits of total throughput, for £3,239 (US$4,500). Need more connections? You can buy extension packs in increments of 500 users/10 megabits for £2,879 (US$4,000) each.

Compare this to Shockwave Multiuser Server 3 (SMS3), which comes free of charge with Director 8.5 Shockwave Studio. According to Macromedia, SMS3 enables 2000 simultaneous connections right out of the box. With FlashCom this capacity would cost a whopping £11,876 (US$16,500). Of course, as we already said above, SMS3 doesn't offer the full range of features that come with FlashCom, but FlashCom will certainly be used to build many of the same types of applications, especially in the beginning.

Macromedia has clearly set its pricing in comparison to other rich-media servers like Real Media's Helix and in the tradition of their own now-discontinued Generator technology. But our experience as a developer trying to sell Generator solutions is that the price was always a major issue, even with global clients. It was hard enough to convince strict IT administrators to introduce a new technology into their carefully managed server parks; tell them they had to drop US$6000 on a server they weren't sure they would use more than once and more often than not it was Game Over.

The dearth of large-scale Generator solutions over the past few years leads us to believe we weren't alone in our experience. And now, to some degree, we're back in the same boat. The question is whether, considering the current market, the time is now right for this type of pricing. We just hope Macromedia doesn't make the same mistake as it apparently did with Generator, and

stifle the market for the fantastic new FlashCom services before it has a chance to take off.

Conclusion

With the release of Flash Communication Server MX Macromedia moves the Internet a huge leap in the direction of ubiquitous, rich-media, multiuser applications. In the process it also transforms Flash from an attractive but largely isolated user environment into a window on a shared media world.

FlashCom heralds a new era of exciting possibilities. Whether you're a hard-bitten scripter or thoroughly non-technical, it should give you plenty of reasons to rejoice.

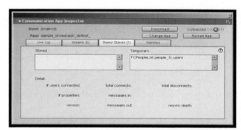

The Communication App Inspector gives a thorough overview of your application while it's running on the server, including details for all streams and shared objects.

Capturing camera input

Connecting your digital camera to Flash is as simple as 1 2 3... okay, 4...

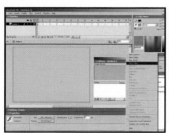

1 Make sure your camera is connected to the computer and open a new file. Open the Options menu in the upper right of the Library panel and choose New Video to create a new Video object. Drag the Video object onto the stage.

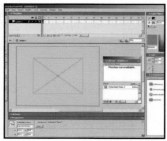

2 Use the Free Transform Tool to scale the Video object to whatever size you like, and position it as desired. Using the Properties Inspector give your Video object the Instance Name myVideoStream.

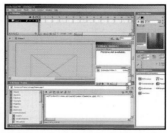

3 Open the Actions panel and insert the following ActionScript at Frame 1: myVideoStream.attachVideo(Camera.get(0)); This tells Flash to connect the stream coming from your camera with the Video object now on the stage.

4 Choose Control>Test Movie. The Flash Player Settings Privacy dialog will appear, asking if you want to allow the use of your camera. Once you click Allow, you should see your camera's stream. You now have a live video player!

Web design book round-up

Now it's time to extend your Flash MX knowledge even further with this selection of guides to learning effective Web animation

Taking Your Talent to the Web

Author
Jeffrey Zeldman

Publisher
New Riders

Price
£30.99

ISBN
0735710732

 ased on the Populi Curriculum training programme in the USA that Zeldman helped to develop, this book will help print designers move their skills to the Web. It is not a technical publication. There are no tutorials covering either Dreamweaver or JavaScript, as it's more a complete and comprehensive overview of all of the skills that you will need to develop before you can move into the online environment.

The advice on offer is solid and follows a formal path that begins with a potted history of the Web's development before moving into more practical advice regarding colour, site navigation and the new tools that you will have to learn to use to take your talent to the Web.

Zeldman's style is what sets this book apart. Speaking to his fellow designers you are always confident that the knowledge he is imparting is timely,

accurate and useful. Jeffrey Zeldman himself states: "I wrote this book for print designers whose clients want Websites, art directors who'd like to move into full-time interactive design, homepage creators who are ready to turn pro, and professionals who seek to deepen their Web skills and understanding."

This book is a superb primer for any designer who has set their sights on the new design challenges that the Web has to offer. Page after page of concise information is presented that is always useful and entertaining. This is a must for all print designers who are looking for one book that will explain what challenges they will face as they move their skills into the online world.

This is an essential reference book for everyone who wants to make the most out of their business or personal Web site, and a useful fountain of information for all print designers who want to move their skills to the Web. All in all, it's a very handy book to have on the shelf!

Homepage Usability: 50 Websites Deconstructed

Author
Jacob Neilsen & Marie Tahir

Publisher
New Riders

Price
£36.99

ISBN
073571102X

 ollowing Nielsen's earlier work, Designing Web Usability, this book attempts to show you how to avoid breaking Jakob's law of Internet user experience that states: "Users tend to spend most of their time on other sites than your site."

Beginning with a refreshingly thorough explanation of each of the 113 design elements that make up the testing structure, you then move onto chapter two's statistical breakdown of each of the design elements covered. What it provides is a well-researched distillation of design attributes that should be present on any Website that wants to be successful.

Where this book scores highly is in imparting a set of guidelines that you can apply to the initial design stages of your own Website. This is the core of this book. Seeing each of the 50 sites in all their glory,

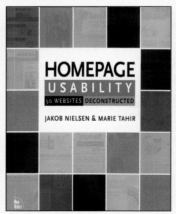

dissected and critiqued is useful to a point, but just serves to illustrate the key points covered in the first chapter of the book and should not be your focus.

This book does suffer in that for the most part the Websites covered are from corporate America: only two of them are from the UK and there are none from other European countries. That said, along with his earlier book this is a Nielsen consultation in book form.

You cannot fail to learn from the advice given here. You may not agree with all that is written, and you may have to modify some of the points made to fit with your own unique design brief, but the usability template will enable you to design a better Website.

Overall, Homepage Usability: 50 Websites Deconstructed will give you a better understanding of how other businesses build their Websites, and how their designs and experiences can be taken on board to enable you to get the most out of Website design.

www.layout

Author
Alastair Campbell

Publisher
Cassell & Co

Price
£18.99

ISBN
0304358010

Profusely illustrated, this latest in the www. series looks closely at Web page layout, but it leaves a lot to be desired. Aimed at the novice Web designer this focuses on basic packages such as FrontPage, while ignoring the likes of Dreamweaver. It's worrying that within the typography chapter, the author says that text viewed on an Atari ST looks different to that on a PC or Mac. This was first published in 2001, but is there really anyone out there still designing on an Atari ST?

If you want a very brief overview of Web technologies and some of the tools and issues encountered, this book would certainly further your understanding to a degree. However, its bright mass of illustrations mask the lack of comprehensive and practical information that you could use to put together your next project.

If you're a novice designer, we suggest you check out a handful of other titles first and decide which is best for you. This could be your Web design book but there's a very large possibility that you'll find something else more suitable.

Web ReDesign

Author
Kelly Goto & Emily Cotler

Publisher
New Riders

Price
£34.99

ISBN
0735710627

If you are about to design a new Website, or redesign an existing one, this book will arm you with tried and tested methodologies that enable you to avoid many of the pitfalls that befall those who rush head-long into the design and coding phase.

Based on what the authors call The Core Process, you will see checklists, surveys, worksheets and hints and tips enabling you to enter the planning phase of your project with confidence. You will also see advice from such Web luminaries as Jakob Nielsen, Lynda Weinman and David Siegel.

This is one of the first books to take a close look at Website development logistics and present real-world examples that successfully implement The Core Process. Overall, this is the missing link between inspiration and the practical realisation of a Website. If you want to learn more about every external aspect of Web building, get this book!

Back to the USER

Author
Tammy Sachs & Gary McClain, PhD

Publisher
New Riders

Price
£27.50

ISBN
0735711186

Based on practical field research, this is an ideal companion to Web ReDesign because it offers an overview of the planning and preparation to build a successful site.

The first of six sections looks at the design process — what the authors call taking the 30,000-foot view. Further chapters delve into more specific topics such as site design and navigation, and things like company branding and marketing considerations.

Ultimately, this is your first step to good user-centric Web design. With research tips, insightful anecdotes and all the hard questions you should ask yourself at the end of each chapter, the authors have written a mantra that Web developers should learn off by heart. Although this book is probably intended mostly for senior management within small to intermediate sized companies who are about to build or rebuild a Website, it can also be of benefit to anyone else who wants to learn about putting a company Website together.

Designing with JavaScript

Author
Nick Heinle & Bill Pena

Publisher
O'Reilly

Price
£24.95

ISBN
156592360X

If you feel that you have hit a creative barrier with HTML, then it's probably time to learn the black art of JavaScript. This is the second edition of this excellent book where you can expect to conclude with a firm understanding of the key concepts of JavaScript and be confident in your abilities to write code that works.

Divided into 11 chapters, you begin with some easy steps that illustrate what JavaScript can do for your Web pages. Proceeding chapters cover more complex coding as you move from controlling windows, through dynamic images and on to combining JavaScript with DOM (Dynamic Object Model) and CSS (Cascading Style Sheets).

Even if your programming knowledge is non-existent you will become a competent JavaScript programmer by the end of the book. And if you already know a thing or two about coding, Designing with JavaScript will almost certainly teach you a few new tricks.

Index

m

n

o

p

r

s

t

u

v

w

x